Fourth Edition

W9-ARV-884

Religion in America

Julia Mitchell Corbett
Ball State University

Prentice Hall, Upper Saddle River, New Jersey 07458

Library of Congress Cataloging-in-Publication Data

Corbett, Julia Mitchell.
    Religion in America / Julia Mitchell Corbett. — 4th ed.
        p.   cm.
    Includes bibliographical references and index.
    ISBN 0-13-020992-9
    1. United States—Religion—1960-   I. Title.
BL2525.C67 2000
200'.973—dc21   99-28719
                                                        CIP

Editorial/Production Supervision and Interior Design: *Barbara DeVries*
Acquisitions Editor: *Karita France*
Prepress and Manufacturing Buyer: *Ben Smith*
Editorial Assistant: *Jennifer Ackerman*
Cover Designer: *Bruce Kenselaar*
Cover Design Director: *Jayne Conte*

This book was set 11/12 Adobe Garamond by Stratford Publishing Services, Inc. and was printed by Courier Companies, Inc. The cover was printed by Phoenix Color Corp.

Printed in the United States of America
10 9 8 7 6 5 4 3 2 1

ISBN 0-13-020992-9

Prentice-Hall International (UK) Limited, *London*
Prentice-Hall of Australia Pty. Limited, *Sydney*
Prentice-Hall Canada Inc., *Toronto*
Prentice-Hall Hispanoamericana, S.A., *Mexico*
Prentice-Hall of India Private Limited, *New Delhi*
Prentice-Hall of Japan, Inc., *Tokyo*
Pearson Education Asia Pte. Limited, *Singapore*
Editoria Prentice-Hall do Brasil, Ltda., *Rio de Janeiro*

Contents

4 Catholics in the United States   70

5 Living a Jewish Life in the United States   92

6 Humanism and the Unitarian Universalists   120

Part Three   ALTERNATIVES TO THE CONSENSUS

7 Christianities That Began in the United States   141

13 Religion as an Individual and Cultural Problem

302

Preface

Far too often, when people discuss religion, the discussion becomes an unproductive and unpleasant argument about who is right and who is wrong. This does not have to be the case. The academic study of religion in the humanities offers a unique opportunity to learn about American communities of faith in an atmosphere free of both judgment and partisan advocacy. It focuses on what each group believes and does and on what these beliefs and practices mean to those who are a part of it. It does not evaluate whether those beliefs and practices are right or wrong, nor does it make judgments about whether a religion is true or false. The academic study of religion does not judge and it does not advocate. It does not present religion as preferable to nonreligion, nor does it favor secularity over religiousness. It does not attempt to make converts to or from any particular community of faith. Each community of faith is presented without its beliefs and practices being judged favorably or unfavorably.

Although religious beliefs and practices are presented impartially in this book, it is important that you know from the outset that this book is not value-free. I believe that religion is an important part of humanity's story. I also believe that nothing in the entire spectrum of human religiousness can be completely strange to any of us, because we are all human. I believe firmly in the freedom of religion that is guaranteed by the Constitution. In the climate of diversity that we have in the United States, respect for those who are different from ourselves is vitally important. I believe in the community of neighbors, not strangers. This is a community of dialogue, based on respect and the appreciation of differences. It is a community based on every individual's commitment to freedom of belief and freedom of religious practice within the boundaries of the law.

You should be aware as you begin your study of religion in the United States that there is a vast distinction between religion as it is described in books—as I describe it in *this* book, for example—and religion as people actually live it. A majority of both Jews and Christians do not attend corporate worship with any regularity. Nor do they pray with the constancy their holy books instruct. Catholics do not necessarily follow their church's teachings about such personal matters as birth control and abortion. Some American Buddhists drink wine with dinner, in violation of a prohibition on intoxicants (which some read as a prohibition on intoxication). So do some Muslims, in the face of a similar prohibition. We choose from our religions' teachings those things that are personally meaningful to us and feel free to leave the rest alone. So when you meet actual Methodists or Hindus or Jews, they won't conform completely to what you have read. Their lives, however, *will* be informed at some level by their religious faith.

There are two things about which I am especially excited in this edition of the book. First, there is increased emphasis on religious diversity in the United States. Less-familiar religions receive more attention than in previous editions. Correspondingly, there is somewhat less emphasis on the religions of the majority. Attention is also given to responding to the religious diversity that surrounds us. The United States is an ideal place to learn about religion, not only in books, but as it is embodied in the people with whom we come into contact every day.

The second thing that I am excited by in the Fourth Edition is that it is "Web-integrated." I have integrated use of the World Wide Web throughout the book, and I have used the Web as a resource in writing the book. References are also given to relevant Web sites for each chapter and Web related assignments have been incorporated into the *Questions for Review, Discussion, and Writing* at the end of each chapter. I have developed and maintain a site on the World Wide Web for students who use the book, as well as for the general public. It contains links to many additional sites in several categories, as well as other material. If you have access to the World Wide Web with your own computer or at a computer lab at your college or university, you can access this site at *http:// bsuvc.bsu.edu/~00jmcorbett/index.htm*.

I hope you will enjoy your study of religion in the United States. Religion, along with families and friends, work and creative endeavors, school and leisure time, helps to make life meaningful and good for most Americans. It is a fascinating and rewarding subject for study. Fundamentally, this is a book about people, because religion is about people. For most people in the United States, religion is also about something that transcends people, such as God or another higher reality. But it is always about people, what people believe and how they act in response to those beliefs. So this is a book about us, all of us.

Books are always the product of far more people than just the author. I want to thank the Prentice Hall reviewers for the fourth edition for their helpful comments: Joan Rottler, *Iowa State University* and Jennifer Rycenga, *San Jose State University.* I am also grateful to all the clergy and religious laypeople who provided information and encouragement. Department Chair David B. Annis and my colleagues in the Department of Philosophy at Ball State University have been, as always, unfailingly helpful and supportive. Karita France, Religion Editor at Prentice Hall, was a pleasure to work with, as was my Production Editor, Barbara DeVries. I wrote this edition under difficult personal circumstances. Special thanks go to Dr. Steve Rousseau and the group of supportive friends without whom it would not have been possible. My husband, Mike, prepared the graphics. As always, he deserves credit for putting up with the amount of time that I invested in writing and for helping to solve computer problems. This edition is dedicated to him, with gratitude for our life together.

Introduction

Responding to Religious Diversity

Before you begin to read this chapter, ask yourself what your attitude is toward those whose religion is different from your own. Do you feel curious, interested to know more about them? Defensive? As if their religion is not "true" or "right"? Would you want to convince them of your own views? Do you think your own point of view might be enriched by dialogue with them?

Religious diversity in the United States and throughout the world is increasing. College students today can expect to be part of a community, a workplace, and social groups that include people of many faiths and of none. The development and growth of this diversity is an important social phenomenon of our time and one that extends far beyond the confines of "religion."

> The radicalism of religious diversity is a fact of contemporary life and may well become the most significant feature in the development of society and culture in the twenty-first century. . . . A Muslim living in the United States today is not a Muslim only when he [or she] visits the mosque, recites *Allah akbar*, or fasts during the sacred month of Ramadan. He is a Muslim when he votes in a local election, goes to market, visits a museum, or reads the newspaper. He is, indeed, a Muslim when he meets a Christian or a Jew in the local park.[1]

We encounter many other kinds of diversity also—racial, lifestyle, political, and sexual preference, to name but a few. Thinking through our responses to religious diversity can help us be more conscious of how we respond to diversity of other kinds, as well. There is also a particular feature of religious diversity that should be noted. Most—although certainly not all—religions make claims to absolute truth. The existence of wide-ranging religious diversity coupled with

[1]Richard E. Wentz, *The Culture of Religious Pluralism* (Boulder, CO: Westview Press, 1998), p. 13.

absolute truth claims poses a particularly interesting challenge for thoughtful, reflective response.

RESPONDING TO RELIGIOUS DIVERSITY

Each of the five responses described below stems from authentic human concerns. Many are grounded in the sacred writings of their proponents' religious tradition or in specific interpretations of those writings. Each has its adherents within most of the religions, as well as among the different religions. Different authors who write on responses to religious diversity may use the terms differently, as well.

We first need to distinguish all of these responses from *tolerance*, which may go along with any of them. Tolerance refers to the willingness to grant basic civil liberties to members of a faith other than one's own, regardless of how one feels about that other faith. Tolerance encompasses such things as willingness to grant the freedom to gather for religious meetings, to speak publicly in the hope of winning other people to one's viewpoint, and not to be discriminated against in matters of employment or housing, for example. A person who is tolerant may disagree, may be convinced that the other's position is simply wrong, but may still be willing to see the other person share these fundamental freedoms.

Exclusivism is the most clearly defined response. The exclusivist holds that, because religion deals with ultimate truth, there can be only one true or correct religion, and the rest are simply wrong. Exclusivism is found within most of humankind's religions. The following statement in *Evangelical Affirmations* provides a good example:

> Without Christ and the biblical gospel, sinful humanity is without salvation. . . . Any "gospel" without the Christ of the Bible cannot be the saving gospel, and leaves sinners estranged from God. . . . We affirm that only through the work of Christ can any person be saved and resurrected to live with God forever. Unbelievers will be separated eternally from God."[2]

Although exclusivism is a more prominent response within the three monotheistic religions of Judaism, Christianity, and Islam, it is not wholly confined to them. Although mainstream Buddhism exhibits a great deal of openness toward other faiths, Nichiren Shoshu Buddhism regards itself as "the One and Only True Buddhism" and "the One True Path of enlightenment."[3]

At the opposite end of the response spectrum lies *relativism*. There are different forms of relativism, but all of them share the premise that all perspectives are limited, even those that lay claim to absolute truth. There is no unlimited viewpoint from which a truth that is relevant for all times, places, and persons

---

[2]*Evangelical Affirmations*, ed. Kenneth S. Kantzer and Carl F.H. Henry (Grand Rapids, MI: Zondervan Publishing House, 1990), pp. 30–31 and 36.
[3]Nichiren Shoshu World Wide Web site (http://www.primenet.com/~martman/).

could ever be known nor expressed. This perception may lead the relativist in one of two directions: One approach is to maintain that, because religions claim absolute truth and absolute truth cannot be known, the religions are all wrong and none is worthy of one's commitment. This approach leads to secularism or irreligiousness. Another kind of relativism, however, holds that, in the absence of knowable absolute truth, the choice of a religion is simply up to individuals to pick the religion that feels right for them. This is the position taken, for example, by the Universal Life Church. "The Universal Life Church . . . recognizes that each person must choose his own path. Each person in the ULC is free to follow any path as long as it does not infringe on the rights of others."[4]

Sociologist Robert N. Bellah's often-cited description of "Sheilaism" illustrates the point nicely:

> One person we interviewed has actually named her religion (she calls it her "faith") after herself. This suggests the logical possibility of over 220 million American religions, one for each of us. Sheila Larson is a young nurse who has received a good deal of therapy and describes her faith as "Sheilaism. . . . My faith has carried me a long way. It's Sheilaism. Just my own little voice."[5]

Sociologist of religion Peter Berger describes another dimension of this situation when he writes about the status of religion in a situation of diversity and disestablishment:

> [R]eligious ex-monopolies can no longer take for granted the allegiance of their client populations. Allegiance is voluntary and thus, by definition, less than certain. As a result, the religious tradition, which previously could be authoritatively imposed, now had to be *marketed*. It must be "sold" to a clientele that is no longer constrained to "buy." The . . . situation is, above all, a *market situation.*[6]

A third approach is that of *inclusivism*. The inclusivist holds that there is one true or best religion, one that holds within itself the fullness of religious truth and human salvation. However, there is something of this truth in some other religions, as well. Most Muslims believe, for example, that the revelation of God to the Jews and the Christians was true and salvific but that it had been distorted by Muhammad's time. God's revelation to Muhammad is believed to confirm the truth of earlier revelations, while eliminating the distortions. The Second Vatican Council of the Catholic Church affirmed an inclusivist view:

> From ancient times down to the present, there has existed among diverse peoples a certain perception of that hidden power which hovers over the course of things and over the events of human life; at times, indeed, recognition can be found of a

---

[4]From the official World Wide Web site of the Universal Life Church (http://www.ulc.org).
[5]Robert N. Bellah et al., *Habits of the Heart: Individualism and Commitment in American Life* (New York: Harper & Row, Publishers, 1985), pp. 220–21.
[6]Peter L. Berger, *The Sacred Canopy: Elements of a Sociological Theory of Religion* (Garden City, NY: Doubleday & Company, Inc., 1967), p. 138.

Supreme Divinity and of a Supreme father too. Such a perception and such a recognition instills the lives of these peoples with a profound religious sense. . . . The Catholic church rejects nothing of what is true and holy in these [non-Christian] religions. . . . Yet she proclaims and is in duty bound to proclaim without fail, Christ who is the way, the truth, and the life (John 14:6). In him, in whom God reconciled all things to himself (2 Cor. 5:18–19), men find the fullness of their religious life.[7]

The fourth position may be called *synthesis*. This view holds that all religions are essentially the same underneath a veneer of cultural particularity. The differences among the religions are downplayed in favor of the similarities among them. Thus, all will—or at least should—come together into a unity. This point of view is often associated with the New Age Movement:

In the New Age, it is believed, people will recognize only one universal religion. While that one religion will assume many different forms . . . the same mystical faith (i.e. the Truth) will underlie each grouping, no matter what label . . . it chooses.[8]

Hindu theologian and former president of India Sarvepalli Radhakrishnan takes a similar position, believing that what he calls *Sanatana Dharma* (the -"eternal religion," a name often used by Hindus to describe their faith) is the one religious reality that encompasses all others and toward which all others will eventually evolve. As human beings collectively mature religiously, the various manifestations of religion will converge on "the One Spirit which takes us beyond the historical formulations," which are only "imperfect halting expressions."[9]

The relatively recent world faith of Baha'i also holds a view that humankind is evolving inevitably toward one world religion. For Baha'is, one world religion is an aspect of a larger view that there will gradually come about a global civilization that includes a worldwide government, judicatory system, and currency. A basic book on Baha'i teachings is titled *The Baha'i Faith: The Emerging Global Religion*. The authors of this book state that "In reality, there is only one religion, the religion of God."[10] Baha'u'llah, the founder of Baha'i, is quoted as saying that "all nations should become one in faith and all men as brothers; that the bonds of affection and unity between the sons of men should be strengthened; that diversity of religion should cease, and differences of race be annulled. . . ."[11]

---

[7]Walter Abbott, ed., *The Documents of Vatican II* (New York: Guild Press, 1966), pp. 661–663.

[8]"Introductory Essay: An Overview of the New Age Movement," *New Age Encyclopedia*, ed. J. Gordon Melton, Jerome Clark and Aidan A. Kelly (Detroit, MI: Gale Research, Inc., 1990), p. xvi.

[9]Sarvepalli Radhakrishnan, "Religion and Religions" in *Relations Among Religions Today*, ed. Moses Jung et al. (Leiden, 1963), pp. 131–32.

[10]William S. Hatcher and J. Douglas Martin, *The Baha'i Faith: The Emerging Global Religion* (New York: Harper & Row, Publishers, 1985), p. 82.

[11]Quoted in J.E. Esslemont, *Baha'u'llah and the New Era: An Introduction to the Baha'i Faith* (Wilmette, IL: Baha'i Publishing Trust, 1950), pp. 117–18.

Figure I-1 The Baha'i House of Worship, located just north of Chicago on the shore of Lake Michigan at Wilmette, Illinois. The nine-sided building symbolizes the unity of all religions. It is listed in the National Register of Historic Places. (*Photo courtesy of Baha'i Publishing Trust.*)

The fifth response might be described as the *affirmation* of religious diversity. Affirmation holds that the different religions are simply different, not headed toward a synthesis and not subsumable under the big umbrella of inclusivism. At the same time, each is ultimately true and must be honored as such. Affirmation has room for both commitment and openness. Describing this perspective, religious studies scholar Harold Coward writes:

> It is a recognition that deep religious commitment is necessarily felt as absolute and, as such, functions as the validating criteria for all of one's personal experience. This, however, does not impose it on others or rule out the recognition that in other persons there is a similar absolute commitment to a particular experience, which . . . will be different from one's own. . . . Thus, one is able to honor one's own commitment as absolute for oneself and at the same time respect the different absolute commitments of others. . . . In a dialogue this would mean the preservation of our differences in dignity and mutual respect.

In discussing how such dialogue could go forward, Coward continues:

> A basic prerequisite for such future dialogue is that all participants have accurate information about each other's religions. Fulfilling this prerequisite is probably the

single largest obstacle to the success of religious dialogue. The majority of people today are illiterate of their own religion as well as the religions of others. The academic discipline of religious studies has a major role to play in overcoming this problem. Intellectual knowledge of the facts of all religions is needed—but alone that will not be sufficient.[12]

The affirming impulse can arise from the recognition of the realities of historical existence. History, according to religious historian Ernst Troeltsch, exhibits a "universal law" that applies in religion as in all of history:

> The universal law of history consists precisely in this, that history constantly manifests itself in always-new and always-peculiar individualizations—and hence that its tendency is not toward unity or universality at all, but rather toward the fulfillment of the highest potentialities of each community.[13]

In her thorough discussion of this stance, which she labels "pluralism," Diana Eck, Director of Harvard University's Pluralism Project, notes these five points that help to clarify what an affirming stance is, as well as how it differs from some of the other views we have described:[14]

- It is not just the fact of religious diversity but "active positive engagement with it."
- It is not simply tolerance and a commitment to insure the rights of the followers of many faith traditions but "the active effort to understand difference and commonality through dialogue."
- While relativism does not allow for commitment, affirmation assumes that members of the different communities of faith are deeply committed to their chosen paths while practicing openness toward the chosen paths of others.
- It does not expect all religious to fuse together but looks for "ways to be distinctively ourselves and yet to be in relation to one another."
- The foundation of affirmation is interreligious dialogue based on understanding rather than on agreement, holding that the understanding of difference is as important as agreement.

In a recent book on religious pluralism in the United States, scholar Richard Evans Wentz highlights three characteristics of the affirming attitude.

- It *respects* the religious "others" who share our space. Respect means being able to imagine their way of being religious as something that might have meaning for ourselves.
- It is *reverent*, a deepening of respect "to the point of honor and caring."

---

[12]Harold Coward, *Pluralism: Challenge to World Religions* (Maryknoll, NY: Orbis Books, 1985), pp. 106–107.
[13]Ernst Troeltsch, "The Place of Christianity among the World Religions," in *Christianity and Other Religions*, John Hick and Brian Hebblethwaite, eds. (Philadelphia: Fortress Press, 1980), p. 17.
[14]Diana Eck, *Encountering God: A Spiritual Journey from Bozeman to Benares* (Boston: Beacon Press, 1993), pp. 191–199.

- Finally, it issues in *refinement*, the capacity to imagine "the kind of existence in which respect and reverence have exalted the human enterprise and lifted that enterprise to a new order of beauty and harmony."[15]

Another way to approach the question of how members of one religion deal with followers of other faiths is to ask whether or not the religious "others" are seen solely as objects for potential conversion or regarded on their own terms. This issue arises in the United States because the official disestablishment of religion means that religions must compete for followers and support in what is essentially a free marketplace. In this situation, religious groups and individuals may respond in one of three ways:

1. It is possible to lay self-interest aside and accept religious "others" as a part of the religiously diverse American religious landscape, respecting their values and beliefs and including them as an equal part of the religious community. Differences are not ignored, but respected.

2. For some, the religious "others" are seen solely as objects for potential conversion. Whether the approach to the other is negative or more sensitive, the intention remains conversion.

3. A third category is between the other two. People and groups in this category try to take seriously both the claims that American religious pluralism makes and the exclusive claims that their religion makes against competing claims. Rather than discount either, they have chosen to live with the tension between the competing claims.

The attitude that we hold toward those whose religion differs from our own has pragmatic ramifications as well as philosophical ones. For example, it influences our willingness to grant freedom of religious expression to them. A Christian pluralist, for example, would be more likely to willingly give a Muslim employee time off from work during Ramadan, Islam's holy month, than would a Christian exclusivist. A public school teacher who takes an inclusivist view might approach teaching the role of religion in world history differently than would one who takes a synthesist position. A college student whose approach was relativistic would respond differently to a roommate of another faith than would a student who was an exclusivist.

QUESTIONS AND ACTIVITIES FOR REVIEW, DISCUSSION, AND WRITING

1. What two features make religious diversity in the United States an especially interesting issue for reflective thought?
2. Describe each of the five responses to religious diversity.
3. Describe the affirmative response in greater detail.

---

[15]Wentz, *The Culture of Religious Pluralism*, pp.114–117.

4. Write an essay in which you describe your own attitude toward religious diversity. Be sure that you include any ideas you may have about *why* you feel as you do.
5. With several classmates, role-play different ways that members of one religion might approach members of another.
6. In the Yellow Pages of your local telephone directory, find listings for churches, religious organizations, and synagogues. How many different categories are listed? If you are from a small town or small city and have access to the telephone book of a major city (at your library, for example), do the same with it and notice the difference.
7. Visit the Yahoo search engine's religion category. Click on *Faiths and Practices*. Which religion has the greatest number of listings? The fewest? Why do you think this is?
8. Visit the Ontario Consultants for Religious Tolerance Web site, and read one of the essays. Write a response to what you have read. Be certain to include the title of the essay that you read.

FOR FURTHER READING

In a book such as this, we look at world religions as they are found in the United States. Any of the following three books provides additional information on world religions.

ELLWOOD, ROBERT, and BARBARA MCGRAW, *Many Peoples, Many Faiths: An Introduction to the Religious Life of Humankind,* 6th ed. Upper Saddle River, NJ: Prentice Hall, 1999. This and the Fisher book that follows are good standard introductory texts.

FISHER, MARY PAT, *Living Religions*, 3d ed. Upper Saddle River, NJ: Prentice Hall, 1997.

SHARMA, ARVIND, ed., *Our Religions*. San Francisco: HarperSanFrancisco, 1993. Professor Sharma's book is a collection of essays written by people who are both religious studies scholars and adherents of the faiths they describe.

Two recent books that focus on religious diversity itself are worthy of attention.

RICHARD E. WENTZ's *The Culture of Religious Pluralism* (Boulder, CO: Westview Press, 1996) places the contemporary situation in the context of religious diversity throughout United States history.

JAMES B. WIGGINS' *In Praise of Religious Diversity* (New York: Routledge, 1998) takes a more philosophical approach, thoroughly informed by the academic study of religion, and suggests that what has been done thus far by way of understanding and honoring diversity is not nearly enough.

Three general encyclopedic works provide information about the range of religion and religions in the United States.

LIPPY, CHARLES H., and PETER W. WILLIAMS, eds. *Encyclopedia of the American Religious Experience: Studies of Traditions and Movements.* New York: Charles Scribner's Sons, 1988. This is a three-volume work that covers both historical and contemporary topics. This book and the Melton book below are basic reference books for religion in the United States.

MELTON, J. GORDON, *The Encyclopedia of American Religions,* 5th ed. Detroit, MI: Gale Research, 1996. This book is a thorough and unbiased presentation of information about both consensus and alternative religions that is carefully indexed.

SWATOS, WILLIAM H., JR., *Encyclopedia of Religion and Society.* Walnut Creek, CA: AltaMira Press, 1998. The author uses a sociological approach throughout.

RELEVANT WORLD WIDE WEB SITES

The Interfaith Alliance: http://www.tialliance.org/

The Ontario Consultants for Religious Tolerance: http://www.religioustolerance.org/

The Pluralism Project: http://www.fas.harvard.edu/~pluralsm

United Communities of Spirit: http://www.silcom/~origin/ucs.html

These and other sites relevant to religious diversity can be accessed through the "Interfaith and Ecumenical Sites" Web page at the *Perspectives on Faith* Web Site (http://bsuvc.bsu.edu/~00jmcorbett/index.htm).

1

Studying and Describing Religion

Before you read this chapter, think about how and where you have learned about religion so far. What kinds of things did you study? What was the purpose of your study? Also, think about how *you* define religion. All of us have some idea of what religion is. What does the word *religion* mean to you?

WHY STUDY RELIGION?

Many, perhaps most, of you reading this are studying religion to receive academic credit for a course. But there are other reasons for studying religion. We study our own religion to learn more about a significant dimension of our lives. Our commitment to it matures as we base our devotion on greater knowledge and understanding.

Why study other people's religions? Doing so can help us to understand other people. Religion is an important, even essential, part of many people's lives, and by understanding and appreciating it, we come to know them better. Prejudice often results in part from a simple lack of knowledge and information. While knowledge and understanding do not guarantee freedom from prejudice, a lack of knowledge greatly increases the likelihood of prejudice.

It is also important that we understand religion because it has had an important role in history and continues to have a significant impact on contemporary events. Religion has had and continues to have an impact on cultural forms such as literature, art, and music. Finally, because all religions have deeply human roots, to understand anyone's religion can help us understand ourselves better. By understanding the similarities and differences between our own religion and those of other people, we also come to know our own better.

Recent statements by notable religious studies scholars highlight several important themes, including the practical applicability of religious studies, that help to relate the study of religion to the discussion of religious diversity in the Introduction.

Religious faith, both in individually packaged and communal forms, while it may not always be deep, is so widespread that it commends itself for study by anyone who wants to understand humans. . . .

In a society marked by what has come to be called multiculturalism, religion serves both to pocket people in enclaves, as in the case of the Amish, the Unification Church, Orthodox Judaism, the Nation of Islam, fundamentalisms, or high-church Anglicanism, *and* to help people engage in crisscrossing between these subcultures. Thus at one moment being an *African American* Baptist defines a person, and a moment later, in a different context, being an African American *Baptist* is the vital identifier. Being a Catholic *feminist* counts for one set of questions, and being a *Catholic* feminist helps account in the case of another. In every case, understanding the lover or the neighbor or the enemy often demands knowledge of religion. . . . Those who *get* to study religion may not necessarily contribute to concord and tolerance, though they also may. But they will understand better than before the Other with whom they coexist in a diverse world. . . .

On the domestic political scene, one need hardly elaborate on the practicality of understanding religion in the form of the putative Catholic vote, the various Christian coalitions, ever-changing Jewish interests, or what African American pastors are thinking. Advertisers blunder when they try to sell a product while being insensitive to the religious sensibilities of potential customers. Marketers include religious data when planning where to sell: hog butchers of the world, to take an obvious case, do not target Jewish communities.

In intimate personal relations, such as providing medical care, promoting support groups in struggles against addiction, or making sense of the person to whom one is married, some understanding of religious impulses and religion is practical. Even the widespread religious indifference and ignorance in much of the culture demands study. . . .[1]

The diversity of American society makes it urgent for our citizens to introduce themselves to one another. That is why the academic study of religion demands a high priority in the academy. The Texaco executives having trouble with Hanukkah and Kwanzaa [Jewish and African American celebrations, respectively] at Christmastime cost their company a big bundle of money. But they also illustrate why in a country in which nearly every religion in the world finds practitioners—in numbers—requires its citizens to learn about one another. . . . The special promise of the academic study of religion is to nurture this country's resources of tolerance for difference, our capacity to learn from the other and to respect the other.[2]

---

[1]Martin E. Marty, "An Exuberant Adventure: The Academic Study and Teaching of Religion," in *Religious Studies News*, Vol. 12, No. 3 (September, 1997), pp. 20 and 48.
[2]Jacob Neusner, "Scholarship, Teaching, Learning: Three Theses for the Academic Study of Religion," in *Religious Studies News*, Vol. 12, No. 3 (September, 1997), p. 20.

STUDYING RELIGION
AS A PART OF THE HUMANITIES

The study of religion has many dimensions. Studying religion as a part of a course of study in the humanities may involve attitudes and methods that are new to you.

Most of us who think about religion first learned to do so in a religious organization or a community of faith, or perhaps within our families. Maybe it was in preparation to become a member of a church or synagogue.[3] Perhaps it was learning about our own religion in Sunday school or Hebrew day school classes. For some, it was probably learning the prayers of our faith from our parents. We can call this method of studying religion a **devotional** or **theological** approach. This is study undertaken by members of a community of faith when they study their own religion. Therefore, we can call it an "inside" perspective. It usually involves the personal faith commitments of both teachers and students. It takes as its beginning point the faith of the community, the "givens" accepted as a part of their tradition. For Christians, for example, the uniqueness of Jesus and Jesus' special role in God's plan for the world is such a given. For Jews, the oneness of God has a similar role. Buddhists[4] take the early teachings of the Buddha as foundational. These starting points are often found in or derived from the group's sacred writings.

The word **theology** is sometimes used for this type of study. Theology takes faith as its starting point. It is, in Saint Anselm's classic definition, "faith seeking understanding."[5] Theology uses intellectual concepts to understand a particular religious tradition and to express its relevance for the present.

The goal of such devotional study is that those who engage in it will become more knowledgeable about and more committed to their faith. It does not necessarily involve attempting to show that one's own faith is superior or correct, although it is sometimes used in this way. Devotional study is an important part of educating people in their faith and helping them to mature as religious persons. It is a significant aspect of the growth and development of any religion. A firm understanding of one's own faith is also one foundation for dialogue with others.

The **academic study of religion** differs from the devotional approach in that it makes no assumptions about the beliefs, or lack of beliefs, of the scholar. Religious studies teachers and students alike may be believers, nonbelievers, or agnostics (people who believe that we cannot be certain whether God exists or not) in their personal religious lives.

Rather than concentrating on one religion, the academic study of religion promotes a lively awareness of the diversity of religious beliefs, practices, and

---

[3]A *synagogue* is a Jewish place of worship and center for study.
[4]You will learn more about Buddhism in chapter 10.
[5]Saint Anselm was a Christian theologian who lived between 1033 and 1109 C.E. The abbreviations C.E. for Common Era and B.C.E. for Before the Common Era have replaced A.D. (*Anno Domini*, the year of our Lord) and B.C. (Before Christ) in most scholarly writing.

experiences that people have. It encourages open-minded acceptance of that diversity. It investigates religions in their historical and cultural settings and examines a broad range of materials to provide the most balanced treatment possible. It distinguishes between things that most people accept as historical facts and other things that are taken as true only within the context of a particular community of faith. For example, most people in the United States would agree that the founder of Christianity was a historical person named Jesus who lived in the area of Nazareth. Non-Christians usually do not accept that Jesus was in a unique sense the Son of God.

In studying religion from an academic standpoint, we may try to *explain* religious behavior and beliefs as well as simply *describe* them. You will see a number of examples of this in Chapter 13. However, such explanations must never become *reductionistic*. Reductionism is an oversimplification that claims to exhaust the meaning of a phenomenon by explaining it in terms of some other, external factor. For example, saying that people are religious because economic deprivation in their earthly lives makes "pie in the sky by-and-by" attractive is a case of reductionism. While there may be some truth to this for some persons, it does not exhaust the meaning of religion.

When we study religion academically, the study takes place in an atmosphere that is free of advocacy. It promotes neither religion nor nonreligion. It educates about all religions and neither favors nor belittles any. It is loyal first of all to the guidelines of public scholarship. Its commitments are to knowledge and understanding for their own sake and to religion as a vigorous dimension of humanity's story (Figure 1-1). It does not involve the personal beliefs of its teachers and students. It is especially important to keep the distinction between the devotional study of religion and the academic study of religion clear in public, tax-supported schools, colleges, and universities. An institution supported by taxes paid by people of all faiths and by those who are not religious cannot

Figure 1-1   The study of religion is an integral part of education in the humanities. (*Photo by the author.*)

favor one religion over others. Nor can it favor either religion or secularity. To do so clearly violates the disestablishment clause of the First Amendment to the Constitution.

Our personal religious views *might* change when we study religion academically, but, if that happens, it is a personal by-product of the study and not its goal.

A Christian or Jew engaged in the devotional study of the Bible would turn to it as a believer studying the Word of God, trying to understand it more fully and grasp its contemporary meaning. People involved in the study of the Bible as literature (an academic class) have commitments, as scholars, to scholarship, whatever their personal religious beliefs may be. They look at the passage as literature, not as the Word of God. In a similar way, religious studies professionals might engage in a comparative study of the sacred writings of several religions. These would be viewed as examples of sacred writings but not as divine revelation.

The 1963 United States Supreme Court decision in *Abington* v. *Schempp* has particular relevance for the academic study of religion. The Court ruled that schools and school personnel could not mandate devotional activities in their schools and classrooms. For example, teachers cannot lead their students in saying grace before lunch. The Bible cannot be read as a morning devotional exercise. People who favored such exercises in the public schools charged that the Court had, in effect, supported the religion of secularism (nonreligion). Justice Clark, in replying to this charge, distinguished between the practice of religion, such as devotional exercises, and study about religion. He went on to say that study about religion as a part of human culture and the humanities is well within the guidelines established by the First Amendment to the Constitution. This Supreme Court decision allows for the academic study of religion at all levels of public education.

Religious groups cannot be barred from using public school facilities or other public buildings, however. If secular groups can use these facilities, then religious groups must have the same privilege. This is the result of the **Equal Access Act**. The Equal Access Act was passed by the 98th Congress in 1984 and upheld by the Supreme Court in *Board of Education of Westside Community School District* v. *Mergens* (1990). For example, if a school board permits such noncurricular clubs as a chess club or Boy or Girl Scouts to use their facilities for meetings, then a Bible study club must have the same right. Usually, interpretation holds that teachers or other school personnel may not be officially involved in such groups. If a city or county building has a public meeting room, then religious groups must be allowed to use it on the same basis as secular groups. The net effect of *Abington* v. *Schempp* and *Mergens* is that schools cannot actively promote religious activities, but neither can they prohibit them.

You may be wondering whether religious studies is defined by having a distinctive method or a distinctive subject matter. Religious studies scholars do not agree on the answer. In my opinion, religious studies is a distinct and identifiable academic discipline because it investigates the subject of religion in all its forms. Its *subject matter* is distinctive. In its investigation of its subject, it uses many methods. Human religious behavior is a very complex phenomenon and calls for many investigative tools.

There is no single best way to study religion. A variety of methods is necessary, and no one of them can claim primary authority.

Within the academic study of religion, we can distinguish two interrelated types of inquiry. The **social-scientific study of religion** is very much an "outside" point of view. It focuses on observation and on data that are quantifiable. Its goal is to be wholly objective. The data that it provides make a crucial contribution to our understanding of religion. Psychologists and sociologists who study human religious behavior often use social-scientific methods. The widespread use of computers for data processing and analysis has greatly enhanced this branch of the academic study of religion.

People **study religion as a part of the humanities** to understand a religious group, belief, or practice from the standpoint of what it is like for those who follow it. This approach encourages students and teachers to enter empathically into the life and experience of the religious "other." It seeks imaginative participation, developing what can be described as an "inside-outside" point of view. We can, with practice, become increasingly able to see religions other than our own *as if* from the inside, while remaining on the outside. We do not become participants, but we learn to value and appreciate the meaning that the religion has for those who are participants in it.

The academic study of religion may come under attack from either of two sides. On one side are traditional believers who are threatened by any viewpoint that takes the position that there is no one true religion and refuses to judge the truth or falsity of religious beliefs. On the other side are those who refuse to take religion seriously and think that it must be "explained away" in terms of social, psychological, or economic factors. As philosopher of religion Ninian Smart writes, in either case, people "forget that religions are what they are and have the power they have regardless of what we may think about their value, truth, or rationality. They also forget that . . . we have to listen to one another"[6] in a nation that is as religiously diverse as is the United States.

Perhaps you have felt one of these two ways at times, or perhaps you do now. You might occasionally find yourself feeling threatened by some of the material studied, by the way it is studied, or by your classmates' comments. Remember that the study of religion from an academic viewpoint allows everyone ideological space in which to exist. All that is required is that you extend to the beliefs and practices of others the same respect that you wish for your own.

---

[6]Ninian Smart, *Worldviews: Crosscultural Explorations of Human Beliefs* (New York: Charles Scribner's Sons, 1983), p. 17.

THE WORLD WIDE WEB:
A RESOURCE FOR STUDYING RELIGION

The World Wide Web is one of the most important—perhaps the most important—information resource to emerge in the twentieth century. Its eventual impact on human culture will rank with that of Gutenberg's invention of the printing press.

There is a great deal of information about religion and religions on the Web, and more appears daily. The Web is about communication—about people sharing information and gathering information. When information about religion, religious groups, and religious issues is presented on the Web, people of faith have the chance to speak for themselves, rather than an "outsider" speaking about them. When we visit Web sites, we have access to this information in whatever way suits us best. We can read and/or listen (many Web sites include sound) without feeling pressured to respond. We can read, reflect, come back and read again if we wish. The nature of the Web is such that we can always explore further along the same path, down a variety of side trails, or in another direction.

Evaluating Resources on the Web

One of the great strengths of the Web, in my opinion, is that anyone who has access to the appropriate hardware, software, and server and even a modicum of skill can create a Web page. It is, in other words, an extremely democratic, egalitarian environment. However, this characteristic brings with it a set of problems that concern evaluating what we find on the Web. When you go to a library to do research, or when you read a textbook, you make certain assumptions: The people who write articles for encyclopedias or for scholarly journals (for example) and the authors of textbooks are qualified to do what they've done. The material has been "refereed" or reviewed by other scholars in the area. It probably has been reviewed by the library staff as a part of its collections development. *You simply cannot make these assumptions about material that you find on the World Wide Web.* Material on the Web is in this respect more similar to articles in "popular" magazines, although even there, editors exercise at least some control over the content of articles. No one "owns" the Internet nor the Web; therefore, no one (other than the consumer of its resources) has a vested interest in the quality of what is published on it. Thus, an important part of becoming a savvy consumer of Web resources is carefully evaluating what you find there.

Perspectives on Faith: A Web Site for Inquiry about Religion

I have developed and maintain a World Wide Web site specifically designed to help students locate Web resources that are relevant to religious studies courses. It provides numerous links to religion-related sites on the Web. It also has an editorial. The URL for this site is:

http://bsuvc.bsu.edu/~00jmcorbett/index.htm

This site is accessed through Ball State University's computer system, which is very busy at times. If the server is busy, you may get an error message. Keep trying.

DESCRIBING RELIGION

Religion is an ambiguous word. People use it to mean various things. Even scholars in religious studies cannot agree on its meaning. The beginning point of understanding its meaning can be ordinary usage. That is, we do have some idea of what religion is. If someone asks, for example, "What religion do you practice?" we know how to answer the question. If someone mentions a religious service, we have a general idea of what sort of activity is meant.

By itself, our everyday, unreflective definition is inadequate. It is probably limited to our own experiences with religion. Our definition might be biased in some way, based on what we have been taught is "true" religion. Different people have different everyday definitions, and the same person may use different definitions at different times.

For purposes of study, we must have a good working definition. A **working definition** or **description** is one that is useful and adequate, but it is not necessarily the only possible one. It should meet the following three criteria.

1. **A good working definition of religion is broad enough to include all religions**. It should not define religion in a way that leaves out some manifestations of religion. Nor should it leave out any specific religion. For example, if we say that *religion* means belief in God (having in mind God as Jews and Christians think about God), we will leave out those people who worship many *deities* (a general word meaning "gods or goddesses") and those who worship none at all. This definition also focuses on belief and excludes other important dimensions of religion.

2. At the same time, **it must be sufficiently specific to distinguish religion from other similar things**, such as a nonreligious philosophy of life or a deeply held and passionate commitment to a social or political cause.

3. **It also needs to be as free of prejudice or bias as we can make it**. Definitions that state what true or genuine religion is often fall into the trap of imposing one person's or group's bias on the definition of religion generally.

In sum, then, our working definition of religion needs to be broad enough to include all religions, yet specific enough to allow us to distinguish religion from other, similar things. It also must not define religion in terms of our own prejudices.

Figure 1-2

A *developed religion* is an integrated system of beliefs, lifestyle, ritual activities, and social institutions by which individuals give meaning to (or find meaning in) their lives by orienting themselves to what they take to be holy, sacred, or of the highest value.

We will use the working definition given in Figure 1-2. It is important to know and understand this definition, because it underlies everything that follows throughout the book.

Religions are also *communities of faith*. They are groups of people knitted together by their shared commitment to a common world view and their participation in shared experiences. The nature of religious commitment and experience means that it often claims its adherents' greatest, most intense loyalties. The ties within communities of faith are frequently among the strongest and most meaningful of human relationships.

Let's discuss this definition of religion in detail. A developed religion is an **integrated system**. Ideally, all the dimensions in a religion hold together to make a comprehensive, coherent whole. Its various parts work together without conflict and with mutual support. The extent to which this is the case varies from one religion to another and from one person to another. But ideally, a religion does have coherence among its various dimensions. These dimensions include beliefs, a lifestyle, rituals, and institutions.

Belief takes many forms. Beliefs are the ideas of a religion. For example, most religions have an idea about what the purpose of human life is. Most have beliefs concerning how the world came into being and what happens to people after death. These beliefs are found in scripture, statements of faith, creeds (official written statements), hymns, stories, and handbooks of belief, to name but a few locations. The beliefs of a community of faith also exist in the minds of its members, although these may not be as well worked out as those found in official statements.

Nearly all religions have guidelines for their members' daily **lifestyle**. These include codes of conduct and standards of behavior, as well as carefully worked out ethical systems. They involve both formal requirements and customs and less formal folkways and habits. Examples include dietary regulations followed by Jews and Seventh-day Adventists and dress codes followed by certain Christian groups and many Muslims.

Religions also include **ritual activities**. These are the ceremonial actions, usually repetitive in nature, that people perform as a part of their religious behavior. The word *worship* suggests that there is a divine being or beings who are being worshiped. Not all religious people worship such a being, although they do participate in other rituals. So *worship* is too narrow a term for our use. Religious rituals include worship, however, along with prayer, chanting, meditation, the lighting of candles, pilgrimages, and the devotional reading of religious books, to name but a few examples. There are religious rituals that are public and corporate, and there are those that individual people and families do privately. For many religious people, the rhythm of regular participation in the ritual life of their religion is more important than is reflection on religious beliefs.

Finally, although religion has to do with individual people, it also includes **social institutions**. Like-minded people join together for instruction, for rituals, and for fellowship. Structures for governance and decision making are necessary. Other things in this category are arrangements for admitting members to the group and expelling them from it, educational functions, and arrangements for the selection, training, and support of leaders.

Religion is one way that **people give meaning to or find meaning in their lives**. A religion is a human creation or development. Its beliefs, lifestyle, rituals, and institutions are the products of human thought and activity. It is continuous with the many other ways that we either create or find meaning in our lives, such as through the personal relationships that are dear to us, the work that we do, and the values, ideals, and causes to which we give our loyalty. Religion is continuous with these other structures of meaning and shares their profoundly human roots.

Religion involves that which people take to be **sacred, holy,** or **of the highest value**. Although religion is continuous with other structures of meaning, it is also unique. Most interpretations of religion hold that its uniqueness is in its reference to the sacred or to the highest value. It reaches beyond the individual and the ordinary concerns of day-to-day living. Religion puts us in touch with the sense of mystery that shines through the cracks of our common world. It has to do with the most comprehensive, fullest expression or embodiment of reality.

QUESTIONS AND ACTIVITIES FOR REVIEW, DISCUSSION, AND WRITING

1. Write a paragraph in which you explain what you hope to gain from your study of religion in the United States. Are your goals academic, personal, or a combination of both? Compare your answer with those of other people.
2. Ask several of your friends how they define religion, and compare their answers. How are they alike? Different?
3. Look up the definition of *religion* in any standard dictionary, and write an essay in which you evaluate it based on what you have learned in this chapter.
4. If you are a part of a religious group, think about how the four dimensions of religion we discussed apply to it.
5. Visit the American Academy of Religion Web site to learn how they answer the question, "Why study religion?" Look at the Overview and Mission Statement especially.

FOR FURTHER READING

CAPPS, WALTER H. *Religious Studies: The Making of a Discipline.* Minneapolis, MN: Fortress Press, 1995. Capps's book is lucid and well-written, a very thorough introduction to the history and methods of the study of religion. Capps is a well-known scholar in the field. This is highly recommended.

CUNNINGHAM, LAWRENCE S., et al. *The Sacred Quest: An Invitation to the Study of Religion.* Englewood Cliffs, NJ: Prentice Hall, 1995. This book, along with the Ellwood and Monk books, are good introductory texts that focus on what religion is and how we can best begin to study and understand it.

ELLWOOD, ROBERT. *Introducing Religion: From Inside and Outside,* 3d ed. Englewood Cliffs, NJ: Prentice Hall, 1994.

MONK, ROBERT C., et al. *Exploring Religious Meaning,* 5th ed. Upper Saddle River, NJ: Prentice Hall, 1996.

There are a number of journals relevant to the study of religion. Representative ones include the *Journal of the American Academy of Religion,* the *Journal of Biblical Literature, Sociology of Religion,* the *Journal for the Scientific Study of Religion,* and *Religion and American Culture: A Journal of Interpretation.*

RELEVANT WORLD WIDE WEB SITES

The American Academy of Religion: http://scholar.cc.emory.edu/scripts/AAR/AAR-MENU.html

The Society for Biblical Literature: http://scholar.cc.emory.edu/scripts/SBL/SBL-MENU.html

The Center for the Study of Religion and American Culture: http://www.iupui.edu/it/raac/home.html

Yahoo! search engine, religion: http://www.yahoo.com/Society_and_Culture/Religion/

Excite search engine, religion: http://excite.com/lifestyle/communities/religion/

AltaVista search engine, religion: http://altavista.looksmart.com/r?li&izf&e53322

There are Web sites about how to think critically about Web sites; one of the most thorough is at http://www.library.ucla.edu/libraries/college/instruct/critical.htm. There are also sites dealing with evaluating sites (http://thorplus.lib.purdue.edu/~techman/eval.html) and evaluating Internet information (http://sol/slcc.edu/lr/navigator/discovery/eval.html).

2

Religion in the Life of the United States

The United States has become known for its freedom of religion. People decide for themselves whether they will be a part of a religious group, and, if so, which one. Before reading this chapter, stop and think about what freedom of religion means to you personally. How important is it to you? In what specific ways does it affect your life? Do you think there should be limits on religious freedom? If so, what should they be, and why do you think they are necessary?

DISESTABLISHMENT AND THE CONSTITUTION

Prior disillusionment with established religion and the existence of religious pluralism worked against the continued existence of established religion in the United States. The American experience with established churches was influenced by the experience of European settlers who were forced to flee from establishments of religion in their home countries. It was also influenced by the experiments with pluralism and freedom of religion that had been carried out in Rhode Island and Pennsylvania. Many people concluded that civil power and privilege for churches led to problems, while toleration and equality under the law was good for both the churches and society at large.[1] In addition, no single religious group had enough support throughout the original thirteen states to make its belief and practice the law of the land. Furthermore, the framers of the Constitution held several views of religion. Some were Protestant and Catholic Christians. Others were advocates of naturalistic religion based on rationality and morality, and still others were nonbelievers or atheists. Freethinkers either questioned or rejected traditional Christianity, and their views helped to bring about the official separation of church and state that we have now. Still others came from those strands of Protestant Reformation thought that advocated strict separation of church and state.

[1] Henry Steele Commager, *The Empire of Reason* (Garden City, NY: Anchor Press, 1977), pp. 210–211.

Matters pertaining to religion are found in three places in the Constitution: Article 6, the First Amendment, and the Fourteenth Amendment.

1.   Article 6 prohibits religious requirements for holding public office: "The Senators and Representatives . . . , and the Members of the several State Legislatures, and all executive and judicial offices, both of the United States and the several States, shall be bound by Oath or Affirmation, to support this Constitution; but **no religious Test shall ever be required as a Qualification to any Office or public Trust under the United States**" [emphasis added]. In other words, someone's religion or lack of religion cannot legally be a qualification for holding public office. In a pluralistic culture in which religion and government are separate functions, affirmations about religion cannot be requirements for holding public office.

2.   The First Amendment to the Constitution contains some of the most important religious liberty legislation in our nation's history. It is part of the Bill of Rights, prepared under the leadership of James Madison: "**Congress shall make no law respecting an establishment of religion, or prohibiting the free exercise thereof**; or abridging the freedom of speech, or of the press; or the right of the people peaceably to assemble, and to petition the Government for a redress of grievances" [emphasis added].

The "establishment clause" says that the United States Congress cannot make any one religion the official religion of the United States. It cannot act in a way that gives preferential treatment or support to one religion above others. Nor can it support religion or nonreligion generally, one over the other. Insofar as possible, it must maintain a neutral stance toward religion.

The second clause is often called the "free exercise" clause. It states that the government cannot interfere with any person's religion. A significant distinction was made in the interpretation of this clause and has remained a part of judicial precedent. In *Reynolds* v. *United States* (1878), Reynolds held that a law against marriage to more than one person at the same time violated his religious freedom, because he was a member of the Latter-day Saints, who at that time advocated the practice. The Supreme Court did not agree with Reynolds. In a landmark opinion, the Court held that the free exercise clause applied to religious beliefs but not necessarily to the actions arising from those beliefs. It held that "actions which are in violation of social duties or subversive of good order" cannot be tolerated, even when they are done in the name of religion.

This is a dilemma that cannot be fully resolved. Because religion is an intimate joining of belief and action, it may seem odd to tell people that they may believe what they please but prevent them from acting on those beliefs. Yet there are actions that no reasonable human being would condone, such as the torture of people or animals. There are actions that, if permitted, would utterly disrupt the social order, such as the refusal to be bound by any laws. These sorts of actions cannot be tolerated, even in the hallowed name of religious freedom.

Freedom of speech, the press, and assembly also contributes to religious freedom. These freedoms mean that people may speak and write openly about their views on religious questions. They may gather peaceably to listen to speakers or to worship in whatever ways they choose.

These two clauses account for most of the freedom of religion cases to come before the Court. The framers of the Bill of Rights could not possibly have known the range of circumstances these first ten amendments might be required to cover. The provisions of the bill are necessarily very broad, both allowing for and requiring constant reinterpretation. The majority opinion in *Walz* v. *Tax Commission of the City of New York* (1970) summarizes the role of the Supreme Court:

> The general principle deducible from the First Amendment and all that has been said by the Court is this: That we will not tolerate either governmentally established religion or governmental interference with religion. Short of those expressly proscribed governmental acts there is room for play in the joints productive of a benevolent neutrality which will permit religious exercise to exist without sponsorship and without interference. . . .

3.   The Fourteenth Amendment is the final Constitutional reference to religious liberty. Added in 1868, this long amendment touches on several issues. The crucial point for religious liberty is in Section 1: "**No State shall make or enforce any law which shall abridge the privileges or immunities of citizens of the United States**; nor shall any State deprive any person of life, liberty, or property without due process of law; nor deny to any person within its jurisdiction the equal protection of the laws" [emphasis added].

Both Article 6 and the religion clauses in the First Amendment deal with what the federal government may not do. The Fourteenth Amendment holds that the states as well are not to "abridge the privileges" of their citizens, including the privilege of religious freedom. When the Constitution was originally written, several of the states did have establishments of religion. Such state interference with religion is prohibited under the Fourteenth Amendment.

LEGISLATING RELIGIOUS LIBERTY

The **Religious Freedom Restoration Act** was signed into law in November 1993. In the early 1990s, freedom of religious practice for smaller and less popular religions appeared to have been jeopardized by certain United States Supreme Court decisions. To cite a well-known example, *Employment Division of the State of Oregon* v. *Smith* (1990) overturned the principle that the government's interest had to be "compelling" to justify restricting freedom of religion. In *Smith*, the Court upheld the denial of unemployment benefits to Native Americans who lost their jobs because they used the illegal drug peyote as a sacrament in religious ceremonies. In its majority opinion, the Court held that the free exercise of religion deserves no special protection, as long as the law applies to nonreligious groups also. This line of argument lays the groundwork for the restriction of any unpopular religious practice.

In response to the perceived threats to religious liberty, a diverse coalition of religious leaders and groups came together to support the passage of the Act. This bill sought to protect the free exercise of religion through a legislative act rather than by judicial means, enhancing protection especially for the lesser-known and less-understood religions.

Many civil libertarians and religious liberty advocates hailed the passage of the RFRA as a restoration of one of our most important freedoms. Others attacked the Act as an unconstitutional protection of conduct motivated by religion and thus an infringement of the establishment clause. The definitive Supreme Court test was the case of *City of Boerne, Texas* v. *Flores* (1997). St. Peter Catholic Church in Boerne requested permission from the city to expand its building. Denied permission because the church is located in a historic district, they sued the city under the Religious Freedom Restoration Act. The city responded that the Act itself could not be binding because it violated the non-establishment provision of the First Amendment. The Religious Freedom Restoration Act was invalidated by the Supreme Court.

This leaves religious freedom in question, especially for smaller and less-understood groups. The government need only demonstrate a *rational* basis for curtailing freedom of religious practice; it does not have to show a *compelling* interest in doing so.

Supporters of the RFRA responded quickly and negatively. In June, 1998, the Religious Liberty Protection Act of 1998 was introduced into the Senate and the House of Representatives. Like its predecessor, this act seeks to restore the compelling interest and the least restrictive means tests. The bill had not come to a vote as this book went to press.

THE ROLE OF RELIGION IN PUBLIC LIFE

There is disagreement in the United States about the role that religion *should* play in the public life of the nation. For example, between 30 and 40 percent of adults think that politicians who do not believe in God are not fit to hold public office and that it would be better for the country if more people with strong religious beliefs did hold public offices. On the other hand, about two-thirds feel that religious leaders should not try to influence how people vote, and over half believe that religious leaders should not try to influence government decisions. While a majority feels that religious institutions have about the right amount of power in this country, nearly one-fourth feel that they have too much, and almost one-fifth think it's too little. The issue of prayer in public schools provides another example of the diversity of opinion about religion in public life. A majority of people think that there should be time in the public school day for silent prayer. Twelve percent, however, think that organized prayer has no place in the public schools, while about one-third want to see some type of organized prayer (22 percent who want group prayers not linked to a particular religion and 9 percent who want Christian prayer required).

There is no disagreement, however, that religion *does* play a very visible public role in the United States. One recent book on religion and politics cites the following:

> There is the vigorous presence of the religious Christian conservative movement, which has entered politics to address abortion, pornography, sex education, prayer in public schools, and family breakdown. We see the growing assertiveness of the Catholic Church, which allies itself with evangelicals on abortion and educational choice and with liberal Protestants on defense and social welfare issues. We observe the increasing politicization of the black church and the presidential campaigns of one of its most prominent ministers, the Reverend Jesse Jackson. We have seen the vigorous lobbying by liberal religionists, Protestant and Catholic, who argued against U.S. military initiatives in Central America and the Persian Gulf but supported intervention in Haiti. We consider the prominent role of Jewish organizations in American politics, especially regarding support for Israel, which sharply contrasts with the as yet fitful efforts of the growing Muslim population to gain political influence. We watch the rising flood of cases in the courts, especially cases brought by religious and antireligious minorities. Everywhere one looks religion and politics are engaged in American public life.[2]

Religious groups and individuals try in many ways to affect American public life. They try to influence how people vote on candidates and issues. They try to shape public opinion by advertising to the culture at large and by trying to mold their own followers' opinions and actions. They lobby public officials, write letters, make telephone calls, and send off e-mails and faxes. They run for public office. Some of these efforts are carried out by organizations (e.g. the Catholic Church, the Presbyterian Church), some by coalitions of groups (e.g. the Christian Coalition, the National Council of Churches of Christ in the U.S.A., the United Jewish Appeal), and some by individuals or local groups of individuals.[3]

A word of caution is in order here. I will be summarizing the relationships between religion and politics. To say that a particular religious view or orientation is *related* to a political view or an opinion or social issues is not to say that the religious view *causes* the political or social view. Both might well be affected by another factor or factors, and the examination of all these intervening factors is far beyond the scope of this book. While linkages do exist, they are often not

---

[2]Robert Booth Fowler and Allen D. Hertzke, *Religion and Politics in America: Faith, Culture, and Strategic Choices* (Boulder, CO: Westview Press, 1995), p. 1.

[3]Michael Corbett and Julia M. Corbett, *Politics and Religion in the United States* (New York: Garland Publishing, 1999), pp. 339–345.

as strong as we might expect, due, for example, to problems people have in translating religious beliefs into specific issue stands or lack of integration between religious beliefs and the rest of life.[4]

Having noted these cautions, there remain some generalizations that can be made that help to define the parameters of religion's role in public life.[5] In terms of their political party identifications, black Protestants and Jews tend to be Democrats, as do Catholics, although to a lesser extent. Republicans have the greatest strength among evangelical and mainline Protestants, and those with no religious preference are the most likely to classify themselves as political independents. Jews are the most likely to identify themselves as political liberals, with seculars and black Protestants liberal but to a lesser extent. A plurality of Catholics, mainline Protestants, and evangelical Protestants consider themselves political conservatives. On the whole, these correlations are much more relevant for whites than for blacks; race has a much greater influence on political orientation among blacks than does religion.

There are also correlations between religion and social views. Mainline Protestants tend toward social-issues liberalism, although the link is much stronger among the leadership than for the average person in the pew. These Protestants think of Jesus primarily "as a moral teacher who told disciples that they could best honor him by helping those in need."[6] Their approach resembles the Social Gospel tradition of the 1800s with its emphasis on making social structures more humane and compatible with the will of God, rather than simply providing assistance for individuals. The National Council of Churches' support for passage of the Equal Rights Amendment and its statement against a military strike in Iraq exemplify this view.

Evangelical Protestants have emerged in recent decades as a substantial morally conservative force on social issues. White evangelicals are the most likely of all the religious groups to oppose abortion under most circumstances. They are least supportive of civil rights for homosexuals. They are among the most likely to believe that women's proper place is in the home. They are least likely to support gun-control laws and most likely to advocate making all pornography illegal. Evangelical Protestants tend to emphasize Jesus as the way to personal salvation for those who put their faith in him,[7] and living a morally upright life, defined in terms of adherence to traditional moral standards. An overwhelming majority of black Protestants are evangelicals, and they do not show the same patterns, instead blending religious conservatism with political progressivism, particularly on economic and race-related issues.

---

[4]For an examination of this issue, see Corbett and Corbett, *Politics and Religion in the United States*, pp. 258–262.

[5]For much fuller discussion of the links between religion and political views and between religion and social views, see the following: Michael Corbett and Julia Corbett, *Politics and Religion in America*; Robert Booth Fowler and Allen D. Hertzke, *Religion and Politics in America: Faith, Culture, and Strategic Choices* (Boulder, CO: Westview Press, 1995); and Kenneth D. Wald, *Religion and Politics in the United States, Third Edition* (Washington, DC: CQ Press, 1997).

[6]R. Stephen Warner, *New Wine in Old Wineskins: Evangelicals and Liberals in a Small-Town Church* (Berkeley: University of California Press, 1988), pp. 33–34.

[7]Warner, *New Wine in Old Wineskins*, pp. 33–34.

Catholic views on the issues of the day resemble those of evangelical Protestants in some respects and those of their liberal Protestant counterparts in other ways. They blend economic and social liberalism born of historic alliances with labor and extensive experience in dealing with immigrant populations with the concern for traditional moral values that has always characterized Catholic moral theology. This makes Catholics "key swing voters" with whom "both liberal Protestants and conservative evangelicals seek political alliances."[8] While Catholics tend to favor federal government intervention in providing welfare services and business regulation, they also favor restrictions on legal abortion. In recent years, they have sided with political liberals on most peace and justice issues. As with mainline Protestants, there is considerably more diversity among the Catholic faithful than there is among the elites (for example, the U.S. Catholic Conference, the staff arm of the National Council of Catholic Bishops).

Historically, those of Jewish faith have tended to be socially and economically liberal and strongly in support of individual liberties with regard to matters of conscience such as legal abortion and civil rights for gay people. There are a number of reasons for this liberalism, one of which is the Jews' long history of persecution and discrimination. This has made them very wary of restricting the rights of any unpopular group. A substantial proportion of Jews in the United States are Reform Jews, whose history includes Enlightenment beliefs about the value and sanctity of each individual's conscience. Jews are also among the most highly educated religious groups, and there is a strong association between education and tolerance, as well. In recent times, an economically conservative movement has developed within American Judaism, particularly among Conservative and Orthodox Jews. This conservatism, however, accounts for a small minority only.

Those with no religious preference or those identified as "seculars" are on the liberal end of the spectrum of views on sociopolitical issues. Socially, particularly when the issue concerns individual liberties, they are either most liberal or second-most liberal (on issues on which Jews are the most liberal). On economic issues, seculars and those with no religious preference are usually the most liberal.

CIVIL RELIGION AND BEYOND

Neither the idea of a **civil religion** nor the use of the concept in the United States began with sociologist Robert Bellah, but his work brought it to scholarly attention and ultimately to the American popular mind. In a 1967 essay, Bellah wrote that in the United States

> There actually exists alongside of and rather clearly differentiated from the churches an elaborate and well-institutionalized civil religion in America. . . . This

---

[8]Fowler and Hertzke, *Religion and Politics in America: Faith, Culture, and Strategic Choices*, p. 43.

public religious dimension is expressed in a set of beliefs, symbols, and rituals that I am calling the American civil religion.[9]

Bellah cited founding documents such as the Declaration of Independence and the Constitution, as well as the inaugural speeches of several presidents, along with holiday observances, in support of his thesis. He included belief in God, belief in America's role in God's plans for the world, commonly accepted standards of morality and civic virtue, and routinely observed holidays among the verities of civil religion.

Bellah's seminal essay gave religious studies scholars a new way of analyzing the roles that religion plays in the public life of the United States. It moved the study of religion beyond the study of ecclesiastical institutions and laid the groundwork for recognition of the importance of popular religion. It also provided great insight into the ways in which civic ideals and the legitimating principles of a culture are expressed powerfully in symbols that link them to divine realities.

Changes in how we view the culture of the United States have made Bellah's assertion that there is a common set of religious and civic convictions that underlies American life increasingly problematic. As one scholar describes the current situation, the sense of national consensus that is required by Bellah's civil religion thesis "flies in the face of observed reality. . . . Instead of a single civil religion harmoniously uniting all Americans, an alternative hypothesis rooted in the pervasive sense of cultural conflict that characterizes much of America's past seems . . . far more persuasive." Another scholar identifies civil religion as interpreted by Bellah as "a vestige of the de facto religious establishment of the nineteenth century" and goes on to note that

> by appealing to a set of overarching religious values, Bellah's concept of civil religion encourages us to make presumptive religious judgments about what it means to be an American. Yet, it is precisely the restraint from making such judgments that allows us to see the contributions religious diversity in America has made to social equality and to social activism.[10]

Rather than a single voice, the vision of what the United States is and ought to be has become a chorus of many voices, each vying for a hearing. Any attempt to describe a single American voice inevitably seems sectarian and exclusive. Increasing cultural pluralism has made the broadly liberal Protestant outlines of Bellah's civil religion misleading when they are used to describe an agreed-upon set of civic standards and virtues. It seems necessary at this point in our history to focus on the variety of religions and cultures that are present in the United States, rather than looking for a unity that many have come to doubt.

[9]Robert N. Bellah, "Civil Religion in America," *Daedalus*, 117, no. 3 (Winter 1967), pp. 1, 4.
[10]Phillip E. Hammond, Amanda Porterfield, James G. Moseley, and Jonathan D. Sarna, "Forum: American Civil Religion Revisited," *Religion and American Culture: A Journal of Interpretation*, 4, no. 1 (Winter 1994), pp. 9–10 and 21.

At the same time, there is a reality behind the civil religion thesis that ought not to be overlooked in any discussion of the role of religion in the life of the nation. Political speeches continue to be laced with religious rhetoric. Debates about "hot button" issues such as legal abortion, homosexual rights, prayer in public schools, and the role of the United States as the world's military police officer continue to be bolstered by appeals to religion from all sides of the discussion. The fact that the debate over the proper role of religion in the political life of the nation continues is itself evidence of the civil religion impulse, however diffuse its content.

There may well be multiple civil religions in the United States. At the very least, it would seem that there are two different versions of it, one more conservative and one more liberal.[11] The *conservative* version of civil religion continues to understand the United States as God's chosen nation and the American political and economic order as the one most aligned with the will of God. The advocates of civil religion in its conservative mode seek an active role for the government in promoting public and private virtue through the promotion of religion, for example by having organized time for prayer in the public schools and posting the Ten Commandments in public buildings. They seek to have laws enacted that enforce a traditional code of private morality, such as limiting the availability of legal abortion and legal recourse in situations of racial or gender discrimination. They are most likely to call for United States military involvement to protect U.S. interests or to protect the world from governments and leaders deemed "ungodly."

Civil religion liberals take the opposite approach on all of these points. The privileged position of the United States in the world is understood as a call to greater service rather than a confirmation of God's unique favor. The political and economic system of the United States is described as one among many, each with strengths and weaknesses, and none identified with the will of God. Believing that the particularities of religion can lead to disruption in the public order, liberal civil religionists want to keep them separate. Valuing diversity above conformity to a single standard, they promote individual civil liberties and call on the government to enact policies that enhance them. If they advocate military intervention, it is usually in the interest of justice and human rights.

Culture Wars?

The discussion of competing civil religions in the United States is related to another thesis about the role of religion in American public life: the belief that the nation is embroiled in a "culture war" that pits liberals against conservatives across a broad spectrum of policy issues and moral choices. Culture war theorists

---

[11]For fuller discussion of America's two civil religions, the following two sources are recommended: Derek H. Davis, "Law, Morals, and Civil Religion in America," *Journal of Church and State*, Vol. 39, No. 3 (Summer, 1997), pp. 411–425; and Robert Wuthnow, *The Restructuring of American Religion: Society and Faith Since World War II* (Princeton, NJ: Princeton University Press, 1988).

identify two rival camps. The exact description and composition of the two camps varies somewhat from author to author, but the outlines are clear.[12]

The *progressive* or *liberal* side includes liberal religionists, secularists, humanists, modernists, and their sympathizers. They draw their inspiration from Enlightenment philosophy and very liberal religion and advocate pluralism and individual rights. They favor a strong role for the federal government in promoting equality and justice. Government and religion should remain separate. Censorship has no place in a free society, no matter how offensive the content of speech or art might be. Discrimination on any basis should be eliminated. Matters of personal morality ought not to be regulated by law. They share many of the beliefs and ideals of liberal civil religion. Organizations usually associated with this perspective include the American Civil Liberties Union, the National Organization for Women, and People for the American Way.

The *orthodox* or *conservative* camp includes more traditional religionists and social conservatives. Their watchword is "traditional values," reinforced by law whenever possible. They are dismayed at the proliferation of "big government." Organizationally, this group coalesced around the Moral Majority, which was dissolved in the late 1980s. Currently, the Christian Coalition is the main organizational locus for this viewpoint.

There can be no doubt that there are dramatic differences of opinion about important issues in the United States, including those as fundamental as the kind of nation that the United States is and ought to be and the best means of enhancing civil life. But do these differences signal a "culture war"? On the whole, I think not, for several reasons.

Perhaps most important is the fact that most people occupy a position somewhere in the middle, avoiding either extreme on the issues that cut across the conservative/liberal divide. There are dedicated partisans on both sides, but they are far outnumbered by moderates. Too, most of us are not true ideologues. That is to say, our views on social and political issues are not wholly consistent. We tend in one direction on some issues, and in another on other issues. Nor is the conservative/liberal division closely associated with demographic characteristics—such as race, socioeconomic class, or region of residence—that would make it even more culturally divisive.

The metaphor of two opposing camps arrayed against each other in a "culture war" is too extreme. It is inaccurate, first of all, and it tends to cut off genuine dialogue before it can begin. It posits a sharp "either/or" that is belied by the facts. There is also some danger that such metaphors will turn into self-fulfilling prophecies. Perhaps a better image for what is going on in the culture is that of a troupe of dancers struggling to learn the intricate dance of pluralism. Few have learned their steps thoroughly yet, and every so often they bump head-

---

[12]Good discussions of the culture war thesis can be found in James Davison Hunter, *Culture Wars: The Struggle to Define America* (New York: Basic Books, 1991), the title of which brought the term to popular attention; Robert Wuthnow, *The Restructuring of American Religion* (Princeton, NJ: Princeton University Press, 1988); and Robert Wuthnow, *The Struggle for America's Soul: Evangelicals, Liberals, and Secularism* (Grand Rapids, MI: W.B. Eerdmans, 1989).

long into each other. Toes get stepped on, and tempers flare. But the dance goes on and becomes smoother with time.

The Search for Common Ground

As the twentieth century evolves into the twenty-first, there are indications of a movement beyond the vehement politics of left and right, a movement to discover values and virtues on which we can agree. Two examples of this changing mood in the culture are described below.

Common Ground Politics

We believe the American people are disgusted with politics as usual and hungry for political vision with spiritual values that transcends the old and failed categories that still imprison public discourse and stifle our creativity. The religious community should help lead that discussion and action toward new political and economic alternatives.[13]

Sojourners represents a grassroots network for personal, community, and political transformation. Rooted in the solid ground of prophetic biblical tradition, Sojourners is a progressive Christian voice that preaches not political correctness but compassion, community, and commitment. We refuse to separate personal faith from social justice, prayer from peacemaking, contemplation from action, or spirituality from politics. Sojourners includes Evangelicals, Catholics, Pentecostals and Protestants; liberals and conservatives; blacks, whites, Latinos, and Asians; women and men; young and old. We are Christians who want to follow Jesus, but who also sojourn with others in different faith traditions and all those who are on a spiritual journey. We reach into traditional churches but also out to those who can't fit into them. Together we seek to discover the intersection of faith, politics, and culture.[14]

The movement toward a politics of the common ground, and with it a new engagement between religion, politics, and culture, has been largely a Christian concern in the United States, because the disagreements between left and right have been stated primarily in terms of Christian thought. Sojourners and Call to Renewal are two examples of this approach. Advocates of this approach believe that politics and the overall public life of the nation desperately need to be informed by religious and spiritual values. But instead of increasing and supporting the old divisions, religious organizations and individuals should manifest a new style of engagement that transcends the old divisions.

The liberal and the conservative sides of the disagreement each have strengths and weaknesses, and many Americans can support elements of both platforms. Peace and justice *and* a strong individual and social fabric of personal

---

[13]The Founding Document of the Call to Renewal, on the Call to Renewal Web site (http://www.calltorenewal.com).

[14]From the Sojourners organization Web site (http://www.sojourners.com/).

morality can go together. Support for government services for those who need them need not undercut the importance of personal responsibility. Support for "family values" need not mean support for only one style of family but supporting whatever styles of families actually exist.

The accent is on cooperation in practical terms, as well. We can no longer expect the federal government, or government in general, to "do it all." Individuals, families, and the private sector all need to work together to ameliorate the host of problems that confront us. Rather than the government providing social services directly, for example, food programs run by religious organizations and addiction-recovery programs sponsored by churches and synagogues should also be eligible for government funding, even if they include a religious dimension. While many people would agree with the theoretical perspectives of common ground politics, it is these pragmatic connections between religion and government that make some people uneasy. Does government money mean government control? Does financial support mean government establishment of religion?

Tikkun Magazine, founded in 1986, and Michael Lerner's book, *The Politics of Meaning*,[15] describe a Jewish attempt to find a common ground between liberalism and conservatism. One advocate of the politics of meaning describes the situation and their response in terms that call for greater balance in the public face of religion in the United States:

> Liberals have fought to keep ethics and spirituality out of the public sphere. But all they have succeeded in doing is keeping their ethical and spiritual values out of the public sphere. The Right's approach to these issues has already entered the public sphere, and the market's commitment to an ethos of materialism and self-ishness already shapes much of the public debate. It's time for liberals and progressives to introduce an alternative vision of ethics and spirituality, one that rejects the demeaning of others and the privileging of market values.[16]

The Interfaith Alliance

Movement toward a common ground beyond division and discord has come from within the religious community, as well. The Interfaith Alliance is one example. It was founded to counteract the efforts of the Christian Coalition and similar groups to claim a monopoly on the voice of faith in American public life. Its Mission Statement and Statement of Principles specifically challenge approaches that seek to divide or to pit religion against democracy:

> The mission of The Interfaith Alliance is to promote the positive role of religion as a healing and constructive force in public life. Therefore we challenge those who manipulate religion to advance an extreme political agenda. Through our shared

---

[15]Michael Lerner, *The Politics of Meaning: Restoring Hope and Possibility in an Age of Cynicism* (New York: Addison Wesley, 1996).
[16]"The Politics of Meaning: A New Bottom Line" Web site (http://members.aol.com/pomeaning/).

religious values, we seek to build a revitalized mainstream religious movement based upon active civic participation. . . .

The Interfaith Alliance believes that religion best contributes to public life when it works for reconciliation, inspires common effort, promotes community and responsibility, and upholds the dignity of all human beings. The Interfaith Alliance will publicly challenge any candidate or political organization that implicitly or explicitly claims to speak for all people of faith. We will openly counter those who, in the name of religion, ignore the basic religious principles that remind us all of our responsibility to ourselves, each other, and our community. We believe these principles are consistent with the highest ideals of American democracy.[17]

POPULAR RELIGION

I defined *religion* in Chapter 1 in a way that emphasizes religions as structured social systems, institutions, or organizations. This aspect of religion can be called **institutional religion**. The words **ecclesial** or **ecclesiastical** are sometimes used to describe this aspect of religion. There is another aspect of religion in the United States that is at least as significant: This is **popular religion**—religion that occurs outside the formal boundaries of religious institutions. The existence of widespread and flourishing popular religion in the United States indicates that, as one scholar puts it, the "determination of what counts as religion is not the sole preserve of academics."[18]

Most people in the United States belong to some sort of religious community—they are Protestants within particular denominations, Catholics, Jews, or Buddhists, for example. Many, however, supplement their formal membership and participation with a variety of other religious activities that do not come directly from their community of faith—revivals, watching religious television, various devotional activities such as private prayer and reading, chanting and meditation, wearing religious jewelry, or placing religious bumper stickers on their cars and trucks. For some, these activities and others similar to them become the primary focus of their religious life.

These examples of "popular religion"—revivals, newspaper columns, radio programs—are all present in the common culture in which most Americans participate, and are familiar enough by hearsay if not by direct experience. . . . They may be popular in two principal senses. On the one hand, they have "mass appeal," they "sell." On the other hand, they are "of the people": they are examples not of the kind of religion that is taught by theologians in seminaries, but rather of that

---

[17]The Interfaith Alliance organizational Web site (http://www.tialliance.org).

[18]David Chidester, "The Church of Baseball, the Fetish of Coca-Cola, and the Potlatch of Rock'n'Roll: Theoretical Models for the Study of Religion in American Popular Culture," *Journal of the American Academy of Religion* 59, No. 4 (Fall, 1996), p. 760.

which appeals to a wide variety of people of no special theological sophistication outside the context of formal "Sunday-morning" worship in the churches.[19]

Popular religion is a "dimension of religious life that is elusive and difficult to describe," as one study of the phenomenon puts it.[20] There is no one agreed-upon definition of popular religion, but we can describe it.[21]

- Popular religion is the religious belief and practice of ordinary people rather than of theologians and religious leaders. It is transmitted through various channels outside of religious institutions.
- It exists alongside institutional religion as a complement to it. It is a supplement to participation in formal religion for some people and a substitute for it for others. People do not abandon formal religion for popular religiosity but use the latter to develop their own personal worldview.
- It offers people more direct access to the sacred than they have through the mediation of formal religious groups. Formal religious organizations impose order and structure on religion. Popular religion is distinguished by a lively sense of the supernatural without the imposition of formal structure. It does not have the "conceptual coherence" of organized religion.
- It draws on the core religious institutions of the culture (in the United States, primarily Christianity) but blends this with other sources and traditions. It often reflects both mainstream and alternative values. It draws heavily on secular popular culture.

[For] the vast majority of Americans, a sense of the supernatural so lively that it cannot be contained in creed and doctrine permeates life. . . . [O]rdinary men and women have sought and continue to seek direct access to the realm of the supernatural in order to use its power to give them control over their lives and to endow their lives with meaning. . . . Sometimes they gain that access through religious traditions and institutions, but more often [they do so] through fusing together an array of beliefs and practices to construct personal and very private worlds of meaning. If we would understand the dynamics of being religious, American style, we must explore the phenomenon of popular religiosity.[22]

Examples of popular religion abound. There is considerable interest in angels, although angel popularity may have peaked. An article in *Good Housekeeping* magazine describes five events in which people believed they or their loved ones had been rescued by angels. A boy emerges from a coma after his father cries out to Raphael, the angel of healing. A man becomes convinced that his late father has become his son's guardian angel. A woman encounters her dead husband's spirit, and she links this to the disappearance of her brain tumor.

---

[19]Peter W. Williams, *Popular Religion in America: Symbolic Change and the Modernization Process in Historical Perspective* (Englewood Cliffs, NJ: Prentice Hall, 1980), pp. 3–4.
[20]Charles H. Lippy, *Being Religious, American Style: A History of Popular Religiosity in the United States.* (Westport, CT: Greenwood Press, 1994), p. 1.
[21]This section draws loosely on Lippy, *Being Religious*, chap. 1.
[22]Lippy, *Being Religious*, pp. 18–19.

Cross-country skiers are guided to safety by rescuers who lead them to safety in a blinding snowstorm and then vanish without a trace. A woman is guided out of her burning house by an angelic presence who had appeared to her in the nights prior to the blaze.[23] Catalogs regularly offer angel-related articles, as do gift shops, evidence that the interest level remains at least fairly high.

Near-death experiences provide what some people believe to be a glimpse into a world beyond this one. Typical is this account reported in a contemporary women's magazine. It concerns a woman whose heart and breathing stopped during childbirth.

> In those few moments, while the doctors worked frantically to revive her, Jayne found herself standing in a gray mist. She says she knew immediately she'd died. She remembers feeling flooded with joy at the knowledge that some part of her lived on. Then she saw a white light coming toward and merging into her. She was filled with what she describes as unfathomable knowledge and love. In that moment, she says she knew two things: that she was immortal, indestructible, safe—she had always existed and always would—and that everything in the universe operates by a perfect plan, even famine and child abuse.
>
> Next, she remembers standing in a meadow filled with brilliant flowers. She saw a group of people in exquisite robes standing on a hill. One bald man in purple, a man of enormous compassion and authority, approached and, communicating telepathically, answered many of her questions. It was at this point she learned she couldn't stay. . . . The next moment she was back on the hospital table.[24]

In the commercially oriented culture of the United States, the strength of popular religion is shown in part by how well it sells. Christian retail is a three-billion-dollar-plus industry. Some people place statues of Jesus, Mary, Saint Francis, or the Buddha in their yards, or cross or fish symbols on their cars or trucks. I regularly see religiously oriented tee shirts in classes. There is religious music in any format people like. The musicals "Jesus Christ, Superstar" and "Godspell" continue to attract audiences. Gift items such as religiously oriented figurines, decorative items, and greeting cards sell well in religious book and supply stores and in "secular" stores as well. There are religious-theme computer games and educational software to help children learn about the Bible.

As noted above, most popular religion in the United States is in at least some sense Christian. However, it is not exclusively Christian. A number of catalogs offer a variety of items for people devising their own spirituality. One such catalog has an umbrella that features the eight major symbols of Tibetan Buddhism, as well as items reflecting Native American (and other) religions. In another catalog, those of Jewish faith can choose from a vast assortment of Jewish religious items such as prayer shawls, menorahs, Passover plates, and mezzuzahs (which are described in Chapter 5). Several sources exist for Buddhists to obtain statues, meditation cushions and benches, and audiotapes or videotapes.

---

[23]Alan Ebert, "Rescued by Angels," *Good Housekeeping*, December, 1995, pp. 128–29 and 237.
[24]Sophie Burnham, "A Glimpse of Heaven," *New Woman*, May, 1994, pp. 93–97 and 146.

Hinduism Today, a magazine for North American Hindus, routinely advertises Hindu religious articles such as deity statues, beads, and incense.

Although a lot of popular religion concerns material culture, it also involves religious practices, many of which are learned and practiced in people's homes. Countless parents pass on to their children the practice of saying bedtime and mealtime prayers, often using those they themselves learned as children. Parents read stories of faith to their children. College students pray for aid on exams. Many of my students wear cloth bracelets bearing the letters "WWJD?" The acronym stands for "What Would Jesus Do?" a reminder to the wearer to ask that question when they cannot figure out the answer to a moral dilemma. The same letters are featured on a large neon-colored billboard in town. Many people read devotional magazines, watch religious television, and listen to religious radio stations.

Two other concrete examples of popular religion in action will round out our discussion of this important topic. One is religious activism around the controversy over abortion rights. Although there is organized support from religious groups on all sides of the issue, other activists are motivated as individuals by their religious beliefs.

Another example is the "March for Jesus" held in Elkhart, Indiana. An intergenerational and interracial group of more than 2000 Christians marched in the rain, carrying banners, clutching balloons, singing hymns, and clapping. About 120 similar marches took place across the United States. "Drench this land with your awesome presence," the crowd prayed as dark clouds gave way to torrential rain. "Let grace and mercy flood this land." The purpose of the marches was to praise Jesus and increase Christian visibility in the communities in which they took place.

Figure 2-1   The conflict over abortion rights often includes a religious dimension. (*Paul Conklin/Monkmeyer Press.*)

Religion in Cyberspace

Perhaps the most notable development in popular religion at the beginning of the third millennium is the rapidly expanding presence of religion on the Internet. There are chat rooms and newsgroups pertaining to a wide range of issues and faith traditions. Some groups conduct "cyber-rituals" in which the "virtual congregation" consists of people throughout the country who are on line at a particular time for that purpose. Local temples, synagogues, and churches have their own home pages on the World Wide Web. One group, the Houses of Worship project, has begun a Web site that they hope will eventually connect the majority of Christian churches worldwide and perhaps include other faiths, as well. There are informational and/or advocacy sites and groups sponsored by individuals and by organizations. Major Internet service providers include religion among the categories or "channels" available to members.

It is probably too early to assess the impact of the revolution in electronic communication on religion in the United States. It seems certain that the impact will be profound. One author compares the impact of electronic communication on religion and spirituality to that of the Protestant Reformation:

> The most significant issue for an inquiry into the implications of computer-mediated religion . . . is the potential comparison between the communication revolution that took place concurrently with the Reformation and our current transition into the digital age. Contemporary scholarship has exhaustively documented the crucial role that printing played in the Reformation, the most significant political and religious movement of post-medieval Western culture . . . ; we may reasonably anticipate that the digital revolution will be accompanied by similarly massive upheavals in the social sphere in general and in religion in particular.[25]

Christian sites predominate on the Internet. This comes about because a majority of users of the Internet are located in the United States and Western Europe, areas in which Christianity is strong. The dominance of U.S. and Western European users can be expected to lessen as more and more areas gain better access to the Internet. However, it is unlikely that all areas of the globe will ever be equally represented. "If information is power," one author notes, "then during the next century Christianity, of all the major world religions, will benefit the most from Internet growth."[26]

However, the Internet also strongly supports religious diversity. Practitioners whose faiths have only a very small percentage of members in the United States population may live far from a meeting place of their faith. If they have access to the Internet, they have the opportunity to find information, keep up on what is happening in their religion worldwide, and even interact with others

---

[25]Stephen D. O'Leary, "Cyberspace as Sacred Space: Communicating Religion on Computer Networks," *Journal of the American Academy of Religion*, 59, No. 4 (Fall, 1996), p. 787.

[26]Jeff Zaleski, *The Soul of Cyberspace: How New Technology is Changing Our Spiritual Lives* (San Francisco: HarperEdge, 1997), p. 99.

of their faith. Dharma Communications, the outreach arm of the Zen (Buddhist) Mountain Monastery in New York state, explicitly seeks to support the religious practice of scattered Buddhists through its Dharma Communications On-Line Services:

> In an effort to make the teachings of Zen available to the widest possible audience, Dharma Communications is committed to use all dimensions of modern tech-nology. The easy accessibility to and the growing reach of "cyberspace" make it an ideal medium for communicating the perennial wisdom of Buddhism and for nurturing the spiritual practice of anyone with access to a computer screen and a telephone line. Currently, more than 6000 people reach Dharma Communications and Zen Mountain Monastery via Internet monthly, asking questions pertaining to their practice, downloading articles from the electronic *Mountain Record* journal, registering for retreats, purchasing their first sitting cushion or hundredth roll of incense, and connecting with other members of the cybersangha.[27]

Such access can be especially useful for practitioners of the less popular and less understood religions in our culture.

> Practitioners of nontraditional religions can run a considerable risk by publicly declaring their allegiances in communities hostile to non-Christians; the network afforded an opportunity to meet with like-minded others and engage in religious activity without ever leaving one's home or alerting one's neighbors to one's nonconformity.[28]

The Internet, with its religiously oriented Web sites and interactive newsgroups and chat rooms, supports the *affirmation* of religious diversity, as well. Having accurate information about religions does not guarantee greater willingness to affirm diversity, but it increases the probability that people will be more understanding of religious differences. The religious presence on the Internet can provide that information.

Having said that, two caveats are in order. Chat rooms and newsgroups are sometimes the locus for religiously motivated animosity. The relative anonymity of faceless participants scattered throughout electronic space can encourage people to express hostilities that they might not express in a face-to-face conversation. People do not always check their facts, and rumors may get passed on as facts. The other caveat has to do with being aware of the *source* of information about a religion. Sites exist that are devoted to attacking unpopular religions, and the accuracy of their information is immediately suspect. Disgruntled ex-members, for example, have a vested emotional interest in making their former faith look bad.

---

[27] *The Monastery Store: Dharma Communications 1998 Catalog* (Mount Tremper, NY: Dharma Communications, 1998), p. 32.
[28] O'Leary, "Cyberspace as Sacred Space," p. 794.

QUESTIONS AND ACTIVITIES FOR REVIEW, DISCUSSION, AND WRITING

1. In your opinion, is government neutrality toward religion a good idea, or not? Why?
2. What are some classroom activities that would be prohibited by the *Abington* v. *Schempp* ruling? What kinds of activities are allowed?
3. Do you think that religious clubs (such as student Bible study clubs or prayer groups) should have the same opportunities to use classroom space before or after school hours as nonreligious groups do? Why or why not? You might want to organize a debate on this topic.
4. Is something like the Religious Freedom Restoration Act necessary in the United States? Why or why not?
5. Which of the views about civil religion—that there is a civil religion, that there are competing civil religions, or that we are in the midst of a culture war—seems to you most accurate? Give evidence to support your view.
6. Write an essay in which you respond to either common ground politics or the work of the Interfaith Alliance.
7. Discuss with others in your class the manifestations of popular religion with which you are familiar. Organize a "popular religion scavenger hunt" in which people are alert for evidence of popular religion for a day or two and then report what they find.

FOR FURTHER READING

CORBETT, MICHAEL, and JULIA CORBETT, *Politics and Religion in the United States*. New York: Garland Publishing, 1999. This book surveys the role of religion in American public life from colonial times through the present, with sections on history, the First Amendment, religion and public opinion, and religion in politics. Contemporary material is based on analysis of survey data.

GREEN, JOHN C.; JAMES L. GUTH; CORWIN E. SMIDT; and LYMAN A. KELLSTEDT, *Religion and the Culture Wars: Dispatches from the Front*. Lanham, MD: Rowman and Littlefield Publishers, 1996. This book surveys the Christian right and political activism from the 1980s through 1996.

GROOTHUIS, DOUGLAS, *The Soul in Cyberspace*. Grand Rapids, MI: Baker Book House, 1997. This is an interdisciplinary (theology, philosophy, and sociology) Christian critique of Internet culture and its implications for religion and the human soul.

MCDANNELL, COLLEEN, *Material Christianity: Religion and Popular Culture in America*. New Haven, CT: Yale University Press, 1995. This book is a fascinating examination of the material objects that are a part of popular Christianity.

SEGERS, MARY, and TED JELEN, *A Wall of Separation? Debating the Public Role of Religion*. Lanham, MD: Rowman & Littlefield Publishers, 1998. The authors examine the impact of organized religion on the political process and its significance in the creation of public policy. Seger and Jelen, both political science professors, do not overlook the complexity of these issues.

SILK, MARK, *Unsecular Media: Making News of Religion in America*. Champaign, IL: University of Illinois Press, 1965. Silk, a journalist and historian of religion, traces the history of how religion has been covered, or not covered, by the news media and demonstrates the extent to which the media reflect common American values.

SWIFT, DONALD C., *Religion and the American Experience: A Social and Cultural History, 1765–1996*. Armonk, NY: M.E. Sharpe, 1997. Swift's book pulls together a large amount of material to integrate American religious, social, cultural, and intellectual history. It provides a good overview.

RELEVANT WORLD WIDE WEB SITES

"Religious Freedom" focuses on issues of religious liberty in the US and worldwide (http://www.religious-freedom.org).

Rather than try to list even a few of the many links to political and religious organization sites, here are two lists of links. The Institute for the Study of Religion in Politics maintains lists of "left" and "right" oriented links (http://www.isrp.org/linksleft.html and http://www.isrp.org/linksrt.html, respectively).

Evangelicals for Social Action (http://www.libertynet.org/~esa), Sojourners and Call to Renewal (http://www.sojourners.com and http://www.calltorenewal.com), and Tikkun (http://www.tikkun.org) all maintain sites representative of the search for a common ground.

There are "popular religion" oriented sites for many faith traditions on the Web. A major one for Christians is the Gospel Communications Network (http://www.gospelcom.net). For examples of such sites for other faiths, see Torah Net (http://torah.net); the CyberMuslim Information Collective (http://www.uoknor.edu/cybermuslim), particularly their bookstore; and Gateways to Buddhism (http://dharmanet.org). At its Dharma Marketplace, for example, you can download five free Buddhist screensavers.

3

Consensus Protestants

What do you think of when you think of "ordinary" religion in the United States? It is probably the style of religion described below as "consensus religion." It is the religion of approximately 90 percent of the population, and its followers may be Protestant or Catholic Christians, Jews, or Unitarians.

CONSENSUS RELIGION

Consensus religion reflects the religious sensibilities of the majority of people in our culture. They are "the dominant, culturally established faiths held by the majority of Americans."[1] Even more important, these are the groups that believe they are responsible for relating religion to the larger culture in positive ways. For example, they have lobbyists in Washington and speak out on the important moral and ethical issues of the day.

What sociologist Robert Bellah writes about mainline Protestantism in the United States applies equally to most consensus religions: These communities of faith

> . . . have tried to develop a larger picture of what it might mean to live a biblical life in America. They have sought to be communities of memory, to keep in touch with biblical sources and historical traditions not with literalist obedience but through an intelligent reappropriation illuminated by historical and theological reflection.[2]

This statement applies to the vast majority of Protestant, Catholic, and Jewish members of the religious consensus. Unitarians, as we shall see, may not share the emphasis on "biblical sources." They nonetheless share the cultural location that defines the religious consensus.

[1]Wade Clark Roof and William McKinney, *American Mainline Religion: Its Changing Shape and Future* (New Brunswick, NJ: Rutgers University Press, 1987), p.6.

[2]Robert N. Bellah, Richard Madsen, William M. Sullivan, Ann Swidler, and Steven M. Tipton, *Habits of the Heart: Individualism and Commitment in American Life* (New York: Harper & Row, Publishers, 1985), p. 237.

Most, if not all, of the consensus religious bodies in the United States recognize themselves as "denominations," as one religion among many. Even as they claim their own authenticity and recognize themselves as clearly bounded, they acknowledge the authenticity of other, competing religions.[3] They also understand religion as a part of the culture and one among many aspects of life with a legitimate claim on people's time and attention. They share most of the characteristics that sociologists identify with denominational religion, including

- friendly or at least tolerant relationships with other religions and with secular groups as well
- reliance on births within the congregation to increase membership, or, if they try to make converts, they focus on people with no religious affiliation, rather than on those who are members of another group
- acceptance of at least some change in teaching and practice as circumstances change, and tolerance of diversity of interpretation within the denomination
- relatively routinized worship without a strong emphasis on innovation and spontaneity
- a professional clergy who must meet specific educational and certification requirements for ordination[4]

There is an important link between this form of religious organization and the religious pluralism described in the Introduction. In a situation of religious pluralism, religion becomes a matter of voluntary participation, and the dominant religious traditions take on a new form:

> The denomination is thus marked perhaps most significantly by this voluntarism of support coupled to mutual respect and forbearance of all other competing religious groups. It is, indeed, this quality of *competition* that is the unique hallmark of the pluralistic religious situation; acceptance of the "free market" situation in religious ideas is the critical operating principle of denominationalism. Denominations are the structural–functional forms that dominant religious traditions assume in a pluralistic culture.[5]

WOMEN IN CONSENSUS RELIGION

Before you read this section, take a moment to reflect on your own experience. Have you thought about the role and status of women in religious organizations? What is your impression? If you attend or have attended worship services, what

[3]Russell E. Richey, "Denominations and Denominationalism: An American Morphology," in *Reimagining Denominationalism: Interpretive Essays,* ed. Robert Bruce Mullin and Russell E. Richey (New York: Oxford University Press, 1994), p. 76.

[4]Ronald L. Johnstone, *Religion in Society: A Sociology of Religion,* 5th ed. (Upper Saddle River, NJ: Prentice Hall, 1997), p.91.

[5]Swatos, William H., Jr., ed., *Encyclopedia of Religion and Society* (Walnut Creek, CA: AltaMira Press, 1998), p.134.

roles did women play? Have you heard a female minister or pastor preach? If so, how did you feel about that? If you had a personal problem that you wanted to discuss with a religious counselor, would it matter to you if that person were a woman or a man? Why or why not? How much do you think your answers to these questions are influenced by your own gender?

An American Paradox

Recently, a lot of attention has been paid to the role and status of women in American religious organizations. Religion has often limited women to traditional female roles. It has often supported and encouraged the belief that women's proper roles were those of wives and mothers. The home was often believed to be women's only proper sphere of action. Until the last half of the twentieth century, women usually were unable to be ministers, pastors, rabbis, or priests in most of America's communities of faith. Nor have they been able to be deacons, elders, or other lay officers of their congregations. Religion has also offered encouragement and comfort to those women who themselves support traditional female roles in the face of cultural demands for change.

But this is only one side of the story, because religion has also been a catalyst for change. Women have found encouragement in the scriptures of both Judaism and Christianity to work toward full equality and rights. Churches and synagogues have supported movements for women's rights. Although many communities of faith denied official roles to women, in others men and women functioned as equals. It is very important to evaluate the role that religion has played in the context of its own time. Feminist theologian Rosemary Radford Ruether cautions us that if we approach history from the viewpoint of the twentieth century, religion's tendency to support traditional roles will loom larger than it actually was, and we will be in danger of missing the extent to which religion has encouraged change.[6]

A Very Brief Historical Overview

It is not possible to go into how women's roles in religion in the United States have evolved over time. That topic is a book in itself, as many authors have demonstrated. Feminist historian of religion Rosemary Skinner Keller summarizes that evolution briefly:

> At the obvious risk of oversimplifying, the evolution of women's leadership in religious institutions in colonial and national North American history may be broadly characterized in this way. During the colonial and revolutionary periods of the seventeenth and eighteenth centuries, individual women and small groups of females occasionally challenged male domination and usually were put down or

---

[6]Rosemary Radford Ruether and Rosemary Skinner Keller, eds., *Women and Religion in America, Volume I: The Nineteenth Century* (San Francisco: Harper and Row Publishers, 1989), p. x.

at least not taken seriously. Voluntary societies and orders "for women only" characterized the organizational work of women, first at local levels in the early nineteenth century and, later, at regional and national levels in the late nineteenth century. In the preaching tradition, some women sought to be ordained during the nineteenth century, but their efforts were usually individual, isolated, and ineffective. In the early twentieth century, these patterns continued, while the late twentieth century has been marked by increasing gains by women, clergy and lay, coming into professional and voluntary leadership in the mainstream of established institutional bodies. Simultaneously, women's societies often have faded out or become absorbed or incorporated into mainstream institutional organizations.[7]

Women's Responses

Women, and men who share their concerns about continuing male predominance in the consensus religions, respond in a number of ways. The tradition-supporting response remains the most common, whether in an active or passive mode. People remain in their religious institutions and do not challenge practices and policies. For example, women continue to worship in services that use gender-exclusive language, either actively affirming that tradition or simply not challenging it. Catholic, some Protestant, and some Jewish women affirm or choose not to challenge their exclusion from ordination. In Catholicism, separate religious orders for women continue to gain participants, although in reduced numbers. Among conservative and fundamentalist Protestants, many women and men continue to affirm or at least accept traditional gender role definitions.

Others remain in their religious traditions and work actively for change. One approach entails renewed examination of the scriptures and traditions of a group from the standpoint of women's experience to reconstruct beliefs, rituals, and history that have been obscured and neglected by male history and interpretation having been taken as universal. For example, while parts of the Christian New Testament have been used to justify "keeping women in their place," other passages can be shown to challenge that view in favor of greater equality. Other men and women in those groups that do not ordain women to the clergy work actively to change that policy. Still others remain active in their community of faith but supplement that involvement with participation in a variety of distinctively women's spirituality groups in which clearly feminist ideas and rituals are embraced. For most people within a community of faith, its scriptures and history have to be taken into account. They may have to be reinterpreted, parts may simply have to be discarded, but scripture and history set the boundaries and must be dealt with.

Some Catholic nuns, while remaining in their orders and loyal to the church's hierarchy, have worked untiringly to broaden the scope of their influ-

[7]Rosemary Skinner Keller, "Forum: Female Experience in American Religion," *Religion and American Culture: A Journal of Interpretation*, 5, no. 1 (Winter, 1995), 5.

ence within the church and gain greater autonomy for themselves. Jewish women have developed rituals for important holidays such as Passover and life transitions such as birth and coming of age that reflect more clearly the role that women have played in the life of Judaism and provide rituals for girls that parallel those for boys.

One particular example of this type of response was the "Re-Imagining" conference in 1993. Nearly 2000 women and men from around the United States and around the world, including Catholics, Protestants, and others, about two-thirds lay and one-third clergy, met in Minneapolis "to explore feminist theology and liturgy and freely to give expression to the creative feminist theological imagination in reshaping and transforming the Christian tradition."[8] The women and men who participated were not interested in developing a feminist alternative *to* the Christian church, but rather in developing feminist alternatives *within* the Christian church. The conference both energized the participants and led to a backlash from more conservative forces within the denominations involved.

It is especially important to note that *most* of the women (and men) who feel alienated from their communities of faith are not leaving but are "defecting in place," choosing the difficult path of working actively for change within their local, regional, and national organizations.[9]

However, there are those for whom their traditions seem so alienating and bankrupt that they do make the equally difficult decision to abandon them altogether. Some become secular persons, without religious affiliation or participation. Others develop their own spirituality essentially in solitude, working out values, ideas, and sometimes rituals that provide spiritual sustenance without a group context. Still others find their way to, or form, women's spirituality groups that focus on goddess worship or espouse a nongendered view of the sacred.

Continuing Issues

While great strides have been made to redress the grievances that feminist Protestants, Catholics, and Jews have with their communities of faith and the institutions that undergird them, for many feminists, a lot more needs to be done. The key issue for Catholic women is ordination to the priesthood and the opportunity to rise through the ranks of the hierarchy. For many consensus Protestants ordination and participation in the higher ranks of church leadership are a reality, but there are still limits. Writing on the basis of interviews with

---

[8]Catherine Wessinger, "Women's Religious Leadership in the United States," in *Religious Institutions and Women's Leadership*, ed. Catherine Wessinger (Columbia, SC: University of South Carolina Press, 1996), p. 20. For a fuller account of this conference and the responses to it, see Nancy J. Berneking and Pamela Carter Joern, eds., *Re-Membering and Re-Imagining* (Cleveland, OH: The Pilgrim Press), 1995.

[9]Miriam Therese Winter, Adair Lummis, and Allison Stokes, *Defecting in Place: Women Claiming Responsibility for Their Own Spiritual Lives* (New York: Crossroad, 1994).

clergy women in several Protestant denominations and with concerned Catholic women, one author concludes the following:

> Women are permitted to discuss women's issues, forge professional identity, and nurture the growth of a few struggling parishes. Occasionally, they are admitted to the second or third tier in larger churches. Less frequently, they are granted the opportunity to make the choices that shape some small part of the "performance." By and by, however, they are forced to live on the fringes of a church where men discuss the church's theology and its ministry, shape their professional identity in close proximity with the centers of ecclesiastical power, and govern the affairs of the largest churches.[10]

PROTESTANT CHRISTIANITY

Protestant Christians make up the majority of consensus religion in the United States. Protestant belief and practice varies somewhat among denominations and among congregations within a denomination. There are features of Protestantism that make it distinct, however, and that transcend denominational differences. Despite the diversity, there were, and still are, certain beliefs and practices that, although with modifications, have been a part of Protestantism since the Protestant Reformation in the 1500s. We will use the now-familiar four elements of religion to organize our thinking about what most Protestants hold in common.

Belief

We can identify a core of **beliefs** that most Protestants share. Like Catholic, Eastern Orthodox, and other Christians, **the religious life of Protestants centers on the person, life, death, and resurrection of Jesus**. Christians, including Protestants, are those people who are defined religiously by their faith in Jesus as their Lord and Savior. The story of Jesus is made accessible in the Bible. Through the action and influence of the Holy Spirit, Christians believe that the words of the Bible become the Word of God for the believer, God's direct and personal communication to each and every individual.

The Bible plays a central role for Protestants. It is the only authority for religious faith and practice. For Protestants, the authority of any creed or confession of faith is subordinate to that of the Bible, and any such document is valid only insofar as it is an accurate representation of what the Bible teaches. Some Protestant communities of faith have written creeds or statements of faith that express the essence of their beliefs, but these are secondary to the authority of the Bible itself.

Other communities of faith do not have a formal creed as such, although some of them may make occasional use of creeds, especially of the early ones.

---

[10]Frederick W. Schmidt, Jr., *A Still Small Voice: Women, Ordination, and the Church* (Syracuse, NY: Syracuse University Press, 1996), pp. 169-70.

Adherence to a creed is not a prerequisite to membership in these groups. Communities of faith that do not have a formal creed take this position for a variety of reasons. Some believe that formal creeds are too restrictive and violate the right of individual conscience in religious matters. Others fear that acceptance of a creed can too easily become a substitute for faith in Jesus.

Protestants believe that **salvation is a gift from God**, an effect of grace and grace alone. There is nothing that people can do to earn salvation. At the same time, there is nothing that people need to do to earn salvation, because God has made it a gift of his grace in and through Jesus, who for this reason is known by Christians as Savior (Ephesians 2:8–9).

The church is the gathered fellowship of believers. It is the people meeting together to hear the Word preached, to participate in the sacraments of baptism and communion, and to encourage and help each other. In a very real sense for Protestants, the church is not a "something" that "is" as much as it is an event that happens each time and place that believers gather. This gathered fellowship is a **priesthood of all believers**. Protestants find support for this belief in the New Testament and in the writings of the Reformers. In the first letter to Peter, the faithful are called a "chosen people, a royal priesthood" (1 Peter 2:9). Each Christian has the responsibility to pray for, teach, and encourage every other Christian and to tell God's story to nonbelievers. Each Christian shares with all others the same authority. No one has an inside track, and no one is relegated to outsider status in matters of religious authority. All are equal, because all have equal access to the Word.

Protestants, in other words, distinguish between priesthood and ministry. Baptism makes all Christians priests, some of whom are then called to preach, administer the sacraments, and govern as ministers. The minister is one who is chosen to serve a congregation, rather than one given special powers by God or special honor by the institution.

Lifestyle

What of **Protestant lifestyle**? Their faith directs consensus Protestants squarely into the middle of the world. Christian faith, say most followers of its Protestant branch, must be lived out in the midst of the world, not in retreat from it. God provides all the various arenas of human activity, such as marriage and family, vocation and work, civil government and politics, leisure and play. Each in its place is equally good, equally capable of being transformed by grace. One is not to turn one's back on the world but to live in it, glorifying and obeying God in all things.

For all Protestants, living decently, charity toward others, upholding the law, and being faithful in one's commitment to God and to the community of God's people are important virtues. Freed from its role in bringing about salvation, morality became a central feature of Protestants' lifestyle, as a joyful and obedient response to God's freely given gift of salvation.

Ritual

Baptism and **the Lord's supper or communion** are the only two acts that Jesus told his followers to carry on after his death, according to the Protestant understanding of the New Testament. Among most Protestants, these are the only rites of the church recognized as sacraments.[11] The age for baptism varies; many Protestants baptize babies, but not all do. Immersion, pouring, and sprinkling each have their advocates within the Protestant community. Likewise, the exact understanding of the Lord's supper varies, but Protestants are united in their denial of its sacrificial character. Architecturally, its context is that of a table that echoes the one around which Jesus and the disciples are said to have gathered, rather than the altar of sacrifice. Some congregations pass the elements through the pews, and some come to the front of the church. The roles played by the minister and laypeople vary somewhat. All use bread, leavened or unleavened; some use wine, and some use unfermented grape juice.

A second distinctive aspect of Protestant ritual is the **importance of preaching**. The pulpit occupies a prominent place in Protestant churches, and the sermon is considered the focal point of worship. Ministers usually receive extensive training in biblical preaching, and a potential minister's skill as a preacher plays a large role in the selection process when it is time to call a new pastor.

Organization

Each Protestant denomination is self-governing. There is no worldwide organization. Individual denominations have various organizational patterns. The *congregational* form of organization places most of the decision-making power in the hands of the local congregation, and important decisions are usually made by a congregational vote. The *connectional* form of organization is a representative form of organization. Local congregations make many decisions, but major decisions are made by higher governing bodies to which local congregations send delegates. Within local churches, boards elected by the congregation are the primary decision-making group. The *hierarchical* form of organization centers on bishops, who are officers appointed by those higher up the organizational ladder than themselves, rather than being elected at the local level. In individual congregations, decision making is strongly influenced by the ordained leaders, in consultation with elected boards.

Especially among consensus Protestants, ecumenical organizations provide a forum and a method for working together to achieve commonly shared goals. The **National Council of Churches of Christ in the U.S.A.** came into being in 1950 when a group of churches agreed to try to demonstrate in their organization the unity they believed the Christian church should have. It was the succes-

---

[11]Among the Protestant Christians discussed in this chapter, Episcopalians do recognize all seven traditional sacraments of the church.

sor to the Federal Council of Churches, which had begun in 1908. It has become known as an organization of liberal Protestant denominations and includes many Eastern Orthodox and other Christian churches as well. Its position statements characteristically have affirmed social action and justice while downplaying evangelism and doctrinal precision. The magazine *Christian Century* is an important national voice for this perspective. *Sojourners* focuses on social issues, while the *National Catholic Reporter* embodies this perspective in Catholicism.

The **National Association of Evangelicals** was formed in 1942 in response to the liberal theological and social positions and perceived doctrinal looseness of the Federal Council of Churches. Its aim is to promote and uphold conservative Christianity while at the same time overcoming the separatist and isolationist tendencies present in much of the evangelical and fundamentalist movement. It is a cooperative association of denominations, independent churches, Christian schools, and some individuals who affirm a creedal statement that begins with the affirmation of the Christian Bible as "the inspired, the only infallible, authoritative Word of God." The creed also requires belief in the doctrine of the Trinity, the virgin birth of Jesus, the substitutionary theory of the atonement, and the unity of all true believers in Christ. *Christianity Today* has long been a significant national journalistic expression of this viewpoint in the United States.

Perhaps the most dramatic ecumenical effort came in December 1960. The Reverend Eugene Carson Blake, at the time Stated Clerk[12] of the United Presbyterian Church in the United States of America, preaching in the Episcopal Grace Cathedral in San Francisco, proposed an organizational merger of the Presbyterian, Methodist, Protestant Episcopal, and United Church of Christ churches. The first meeting of representatives from the four churches took place in 1962. In 1970, the **Consultation on Church Union**, with nine member churches in full support, drafted *A Plan of Union for the Church of Christ Uniting*. The organization is still alive, although no major organizational realignments have come out of that historic effort. However, the impact of the COCU documents on the thinking of consensus religious groups in America remains. One example is that some of the member denominations accept as valid ordination in any of them. People ordained in one of these denominations could become ministers in another without being ordained again.

Most ministers are married rather than celibate. The rejection of monasticism goes together with a rejection of celibacy as the proper lifestyle for ministers. Many Protestant denominations, although not all, **ordain women** as well as men to the ministry.

Many of the consensus Protestant denominations maintain ministries on college campuses, either individually (for example, the Wesley Foundation sponsored by the United Methodist Church) or ecumenically (for example, a United

---

[12]The Stated Clerk is the "chief executive officer" of this denomination.

Christian Foundation sponsored by the Methodists, Presbyterians, and United Church of Christ).

We will now turn our attention to several major representative Protestant communities of faith. Catholics, Jews, and Unitarians will be the subject of subsequent chapters.

DENOMINATIONAL DISTINCTIVENESS

Denominational differences play a much smaller role in religion in the United States than they did a few decades ago. American religion has been "restructured" along a different set of lines. As sociologist Robert Wuthnow points out, the "symbolic boundaries have changed." "These changes . . . involve new modes of religious identification, new distinctions in the web of religious interaction, alterations in the lines of moral obligation that define religious communities, changes in the categories that are taken for granted in religious discourse."[13] At least in a sense, we are a postdenominational religious culture. The distinctions between Protestant and Catholic Christians, and those between Christians and Jews, are not as central to religion in the United States as they were in earlier decades. Neither are the distinctions between the various Protestant denominations. Nonetheless, there remain distinguishing features of denominations that are important to those who are a part of them. It is to those that we now turn.

About 60 percent of adults in the United States are Protestant. About one-third of these are Baptists. Methodists account for about 15 percent and Lutherans about 12 percent. About 6 percent are Presbyterians, and 5 percent are Episcopalians. The last three groups described below each account for less than 1 percent.

Baptists

About two-thirds of Baptists in the United States are members of the Southern Baptist Convention, and about another 10 percent are in the American Baptist Convention. The rest are part of any one of many smaller Baptist groups or are independent Baptists.

Baptist churches are a part of what is known as the *free church movement*. They believe that the church should be a free or voluntary association of adult believers. They are the largest Protestant denominational family in the United States and second only to the Roman Catholic population in size. Baptists in the United States are distinguished by their belief in a regenerate church membership, their emphasis on the New Testament as interpreted to each individual through the Holy Spirit, the absence of an official creed, and their passionate

[13]Robert Wuthnow, *The Restructuring of American Religion: Society and Faith since World War II* (Princeton, NJ: Princeton University Press, 1988), p. 10.

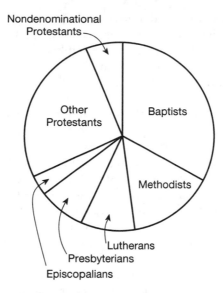

Figure 3-1   Among those who are Protestants, about 38 percent are Baptists, 15 percent Methodists, 12 percent Lutherans, 6 percent Presbyterians, 5 percent Episcopalians, and 6 percent nondenominational Protestants; 18 percent identify with some other Protestant group. *(Data from the 1996 National Opinion Research Center General Social Survey.)*

interest in the separation of church and state. Baptists believe that the church should be made up of only those who are spiritually reborn and fully sincere in their pursuit of the Christian life. This is what is meant by the concept of a *regenerate church membership*, which is a basic Baptist teaching. Church members are people who have been baptized upon their profession of faith in Jesus Christ as Lord and Savior. It is sometimes said that people are "not Baptist by birth, but by rebirth."

Baptists have no official creed. Although some local congregations and associations of congregations have written creeds or statements of faith, no convention of Baptists has ever set forth a binding creed. This reflects their belief in the guidance of the Holy Spirit as each person reads the Bible. Baptists support the right of private judgment and freedom of conscience in belief. They regard all creeds as inadequate because they believe that no creed can adequately express the fullness of the Christian gospel and that the full significance of vital, living faith cannot be bound by any statement. Some early Baptists experienced persecution at the hands of those who would make and enforce creeds, and some died in defense of their faith.

Baptists are passionate supporters of religious liberty. Freedom of religion is an inherent right of the human soul, say the Baptists, because human beings are created to be both free and responsible. For freedom of religion to be a reality, religion and the civil government must be kept strictly apart. Because of this belief, early Baptists encountered persecution. They also played a decisive role in the achievement of civil and religious liberty for all persons, especially in colonial New England and Virginia. Baptists certainly are not alone in their support of religious liberty and the official separation of church and state. However, these concepts play an especially significant role in both Baptist history and present-day concern.

Baptists are the most likely of any of the Protestants to be fundamentalist in their religious outlook. Some, particularly in the South, in rural areas of the country, and in the smaller, more conservative Baptist groups, advocate a stricter personal morality than is the prevailing custom in the culture. Individual congregations can and sometimes do set standards for their members, and these standards may include opposition to drinking alcohol, theatergoing, and dancing, as well as a code of modesty and moderation in women's dress.

In worship, many Baptists emphasize openness to the leading of the Holy Spirit over the use of set format and ceremony. Their worship tends to be somewhat more emotional and evangelistic than that of the other consensus Protestants, although this is not always the case. Each congregation develops its own patterns of ritual activity, blending repeated common elements with innovation.

Baptists practice two ordinances: baptism and the Lord's supper. By calling these two rites of the church *ordinances* rather than sacraments, Baptists describe their belief that these are acts that Jesus told his followers to continue after his death, but they have no sacramental significance.

Baptism as it is practiced in most Baptist churches has two distinctive features. Most important, those receiving baptism must be old enough to know what it means for themselves and to make their own declaration of faith in Jesus and intent to live by his standards. Thus, in contrast with those Protestant churches that grew out of the Lutheran, Calvinist, and English reformations, Baptists do not baptize infants or young children. It is a rite of incorporation into the church community, and this must be a free and knowledgeable act of the one participating in it, not something done on behalf of a child too young to understand. Baptism in the Baptist tradition is by full immersion of the person into water. It may be performed in a tank built into the church for that purpose or in an outdoor lake or stream if one is available. Immersion is believed to be the only truly scriptural mode of baptism. Immersion also is regarded as an enacted parable of spiritual regeneration, a symbolic burial of the former life and resurrection to the new life in Christ, as well as echoing Jesus' burial and resurrection. Baptists differ in their willingness to accept baptism by modes other than immersion as valid. Nearly all agree, however, that, whatever the form, it must be performed with the full consent of the baptized person.

The Lord's supper is believed to be a remembrance of Jesus' last supper with the disciples and a memorial of his sacrificial death. Like baptism, it is not a sacrament, and the elements of bread and unfermented grape juice remain simply what they are. Baptists do not believe that Jesus is present spiritually or symbolically in the elements. Some Baptist congregations restrict participation in this ordinance to those who are members of that specific church. Others, most notably the large American Baptist Churches in the U.S.A. convention, practice open communion.

The church, as it is understood by free church Christians, *is* the local congregation. Denominational organizations, made up of representatives from local congregations, plus professional and support staff, act in an advisory capacity only. They have no authority over the local congregations. Although Baptists cherish their congregational independence, they are also interdependent, and these larger denominational organizations (frequently called *conventions*) are important for the whole fellowship of Baptists. The conventions also perform activities that cannot be maintained efficiently by local congregations alone, such as higher educational, missionary, and social service work and retirement programs for church employees. Some local congregations, however, do refuse to join any larger group, maintaining a strict independence.

Many denominations in the Baptist family of churches joined in 1936 to sponsor the Baptist Joint Committee on Public Affairs in Washington. This committee reflects the Baptists' commitment to religious liberty. It is the only church office of any faith that works full time on religious liberty and church-state issues.

The Southern Baptists are distinguished by being considerably more conservative theologically than their American Baptist counterparts. For example, in 1996, the convention adopted a resolution to evangelize among Jews, seeking to convert them to Christianity, and appointed a missionary to direct that effort. In 1998, the convention passed a statement strongly supporting traditional roles for women and men.

To summarize the Baptists' place in the religious culture of the United States:

> A key to Baptist identity, then, is a certain passion for spiritual freedom, not only in faith and order but also in piety and worship. The ideal of a congregation thriving in spiritual fellowship of "newly born" regenerate believers, each one personally experiencing divine grace through Jesus Christ, is a recurring theme in Baptist history. Preaching, praying, and singing freely without uniform directive or constraint, balancing ordered formality with spirit-moved spontaneity, have framed most kinds of Baptist worship. The ordinances . . . of baptism and the Lord's Supper . . . likewise are practiced with a minimum of liturgical formality. At the center of worship is the Bible, which through the guidance of the spirit is expected to provide sufficient resource for understanding and practicing the faith.[14]

Methodists

Methodists are distinguished by a great latitude and variety in what is acceptable belief. They affirm the central beliefs of Western Christianity with specific emphases derived from the teachings of their founder, John Wesley. One of these

[14]Eldon G. Ernst, "The Baptists," in *Encyclopedia of the American Religious Experience: Studies of Traditions and Movements*, vol. 1, ed. Charles H. Lippy and Peter W. Williams (New York City: Charles Scribner's Sons, 1988), p. 576.

features is a focus on the practical: "The underlying energy of the Wesleyan theological heritage stems from an emphasis upon practical divinity, the implementation of genuine Christianity in the lives of believers. . . . The Wesleyan emphasis upon the Christian life—faith and love put into practice—has been the hallmark of those traditions now incorporated into The United Methodist Church."[15]

Wesley combined traditional Christian themes dealing with salvation in a distinctive way, as well. "Grace" is the completely undeserved action of God through the Holy Spirit. Manifest in all of life. "Justification" means the forgiveness of sins through God's grace and the restoration of the individual to a right relationship with God. "Assurance" denotes the confidence in salvation that is given by the Holy Spirit. Finally, "sanctification" describes the process of the Christian's growth in grace, enhancing their personal relationship with God and manifesting in ever-increasing Christ-likeness.[16]

Methodists have also highlighted the social dimension of the Christian life. As with most Methodist teachings, this is a particular emphasis on a theme widely shared among Christians, as well as among many non-Christians.

> We insist that personal salvation always involves Christian mission and service to the world. By joining heart and hand, we assert that personal religion, evangelical witness, and Christian social action are reciprocal and mutually reinforcing.

> Scriptural holiness entails more than personal piety; love of God is always linked with love of neighbor, a passion for justice and renewal in the life of the world. . . .

> For Wesley, there is no religion but social religion, no holiness but social holiness. . . .

> The Social Principles provide our most recent official summary of stated convictions that seek to apply the Christian vision of righteousness to social, economic, and political issues. . . .

> Our struggles for human dignity and social reform have been a response to God's demand for love, mercy, and justice in the light of the Kingdom [of God]. We proclaim no personal gospel that fails to express itself in relevant social concerns; we proclaim no social gospel that does not include the personal transformation of sinners.[17]

Most churches in the Methodist family fit easily into the culture of which they are a part. Their members' lifestyles differ little from those of others in their

---

[15]"Doctrinal Standards and Our Theological Task," The United Methodist Church Web Site (http://www.umc.org/).

[16]"Doctrinal Standards and Our Theological Task," The United Methodist Church Web Site (http://www.umc.org/).

[17]"Doctrinal Standards and Our Theological Task," The United Methodist Church Web Site (http://www.umc.org/). The United Methodist Social Creed can be found on this site.

communities. John Wesley formulated three guidelines for members of his religious societies:

- Do no harm and avoid evil of all sorts.
- Do good of every possible sort, and insofar as possible to all people.
- Observe the ordinances of God, including public worship, the ministry of the Word both read from Scripture and explained in preaching, participation in the Lord's Supper, family and private prayer and Bible reading, and fasting and abstinence.

With the exception of fasting and, in some instances, abstinence from alcohol, many Methodists' lives today can be described in the same way.

Like their beliefs, Methodists' patterns of worship vary widely. There is no required form of worship, although the *Book of Worship* gives suggested forms for Sunday services as well as for several special services, including those for the special occasions of the church year, the significant passages of human life, and a new service of healing. Local congregations make use of it and modify it as they adapt it to their particular needs.

Methodists baptize people of all ages. Water is usually sprinkled on the head of the person being baptized. It is a rite of incorporation into the community of faith. As is always the case, people baptized as infants or young children are expected to make their own profession of faith and declaration of intent to live a Christian life within the church when they are capable of understanding what it means to do so. At that point the person becomes a full church member. This confirmation of the promises made on one's behalf at baptism usually occurs at twelve or thirteen years of age and is preceded by a period of instruction.

Most Methodists believe that Christ is symbolically present to the faithful in the elements of bread and grape juice in the communion service in a "heavenly and spiritual manner." It is a solemn yet joyful service, taken with great seriousness by most members of this diverse group of Protestants.

Like the Baptists, though to a somewhat lesser extent, Methodist organization is marked by its being a large family of related church groups. There are more than twenty separate religious bodies that claim the Methodist heritage. Those Methodists who are a part of the religious consensus in the United States make up the United Methodist Church. The United Methodist Church came into being in 1968 with the merger of the Methodist Church and the Evangelical United Brethren, both of which were themselves products of earlier mergers. The United Methodist Church includes approximately 80 percent of the Methodist population.

Besides the United Methodist Church, there are three large, predominantly black churches in the Methodist group: the African Methodist Episcopal Church, the African Methodist Episcopal Zion Church, and the Christian Methodist Episcopal Church. These churches have begun discussions with the United Methodists concerning an eventual merger.[18] In addition, there are several smaller

---

[18]"Methodist Bodies Take First Steps toward Possible Merger," *EcuLink*, no. 33 (May–September 1991), 3.

groups, the names of which often point to either their geographic region or a particular point of view, such as the Free Methodist Church of North America, the Southern Methodist Church, and the Evangelical Methodist Church. Others use the name *Wesleyan* to refer to their link with John Wesley and his teachings.

The Methodists are a religiously diverse people noted for their tolerance and their involvement in social action, who strongly believe with their founder that religion is a matter for both heart and will as well as for the intellect.

Lutherans

The Lutheran family of churches, including the large Evangelical Lutheran Church in America (ELCA) and the more conservative Lutheran Church–Missouri Synod, embrace the basic teachings and practices of Protestant Christianity as interpreted by the founder, Martin Luther, the German "Father of the Protestant Reformation." Luther's *Small Catechism* is still used, along with the Augsburg Confession, to introduce people to the basics of Lutheran thought.[19]

Some of the things that help to distinguish Lutherans from other Protestants include:

You don't hear Lutherans say, "It doesn't matter what you believe, just so you live right." Lutherans think that a way of living is a by-product of a way of believing.

Since Lutheranism developed from Luther's intense experience of salvation through faith, it has been marked by a concern for faith as the essential part of religion. So Lutherans, more than most other Protestants, emphasize doctrine. They insist on unusually thorough education of their pastors and require young people to engage in a long period of study of the Lutheran Catechism before being admitted to full church membership. . . .

Since Luther had been an ardent Roman Catholic before his excommunication, he was less drastic than some later reformers in abandoning Catholic forms of worship. These are retained among Lutherans in a simplified form.

Lutherans observe the festivals and seasons of the historic church year. In their churches, they have the altar, cross, candles, vestments, and other equipment of worship that most other Protestants discarded as "too Catholic." Lutherans believe that these forms of liturgy . . . are valuable because of their beauty and because, through them, we share in the experiences of the family of Christian worshipers of all ages.[20]

Unlike Baptist and Methodist Christians, Lutherans are a creedal denomination. For Lutherans, the Bible is the inspired Word of God, containing God's

---

[19]Evangelical Lutheran Church in America Web site (http://www.elca.org/). The text of both the *Catechism* and the Confession can be found at this site.
[20]G. Elson Ruff, "What Is a Lutheran?" in *Religions of America: Ferment and Faith in an Age of Crisis*, ed. Leo Rosten (New York: Simon and Schuster, 1975), p.159. This older statement is still accurate.

full revelation to humankind. It is the only source of true Christian teaching and the only rule and norm of Christian faith and life. Alongside the Bible, certain creeds and confessions of faith are said to express correct belief. The three **ecumenical creeds** of the whole church are among them: the Apostles, Nicene, and Athanasian creeds. The creeds have no authority in themselves but are of value only as they reveal the true Word of God. The **Augsburg Confession**, written in 1530, is a central statement of Lutheran essentials. It was written as a statement that set forth Luther's position on points wherein he differed from the Roman Catholic Church. In addition to the Augsburg Confession, Lutherans hold that the Apology[21] for the Augsburg Confession, the Smalcald Articles, the Formula of Concord, and Luther's *Large* and *Small Catechisms* contain true Christian teaching. Many of the important creeds of Lutheranism are drawn together in the *Book of Concord*, first published in 1580.

Lutherans teach that both the law and the gospel are necessary. The law is necessary to awaken sinners to their sinful condition and to arouse them to repentance and a longing for redemption. The gospel assures the repentant sinner of God's forgiveness in Christ. Thus, both must be held together. Like so much in Lutheranism, this belief follows Luther's own teaching closely.

Lutherans' lifestyles are usually culture affirming. Some smaller and more conservative groups impose restrictions on their members that go beyond the prevailing standards of the culture, but usually, Lutherans are very much like their neighbors.

One of the more conservative branches of the Lutheran family, the Missouri Synod Lutheran Church sponsors a church-related school system in the United States that is second in size only to the Roman Catholic school system. Like the Baptists, who are involved in the Christian school movement, these Lutherans want the education their children receive at school to reinforce and complement that which they receive at home and at church.

Worship is very important to Lutherans. Lutheran worship follows a precise liturgical format. Worship is orderly, using an adaptation of the worship of the early church as interpreted through Luther's modifications. Lutherans believe that weekly worship is central to the life of faith, and churches may hold services during the week so that those who cannot worship on Sunday may do so at another time. Many hymns are used. Prominence is given to hymns written by Luther, who is often regarded as one of the greatest hymn writers the Christian church has ever known. He is probably best known for "A Mighty Fortress Is Our God," which became a key hymn of the Reformation.

Preaching and the sacrament of communion are both very important elements in Lutheran worship. The altar, a symbol of Christ's presence in the sacrament, and the pulpit, symbolizing God's presence through the Word, are equally important in their church architecture. This contrasts with many Protestant churches, in which the pulpit (perhaps along with a lectern from which the Bible is read) vastly overshadows the altar, which is frequently a simple table.

---

[21]Here, *apology* means a defense.

Communion is an important part of Lutheran worship. Lutheran congregations are encouraged to include communion as a part of each Sunday's worship. While some churches include it weekly, most celebrate the Eucharist either monthly or biweekly. Usually, people come to the front of the sanctuary and kneel at the altar to receive the elements. Many Lutherans also receive communion privately in times of personal difficulty or emergency. The Lutheran view of what takes place in the communion incorporates images of remembrance, fellowship, thanksgiving, confession and forgiveness, and celebration. The distinctive Lutheran view differs from both the Catholic belief in transubstantiation and from those who hold that Christ is not present in the elements themselves. They believe that the risen Christ is truly present in the bread and wine. The bread and wine continue to exist as bread and wine, but along with this, Christ is actually present. This teaching is sometimes referred to as the "Real Presence." This, Lutherans believe, is what Christ promised at the Last Supper.

The Evangelical Lutheran Church in America, the largest Lutheran body, is firmly within the sphere of consensus religion. As the religious consensus in the United States has become more conservative, religious groups that would have been outside the consensus a decade or two ago are now within it. The Missouri Synod Lutheran Church is one of two major evangelical and conservative Protestant groups in the United States that is now a part of the broad consensus, along with the Southern Baptist Convention. Neither completely fits the description of consensus Protestant churches. For example, both have remained outside the National Council of Churches. However, their size and the increased conservatism of the consensus warrants their inclusion here.

Presbyterians

John Knox founded the Presbyterian Church, based on the teaching and organizational pattern developed by the Genevan reformer John Calvin. Presbyterianism became the established church in Scotland. Presbyterian churches are distinguished by their theology, which is usually called "reformed," and their form of church government, which is strongly connectional, so much so that this type of church organization is sometimes called *presbyterian* (lowercase *p* to distinguish it from the denomination). The Presbyterian Church (U.S.A.) is the largest embodiment of reformed theology among churches in the United States. Another consensus denomination in the reformed theological tradition is the United Church of Christ, discussed later in this chapter.

A recent statement about the uniqueness of the Presbyterian Church describes its theology and organization:

> Reformed theology . . . emphasizes God's supremacy over everything and humanity's chief purpose as being to glorify and enjoy God forever . . . Central to this tradition is the affirmation of the majesty, holiness, and providence of God who creates, sustains, rules, and redeems the world in the freedom of sovereign righteousness and love. . . .

Calvin developed the *presbyterian* pattern of church government, which vests governing authority primarily in elected laypersons known as elders. The word *presbyterian* comes from the Greek word for elder.[22]

Like Lutheranism, Presbyterianism is a creedal faith. A group of religious leaders gathered at Westminster Abbey from 1643 to 1648 to write the Westminster Confession of Faith, as well as the Larger and Shorter Catechisms that are based on it. A later *Book of Confessions* (1967) contains the creeds and confessions. Following a merger in 1983, a new statement of faith was written for the newly formed Presbyterian Church (U.S.A.). It is not intended to stand apart from the other confessions of faith included in the *Book of Confessions* but to continue them. The preface describes the Presbyterian affirmation of essential Christian belief in its reformed interpretation.

> The new Statement of Faith celebrates our rediscovery that for all our undoubted diversity, we are bound together by a common faith and a common task. The faith we confess unites us with the one, universal church. The most important beliefs of Presbyterians are those we share with other Christians, and especially with other evangelical Christians who look to the Protestant Reformation as a renewal of the gospel of Jesus Christ. . . . We are convinced that to the Reformed churches a distinctive idea of the catholic faith has been entrusted for the good of the whole church.[23]

In general, biblical and theological interpretation among Presbyterians ranges from fairly conservative and literal to more liberal and figurative. The larger denominations within the Presbyterian family of denominations tend toward the liberal, while the smaller ones, many of which grew out of doctrinal disputes, tend to be more conservative.

Presbyterians can be found everywhere and in all walks of life, living very much like others in their culture. The belief that God is sovereign over all of life propels Presbyterians directly into the world as they find it, with the mandate to make it better.

Calvinistic teachings about the value of hard work and frugality made Calvinism a useful element in the life of the colonies and the new nation. Presbyterians are to this day found in the ranks of the more highly educated and the economically better off. They count among their members a disproportionate number of society's leaders, whether in government, business and industry, or education.

Presbyterian worship is usually carried out with great dignity and order. It is stately, as befits the worship of a sovereign God. It is centered on the sermon, including the exposition of the Scriptures and the ordered presentation of the great truths of the Christian faith as Presbyterians understand them. The sermon

---

[22]The Presbyterian Church (U.S.A.) Web site (http://www.pcusa.org/).

[23]Preface to *A Brief Statement of Faith*—Presbyterian Church (USA) (Atlanta: Office of the General Assembly, PC(USA), 1983).

has mainly a teaching function. Presbyterian ministers are formally called "teaching elders," to distinguish them from the "ruling elders," whose function is church governance.

Hymns and prayers center on the main beliefs of the faith, such as confession and forgiveness and praise to the sovereign God. Presbyterian worship is usually more intellectual than emotional and gives the worshiper an experience of logical thoughts, ordered behavior, and a restrained atmosphere. According to Presbyterians, worship is not something done for God, who does not need to be worshiped, nor is it something done for the people themselves. It is preeminently a part of God's work in the world, one of the means whereby God interacts with the created order.

Presbyterians believe very strongly that children, along with their parents, are members of the "household of faith," and they baptize people of all ages. Parents are encouraged to have their children baptized. While baptism is not thought to be necessary for salvation, it is considered a sacrament and is important as the rite of incorporation into the church. It is usually performed by sprinkling.

Presbyterians reject, as did Calvin and Knox, Luther's view of the real presence of Christ in the elements of communion. They also reject the view of some of the reformers that the communion is only a memorial. In the elements of bread and (usually) unfermented grape juice, Christ is spiritually present and is known by faith. Being in a proper frame of mind and spirit to receive communion is important to Presbyterians, for whom this is a very solemn service of worship.

The Presbyterian Church in the United States of America (PC,USA) was formed in 1983 by a merger of the Presbyterian Church in the United States (PCUS, the southern branch) and the United Presbyterian Church in the U.S.A. (the northern branch). In addition, there are several smaller groups that are part of this denominational family, such as the Cumberland Presbyterian Church, the Orthodox Presbyterian Church, and the Reformed Presbyterian Church. Most of these smaller branches are more conservative to fundamentalist in their thinking and are not regarded as part of the consensus.

Episcopalians

The Episcopal Church is regarded as a bridge between Protestantism and Catholicism and is sometimes said to be Protestant in belief while being Catholic in worship. Some interpreters describe it as "a different way of being Christian than Protestantism, Roman Catholicism, or Eastern Orthodoxy."[24] It accepts the Apostles and Nicene creeds as accurate reflections of the teachings of

---

[24]David L. Holmes, "The Anglican Tradition and the Episcopal Church," in *Encyclopedia of the American Religious Experience*, vol. 1, ed. Lippy and Williams, p. 392.

the Bible. "The Thirty-Nine Articles of Religion" is a distinctive statement of Episcopal belief in the United States. The Episcopal Church accepts a wide range of opinion in matters of theology and doctrine. It stresses the importance of "loyalty in essentials and liberty in nonessentials," and the smaller points of theological difference fall into the nonessential category.

The *Book of Common Prayer* is the product of the service books used in the church throughout the centuries and contains orders for Sunday worship and for many other services of worship. A contemporary American revision that was approved in 1980 was the first major revision since 1928.

The Episcopal Church honors the saints of the church in ways similar to what is done in the Catholic church. Churches are frequently named for saints, and saints' festival days are celebrated in worship. Oftentimes, Episcopalians name their children for saints.

Most Episcopal priests are married, and whether to marry or not is left up to the individual. Women also can be priests. The Episcopal Church does have a few groups of nuns and monks who take the traditional three vows of poverty, chastity, and obedience.

Along with the Presbyterians, Episcopalians rank at the top of such socio-economic status indicators as education and income. They are often leaders in their communities. They are among the most liberal of Protestants both theologically and morally, and they are among the strongest advocates of civil liberties for all people.

The sacraments are at the center of Episcopal worship. Episcopalians believe that the sacraments are "visible signs and effectual means" of God's acting in people. The understanding of the sacraments as "effectual means," having power in and of themselves to convey God's grace, sets Episcopalians apart from other Protestants.

The principal act of Christian worship on Sundays and on other significant church festivals is the Holy Eucharist, which is very similar to the Catholic mass. The Eucharistic service is frequently called a mass. The Eucharist is the most frequently used term for holy communion among Episcopalians. They believe that Christ is actually present within the elements of bread and wine, although they refrain from trying to express or explain what they consider to be a holy mystery. In this, they are similar to Lutherans, while differing from those Protestants who regard the presence of Christ as symbolic only.

Infants, as well as children and adults, are baptized, usually by sprinkling. Baptism is believed to cleanse from sin, unite the person with Christ in Christ's death and resurrection, bring about rebirth by the action of the Holy Spirit, and make people adopted children of God the Divine Parent. These two sacraments are understood to have been instituted by Jesus as the chief sacraments of the church.

Episcopalians also believe that other traditionally important rites, including confirmation, reconciliation of a penitent (also called confession and forgiveness), marriage, ordination to the priesthood, and the anointing of the sick, have sacramental significance. The importance placed on the seven traditional sacraments is distinctive for this group of Christians.

The services for morning and evening prayer are frequently used, often being held daily in large churches. There are also services for special times in the church year, such as saints' days and other holy days such as Christmas and Easter, and for special times in peoples' lives.

The Episcopal Church is both hierarchical and connectional in its organization. There are bishops, whose authority is believed to have been handed down across the centuries in an unbroken line of succession. They trace this back to an account in Matthew 16, in which Jesus is said to have given Saint Peter the keys to the kingdom of heaven. Usually, the clergyperson is called a priest. In recent years, the Episcopal church has involved laypeople more at all levels. Each congregation elects a vestry to govern the local church. In consultation with the bishop, the vestry is responsible for calling a priest to the congregation. The spiritual head of the Episcopal church worldwide is the Archbishop of Canterbury, England. Although the American church is self-governing, its members honor the head of the whole Church of England.

In 1979, the Episcopal Church voted to ordain women to the priesthood and also revised the *Book of Common Prayer*. These two actions gave rise to the Anglican Church of North America (or Anglican Catholic Church; both names are used), dedicated to upholding traditional Episcopalianism. There are also several other small Episcopal denominations. In spite of this, the Episcopal Church in the United States is remarkably unified. Latitude in belief is complemented by uniformity in worship, and this shared worship has made for the greatest amount of cohesion in this Protestant community. There are differences of emphasis. High-church congregations emphasize liturgical worship, whereas low-church ones have a simpler service with greater emphasis on the Bible (in a sense, a more Protestant service). Broad-church Episcopalians may be in favor of either way of worship but emphasize a liberal approach to theology and place a great deal of importance on social ethics. In England, these differences have led to a divided church, but in the United States they have remained differences of style.

The Episcopal Church is the Church of England in the United States. Although it has spiritual ties to England, it is independent. Its churches combine wide latitude and tolerance in matters of belief, with uniformity in dramatic, liturgical worship that is centered on the seven sacraments.

Other Consensus Protestants

We now turn to a consideration of three more Protestant denominations that are not as large as the major five but which clearly fit into the category of consensus Protestantism. These include the United Church of Christ, the Christian Church (Disciples of Christ), and the Friends Yearly Meeting, also known as the Quakers.

The United Church of Christ

The United Church of Christ, like the Presbyterian Church, has its roots in Reformed theology and connectional church government.

The beliefs and practices of the United Church of Christ are very similar to those of other consensus Protestants. Its statement of faith, adopted in 1959, loosely follows the format of the Apostles Creed, with sections on God the Father, Jesus Christ the Son, and the Holy Spirit. Concluding paragraphs discuss the nature of the church and the role of Christians and affirm the two Protestant sacraments and eternal life in the Kingdom of God. The statement of faith is not binding on any local congregation, nor is it used as a test of faith for individual members. Its beliefs bring together the various emphases of the churches that make up its heritage. Concerning belief, the UCC affirms, "in essentials, unity; in nonessentials, liberty; in all things, charity."

Its patterns of worship, decided on by local congregations, vary considerably. Sermons frequently address social problems and crises, seeking to apply the historic beliefs of Christianity in the modern world. There are educational activities for all ages, and, especially in larger churches, a variety of specialized ministries and outreach efforts.

This denomination is a strong supporter of ecumenism, and, with other consensus Protestants, is a member of both the World and National Councils of Churches. The United Church of Christ is one of the most socially liberal and activist churches in the United States. Nationally, its Council for Racial and Ethnic Ministries is responsible for coordinating the efforts of councils and boards that focus on the church's ministry to Asian American and Pacific Islands immigrants, Hispanics, Native Americans, and blacks, as well as for overseeing its Ministers for Social and Racial Justice.

The Christian Church (Disciples of Christ)

The Christian Church (Disciples of Christ) is one of the communities of faith that grew out of what we now call the **Restoration Movement** in American Christianity. It is the only one of the denominations in this chapter that began in America.

Prior to the Civil War, religious thinkers in many parts of the country found themselves dismayed over the divisions within the Christian churches. They believed that the Bible taught that there was to be but one Christianity, yet there were many churches. As often as not, the relationships between these churches were not friendly, marred by arguments over creeds and church structures. The Restoration Movement sought to end these divisions.

A passionate desire for Christian unity lay behind the Restoration Movement. Everyone in the movement believed that the multitude of divisions in the Christian Church was offensive to Jesus' intentions for his followers. They believed that the unity that they sought could be achieved by a return to the

New Testament as the only guide to faith and practice, down to the smallest detail of church government. The Restorationists said that division had come about through creeds and organizations invented by human beings, rather than given by God. Thus, the way to peace and purity was a radical return to the past and to the church as it had been in New Testament times. An early slogan, "No creed but Christ," highlights their belief in the importance of avoiding humanly invented creeds.

The Restorationists believed that each local congregation should be autonomous or self-governing. They held that each local gathering of believers was, in fact, the church. There should be no structures that took over things that were properly the responsibility of the local church (such as mission boards), nor any that limited the authority of each local fellowship of believers (such as presbyteries). They had other beliefs in common, including the following: All people have the capacity and the responsibility either to accept or to reject God's offer of salvation in Jesus the Christ; there is no predestination. While God is properly thought of as Father, Son, and Holy Spirit, the actual term *Trinity* is not biblical and therefore ought not to be used. Communion, for which they preferred the term *Lord's supper*, was understood to be a memorial only. Some advocated weekly celebration, and others spoke in favor of less frequent administration.

The Restoration Movement gave birth to two other groups of churches that continue to claim the allegiance of significant numbers of Americans. These two, the Christian Churches/Churches of Christ and the Churches of Christ, are discussed in Chapter 8. It also produced many smaller, independent churches.

The Christian Church (Disciples of Christ) includes both religious conservatives and liberals among its members, giving it a wider range of religious attitudes than is true of the other two. As with all of the Restoration Movement churches, there is no creed, and freedom of personal interpretation is the rule. Although the Disciples believe that all persons are sinful and in need of redemption through Jesus, they do not believe in original sin that is inherited in some way from Adam and Eve. Church membership is based on a simple affirmation of the Lordship of Christ. Congregational worship is dignified and rather formal, with both instrumental and vocal music. The Lord's supper is celebrated every Sunday. The Disciples support a network of schools and colleges as well as other institutions for the betterment of society. They maintain residence halls on many university and college campuses, called Disciples Divinity Houses. They are members of both the National and World Councils of Churches and support ecumenical efforts of many types. On several campuses they are involved in ecumenical campus ministries. A strong national structure has been developed, beginning in 1968, but the local congregation remains the basic unit.

The Friends

The Religious Society of Friends, also known as the **Quakers**, is the last community of faith we will consider in this chapter. The name "Friends" comes from John 15:15 in the Christian New Testament, in which Jesus says to his followers,

"I have called you friends." The Friends began in England in the 1600s. The cofounders, George Fox and his wife, Margaret Fell, were sincere seekers who had failed to find religious peace in any of the churches of their time. They did find it in a quiet, personal relationship with God, and this trait has been a part of the Quaker heritage ever since. Fox, Fell, and their followers came to believe in the presence of an Inner Voice or an Inner Light in every person. The Inner Light is each individual's capacity to know and respond to God and to truth.

The belief in the Inner Light has two very important consequences. It means that the individual's conscience is absolutely sacred and cannot be violated. The unusual religious liberty in William Penn's colony of Pennsylvania was a direct result of Penn's conviction that every person had an absolute right to worship God according to the leading of the Inner Light. It also meant that all persons were, without exception, equal.

These beliefs led to some of the distinctive attributes of the Society. The sanctity of individual conscience means, for example, that people cannot be drafted into the military against their will. The Society of Friends is among the best known of the historic peace churches. They advocate conscientious objection to military service and the pursuit of peace in all of life. A colleague of mine, for example, whose outlook is strongly influenced by Quaker teachings, has helped make us all more aware of the violence implied in certain expressions that are very common in our language, such as "I could have killed him!" or even "That was a killer exam!" The Friends' commitment to the sanctity of individual conscience, however, leaves room for participation in the military for those to whom it seems right, and there are Quaker chaplains in military service.

The emphasis on the equality of all people has made the Friends leaders in the movement for racial justice. It also relativizes such social customs as the use of titles. Letter salutations often read "Dear Jane Smith" or "Dear John Jones" rather than "Dear Dr. Smith" or "Dear Professor Jones." Among strict Quakers, even titles such as Mr. and Mrs. are not used.

Another result of this same conviction was traditional Quaker worship, in which there was no programmed worship and no worship leader. People sat in quiet meditation, speaking as they felt moved by the Holy Spirit to do so. Today, the Friends United Meeting (the largest church in the Quaker family in the United States) usually has ministers and programmed worship. Other churches retain the unprogrammed style, at least in some services. In any case, all members are considered ministers. Those who are "recorded ministers" are set apart for specific service to a congregation, or "meeting." Communion and baptism are taught to be spiritual ordinances, and no outward elements are used.

A hallmark of Quaker practice is that they do not vote in meetings for business in local congregations or larger assemblies. They seek spiritual consensus among themselves, based on the will of God as they perceive it. Not just a meeting of the minds or even of the hearts, this consensus grows out of the Inner Light within each person present.

The American Friends Service Committee (often known by its initials, AFSC) has an outstanding record of relief work in both wartime and peace.

Wherever there is a disaster, at home or abroad, AFSC volunteers can usually be found helping people pick up the pieces and begin to put shattered lives back together again. The committee was awarded the Nobel Peace Prize in 1947.

The Friends have never actively sought converts. They are content to be a quiet presence in the culture, seeking to worship and live in their own way, free from interference, and granting the same privileges to others. Although the "thee" and "thou" of plain speech and the simplicity of traditional Quaker dress have largely disappeared, the Friends remain distinctive in their emphasis on the Inner Light and their witness to peace.

WOMEN IN CONSENSUS PROTESTANTISM

Consensus Protestantism usually has been receptive to the cultural and social changes that have brought about new opportunities for women. Most consensus Protestant churches ordain women to the ministry. Examples include many Baptist congregations, the United Methodists, the Presbyterian Church, U.S.A., many of the Lutheran churches, the Episcopal Church, the United Church of Christ, the Disciples, and the Friends. Women are entering the ministry in increasing numbers. By and large, the opportunities have never been better for women who want to enter the professional ministry. "Women in the late twentieth century are experiencing their day in the sun in many areas of institutional church work. More positions of greater responsibility and authority are being opened to them than ever before. For the first time in history, a woman often receives preferential treatment for posts of leadership in volunteer and professional capacities."[25]

Women are also successful in gaining placements in churches, although a disproportionate number are employed in smaller churches that pay less than their larger counterparts. Most of the churches that have called a woman as minister or pastor are well satisfied with that choice. Women have also moved into the ranks of church officials in larger numbers than before.[26]

Lay positions that historically had been closed to women, such as usher, communion server, and membership on the board of trustees or board of elders, usually are open to both sexes equally. Some local churches have made it a policy to have equal numbers of women and men in such capacities.

The communities of faith described in this chapter attempt to use gender-inclusive language in worship and in publications. They have supported publication of revisions of the biblical books of Psalms, the Gospels, and the Pauline

---

[25]Rosemary Skinner Keller, "Patterns of Laywomen's Leadership in Twentieth-Century Protestantism," in *Women and Religion in America, Volume III: 1900–1968*, ed. Rosemary Radford Ruether and Rosemary Skinner Keller (San Francisco: Harper & Row, Publishers, 1986), p. 276.

[26]Edward C. Lehman, Jr., *Women Clergy: Breaking through Gender Barriers* (New Brunswick, NJ: Transaction Books, 1985).

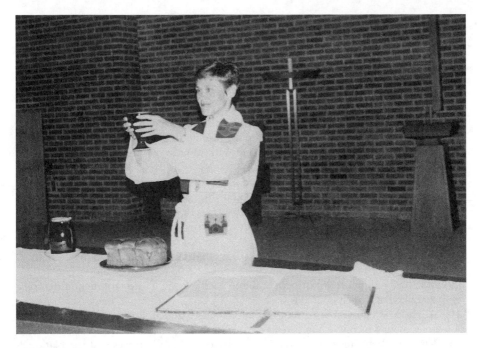

Figure 3-2 Presbyterians, like most consensus Protestants, ordain women to the ministry. (*Courtesy of Pastor Jean Holmes, Nauraushaun Presbyterian Church, Pearl River, NY.*)

Letters in which inclusive language is used. They have also supported publication of inclusive language lectionaries.[27]

The following examples are representative of the ways in which these churches address the need for gender-inclusive language. In United Church of Christ publications, it is no longer permissible to use language that refers to God as "Father, Son, and Holy Spirit." An acceptable alternative is God as "Creator, Redeemer, and Sanctifier." A new *Book of Worship* endorsed by the United Methodist General Conference includes prayers addressed to God as "Mother and Father." The United Church of Christ revised its statement of faith to eliminate gender-specific language. The language of the new Presbyterian statement is inclusive as well.

Consensus Protestant churches have been instrumental in supporting women's rights in general. Most have national boards that focus on women's issues, both within and outside the church. For example, most of them do not discourage women who want to work outside the home or who want to remain single. Many also help sponsor day-care centers. The National Council of Churches of Christ in the U.S.A. formally supported the passage of the Equal Rights Amendment to the U.S. Constitution, unanimously passing a resolution urging its passage.

[27]A *lectionary* is a book of biblical readings arranged for use in worship.

QUESTIONS AND ACTIVITIES FOR REVIEW, DISCUSSION, AND WRITING

1. Describe consensus religion in your own words. How is it related to religious pluralism and diversity?
2. What is the National Council of Churches? The National Association of Evangelicals? In what ways are they similar? Different?
3. What is the "American paradox" concerning women and religion?
4. Describe the variety of responses to male predominance in religion.
5. What roles do you think women should be able to play in their communities of faith? Why do you feel as you do? You might want to organize a discussion of this issue as a class project.
6. If you had a problem that you wanted to discuss with a pastor, minister, priest, or rabbi, would it make a difference to you if this person were female or male? Why?
7. With your professor, invite a female minister, priest, or rabbi to discuss with your class how she perceives the situation of women in consensus religion. Or organize a panel discussion on this topic.
8. Why are denominational differences less important in American religion than they were formerly?
9. What is unique and distinctive about each of the Protestant denominations described in this chapter?
10. Attend a worship service at both a Baptist church and an Episcopal one, and write an essay in which you compare and contrast them.
11. Visit the Web sites of both the National Council of Churches and the National Association of Evangelicals. Write a paragraph in which you describe the differences in how these two ecumenical organizations describe themselves.
12. Visit the Web sites of each of the denominations described in the chapter. From each, discover something about each denomination that you had not learned from the book.

FOR FURTHER READING

Balmer, Randall, *Grant Us Courage: Travels along the Mainline of American Protestantism*. New York: Oxford University Press, 1996. This book is an ethnographic study of twelve consensus churches, focusing on how they have changed and stayed the same in the last half of the twentieth century.

Bradshaw, Paul F., and Lawrence A. Hoffman, eds., *The Changing Face of Jewish and Christian Worship in North America*. South Bend, IN: University of Notre Dame Press, 1992. This book, a careful examination of recent changes in Jewish and Christian worship, includes critiques of these developments from a feminist perspective.

Melton, J. Gordon, *The Churches Speak On: Women's Ordination: Official Statements from Religious Bodies and Ecumenical Organizations*. Detroit: Gale Research, Inc., 1991. Like most of Melton's encyclopedic works, this is a thorough collection that includes Protestant, Catholic, Mormon, and Eastern Orthodox Christian statements, as well as several Jewish ones.

Miller, Donald E., *Reinventing American Protestantism: Christianity in the New Millennium*. Berkeley: University of California Press, 1997. Miller's thesis is that changes occurring in Protestantism as the millennium draws to a close are so extensive that they will "reinvent" Protestantism in the United States, amounting to a "new Reformation."

Mullin, Robert Bruce and Russell E. Richey, eds., *Reimagining Denominationalism: Interpretive Essays*. New York: Oxford University Press, 1994. The editors include a variety of essays dealing with both Christian and Jewish themes that examine the role and interpretation of the denomination as a distinctively American form of religious organization.

NESBITT, PAULA D. *Feminization of the Clergy in America: Occupational and Organizational Perspectives.* New York: Oxford University Press, 1997. Nesbitt presents a 70-year study of women's ordination, primarily in the Episcopal and Unitarian Universalist churches, that compares the patterns before and following the large influx of female clergy in the 1970s.

SCHMIDT, FREDERICK W., JR., *A Still Small Voice: Women, Ordination, and the Church.* Syracuse, NY: Syracuse University Press, 1996. The value of this particular study of the women's ordination issue in several Protestant denominations and the Catholic Church is twofold: It relies heavily on first-person interview material, and it expands the discussion to include the impact of this "women's issue" on men.

WESSINGER, CATHERINE, ed., *Religious Institutions and Women's Leadership: New Roles Inside the Mainstream.* Columbia, SC: University of South Carolina Press, 1996. Wessinger studies women's movement into leadership roles in Protestantism, Catholicism, and Judaism from the nineteenth through the end of the twentieth centuries and how this trend is changing religion in the United States.

RELEVANT WORLD WIDE WEB SITES

National Association of Evangelicals (http://www.nae.goshen.net/contents.html).

National Council of Churches (http://www.nccc.usa.org).

American Baptist Churches (http://www.abc-usa.org).

Disciples of Christ (http://www.disciples.org).

Episcopal Church (http://www.ecusa.org).

Evangelical Lutheran Church (http://www.elca.org).

Friends (http://www.quaker.org).

Lutheran Church–Missouri Synod (http://www.lcms.org).

Presbyterian Church in the U.S.A. (http://www.pcusa.org).

Southern Baptist Convention (http://www.sbcnet.org).

United Methodist Church (http://www.umc.org).

United Church of Christ (http://www.ucc.org).

4

Catholics in the United States

If you are not a Catholic Christian, ask yourself what your attitudes and feelings about Catholic people are. If you are a Catholic, are you aware of any anti-Catholic prejudice? You might want to discuss these questions with friends who are and are not Catholic.

Catholics make up approximately one-fourth of the population of the United States, making this group the largest single community of faith in the nation. It is these people's story, or rather, stories, to which we now turn in our exploration of consensus religion. We will look briefly at the history of Catholics in America, then at core beliefs and practices, and, finally, we will investigate contemporary issues that occupy the Church's thinking.

Before doing so, it is important to locate Catholicism within the larger environment of which it is one aspect. Catholic theologian Richard P. McBrien helps us to do that: "Catholicism is not a reality that stands by itself. The word *Catholic* is not only a noun but an adjective. As an adjective it is a qualification of *Christian*, just as Christian is a qualification of *religious*, and religious is a qualification of *human*."[1] To be a Catholic, then, is to be a religious human being whose faith and life are guided by the particular Catholic interpretation of Christianity.

CATHOLICS AND PROTESTANTS:
MORE SIMILAR THAN DIFFERENT

The religious life of Christians—Protestant, Catholic, Eastern Orthodox, and others as well—centers on the person, life, death, and resurrection of Jesus. Christians are those people who are defined by their faith in Jesus as their Lord and Savior. This means that Protestant and Catholic Christians have a great deal in common. Indeed, their similarities outweigh their differences. The vast majority affirm the basic beliefs and practices in the Apostles Creed, for example.

[1]Richard P. McBrien, *Catholicism,* 3rd ed. (San Francisco: HarperSanFrancisco, 1994), p. 6.

Figure 4-1

THE APOSTLES CREED

We believe in God, the Father Almighty,
Creator of heaven and earth.

And in Jesus Christ, his only son, our Lord,
Who was conceived of the Holy Ghost,
And born of the Virgin Mary.
He suffered under Pontius Pilate,
Was crucified, dead, and buried.
He descended into Hell.
[Alt: "He descended to the dead."Some omit completely.]
On the third day he rose again from the dead.
He ascended into Heaven
And sits at the right hand of God the Father almighty,
From whence he will come
To judge the living and the dead.

We believe in the Holy Spirit, the holy catholic church,
The communion of saints, the forgiveness of sins,
The resurrection of the body, and the life everlasting.

The **Apostles Creed** (Figure 4-1) is so named because it is a summary of essential Christian beliefs as held by the Church at the time of the Apostles. It was not written by the Apostles, as legend has it, but goes back to the very old Roman Creed. In its current form, it probably dates from the seventh century C.E.

When the creed refers to "one holy catholic church," the word *catholic* is being used to mean "universal," rather than referring to the Catholic Church. In spite of the many divisions within Christianity, it is understood to be but one Church, having one Lord, and continuing back to the time of the twelve apostles whom the Christian New Testament says that Jesus gathered around himself during his earthly life. The followers of Jesus the Christ are called into a community, the Church.

The Apostles Creed and other classic creeds of Christianity reflect the teachings that are found in the Christian Bible. Although Protestant and Catholic versions of the Bible are very similar, the Catholic Church had not until recently given its approval to any of the translations of the Bible commonly used by Protestant Christians. In late 1991, the National Council of Catholic Bishops gave their Church's official approval to the *New Revised Standard Version* of the Christian Bible. This means that Catholic and Protestant Christians (as well as Eastern Orthodox Christians, whose leadership had approved the new translation earlier) now have a translation of the Christian Bible that all can use.

FROM IMMIGRANT CHURCH
TO CONSENSUS RELIGION

In one sense, all religions except those of the Native Americans in the United States are immigrant faiths, because the only indigenous religions were those of the various Native American peoples who lived on the North American continent long before the arrival of the first European explorers. Because the union that eventually became the United States included most of the Spanish territories, the oldest non-native religion in the United States is Catholicism, not the Puritanism of the Pilgrims. It is particularly true of Catholics that their history has been, and in many ways continues to be, influenced by being an immigrant church.

Catholics were among the first, if not the first, Europeans to set foot upon the shores of America. It is likely that the first Catholic mass[2] in what is now the United States was celebrated by an early Spanish missionary priest. French missionaries traveled throughout what we know as New York, Maine, Pennsylvania, Wisconsin, Michigan, and Illinois, as well as down the Mississippi River to Alabama and Louisiana. The Spanish and French Catholic explorers came to the New World with two goals: territorial conquest and evangelization of the native peoples. Catholics from England arrived here for a different reason.

English Catholics were the next Catholics to colonize in the New World. There was an important difference between them and the Spanish and French. The English came as settlers and not as missionaries and territorial conquerors. They came to the eastern seaboard area after the persecution of Catholics in England, launched by King Henry VIII, forced many to flee for their lives. The English disliked the Native Americans, whose lands they took over whenever possible. Nor did they get on well with the French or Spanish, bringing Old World hostilities with them to their New World.

Throughout the colonial period, as before, the number of Catholics remained small, less than one percent of the population. Most were English or Irish, but this was soon to change. Land acquired in the South and West added numbers of Spanish Catholics, and European immigrants later arrived in great waves. A huge wave of Irish immigrants escaping famine in the 1840s and beyond became an important dimension in American Catholicism.

The 1924 Immigration Act sharply reduced immigration until Congress removed the restrictive quota system in 1965. After 1965, a great influx of immigrants from Asian countries devastated by war, from the Philippine Islands, from Haiti, and from Mexico again swelled the ranks of immigrant American Catholics. The immigrant membership of the church continues to increase

---

[2]The *mass* is the central act of Catholic worship.

today, and the church continues to face the two monumental tasks that have occupied it during much of its history: caring for the spiritual and oftentimes the physical, educational, and social needs of a vast immigrant membership and integrating within itself the varying styles of religion and spirituality brought to it by these immigrants.

Along the way, and despite tremendous obstacles, the Church has grown, prospered, and become a central element in American life. The parish, or parochial, school system (described below) developed and grew, providing quality education consistent with Catholic values for a multitude of children, not all of whom were Catholic. Colleges and universities were established, many of which have attained national recognition as among the best in the nation. Seminaries for the training of an American priesthood were built. Hospitals, orphanages, and shelters for unwed mothers and abused women and children have been an outgrowth of the Catholic concern for the plight of the unfortunate in society. Social service agencies have contributed to the assistance of Catholic and non-Catholic alike, especially in urban areas. The American Church has met the needs of a growing number of Catholics on a day-to-day basis. It provides centers for worship and community life, counsel in times of trouble and crisis, and celebrations for important life passages such as birth, marriage, and death.

The decade of the 1960s had a tremendous impact on Catholicism. Five events are especially noteworthy: John F. Kennedy became the first Catholic to be elected to the presidency. His popularity, charisma, and the integrity with which he was both American and Catholic reassured non-Catholic Americans that Catholicism was legitimate and that Catholics could be trusted. It also buoyed Catholic confidence. Pope John XXIII, who had been elected two years earlier, became one of the most popular Catholic Popes in history, and reached out with friendship and understanding to non-Catholics and non-Christians. He also convened the Second Vatican Council, or Vatican II, which brought about substantial innovations in the church. Many of these made Catholicism seem less foreign to non-Catholics.

His successor, Pope Paul VI, issued *Humanae Vitae* (*On Human Life*). Its strong reaffirmation of the ban on artificial contraception eclipsed nearly everything else in the document and drew sharp criticism from both Catholics and non-Catholics. The larger cultural revolution of the 1960s permanently affected the church, as it did everything else in the nation.[3]

The majority of people in the United States consider Catholics to be a part of consensus religion. Catholicism is not viewed as "out-of-the-ordinary" religion. This has not always been the case. The history of Catholics in America is in part a history of prejudice and discrimination. In some of the original thirteen colonies, Catholicism was illegal. In all of the colonies, there were times when Catholics could neither vote nor hold public office.

---

[3]William V. D'Antonio, James D. Davidson, Dean R. Hoge, and Ruth A. Wallace, *Laity American and Catholic: Transforming the Church* (Kansas City: Sheed and Ward, 1996), p. 9.

Unorganized and informal anti-Catholic sentiment has existed in the United States for as long as Catholics have been here. An attitude of "America for Americans" has all too often meant America for *Protestant* Americans.[4] Non-Catholic Americans have often feared that, should Catholicism ever become dominant, religious liberty would be lost. This fear overlooks the constant and outspoken support that America's Catholic people, both lay and clergy, have given to the separation of church and state. Some people have also thought of Catholics as subjects of a foreign ruler (the Pope) and hence as less than fully loyal to the United States. This, too, overlooks the historical record. Protestant Americans, accustomed as they are to a style of worship that values words above ceremony and ritual, have looked with suspicion, born of a lack of understanding, upon Catholicism's ornate ritual and have often regarded beliefs such as transubstantiation (to be discussed later) as "superstitious mumbo jumbo." Vigorous anti-Protestant sentiment on the part of some Catholic people, including leaders, at times has compounded the problem of relationships between the two faiths.

This informal anti-Catholic sentiment has become organized into specific groups at various times throughout American history. The American Party, also known as the Know-Nothing Party, actively opposed Catholics in the 1800s. The American Protective Association formed in 1887. Although its stated goals were political rather than religious, its aim was said to be to change the minds and hearts of those who were in "the shackles and chains of blind obedience to the Roman Catholic Church." There was another outburst of organized activity in the first half of the 1900s. A resurgent Ku Klux Klan directed its energies as much against Catholics as against blacks and Jews.

Most of the prejudice against Catholic Americans today originates with a minority of Protestants who do not recognize Catholics as fellow members of the Christian community of faith. Many Americans are also critical of the Catholic Church's stand on issues such as abortion, the use of artificial birth control, and the role of women in the Church. This criticism comes not only from non-Catholics but from within the ranks of Catholic Americans as well.

THE SECOND VATICAN COUNCIL, 1962–1965

Prior to Vatican II, the boundaries that marked Catholicism off from other Christian communities of faith were drawn quite clearly, or at least so it seemed. Those boundaries became much less distinctive after the Council. There is continuity between the pre-Vatican II church and the post-Vatican II church, but they are also clearly different, and the differences make the post-conciliar church less distinctive.

---

[4]Catholics have not been the only ones to encounter this attitude. It has also affected how Jews, Muslims, black Americans, Asian Americans, and other ethnic groups have been and are treated.

The council "solved some of the lingering problems of being a Catholic in the United States." Catholics no longer felt as "different," nor did their non-Catholic neighbors regard them as such.

> Most important, the Council reversed earlier Catholic teaching by affirming the separation of church and state and religious liberty for all. In one stroke a major sore point for American Catholics was removed. Also, the Council redefined the Church as the "People of God" and advocated increased democratization of church structures, a more participative liturgy [worship], use of the vernacular in worship, reduction of rules of abstinence [here, from meat], ecumenical goodwill with other Christians, an open door to biblical scholarship, and greater self-determination for men's and women's orders. . . . The siege mentality of the early twentieth century was gone. Ever since, the dominant mood of Catholics has been to embrace American society with little reservation . . . and to feel like full participants in American life.[5]

THE DISTINCTIVENESS
OF AMERICAN CATHOLIC CHRISTIANITY

Catholic theologian Richard P. McBrien suggests that Catholicism can best be understood by

> . . . identifying and describing various characteristics of Catholicism, each of which Catholicism shares with one or another Christian church or tradition. But no other church or tradition possesses these characteristics in quite the same way as Catholicism. . . . Catholicism is distinguished from other Christian churches and traditions especially in its understanding of, and practical commitment to, the principles of sacramentality, mediation, and communion. Differences between Catholic and non-Catholic (especially Protestant) approaches become clearer when measured according to these three principles.[6]

The Sacraments

Catholic worship, usually called the mass, centers around the **seven sacraments**. Catholics believe that participation in the sacraments changes people inwardly, as a result of the special grace conveyed by the sacraments. They are not only signs and symbols, as most Protestants believe, but effective means by which God acts. "Celebrated worthily in faith, the sacraments confer the grace that they signify."

> They are *efficacious* because in them Christ himself is at work: it is he who baptizes, he who acts in his sacraments in order to communicate the grace that each

---

[5]D'Antonio et al., *Laity American and Catholic*, pp. 9–10.
[6]McBrien, *Catholicism*, p. 9.

sacrament signifies. . . . This is the meaning of the Church's affirmation that the sacraments act *ex opere operato* (literally: "by the very fact of the action's being performed") . . .[7]

Catholic sacramentality, then, is grounded in the conviction that it is God in Christ himself who works in and through the physical sacraments to bring about a spiritual reality, to impart the grace that the sacraments signify.

The first sacrament in which Catholics participate is **baptism**. "Baptism is birth into the new life in Christ. In accordance with the Lord's will, it is necessary for salvation, as is the Church herself, which we enter by baptism."[8] Catholics believe that baptism is necessary for the removal of the inborn sin that is a part of all persons simply because they are human. Most Catholics are baptized when they are babies. When the sacrament is performed for an adult, it is often called the Rite of Christian Initiation, a name that points to its other function as the ritual of incorporation into the Church.

The sacrament of **confirmation** completes what is begun in baptism. It signifies that the person has become an adult in the eyes of the Church and confirms the promises made by others at baptism. The one who is being confirmed is anointed on the forehead with oil that has been blessed to signify the seal of the Holy Spirit. This sacrament is believed to give the grace necessary to live a mature Christian life in the Church.

> Confirmation perfects Baptismal grace; it is the sacrament which gives the Holy Spirit in order to root us more deeply in the divine filiation, incorporate us more firmly into Christ, strengthen our bond with the Church, associate us more closely with her mission, and help us bear witness to the Christian faith in words accompanied by deeds.[9]

The central act of Catholic worship is called the **mass**. The Mass is an integrated experience of worship that is made up of two parts that work together. The **liturgy of the word** includes those parts of the mass that focus on verbal communication, such as Bible readings, prayers, responsive readings, and a sermon, often called a *homily* by Catholics. The Bible readings always include a reading from one of the four Gospels and another reading from either the New Testament or the Old Testament. The **liturgy of the Eucharist** reenacts, in words and actions, Jesus' sharing bread and wine with the disciples at the Last Supper. Catholic worship is highly liturgical, with ornate symbolism; the use of incense and chanting, symbolic colors, and vestments worn by the priest; and an air of high solemnity. Since the Second Vatican Council, many Catholic Churches have experimented with more casual masses that often include folk

---

[7] *Catechism of the Catholic Church* (Mahwah, NJ: Paulist Press, 1994), ¶¶ 1127–1128.
[8] *Catechism of the Catholic Church*, ¶ 1277.
[9] *Catechism of the Catholic Church*, ¶ 1316.

songs and liturgical dance, but the twin elements of the liturgy of the word and the liturgy of the Eucharist are always present.

Catholics believe that in the **sacrament of the Eucharist**, the bread and wine actually become the body and blood of Jesus Christ when the priest speaks the words of consecration ("This is my body . . . This is my blood"—words that the Gospel records Jesus as saying to his disciples at the Last Supper). This belief in **transubstantiation** is based on a philosophical distinction between what something actually is (its substance) and what it appears to be. In transubstantiation, the substance of the bread and wine become the body and blood of Christ, who is fully present under the appearances of bread and wine. This sacrament, received often throughout a Catholic's life, is ordinarily received at mass, but it may also be received privately when circumstances such as illness call for doing so.

> The Eucharist is the heart and summit of the Church's life, for in it Christ associates his Church and all her members with his sacrifice of praise and thanksgiving offered once for all on the cross to his Father; by this sacrifice he pours out the graces of salvation on his Body which is the Church.
>
> As sacrifice, the Eucharist is also offered in reparation for the sins of the living and the dead and to obtain spiritual or temporal benefits from God.[10]

Another sacrament that nourishes Catholics spiritually throughout their lives is the **sacrament of reconciliation, or confession**. Penitents confess their sins to God through the priest who, in the name of God and with the authority of the Church, pronounces forgiveness. Special prayers or other activities may be assigned to assist people in recovering from the effects of their sins. Catholics are expected to confess through a priest at least annually, but many find that the practice helps them be aware of God's forgiving grace and confess more frequently. Non-Catholics often stereotype Catholics by saying that Catholics can confess to a priest and then go out and sin all over again. It needs to be noted here that the rite of reconciliation must be accompanied by genuine sorrow for having sinned and by true intention to avoid it in the future.

The Second Vatican Council revised the Church's understanding of this sacrament somewhat, lessening the emphasis given to the penance performed and emphasizing the rite as one of reconciliation, which is the spiritual reuniting of the penitent with God, other persons, and the Church.

A fifth sacrament is now commonly known as the sacrament of **anointing the sick**; formerly, it was called extreme unction or, simply, the last rites. This sacrament, in which a priest uses oil to anoint a person who is ill or in danger of dying from accident or old age, is a way of mediating the concern of Christ and the Church for the suffering person. Catholics believe that the sacrament gives grace for healing, if that is God's will, or to assist a person in the passage from life

---

[10]*Catechism of the Catholic Church,* ¶¶ 1407 and 1414.

to death and beyond if that is to be the final outcome. The understanding of this rite was broadened by Vatican II to include its use for those who are seriously ill but not in immediate danger of death.

The sacrament of **marriage** is one to which most Catholics look forward. The majority of Catholics, like the majority of all Americans, marry at some time in their lives. Although the stereotype of Catholics having larger-than-average families no longer holds true, marriage and family continue to be very important, because marriage is a sacrament. Blessed by a priest, authorized by the Church, and entered into only after a period of required counseling, Catholics believe that the sacrament of marriage gives the couple the special grace necessary to carry out the promises they make to each other. Because marriage is a sacrament in which two people are believed to be joined by God, the Catholic Church teaches that it is a lifelong commitment.

> The sacrament of Matrimony signifies the union of Christ and the Church. It gives spouses the grace to love each other with the love with which Christ has loved his Church; the grace of the sacrament thus perfects the human love of the spouses, strengthens their indissoluble unity, and sanctifies them on the way to eternal life.[11]

The Church does not recognize divorce and teaches that persons who divorce and remarry are living in sin and are barred from receiving the sacraments. There is a process through which a couple can obtain an annulment of their marriage. If an annulment is granted, it is as if the marriage had never happened. People whose marriages have been annulled can remarry in the Church. Because the marriage bond is sacred, however, such annulments are difficult to obtain. Statistical data indicate that, in actual practice, American Catholics divorce and remarry in about the same proportions as do non-Catholics. In this matter, American Catholics are influenced more by the culture of which they are a part than they are by the teachings of their Church.

The sacrament of orders, or **ordination to the priesthood**, sets a man apart for the official sacramental ministry of the Church. Catholics believe that it gives the priest the grace required to carry out the demands of his priesthood. Only men are ordained to the priesthood.

> Holy Orders is the sacrament through which the mission entrusted by Christ to his apostles continues to be exercised in the Church until the end of time; thus it is the sacrament of apostolic ministry.

> Through the ordained ministry, especially that of bishops and priests, the presence of Christ as head of the Church is made visible in the midst of the community of believers.[12]

---

[11]*Catechism of the Catholic Church,* ¶ 1661.
[12]*Catechism of the Catholic Church,* ¶¶ 1536 and 1549.

The Church as the Mediator between God and Humankind

The Catholic Church shares with Protestants the belief that **salvation comes to people by the grace of God. However, a great deal more emphasis is placed on the role of the Church as the official agent and mediator of God's grace**. The Church mediates by its official teaching and interpretation of the Bible, and it mediates through its administration of the sacraments. The sacraments as administered by the Church are believed to be channels through which the grace of God flows to people.

Catholics, although they regard the Bible as the original revelation, also teach that the tradition of the Church is equal with the Bible in authority. They believe that the Church is the official interpreter of the Bible. **Tradition and scripture together are accorded the same respect and veneration**. The writings of the Church Fathers, the decisions of Church councils, and the pronouncements of the Popes from Peter onward are all regarded as genuine sources of religious truth and as a part of the whole revelation of God to the Church. The Second Vatican Council placed greater emphasis on the Bible. For example, it said that the liturgy of the word, in which the Bible is read, is not just preparation for the liturgy of the Eucharist in the mass but is an integral part of a single act of worship. It also urged people to seek renewed spiritual vitality through increasing attention to the word of God in the Bible, as well as through continued participation in the Eucharist. The sharing of authority between the Bible and the Church and the Church's role as the official interpreter of the Bible are distinctive Catholic beliefs.

The doctrine of **papal infallibility** is unique to the Catholic Church. Many non-Catholic people misunderstand this teaching of the Church. It does not mean that the Pope never makes a mistake or never sins. In reality, this doctrine applies in only a very few circumstances. When the Pope speaks officially on matters of faith and morals that are absolutely central to the life of the church, it is believed that God prevents him from making errors. The current *Catechism of the Catholic Church* describes infallibility in a way that relates it to the whole church and its founding:

> In order to preserve the Church in the purity of the faith handed on by the apostles, Christ who is the Truth willed to confer on her a share in his own infallibility. . . . The Roman Pontiff, head of the college of bishops, enjoys this infallibility in virtue of his office, when, as supreme pastor and teacher of all the faithful—who confirms his brethren in the faith—he proclaims by a definitive act a doctrine pertaining to faith or morals. . . . The infallibility promised to the Church is also present in the body of bishops when, together with Peter's successor [the Pope], they exercise the supreme Magisterium [authority].[13]

---

[13]*Catechism of the Catholic Church*, ¶¶ 889 and 891. This document itself is an excellent example of the official nature of the Magisterium of the Church, in that it is the English version of the official teaching of the Church.

Catholics also believe that authority in the Church has come down in a direct line from Peter and hence from Christ himself. This view is called **apostolic succession**. This doctrine, operative through the sacrament of holy orders by which men are ordained to the priesthood, is the temporal foundation of the church. The principal biblical support for apostolic succession comes from a passage in the Gospel of Saint Matthew. In these verses, Jesus is speaking to one of the apostles: "You are Peter, and on this rock I will build my church, and the powers of death shall not prevail against it. I will give you the keys of the kingdom of Heaven; and whatever you bind on earth shall be bound in heaven, and whatever you loose on earth shall be loosed in heaven" (Matthew 16:17–19). "The Lord made Saint Peter the visible foundation of his Church. He entrusted the keys of the Church to him. The bishop of the Church of Rome [the Pope], successor to Saint Peter, is head of the college of bishops, the Vicar of Christ and Pastor of the universal Church on earth."[14]

There are other mediators as well. Any discussion of Catholic belief and practice would be incomplete if the Catholic **devotion to Mary**, the mother of Jesus, **and to the other saints** were not mentioned. Unlike Jesus, who, the Church teaches, was both divine and human, the saints and Mary were fully human and no more while alive on earth. A good deal of Catholic private devotion centers on these figures, who are in a sense "closer" to the believer because of having shared their human condition without benefit of simultaneous divinity. Catholics teach that Mary and the other saints pray to God on the believers' behalf and watch over the needs and concerns of the faithful. As the author of a recent study of Catholic women stated,

> For Catholics . . . Mary the mother of Jesus has been the feminine face of God. To be sure, Mary is not God, according to orthodox Christian theology. . . . Nevertheless, people pray to Mary. She may not be God in their spoken creed, but in the language of the heart, she functions as God.[15]

The unique Catholic doctrine of **purgatory** illustrates the mediating role of the church, as well. Catholics believe with other Christians that the faithful will have life after physical death. Purgatory is believed to be **a place or condition of further purification after death in which some must exist before they attain the beatific vision of God.** Upon death, individuals without any taint of sin may enter heaven directly. However, few people are this pure. In purgatory, people make amends for less serious sins that were not forgiven or for more serious sins that had been forgiven prior to death. Freed from guilt and punishment, the soul can enter into heaven, not only beholding God directly but being of the same mind and heart with God. The justice of God that requires that sin be punished and the mercy of God that seeks the salvation of all are thus reconciled.

---

[14]*Catechism of the Catholic Church*, ¶936.
[15]Jane Redmont, *Generous Lives: American Catholic Women Today* (Liguori, MO: Triumph Books, 1992), p. 102.

The doctrine of purgatory also provides a means by which the living may assist the souls of the dead through prayers and good works, because it is taught that such prayers and works may shorten the length of time a soul spends in purgatory. In this way, the belief in purgatory can help those who grieve for a loved one to work out their grief. It is important to note here that Catholics believe that God is an infinitely loving parent who will not reject anyone who does not reject God. God creates people with free will and the freedom to sin or to obey, and God goes to great lengths to see to it that disobedience does not result in condemnation unless there are no other alternatives.

Communion: The Centrality of the Church in Catholicism

Protestant Christians strongly emphasize the individual's personal relationship with Jesus, unmediated by the organization of the church or by its priesthood and its sacraments. Catholics, on the other hand, emphasize equally strongly the communal nature of the encounter between God and humankind. There can be no relationship with God, with Christ, that exists entirely without the church.[16]

The Catholic Church is hierarchical in its organization. The **Pope** is the worldwide leader and is revered by Catholics as the **Vicar**[17] **of Christ on Earth**. He is also **Bishop of Rome** (Figure 4-2). The Pope is assisted by the College of Cardinals and by the Roman Curia. The College of Cardinals advises the Pope and is responsible for electing a new Pope upon the death of the previous one.

Figure 4-2   The Pope is the leader of worldwide Catholicism. (*Corbis-Bettmann.*)

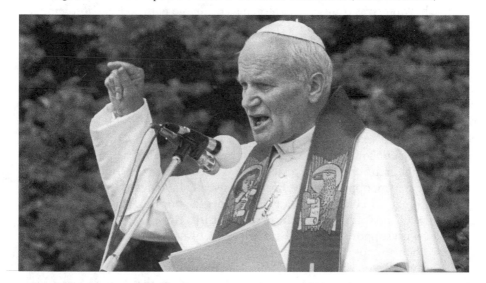

[16]McBrien, *Catholicism*, p. 13.
[17]"*Vicar*" means "official representative."

The Curia has a more administrative function. Archbishops and bishops are appointed by the Pope, taking into account the recommendations of local leaders. Archbishops are in charge of large geographical or population units, and bishops have authority over smaller areas. Local priests have jurisdiction to the extent that it is delegated to them by their bishops. In the Catholic Church in America, local councils of priests and bishops meet in an advisory capacity, and lay parish councils in the local church advise the priest and serve as a link between the ordained leadership and the laypeople who make up the broad base of the organizational pyramid.

The Catholic Church has many male monastic orders and many orders of nuns for women. Nuns and monks serve as full-time religious workers in parochial schools, in Church-sponsored hospitals and other agencies, as teachers in Catholic colleges and universities, and in a variety of other tasks. Much of the outreach work of the Church is done by these dedicated men and women who, while not priests, have a ministry that is of equal importance in the life of the Church. The requirement that priests remain unmarried is an important part of Catholic practice. Although this practice has not always been a part of the Church's teaching, and its historical development is somewhat confusing, its present-day practice seems to have two main functions: The priest is understood to be in the likeness of Christ, and, as far as we can know from the biblical accounts, Jesus never married. Not having the responsibility for a family also frees the priest to devote his full attention to his priesthood.

There are many laymen and laywomen who work professionally in Catholic churches, as well. They often have seminary training, as do the ordained. They serve as chaplains in hospitals, schools, and prisons; as parish outreach workers; as counselors; as teachers of theology in colleges and seminaries; and as leaders of retreat centers and other organizations.

Additional Catholic Distinctives

In the main, the moral views of Catholic people in the United States differ little from those of their non-Catholic counterparts. This is true even in those areas in which the church speaks the most forcefully: artificial conception control, abortion, premarital sexual activity, and homosexuality. However, these concerns are set in a different context than they are for many Protestants.

The church's opposition to abortion is a useful case in point. In Protestant fundamentalism, opposition to abortion is usually linked with support for capital punishment, welfare conservatism, support for nuclear arms and for defense spending. In the Catholic church's **consistent life ethic**, opposition to abortion is linked with support for both private and government-funded services for pregnant women and for the children of single mothers and with opposition to capital punishment, nuclear weapons, and excessive funding for the military. Except for questions of personal sexual morality, the positions that United States bishops take are usually to the left end of the continuum of American views, particularly on economic and defense issues.

Another example is the noteworthy range of things covered under the discussion of the fifth commandment ("you shall not kill") in the contemporary *Catechism*: The core point is that no one can claim the right to end a life because God alone is Lord of life from beginning to end. Killing when necessary in self-defense or in defense of another is upheld. The death penalty is held not to violate the commandment "in cases of extreme gravity" to protect society, but "if bloodless means are sufficient" then "public authority should limit itself to such means." Refusing assistance to people in danger violates the commandment. Societal acceptance of widespread famine is given as an example. Direct abortion is of course included among violations, as is direct euthanasia. Discontinuing heroic medical measures and the use of painkillers to alleviate suffering even when such use may shorten life is, however, acceptable. Suicide is an offense against the commandment. Society is charged with the responsibility to help all of its citizens to attain "living-conditions that allow them to grow and reach maturity: food and clothing, housing, health care, basic education, and social assistance." Temperance and the avoidance of excess is mentioned, and it is noted that people "who, by drunkenness or a love of speed, endanger their own and others' safety on the road, at sea, or in the air" are said to "incur grave guilt." Kidnaping, hostage taking, and other terrorist acts are forbidden by the commandment, as are any but therapeutic amputations, mutilations, and sterilizations performed on innocent people. Autopsy and organ donation are acceptable. Safeguarding peace and avoiding war is encouraged. In conjunction with this, acts of war that destroy entire cities or vast areas and the people in them are condemned, and the specific danger of weapons of mass destruction is addressed.[18]

A key feature of life for some Catholic youngsters is that they attend **parochial schools** sponsored by their Church. Parochial schools provide education within the context of Catholic values. Education about their faith and regular participation in mass are included in their school experience. So is learning about religions other than Catholicism. They may be taught by nuns or brothers or by lay teachers. A flourishing parochial school is a focal point of the parish and a center for its social life.

Fewer Catholic youngsters attend parochial schools now than in the past, a part of the loss of distinctiveness of Catholic life in the United States. Slightly over one-fourth of Catholic elementary- and middle-school children and under one-fifth of Catholic high-school students attend parochial schools. Among Catholic college students, only 10 percent attend colleges sponsored by their Church.[19]

Catholic education is not limited to parochial schools. About 600,000 students are enrolled in 236 Catholic institutions of higher education. These include one of the historically black universities and 49 women's colleges, which account

---

[18]*Catechism of the Catholic Church*, ¶¶ 2258 through 2317.
[19]Dean R. Hoge, "Catholics in the U.S.: The Next Generation," in *The Public Perspective: A Roper Center Review of Public Opinion and Polling*, vol. 2, no.1 (November/December 1990), p. 11.

for half of the women's colleges in the country.[20] Although the question of what exactly is *Catholic* about education in these institutions is difficult to answer, their place in the overall picture of American higher education is important.

In addition, the Catholic Church maintains an active ministry to Catholic students on both Catholic and non-Catholic campuses. In the late 1800s, a society where Catholic students could meet regularly for fellowship and support was organized. Cardinal Newman was a well-known name in Catholic circles and was associated with university education, having been involved in the founding of the Catholic University of Ireland in Dublin, and his name was picked for the organization. By 1920, there were "Newman Clubs" on many campuses. Following the Second Vatican Council, the name was changed to the Catholic Campus Ministry; many local groups still retain a reference to Cardinal Newman in their name.[21]

CONSERVATIVE AND TRADITIONALIST DISSENT IN AMERICAN CATHOLICISM

The situation in which the American Church found itself—pluralism, disestablishment, and freedom of religion in a democratic state—differed greatly from that which had prevailed throughout most of its worldwide history. This led directly to a process that has been called *inculturation*. Inculturation, according to one Catholic author, is "the process of deep, sympathetic adaptation and appropriation of a local cultural setting in which the Church finds itself in a way that does not compromise its basic faith in Christ."[22] Inculturation, then, is something the Catholic Church has done worldwide. In the United States, it has taken place almost from the beginning of the Church's presence here. However, in the United States, this process has more often than not brought the Catholic Church in the United States into conflict with Rome.

Nor is it simply a conflict between the "American Church" and "Rome." Although the Catholic Church in the United States is predominantly under the influence and control of those who favor Americanization, there is a contingent of people, both lay and clerical, who disagree. They believe that the route taken by the Church in the United States has in fact "compromised its basic faith in Christ." Catholic sociologist Joseph A. Varacalli describes it this way: Those who favor inculturation are "attempting (quite successfully) to incorporate secularism into the Church with contemporary anti-Americanizers trying to uphold the autonomy of the Catholic tradition and the unchanging foundational principles of the Faith. . . . The vast majority of American Catholics . . . are a scattered

---

[20]David J. O'Brien, *From the Heart of the American Church: Catholic Higher Education and American Culture* (Maryknoll, NY: Orbis Books, 1994), p. 70.

[21]Thanks to Rev. James R. Bates, Pastor, Our Lady of Grace Parish, Noblesville, IN, for information on the Catholic Student Ministry.

[22]William Reiser, "Inculturation and Doctrinal Development," *Heythrop Journal*, no. 22 (1981), p. 135.

flock presently being highjacked by various secular ideologies and commitments."[23]

There is greater diversity in the church because there are now essentially three generations of Catholic laity, each of which had a distinctive religious upbringing:

- Pre–Vatican II Catholics who matured before the council tend to prefer the older model of the church with which they are familiar, hierarchical and traditional in its ways of doing things and having a great deal of authority in the lives of believers. Being Catholic and being Christian are the same thing, and God's law and the Church's law are one. They tend to take their Church's teachings "whole," without distinguishing among them.
- Vatican II Catholics, those who came of age during the council, have one foot in each Church, so to speak, and their views tend to lie between those of the younger and the older generations.
- Post–Vatican II Catholics have experienced only the postconciliar Church, prefer the more democratic and less institutional Church of their formative years, and are much more individualistic in their interpretation of what it means to be Catholic. They distinguish between being Catholic and being Christian, and between God's law and the laws of the Church.[24]

Diversity of opinion in the Church has led to the development of conservative/traditional dissent from the predominantly democratized, deinstitutionalized and individualistic style of being Catholic in the United States. According to the traditionalists, conservatives, or restorationists (so called because they seek to restore the earlier ways of the Church), the Church, under the combined influences of Vatican II, the decade of the 1960s, and the progressive secularization of American culture, "has fallen into a state of profound crisis," and "has lost its passion and its zeal, its self-confidence and sense of direction, and, most important of all, its privileged claim to ultimate authority."[25] Standards within the Church are collapsing, and compromises with Protestantism and with secularization have led the Church far from the reality of what conservatives think it should be.[26]

Although the conservative/traditionalist movement is not a single movement but one that incorporates a number of different perspectives, there are common themes that help to describe what it is.

- Conservatives agree with their less conservative counterparts that Vatican II and its work were legitimate. However, they favor an interpretation and implementation

[23]Joseph A. Varacalli, *The Catholic and Politics in Post-World War II America: A Sociological Analysis* (Garden City, NY: Society of Catholic Social Scientists, 1995), pp. 9–10 and 45–46.

[24]D'Antonio et al., *Laity American and Catholic*, chapters 4 and 5.

[25]Michael W. Cuneo, *The Smoke of Satan: Conservative and Traditionalist Dissent in Contemporary American Catholicism* (New York: Oxford University Press, 1997), p. 179.

[26]Mary Jo Weaver and R. Scott Appleby, *Being Right: Conservative Catholics in America* (Bloomington: Indiana University Press, 1999), p. 79.

of the council's work that emphasizes continuity rather than change. The council itself is not the problem, but the implementation of it in the thirty years after.

- Because the American bishops and Catholic theologians have taken a very change-oriented approach to the council, it is the responsibility of the laity to uphold the standards of the true Church.
- Moral laxity, particularly in matters of sexual morality, is one of the major problems. Laxity in the nation as a whole is bad enough, but worse is its infiltration into the ranks of the faithful.
- There has been far too much adjusting of traditional Catholic theology to cultural circumstances, especially to pluralism. Conservatives see themselves in the position of having to defend the Church against its own theologians.
- The Church in the United States retains only a symbolic connection to the authority of Rome, seriously eroding its authority.[27]

There are a number of organizations associated with this conservative thrust in the Church. One of the best known is CUF, Catholics United for the Faith. Founded in 1968, it is composed of Catholic laypeople dedicated to defending a traditional view of the Church's teachings as expressed in official documents. They support cautious implementation of the work of Vatican II that does not go beyond the officially expressed views of the council. The Fellowship of Catholic Scholars is made up of scholars who have rallied behind a similarly cautious interpretation of the Vatican II documents. They are particularly concerned that their more conservative scholarly voice be heard alongside that of the more liberal Catholic scholars in the United States.

WOMEN AND THE CATHOLIC CHURCH

The Catholic Church's attitude toward women has always been complex. Mary, as the mother of Jesus, has been given great respect and honor and is looked upon as the first among women. Her status comes from her motherhood. She fulfilled in a very special way the role traditionally held up as the most important one for women. Traditional Catholic teaching also emphasizes Eve, the temptress, as the key figure in the drama of original sin and the human fall from grace, partially offsetting the effect of the veneration of Mary.

Catholic orders of nuns are another example of this complexity. These orders were the first institutional opportunity for the involvement of women in religion in America. They provided a setting in which women could carry out specific duties within the context of a close-knit community of women. Especially for those who did not have the desire or the opportunity to marry, these orders were a means to security and respectability. Negatively, the female orders were closely governed by male superiors in the Church and had little, if any, autonomy in their early years.

[27]Michael W. Cuneo, *The Smoke of Satan*, pp. 24–30.

In the nineteenth century, many nuns taught in public and private schools, as well as in parochial schools. Others worked as nurses in hospitals and other institutions and in private homes. They served heroically as nurses during the Civil and Spanish-American Wars. They played a major role in overcoming American suspicion and hostility toward Catholicism and Catholic people because of their dedicated work in these areas.[28]

During the nineteenth century, nuns in America sought ways to adapt to democracy. They often broke with their European motherhouses (the American nuns were branches of European orders and responsible to them) in order to adopt regulations that were better suited to their new environment.[29] They also founded American orders. **Mother Elizabeth Bayley Seton** was the first American to be officially declared a saint by the Catholic Church. Seton established the **Sisters of Charity**, the first religious order founded in the United States, in 1809. She is also remembered as the founder of the American Catholic parochial school system.

In the twentieth century, nuns have demonstrated continued commitment and service in the areas of nursing, education, and social work. They have also broadened their participation in the cause of international peace and in addressing the plight of the Third World nations. They are in the forefront of a more general Catholic concern for personal spiritual formation, developing and practicing new ways of personal and community devotion that are compatible with life in the modern era.

The Second Vatican Council brought about new opportunities for nuns. It permitted greater self-government in religious orders. It allowed nuns to increase their contact with the world outside their convents. They no longer had to live in communities with groups of nuns but could live much more on their own in the society. They could find employment in agencies that were not related to the Church. Nuns began attending graduate schools in significant numbers and went on to teach in colleges, universities, and seminaries. In many orders, being a nun no longer meant wearing the distinctive clothing that set them apart from other women in the population.

A cluster of reproductive issues has been at the forefront of much of the discussion about the Catholic Church's attitude toward women. The U.S. Catholic Conference (USCC), the official Washington lobby of U.S. Catholic bishops, has consistently worked to have abortion and abortion funding banned. It has voted to work to eliminate clinics that make contraceptive information available in public high schools. The Church continues to restate its well-known teaching that the use of artificial birth control is sinful. The Church teaches that the natural result of sexual intercourse is the procreation of children and that any

---

[28]Mary Ewens, "The Leadership of Nuns in Immigrant Catholicism," in *Women and Religion in America, Volume I: The Nineteenth Century*, ed. Rosemary Radford Ruether and Rosemary Skinner Keller (San Francisco: Harper & Row, Publishers, 1981), pp. 101–102.

[29]Ewens, "The Leadership of Nuns," p. 105.

method of contraception that interferes with this end is against the laws of God and the Church. The Church also teaches that the fetus has a soul and is a human being from the moment of conception. Therefore, abortion is murder. Feminists see the Church's position on all these issues as a violation of women's rights to control over their own bodies.

Many women view traditional Catholic teaching about marriage and divorce as yet another unwarranted intrusion of the Church into areas that are best left up to individual morality. The Church's teachings limit women's (and men's) options to lifelong marriage or celibacy. The presence and at least partial acceptance of other options in the larger culture has caused many Catholics to question and sometimes openly challenge their Church's official teachings.

Ordination to the priesthood is a particularly troublesome issue. As it is now, only men can be ordained priests. The Church's teaching on the ordination of women to the priesthood, repeatedly restated throughout Pope John Paul II's papacy, is unequivocal: Jesus chose men to be his apostles, and they did likewise when they chose their successors. The sacrament of ordination links the priests with the twelve apostles, making them, in effect, present today. "For this reason, the ordination of women is not possible."[30]

Many women are particularly distressed that full priesthood is denied to them. The Second Vatican Council did not prohibit women from engaging in many important lay ministries such as assisting with the Eucharist and reading the Bible during Mass. As a result, many, if not most, Catholic churches in the United States permit this. Girls as well as boys can now be altar servers. In most instances, any lay position available to men is now also available to women. Progress? Yes, say the women who want full ordination as priests in the Church—but not enough. For many, the only way for their Church to make good on its pronouncements about the equality and full personhood of all people is to grant women full ordination to the priesthood and accept women as equals for ordination to the higher ranks of bishop, archbishop, and cardinal. According to these women, the necessary changes will not have been made until it is possible for a woman to be elected Pope.

Many Catholic women also think that the ordination of women would help to solve the severe shortage of priests that the Church faces. Fewer and fewer men have entered the priesthood in recent years, leading to shortages that are nearing crisis proportions. These women claim that the Church can ill afford not to use the additional resource that their ordination would make available. Often, people who urge the ordination of women also urge that priests be allowed to marry, another move that many feel would help to increase the number of candidates for ordination.

For some Catholic women, the quest for ordination has transformed into a quest for an entirely new approach to worship and liturgy, one that does away with the need for priests altogether. The *Woman-Church* movement understands

---

[30]*Catechism of the Catholic Church,* ¶1577.

all Christians to be engaged in equal ministry to each other, with no hierarchy. While it is difficult to say exactly how many women are involved, such communities are being formed nationwide, and national Woman-Church conferences draw thousands of attendees.[31]

All this having been said, two things bear noting. While some Catholic women are dissatisfied with how their Church deals with their specific concerns as women, most are not talking about leaving the Church. Second, the conservative/traditionalist movement, discussed above, includes women among its strong supporters. Specifically, Women for Faith and Family organized in 1984 as a voice for such women. One point in their "Affirmation for Catholic Women" document reads, "We affirm and accept the teaching of the Catholic Church on all matters dealing with human reproduction, marriage, family life and roles for men and women in the Church and in society."[32]

The Church's position on these issues is not likely to change in the foreseeable future. Someone once remarked that people would know that the Catholic Church had made progress when bishops were permitted to bring their wives to Church conferences. They would know that even more progress had occurred when bishops brought their husbands to these conferences.

All in all, it would seem that the Pope's stated goals of "discipline, order, commitment, and obedience" for the Catholic Church will not meet with easy acceptance in the United States. On the other hand, it must be noted that American Catholics, as they have always been, are loyal to their Church. They are a people of two clear loyalties, to their nation and to their Church. Neither has wavered over the course of Catholic presence in America.

We have seen that American Catholics share a great deal with Catholics around the world, as members of the one Catholic Church. They are also unique, and in many ways this uniqueness has come about as a direct result of the conditions under which American Catholicism has developed.

QUESTIONS AND ACTIVITIES FOR REVIEW, DISCUSSION, AND WRITING

1. If you are not Catholic, try to attend a Catholic Mass. If you are Catholic, try to attend a Protestant service. Notice both the similarities and the differences.
2. If you are not Catholic, talk with friends who are about what being Catholic means to them. If you are Catholic, talk with someone about what being a Protestant Christian means.
3. Look at a good road atlas of the United States. Note the prevalence of place names that reflect the Spanish and French Catholic influence in the Southwest, Florida, Louisiana, and the upper Midwest.
4. Are you aware of any anti-Catholic prejudice in your community? Elsewhere? Among other students? What forms does it take? Is it organized or informal? What might be done to end it?

---

[31]Rose Solari, "In Her Own Image," *Common Boundary*, July/August 1995, pp. 18–27.
[32]Mary Jo Weaver and R. Scott Appleby, *Being Right: Conservative Catholics in America*, pp. 177–78.

5. In what ways is the Catholic Church distinctive?
6. Describe the Catholic sacramental system. In what way is it a "sacred materialism"?
7. Think about the issue of how much authority a community of faith ought to have over the lives of its members. Should it have a little or a lot? Are there things that you believe should be left up to the individual? What are the advantages and the disadvantages of a community of faith having great authority? Little authority? You might also discuss this issue with other people in your class.
8. In your opinion, should women be able to be ordained as priests in the Catholic Church? Why do you think the way you do on this issue?

FOR FURTHER READING

ALLSOPP, MICHAEL, and JOHN J. O'KEEFE, *Veritas Splendor: American Responses*. Kansas City, MO: Sheed and Ward, 1995. Pope John Paul II's encyclical, *Veritas Splendor,* is an extensive analysis of Catholic morality. In this book, Allsopp and O'Keefe collect a series of essays dealing with the response of American Catholics to this controversial document.

BUTLER, FRANCIS J., *American Catholic Identity: Essays in an Age of Change*. Kansas City, MO: Sheed and Ward, 1994. This book contains twenty-two addresses concerning what it means to be Catholic in postmodern America and provides a good overview of late twentieth-century American Catholicism.

CHITTISER, JOAN, *Womanstrength: Modern Church, Modern Women*. Kansas City, MO: Sheed and Ward, 1990. This is a wide-ranging and provocative collection of essays on the role of women in today's Catholic Church.

CUNEO, MICHAEL W., *The Smoke of Satan: Conservative and Traditionalist Dissent in Contemporary American Catholicism*. New York: Oxford University Press, 1997. Cuneo's thorough treatment makes careful distinctions between different types of dissent and their impact.

DAVIDSON, JAMES D., et al., *The Search for Common Ground: What Unites and Divides Catholic Americans*. Huntington, IN: Our Sunday Visitor Press, 1997. This sociological analysis of pre– and post–Vatican II Catholics discusses how the Council affects American Catholicism.

HURLEY, BISHOP MARK J., *The Unholy Ghost: Anti-Catholicism in the American Experience*. Huntington, IN: Our Sunday Visitor, 1992. This is a carefully documented study of prejudice against Catholics in the United States throughout history and in the present. There are three sections: (1) 1776 to Vatican II; (2) post–Vatican II; and (3) focused specifically on the abortion issue and support for parochial schools.

REDMONT, JANE, *Generous Lives: American Catholic Women Today*. Liguori, MO: Triumph Books, 1992. In this excellent study of American Catholic women, discursive chapters alternate with first-person accounts by women of all ages, nationalities, and economic backgrounds, both lay and ordained.

WILHELM, ANTHONY, *Christ among Us: A Modern Presentation of the Catholic Faith for Adults,* 6th ed. San Francisco: HarperSanFrancisco, 1996. This very straightforward and accessible introduction to Catholic faith and life is intended for adults but makes no assumptions about prior knowledge.

RELEVANT WORLD WIDE WEB SITES

Catholic Information Center on the Net (http://www.catholic.net/RCC/).
Catholic On-Line (http://www.catholic.org/).

Vatican Web Site (http://vatican.va).

Catholic Campaign for America (http://www.cathcamp.org/).

True Catholic (http://www.truecatholic.org/).

The Pope Page (http://www.catholic.net/RCC/Pope/Pope.html).

National Conference of Catholic Bishops/United States Catholic Conference (http://www.nccbuscc.org/).

5

Living a Jewish Life
in the United States

Are you aware of any stereotypes about Jewish people? Many of us grow up with such stereotypes. What might cause people to believe them?

WHO IS A JEW?

To a greater extent than any other religion in the United States, the term *Judaism* encompasses many different things, not all of them religious. Different aspects vary in their importance to individual Jews. One can, of course, be a Jew *religiously*. In this sense, which will be the primary one for our purposes, a "Jew is one who seeks a spiritual base in the modern world by living the life of study, prayer, and daily routine dedicated to the proposition that Jewish wisdom through the ages will answer the big questions in life—questions like, Why do people suffer? What is life's purpose? Is there a God?"[1]

The Jewish faith has given rise to literature, music, foods, folkways, a rich and complex cultural heritage. To be a Jew *culturally* is to identify with this cultural heritage of Judaism with or without claiming formal religious affiliation.

Judaism is also in part about *ethnicity*, about ties that reach in a biological sense to the people of Israel. Ethnicity and religion have in the past been closely tied together. Jewish ethnicity meant Jewish religion. Not all Jews share this ethnic link, because Judaism accepts Gentiles who want to convert to Judaism. About 10,000 Gentiles annually become "Jews by choice," which is the preferred term for those who choose Judaism rather than being born into the faith.[2] Once a person becomes a Jew, no distinction is made between Jews who are born Jewish and those who are not. In a sense, "all Jews are Jews by choice today, since

---

[1]Rabbi Morris N. Kertzer (revised by Rabbi Lawrence A. Hoffman), *What is a Jew? New and Completely Revised Edition* (New York: Macmillan Publishing Company, 1993), p. 7.
[2]David C. Gross, *1,201 Questions and Answers about Judaism* (New York: Hippocrene Books, 1992), p. 277.

Figure 5-1 *The Magen David* (Star of David): The origin of the Star of David is lost in the mists of early history. It appears on synagogues as early as the second or third century C.E. In the early fourteenth century, it was used as a protective amulet or magical symbol. Apparently, it came into widespread usage as a symbol of Judaism (in the nineteenth century) because there was a desire to have a sign that would symbolize Judaism in the same way that the cross symbolizes Christianity.

even born Jews have to make the conscious decision that they will remain Jewish, rather than join another religion or become nothing in particular."[3]

Jews are also not a race, because there are Jews of many races. Nor are they a nation, although early in their history they were identified with the nation of Israel.

Jews immigrated to the United States from many different Jewish cultures in Europe. Because of this, American Judaism was fragmented into a mosaic of languages and patterns of belief and practice, overlaid by glaring cultural differences. This fragmentation challenged the strong Jewish sense of peoplehood and unity and set the stage for the development of the varied styles of Judaism that have remained important into the present. A rather clear-cut pattern has emerged in the development of Judaism in the United States. The first generation, the immigrants themselves, largely remained close together, seeking comfort and protection among those most like themselves. At the same time, and somewhat ironically, they did not take many steps to preserve their heritage, taking it for granted that their children in the next generation would become more American and thereby less Jewish.

The urge toward integration and assimilation was greatest among the second generation, the largest segment of adult Jews during the period 1935 through about 1970. Many were willing to pay a high price for assimilation, feeling that their acceptance was based on an unspoken demand: They would not be treated as if they were Jewish, providing that they would cease acting as if

[3]Rabbi Morris N. Kertzer (revised by Rabbi Lawrence A. Hoffman), *What is a Jew,* p. 8.

they were. It is difficult to determine to what extent this attitude actually existed in the gentile culture, although it certainly did. Some of it was undoubtedly in the minds of the Jews themselves.

This situation left the third and fourth generations with the task of recovering what had been lost in the struggle for acceptance. By about 1960, the majority of Jews in America had achieved the acceptance they sought. Today, they continue to lead the nation in education, professionalization, and income and are a noteworthy presence in politics and culture. Tolerance has increased also, at least to some extent. With acceptance has come the realization that the price has been high and that it is necessary to recover what has been lost if Judaism is to remain a vital faith and culture.[4] There is a saying, "What the son wishes to forget, the grandson wishes to remember," and this has been very much the case with third- and fourth-generation American Jews. Among all sectors of Judaism in this country, there is renewed interest in Jewish life and culture. Religious observance is increasing, even among liberal Reform Jews. Attention to the dietary laws and to holiday observances is growing. The Hebrew language is being taught more, learned more, and used more in the synagogues. There is a lively interest in Orthodoxy among younger Jews, as well as in the Jewish mystical tradition of Hasidism.

JEWS AND CHRISTIANS

As many of you know already, Christianity began as a small sect within Judaism, as a variation on the teaching and practice of that ancient religion. The two share a common history, up to a point, and a common geography. The cultural conditions out of which Christianity was born were those of the Judaism of its time. It is not surprising, therefore, that Jewish and Christian members of the religious consensus have many things in common.

To begin with, they have some of the Scriptures in common. The Jewish Bible[5] and the Christian Old Testament are nearly the same in content, although the books are not in the same order. The history that is recounted and the religious teachings that are contained in both are quite similar. In most Christian churches today, the Christian Old Testament is used for one of the regular Bible readings during worship.

These common scriptures tell of one God who commands that people worship no other gods. Judaism originated in an area in which it was most common for people to worship many gods and goddesses. The Jewish, and later the Christian, view held that there was but one God. This God is believed to be the

---

[4]Stephen M. Cohen and Leonard J. Fein, "From Integration to Survival: American Jewish Anxieties in Transition," *Annals, The American Academy of Political and Social Science*, no. 480 (July 1985), pp. 75-88; and Jacob Neusner, *Israel in America: A Too-Comfortable Exile?* (Boston: Beacon Press, 1985).

[5]The preferred name among Jews themselves for the Jewish scriptures is **Tanakh**, an acronym for the Hebrew names of its three major divisions: the Law (*Torah*), the Prophets (*Nevi'im*), and the Writings (*Ketubim*).

creator of all that was, is, or ever will be. God is righteous and holy and acts in a just, upright, moral manner. God is personal; it is appropriate to talk of God's will, wrath, love, mercy, and judgment. God hears and responds to peoples' prayers, according to both Judaism and Christianity. Above all, God's character and will for people are shown to them by God's self-revelation.

History is important, because it is believed to be the record of God's continuing involvement with people. God is intimately involved in history, primarily through **covenants** with people. There are covenants with Noah and with Abraham, for example, described in Tanakh, and Jesus is referred to in the Christian New Testament as the bearer of a new covenant. These covenants define a people by their relationship with God. Judaism teaches that Israel was called into being as a people by God. Christianity teaches that the entire church is the Body of Christ, called into being by God.

Because the God whose story is told in the Bible is righteous and holy, the people who live in covenant with God are to live holy and righteous lives themselves. Their special relationship with God is to be embodied in all that they do. The well-known Ten Commandments are revered in both Judaism and Christianity. Some of these commandments deal with people's actions with respect to God: having no other gods, keeping the Sabbath day holy, and not taking God's name in vain. Others have to do with relations between persons and groups of people: not murdering or stealing, not lying, and not wanting what is not one's own, for example. In both Judaism and Christianity, the way people relate with God and the way they relate with each other cannot be separated. For both, a lifestyle defined by the proper worship and attitude toward God as well as by loving and morally upright relations with other persons is basic.

Although this is what is called for, both faiths teach that people will fall short of the goal. They will, in a word common to both, *sin*. If they are truly sorry and committed to doing better and wholeheartedly seek God's forgiveness, then God will forgive.

Worship in each community of faith is both individual and corporate. Individual worship usually takes the form of prayer and devotional reading. Corporate worship provides time for the entire community of faith to focus on God. Prayers are said and praises given. Instruction is given to the faithful in a sermon. It is usually based on one or more readings from the Bible. The importance placed on history creates many holidays and festivals that recall and celebrate God's actions. For example, the Christian holidays of Christmas and Easter keep the stories of the birth and resurrection of Jesus alive in that community of faith. The Jewish Passover celebrates the rescue of the Hebrews from slavery in Egypt, and the giving of the Ten Commandments is recalled in the Festival of Weeks. Corporate worship also includes rites of passage. These are religious ceremonies that mark transitions from one stage of human life to another. Both faiths mark birth, coming of age, marriage and death, for example.

We have seen that there are a variety of organizational styles to be found in consensus religion in the United States. In both Judaism and Christianity, the fundamental point is that the people of God are not to exist in isolation but are gathered together by God into communities for mutual support and instruction and to carry out God's will. In both instances, the group—the people of Israel or the Church—is thought to be not simply a human invention but something brought into being and guided by God.

There are many smaller points of agreement that could be discussed. These major points, however, clearly demonstrate that the two major religions found in the United States—Judaism and Christianity—have a great deal in common. Their common heritage and devotion to the same God means that they are neighbors and not strangers.

PRINCIPAL BELIEFS AND PRACTICES
OF JEWISH PEOPLE

Judaism in the United States has many variations in belief and practice. However, there are certain features that nearly all Jews share, in one way or another. Interpretations vary, but the basics are the same. Lists of what these basics are will be different from one author to another; what is included here is a minimal listing of very fundamental points.

It should first be said that Judaism is primarily a religion of action; characteristically, it has emphasized proper *obedience* to the God of the covenant over proper beliefs *about* God. Samuel Belkin, President of Yeshiva University, the principal Orthodox Jewish educational institution in the United States, has stated this emphasis this way:

> Many attempts have been made to formulate a coherent and systematic approach to Jewish theology. All such attempts, however, have proved unsuccessful, for Judaism was never overly concerned with logical doctrines. It desired rather to evolve a corpus of practices, a code of religious acts, which would establish a mode of religious living. . . . The theology of Judaism is contained largely in Halakha . . . which concerns itself not with theory but primarily with practice.[6]

Nevertheless, there are beliefs that can be identified as core in the Jewish way of thinking.

Beliefs

Jews define themselves in part by their special relationship to the Torah and the Talmud. In a broad sense, **Torah** refers to a guide for life, instruction in living as a Jew, the whole of what it means to live a proper Jewish life. In a more specific sense, it refers to the first five books of the Bible—Genesis, Exodus, Leviticus, Numbers, and Deuteronomy (Figure 5-2). These five books, which for Jews are the core of God's revelation, are believed to have been revealed to Moses and are

[6]Samuel Belkin, *In His Image* (New York: Abelard-Schuman, 1960), pp. 15–16.

Figure 5-2 A Torah scroll is an important part of any synagogue or temple. *(Bill Aron/Photo Researchers, Inc.)*

known as the **five Books of Moses**. They are also known as the *Pentateuch*, a Greek word that means "five books."

The Hebrew Bible is very similar to the Old Testament in the Christian Bible, containing the same books, although in a different order. However, it is inappropriate to refer to the Hebrew Bible as the "Old Testament." That collection of writings is called the Old Testament by Christians because, for them, the New Testament is a part of the Bible. The Christian New Testament is not a part of the Jewish Bible. It has no authority and does not contain the revelation of the God of Abraham, Isaac, and Jacob. To refer to the Torah as the "Old Testament" is offensive to persons of Jewish faith, for whom the revelation of God recorded in the Hebrew Bible can never be superseded by another revelation such as Christians believe is contained in their New Testament. The word **Tanakh** is often used for the Hebrew Bible. *Tanakh* is an acronym taken from the Hebrew first letters of its three divisions.

After the five Books of Moses are the Books of the Prophets. The rest of Tanakh is made up of the Writings and includes such well-known books as Psalms, Proverbs, Job, and Ecclesiastes, along with several others. In addition to the Tanakh itself, there is the **Talmud**, which is the written record of several centuries of discussion, interpretation, and commentary on Torah by the earliest rabbis, who were primarily scholars and teachers of Torah. In spite of differences in interpretation and varied understandings of exactly what authority the Talmud has, Jews are united in their self-understanding as the people of the history and way of life described therein.

The cornerstone of the Torah is the **commandments** that Jews believe God gave to Moses at Mount Sinai. They are found in the Book of the Exodus, chapter 20 (paraphrased in Figure 5-3).

Figure 5-3

THE TEN COMMANDMENTS

1. You shall not worship any other gods.
2. Do not make images of God.
3. Do not take God's holy name in vain.
4. Remember to keep the Sabbath holy; in particular, you are not to work on this day.
5. Honor your parents.
6. Do not murder.
7. Do not commit adultery.
8. Do not steal.
9. Do not bear false witness against anyone.
10. Do not covet [i.e., be envious of] that which is your neighbor's.

The core commandments can be divided into two groups: The first four deal with how one ought to relate to God, and the latter six with how one is to relate with other persons. These commandments are the heart of the Torah and of Jewish life and living.

Most Jews agree on the basic understanding of God. **In Torah, God reveals God to the Jewish people**. It is not a matter of people discovering God through a process of human searching; rather, God chooses to reveal God to people. People of Jewish faith believe that there is but one God. The Jews are a people of uncompromising **monotheism**. This central point is learned by Jewish children early in life and repeated daily by many Jews as the **Shema**: "Hear, O Israel! The Lord is our God, the Lord alone," (Deuteronomy 6:4, *Tanakh*). The passage goes on to prescribe that this God is to be loved with one's entire self, holding nothing back. Monotheism was a part of Judaism from its earliest beginnings. In the area in which Judaism began, it was customary for a tribe to worship many deities. The biblical accounts of the founding of Israel describe how Abraham turned from the worship of many deities to the worship of only one, who is described as *the* God.

Because the Jews are ever watchful to guard the uniqueness of God, they will not represent God in any material form; to do so would be to make an idol. Nor is there any way, in the Jewish understanding of God, that any human being could ever be God. This is one reason that **people of Jewish faith do not accept the Christian teaching that Jesus is the Messiah whose coming is foretold in Isaiah**. The idea of a person who is at once divine and human is utterly repugnant to Jewish sensibility. We must remember that the link between the verses in Isaiah that speak of the coming of the Messiah and the person Jesus are found in the Christian New Testament and are not a part of Hebrew scripture. The Messiah as understood by those of Jewish faith will be a leader who will bring freedom and restoration to the entire people of Israel in more political than individual terms. Jesus as described by the early Christian church—the savior of individual persons from sin and separation from God—is a different sort of savior than that expected in Judaism. According to most Jews, Jesus was a religious leader and teacher, perhaps a prophet, but not God.

> Simply put, Jews do not believe that God had a son or appeared in human form. We do not thus accept Jesus as the Christ, as our Lord, as the son of God, as the word of God incarnate, or as our savior. These and other ways in which Christianity has expressed its faith in Jesus as more than just a man, even a great man, are what Judaism has consistently denied. . . .

> People sometimes ask why Jews do not accept Jesus as their savior. Jews answer that question by pointing to the unrelieved misery in the world as we know it, and say that classical Jewish doctrine teaches that the messiah will arrive only once, and will be recognizable by the fact that the world's suffering will be ended then. As long as we see hunger, inequality, and injustice in the world, we are forced to conclude that the messiah has not yet arrived.[7]

The character of God has definite implications for how people treat each other. God is a just, loving, holy, and righteous God, according to the Hebrew Bible, and God's people must reflect these qualities in their lives and in their dealings with others. **Peoples' actions with other people must be characterized by an attitude reflective of God's own nature**. Under the terms of the covenant, people are responsible to and for one another. One's fellow human being is God's son or daughter and hence is one's brother or sister. Righteousness, love, and tolerance must be the rule, not only among Jews but with all persons. It extends to strangers, servants, and animals. Special concern is to be given to the less fortunate, such as widows, orphans, the poor, and the ill. Fair treatment is to be given even to one's enemies.

Jews are united in their understanding of themselves as a people. In spite of being scattered around the world, and, in spite of speaking many languages and following different practices and beliefs, **the people of Israel are one people**. They are linked by the love they have for each other, by their common tradition and history, and by their shared past and present experience. The Jews understand themselves to be the people of the covenant. They came into being as a people because a covenant was forged between them and God. In Exodus 19, it is recorded that God said to the people of Israel that if they would keep the commandments of God, then God would be their God and they would be the people of God. This brings up the frequently misunderstood concept of the Jews as God's **chosen people**. The language of Exodus speaks clearly of this chosenness. The normative Jewish understanding of chosenness is that the Jews are a people with a special mission in the history of humankind. They have specific responsibilities and obligations under the covenant, even when following these

[7]Rabbi Morris N. Kertzer (revised by Rabbi Lawrence A. Hoffman), *What is a Jew?*, pp. 275–276.

obligations means suffering and death. It means living under the watchful eye of God. It does not indicate that the Jews see themselves as somehow better or more important to God than are gentiles.[8]

The Jewish belief in peoplehood takes on concrete form in widespread support for the state of Israel. Since the destruction of the Temple in Jerusalem in 70 C.E., the Jews have been a wandering people. But they have maintained the conviction of belonging to the land into which the Bible records they wandered under God's leading. For centuries, Jews have prayed for the restoration and rebuilding of Jerusalem. "Next year in Jerusalem!" is spoken at the end of the Seder meal every Passover. Land and covenant are linked; the people of the covenant are the people of the land. This linking of land and people took political form in the Zionist movement. The founding of the state of Israel in 1948 is numbered among the most significant events of Jewish history.

Practices

What can we say about Jewish **lifestyles**? Especially in the United States, Jews live as many different lifestyles as do their neighbors. Overall, survey data tell us two factors that are important in understanding what it means to be a person of Jewish faith in modern day America. Of all the religious preference groups, Jews lead the nation in both education and income. Judaism has always fostered a love of learning, and there is no conflict between faith and reason. The second outstanding feature of the American Jewish population is that, across the board, Jews are more tolerant and broad-minded about moral issues, civil liberties, and nonbelievers than are their Christian neighbors. Yet another general feature that can be mentioned is the heavy involvement of Jews in social reform and assistance programs and in occupations such as social work and professional psychology and psychiatry. The terms of the covenant and responsibility for one's neighbor translate into vocational terms, for both religious and nonreligious Jews.

Judaism in its traditional form has a very rich **ritual life**. A set of rituals pace individual Jews through their lifetimes, and another set paces the community through its collective life. Differences in observance abound, but Judaism is united by these individual and collective religious practices. They are the people whose life, both corporate and private, is demarcated by these ritual observances. Here we will note the principal ones.

We will first turn to those rituals that pace the individual through the life cycle. The circumcision of male babies and the Bar or Bat Mitzvah are two of the best-known. As is the case with every religion, birth is the first step of the life cycle to be ritually marked. After the birth of a girl, it is the father's responsibility and honor to read the Torah at the next synagogue service. He recites the usual benedictions before and after reading and officially announces his daughter's name. For a boy, it is more complicated; **circumcision** is a major Jewish cere-

---

[8]As used in this context, a *gentile* is anyone who is not Jewish.

mony. Although other peoples circumcise infant boys, Judaism understands this as a visible sign of the covenant between Abraham and God, made again in each generation (Genesis 17:9–14). It takes place on the eighth day after birth. The ceremony involves both religious and surgical elements and may be performed by a physician or by a specially trained **Mohel** who has both the necessary surgical and religious knowledge. A festive meal follows.

The next life cycle rite in the life of a Jewish youngster is the **Bar Mitzvah**. Some Jews, although not all, celebrate the **Bat Mitzvah** for girls also. The words mean "son or daughter of the commandment" and mark the coming of age of the child. The child is then considered to be an adult, responsible for observing the commandments and able to fill adult roles in the congregation, although the ceremony traditionally occurs on the Sabbath following the child's thirteenth birthday. The highlight of Jewish life for many, it is preceded by intensive study. The young person is called up to read Torah before the congregation for the first time. This is a great honor. The young person may also make a speech in which parents and teachers are thanked. Especially in the United States, this ceremony has grown in importance and is frequently the occasion for a lavish party with family and friends to recognize the person's new status. In some congregations that practice the Bat Mitzvah, the ceremony parallels that for boys, while other congregations have developed distinctive practices for it.

Some Reform Jewish congregations have an additional ceremony of **confirmation** at about age fifteen or sixteen. Although originally intended as a replacement for the Bar or Bat Mitzvah, it is now a separate ceremony for Reform and Conservative Jews, in which the now somewhat older youths reaffirm their intention to live as Jews in the household of Israel.

Marriage is the next life-cycle ritual in the lives of most Jewish women and men. Judaism places a very high value on marriage and family, and celebrating the beginning of a new family unit in marriage is very important. The **Ketubah**, or marriage contract, which spells out the responsibilities of both spouses, is signed during the ceremony. It is a legally valid document as well as a religious one. The wedding ceremony itself is complex and reflects the sacred nature of marriage and family life. A celebration with family and friends follows. Although divorce is permitted by Jewish law, it is strongly discouraged. In practice, actual divorce statistics among Reform Jews differ little from those among their gentile neighbors; for Conservative and, especially, Orthodox Jews, the rate is somewhat lower. To be recognized as valid among traditional Jews, there must be a religious divorce as well as a legal one.

As well as marking the stages in the individual's life with celebration and consolation, Judaism hallows time through a yearly cycle. This cycle lifts time out of the realm of a merely mechanical tracking of days and hours and uses it to keep history and tradition alive in the present.

The **Sabbath** is a high point in every week. In line with the accounts of creation in Genesis, the Jewish Sabbath is observed from sundown on Friday until nightfall on Saturday. The Sabbath is considered one sign of the covenant between God and Israel. God is said to have rested after the creation, and people, too, are to devote one day per week to rest. The Sabbath meal is prepared in advance. The Sabbath begins when the mother lights special Sabbath candles and recites the appointed blessings. There may be a synagogue service to welcome the Sabbath. The following morning, the family may attend the synagogue together, although in some congregations it is customary for the women to remain at home with the children.

A quiet day follows. Perhaps the best-known feature of the Jewish Sabbath is that any kind of work is strictly forbidden. To understand what it means to "keep the Sabbath," however, we must see beyond the prohibition of work. The Sabbath is intended as a way of separating oneself from the cares and toils of everyday living to make time for what is truly important. It is a time to be with one's God, with one's family, and with oneself, and, for that to be possible in our busy world, a special effort must be made to make it so. Torah study is an important part of what may be done on the Sabbath. Prayer and meditation are encouraged. Taking moderate walks with the family, doing quiet family things together, and visiting friends who live close by are often done.

Like the individual life, the year is marked throughout with festivals and days of great significance. Although each of the festivals leads naturally into the one that follows it, the most reasonable place to begin is where the Jewish religious calendar (which differs from the one we use to follow secular time) itself begins, with the Jewish New Year.

Rosh Hashanah (literally, the "head of the year") takes place in early autumn (September or October). Preparation for it begins the month before, which is used as a time of contemplation and spiritual self-searching. The Jewish New Year is not a time of partying and rowdiness, as the secular New Year often is. Rather, it is a time for looking back over the past year, for reflecting on deeds done and left undone. Judaism emphasizes human beings' free choice in whether we will do good or evil and our responsibility for that choice. With responsibility comes accountability, and God is known as the judge of human actions. It is this sense of judgment that pervades the Jewish New Year and the period that follows it. The oldest and probably best-known of the rituals connected with this festival is the sounding of the **shofar**, an instrument made from the horn of a ram, which makes a sound some have likened to the wailing of the heart of the human race.

Rosh Hashanah is the beginning of a time of intense reflection. Taking stock of one's life and behavior over the preceding year is accompanied by the resolve to do better. Two types of sin must be dealt with: those against God and those against other people. People can be forgiven for those against God by the rituals of **Yom Kippur**, the Day of Atonement, which follows the days of penitence. For those sins in which one has wronged another person as well, forgiveness must be sought not only from God but from the person wronged, and one must seek to make amends if at all possible. There is no savior in Judaism except God, and no mediator between God and people. Jews stand before God as individuals and as members of the household of Israel with their prayers for forgiveness and their resolve to live a better life. Given these factors, Judaism teaches, God will forgive the sincere penitent. The entire day of Yom Kippur is spent in fasting, prayer, and contemplation. Thus cleansed of previous sin and strengthened to live the Torah more fully, the Jew begins another year.

The next holiday is one that has come to be celebrated much more in the United States than it is elsewhere: **Hanukkah**, the Festival of Lights. It comes in November or December, and the increased emphasis it has received in the United States has come about in part because it is close to the time that the Christian majority and the culture in general celebrate Christmas. The word *Hanukkah* means "rededication" and refers to the rededication of the Temple after the Maccabean revolutionaries successfully recaptured it from the Greco-Syrians in approximately 160 B.C.E. Legend has it that only enough oil could be found to keep the Temple lamp burning for one day. Miraculously, the oil lasted for eight days, the time required to prepare and consecrate new oil. Thus, the Hanukkah candle holder, or **menorah**, has eight branches plus a ninth that holds the lighting candle, whereas the regular menorah holds seven candles (Figure 5-4). Another candle is lit every night of the eight-day celebration. There is another very beautiful Hanukkah story that the rabbis tell. When the Maccabees entered the Temple, they found that the menorah was not usable, having been destroyed by the raiding pagans. The Maccabees took their spears and used them to make a new menorah, turning the weapons of war into a symbol of peace.[9]

Figure 5-4   The Menorah

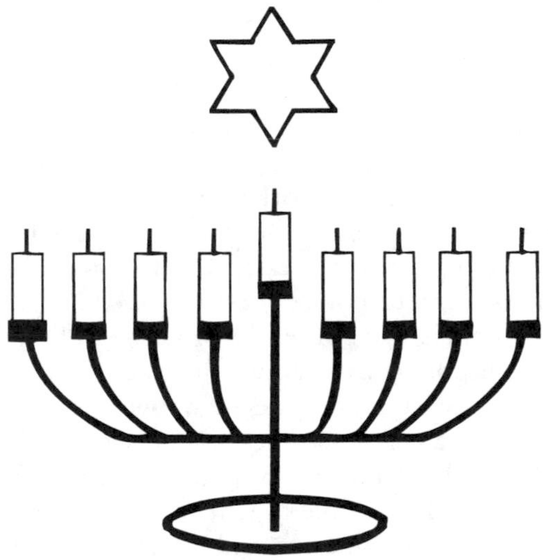

[9]Leo Trepp, *Judaism: Development and Life*, 3rd ed. (Belmont, CA: Wadsworth Publishing Company, 1982), p. 303.

The Jewish holiday that gentiles probably know best is **Passover**, which comes in the spring. It has both associations remaining from the early times when the Israelites were an agricultural people and the historical significance that was given to it later. It exemplifies the way that religious rituals keep the important stories of the faith alive and assist in transmitting them to each new generation. As an agricultural festival, it recalls the spring harvest. Its primary significance is now the historical one, however, in that it commemorates the exodus of the Hebrews out of slavery in Egypt. This is one of the two foundational events of Jewish history. It is sometimes called the Feast of Unleavened Bread, and **matzoh**, a crackerlike bread, is eaten. Unleavened bread is eaten because the hurried flight of the Hebrews left no time for bread to rise (Exodus 12:37–39, 13:3, 6–8, Deuteronomy 16:1–4). The name Passover comes from the biblical promise that the angel of death would pass over those houses marked on the doorpost with the blood of a sacrificial lamb (Exodus 12:12–14). The central ritual of Passover is the **Seder** meal in which the story of the Exodus is retold. Special foods are eaten that help to bring the story alive. This ritual involves everyone present and uses virtually all the human senses, mixing food, fun, and serious intention to serve as an outstanding educational and community-reinforcing tool. Jews who must be away from home at this special time may count on being taken into the home of another Jewish family wherever they may be for the Seder.

Following Passover is another ritual calling to mind a founding event. The **Feast of Weeks (Shavuot)** has roots as a harvest festival, but its contemporary meaning is as a celebration of the giving of the Ten Commandments to Moses on Mount Sinai. Thus, the two interwoven themes of Jewish life, God-given freedom from slavery and the giving of the Torah, are celebrated and remembered. Either one without the other is incomplete and does not do justice to the fullness of Jewish understanding.

The final festival to be described also has its roots in the agricultural experience of the early Israelites and in the later historical interpretation given it by the rabbis. **Sukkot**, or the **Feast of Booths**, comes in September or October. As a harvest festival, it is the fulfillment of the agricultural year. Historically, it refers to the Israelites wandering for forty years from Egypt to the Promised Land, without having any permanent homes (Leviticus 23:42–43). The booth, constructed of natural materials, symbolizes the protection of God during this perilous period in Jewish history. Jewish families may build such a structure at their homes, or they may visit one built outside the synagogue.

Yom Ha Shoah is a Jewish observance of more recent origin. It is also called Holocaust Remembrance Day and takes place in the spring. The activities on this solemn day have two foci: It is a time to remember those people—both Jewish and gentile—who died in the Holocaust, and it is also a time for rededication to the principle that such a thing can never be allowed to happen again. In many communities, Jews and Christians sponsor joint Yom Ha Shoah observances.

Whether in the individual's life or the life of the community as a whole, Jewish festivals and ritual practices pace life, marking off transitions and recalling significant events. They keep the founding events alive, offer opportunities for education and celebration, integrate the individual into the community of Jews past and present, and, most important, offer ways for each person and the community to relate to the God of Abraham, Isaac, and Jacob.

JEWISH WOMEN

According to Tanakh, it was God's intention that men and women be equal. In the first account of creation, both are created in God's image. Woman is created from man in the second account, not as his subordinate but as one who is capable of fulfilling him. When Adam and Eve together violated God's commandments, however, their equality and mutuality was lost.[10] The Jewish tradition is characterized by a dialectical view of women. They are equal to men in essence, yet derivative in power and position.

The current status of women in Judaism, like women's status in Catholicism and Protestantism, is complex. Women's roles and status have changed dramatically in the twentieth century. Jewish women have responded to these changes in the same ways that Christian women have. Some have left Judaism as they have come to feel that the changes did not occur fast enough or go far enough. Some have remained within their synagogues to work for change. And some have chosen to fight against changes that threaten to make their familiar traditions less meaningful to them.

As you might expect, women's roles in Orthodox Judaism have changed the least. Even here, however, the situation is complex. On the one hand, Orthodox women's roles center on home and family, and the role of wife and mother is highly respected. Women are required to perform three religious duties. One is to visit the ritual bath after her menstrual period. The other two, baking the Sabbath bread, or **challah**, and lighting the candles that officially begin the Sabbath observance are among the most important rituals in Judaism. Children are very important in Judaism and especially so in Orthodoxy. Women's role as the bearers and nurturers of children earn them great honor.

Women also play the central role in maintaining a kosher home. Following all the kosher observances is complicated and time consuming. It is also considered one of the most important Orthodox observances because it serves to set the Orthodox apart from other people and reminds them on a daily basis of their life as the covenant people. The contribution of the wife and mother in the family is indispensable.

On the other hand, women cannot be ordained as Orthodox rabbis, nor can they serve as cantors.[11] Nonetheless, they can and do teach in Orthodox Jewish schools. Groups for women's study of both Tanakh and Talmud have

---

[10]William A. Young, *The World's Religions: Worldviews and Contemporary Issues* (Englewood Cliffs, NJ: Prentice Hall, 1995), p. 296.
[11]Cantors assist the rabbi by chanting some of the prayers.

increased rapidly. Women may lead prayer services for women's groups, services that differ little from those for men.

The principle used by modern Orthodox Jews to decide what can and cannot be done illustrates well the difference between their approach and that of the more "modernized" branches. Motivation is central, and the entire body of Jewish law—Halakah—is the ultimate authority. Liberalization of women's roles cannot be justified on the basis of appeal to feminist ideology or modern culture. As one Jewish author notes,

> We are committed to the basic halakhic structure of distinctiveness of obligation. . . . This may go against the contemporary sensibility that regards . . . egalitarianism as a fundamental religious value; but it is a cornerstone of halakhic reasoning.[12]

On the other hand, no exclusion can be justified if inclusion is appropriate in light of Halakah. If the motivation is religious growth, and it increasingly is, then inclusion, within the bounds of Halakah, should be the norm.

There is also in Orthodoxy the phenomenon of the newly Orthodox Jewish woman, the *ba'alat teshuvah*, women who have returned to strict Orthodoxy. Most are of middle-class background, well educated, and had assimilated into the secular culture. For them, Orthodoxy provides meanings that they had been unable to find in the secular culture: a way of making moral sense of their lives, a hedge against relativism, boundaries where there had been none, valuation of the feminine virtues of nurturing, family, and motherhood, a sense of dignity and control.[13]

The attitude toward women in **Reform** and **Reconstructionist** Judaism is much more liberal by present-day standards. The first woman to be ordained as a rabbi was Sally J. Preisand, daughter of Reconstruction founder Mordecai Kaplan. A significant number of women have been ordained as rabbis and as cantors. Women apply to non-Orthodox rabbinical schools in numbers equal to those of men. Reform and Reconstructionism have eliminated the distinctions between men and women in synagogue seating and in the performance of religious ritual. Reform and Reconstructionist women have led in developing new forms of traditional rituals, such as the Passover ritual. The newer rituals include women's contributions to the story of Judaism in explicit ways. These branches of Judaism also pioneered the development and celebration of the Bat Mitzvah to mark a young girl's attainment of religious responsibility. The old ideas and practices concerning ritual impurity have been discarded. Women in these two branches of Judaism have been among the leaders of the women's rights move-

---

[12]Joel B. Wolowelsky, *Women, Jewish Law and Modernity: New Opportunities in a Post-Feminist Age* (Hoboken, NJ: KTAV Publishing House, 1997), pp. 15–16.

[13]Debra Renee Kaufman, *Rachel's Daughters: Newly Orthodox Jewish Women* (New Brunswick, NJ: Rutgers University Press, 1991).

ment in the United States. While motherhood remains important in the more modernized forms of Judaism, there is no bias against women holding jobs outside their homes.

Conservative Judaism has tried to maintain a middle-of-the-road position where women are concerned. Actual observance varies a good bit from family to family and from woman to woman. Men and women sit together in worship. Although the Conservative rabbis voted officially some time ago to ordain women to the rabbinate and as cantors, the actual practice varies from congregation to congregation, and the degree of acceptance of female rabbis is uneven. While many Conservative Jews welcomed the ordination of women as a needed step forward, a significant number refuse to recognize those women who have been ordained.

Observance of the kosher laws and the laws concerning ritual uncleanness varies considerably. While not required, it is strongly supported by many Conservative congregations. Freedom from compulsion makes it possible for some women to observe the tradition without experiencing it as an oppressive burden. For many, Conservatism has been a way to uphold aspects of the tradition that are meaningful while moving toward greater male–female equality.

ONE JUDAISM WITH SEVERAL EXPRESSIONS

Judaism in America is a single religious tradition that is spread across a wide range of practices and, to a lesser extent, beliefs. It remains, however, a "unified and unitary structure," and its varieties are "sectors of one tradition."[14] Due regard must be given to both the differences and the commonalities. The previous section described many of the commonalities. We will look at the differences in this section.

Both the continuities and the distinctiveness are important among Jews themselves.

> In Jewish teaching the Jewish people constitute a unity as descendants of the revered patriarchs whose sagas are told in the Scriptures. Most Jews . . . think of themselves simply as Jews. . . . Although most Jews subscribe to the conviction that they are one people, many who are active in the work and leadership structure of particular synagogues or religious movements take great pride in the institution that they support. While Orthodox Jews believe that their form of Judaism is the only valid and correct one, people who are active in Reform, Conservative, or Reconstructionist groups look upon their forms of Judaism as being best for them personally and for the community in which they participate. . . . Viewed from a strictly logical perspective, there is probably more that divides the non-Orthodox

---

[14]Jacob Neusner, ed., *Understanding American Judaism: Toward a Description of a Modern Religion, Volume II, Sectors of American Judaism: Reform, Orthodoxy, Conservatism, and Reconstructionism* (New York: KTAV Publishing House, 1975), p. xiii.

Jew from the Orthodox than the teachings they share in common. From an emotional standpoint, however—and from the perspective of history—most Jews place an emphasis on what they share in common.[15]

For Jews, expressing a preference for one or another of the sectors of Judaism is one way to identify how they wish to live a Jewish life in the United States. In part, it involves what balance they choose to seek between the ways of the secular culture and the traditional religious ways. For the time period 1990 to 1996, survey data indicate that, among those Jews expressing a preference, about 5 percent identify as Orthodox, 40 percent as Conservative, and 55 percent as Reform.[16] A 1990 National Jewish Population Survey indicated that about 15 percent express no preference.[17] The major trend visible in the NJPS data across the years has been a steady decline in the percentage expressing a preference for Orthodoxy. This contradicts media claims that there has been an increase among Orthodox adherents.[18]

Orthodoxy

We will begin with Jewish **Orthodoxy**. Orthodox Jews believe that their way of being Jewish embodies the authentic Jewish tradition that has existed since Judaism began. Prior to the nineteenth century, all Jews were in essence "premodern." While there were variations among them, there was no "Orthodox" designation. "In the nineteenth century, some modern Jews, primarily in Germany, undertook to reform their medieval tradition so as to bring it up to date with the optimistic rationalism of their time. Those Jews who objected to such changes in age-old traditions became the first Orthodox Jews."[19]

Orthodox Jews emphasize submission to the Law; the revealed will of God is absolute and is not to be tampered with under any circumstances. Orthodoxy, despite what the name and basic outlook might suggest, is not a monolith. There are a vast number of variations in what Orthodox Jews actually believe and do. There are, however, factors that we can identify as clearly distinctive. The Bible is regarded as divinely revealed and altogether accurate, at least in the Books of Moses. (The Books of Moses are those called the *Torah*, including Genesis, Exodus, Leviticus, Numbers, and Deuteronomy.) It has absolute divine authority. The ceremonial law is as binding as the ethical commandments, because both come from the same source and it is not for human beings to make distinctions among them. They are to be observed simply because they are com-

---

[15]Rabbi Roy A. Rosenberg, *The Concise Guide to Judaism: History, Practice, Faith* (New York: Penguin, 1994), pp. 144–145.

[16]National Opinion Research Center General Social Surveys for 1990 through 1996.

[17]David Singer, ed., *American Jewish Year Book, 1997* (New York: The American Jewish Committee, 1997), pp. 117.

[18]David Singer, ed., *American Jewish Year Book, 1997* (New York: The American Jewish Committee, 1997), pp. 119 and 125.

[19]Rabbi Morris N. Kertzer (revised by Rabbi Lawrence A. Hoffman), *What is a Jew?*, p. 9.

mandments and because they were given to the people of Israel by God with the directive, "Do this." **Halakah**[20] is as authoritative as Torah itself, having sprung from the same source and having divine authority behind it. For most non-Jews, the two most distinctive things about Orthodoxy are the strict Sabbath observance (discussed below) and the keeping of the kosher dietary laws. Work of any kind is strictly forbidden on the Sabbath.

The **kosher dietary laws** are a collection of instructions regarding food, its preparation, and consumption. These regulations divide everything edible into three categories: edible or "kosher," things unfit for consumption, and neutral foods. The laws of *kashrut* or ritual purity are very complex, but they may be summarized this way: All fruits, vegetables, and nuts are kosher and may be eaten with anything else. Fish that have both fins and scales may be eaten. Meat from animals that have a split hoof and chew their cud may be used for food. Permitted animals must be ritually slaughtered and treated to remove as much of the blood as possible. Domesticated fowl may be eaten; wild birds and birds of prey may not. Fowl must be slaughtered and prepared ritually in the same ways as meat animals. All dairy products are permitted but may not be mixed with meat. This goes back to three different places in the Torah in which it is forbidden to cook a baby goat in its mother's milk (Exodus 23:19 and 34:25 and Deuteronomy 14:2). For example, cheeseburgers may not be eaten, and milk may not be drunk at a meal containing meat. In a fully kosher kitchen, the same set of cookware, utensils, and dishes would not be used for meat and milk. Furthermore, a separate set of dishes is kept for Passover, necessitating a total of four completely different sets of dishes. Although they frown on drunkenness, Jews usually do not abstain from alcohol. Foods that are kosher have been prepared under close rabbinic supervision throughout. Foods so certified are marked, often with a "U" (for the Union of Orthodox Rabbis) or a "K" (for Kosher) on the container.

The overall effect of the kosher commandments, of which I have named only a few, is to keep the following of God's commandments uppermost in the minds of faithful Jews in matters as common as cooking and eating. In Judaism, the body is as holy as the soul and must be treated as such; keeping kosher is one way of doing so. The meaning of keeping kosher can be summarized this way: "Rabbis have always 'explained' *kashrut* as something Jews do because God commands it in the Torah. The act of obeying the commandment—of performing the *mitzvot*—is its own reward." Over time, other interpretations have been added, amplifying its meaning. It is a way of hallowing everyday life in the very basic act of nourishing oneself and one's family. It helps teach reverence for life, particularly for animal life. It is a way of expressing connection to countless generations of Jews and of passing that connection on to one's children. It is part of the religious discipline that goes along with being Jewish.[21]

---

[20] *Halakah* is the rabbinic record of the application of Torah law to specific circumstances through history.

[21] Anita Diamant and Howard Cooper. *Living a Jewish Life: Jewish Traditions, Customs, and Values for Today's Families* (New York: HarperCollins Publishers, 1996), pp. 98–100.

The other outstanding effect is to strengthen community among observant Jews and distinguish them from outsiders. Much of the time, they live close together because it is necessary to have ready access to a kosher butcher shop, bakery, and grocery. They socialize together, because full observance prohibits eating at the table of one who does not keep kosher.

Other features also are common among Orthodox Jews. In synagogue, women and men sit separately, and in some communities it is not common for the women to attend. The separation varies from simply being seated on separate sides of a center aisle to being separated by a high partition. All of the service is in Hebrew, and the holidays and festivals are observed to their fullest. Men wear the **kippah**, or skullcap, at all times, out of respect for their always being under the watchful eye of God. They wear prayer shawls and **tefillin**[22] for formal daily prayer. Marriage to a non-Orthodox Jew is regarded as invalid even if performed by a rabbi. Orthodox rabbis do not perform interfaith marriages.

Organizationally, Orthodoxy in the United States is represented by the Union of Jewish Orthodox Congregations (commonly, "Orthodox Union"). Its principal educational institution is Yeshiva University in New York City.

Reform Judaism

Reform is the most modernized and liberal of the main three Jewish groups. According to Reform teaching, Judaism is a fully modern religion that must change to keep pace with changes in the rest of culture. Monotheism and the moral law are constant. Everything else is conditioned by circumstances and therefore changes as circumstances change.

> Reform Jews are committed to the eternal validity of Jewish tradition, but they emphasize the need to interpret that tradition from the perspective of individual conscience and informed choice. They believe, therefore, that Jews must study Jewish tradition. Whenever possible, they should adapt it to modern life. They may question ancient practices or attitudes that are inconsistent with the life of a modern person, and they may reject those ancient or medieval teachings that run contrary to one's moral conscience and contemporary spirituality.[23]

It is this reliance on individual conscience that largely distinguishes Reform Jews in the United States.

Reform began by discarding everything "not adapted to the views and habits of modern civilization" (Pittsburgh Platform) and taught that only the moral law is binding. However, there has been increasing interest in recent years in reappropriating the tradition and affirming the importance of continuity with Judaism throughout the ages. In addition to what has been said above, several

---

[22]*Tefillin* are small leather boxes containing Bible verses. Orthodox Jewish men wear them on their foreheads and left arms during prayer.

[23]Rabbi Morris N. Kertzer (revised by Rabbi Lawrence A. Hoffman), *What is a Jew?*, p.10.

features distinguish Reform. Families sit together in services, and their place of worship is most often called a temple rather than a synagogue. English is often used for at least a part of the service, although certain prayers are most often in Hebrew. Although some people wear the kippah, prayer shawl, and tefillin, many do not. Dietary and Sabbath laws are kept less rigorously, and festival observance may be simpler and shorter in duration. Reform Jews are strong supporters of women's rights and were the first major group within Judaism to ordain women to the rabbinate, as well as being the group that developed coming-of-age rituals for girls.

Hebrew Union College and seminary in Cincinnati, Ohio, is Reform's major educational institution. Its U.S. organization is the Union of American Hebrew Congregations.

Conservatism

Conservative Judaism follows a middle road between Orthodoxy and Reform Judaism. Like Reform, Conservatism believes that Judaism changes with time, but it changes because it is a living religion, and change is a part of that aliveness. American Conservatism is dedicated to preserving the knowledge and practice of historic Judaism without utter refusal to accommodate. The truth of the tradition is maintained through the interpretation of living rabbis, so that the focus is not exclusively on the past (as is the tendency in Orthodoxy) nor on the present (as Reform tends to do).

The dietary laws illustrate the types of accommodation that Conservative Jews may make. Most do keep kosher at home. However, when eating with friends or in restaurants, they do not insist on full observance. Thus, they can dine at the homes of nonkosher friends, and any Jew, even the most observant, can dine at their table.

In addition, there are other practices and beliefs that distinguish Conservatives from others. Family seating is the rule in worship. Men usually wear kippah for worship but not at other times. Much of the service is in Hebrew, and there is intensive emphasis on Hebrew education. A distinction is made between avoidable and unavoidable types of work, with that which cannot be avoided being permitted on the Sabbath. For example, it is permissible to drive to the synagogue on the Sabbath, if distance requires it.

Conservatism emerged in the United States in response to the fragmentation and division brought about by the two large immigrant groups and their differing styles of being Jewish. It was more a reaction to the perceived excesses of accommodation in Reform than to the traditionalism of Orthodoxy. Its goal was to be both fully Jewish (in which its adherents felt Reform had failed miserably) and fully American (which it felt Orthodoxy's strictness prevented happening in a meaningful way). This remains its goal today.

The Jewish Theological Seminary in New York City is its major educational arm in the United States. Organizational embodiments include the

United Synagogue of America, which is the largest formal synagogue organization in the United States, and the United Synagogue of Conservative Judaism, founded in 1913 by Solomon Schechter.

Reconstructionism

Conservatism did not unify American Judaism as much as its proponents had hoped. The **Reconstructionist** movement was another attempt at unification. Reconstructionism's founder, Rabbi Mordecai Kaplan, was a teacher at the Jewish Theological Seminary. When he looked out over the whole of American Judaism, he saw two things. As we have indicated earlier, it was still rather fragmented. More seriously, by 1920, those Jews not affiliated with any synagogue at all far outnumbered the total of Orthodox, Conservative, and Reform Jews combined. In 1934, Kaplan wrote a book entitled *Judaism as a Civilization*. In it, he said that Judaism should be thought of as an evolving religious civilization. It is a civilization that has evolved through the ages, based not so much on belief or practice as on the continuous life of the Jewish people themselves. It has come about as the Jewish people have expressed their values through the patterns of behavior, religious and otherwise, that they have developed. Its focus, then, was not religion but Jewishness in all of its forms, and Kaplan sought to bring about an organic community centered in school and synagogue, one that would meet all the needs of its members. In other words, it was to express in organizational form the unity of the Jewish people.

Reconstructionism is the only expression of Judaism that has been produced solely in America. It was a response to the situation of Jewish people in this country. Despite its small numbers, it has had a large impact on Judaism in the United States.

Zionism

The last sector of American Judaism we will consider here is **Zionism**. Zionism is based upon the importance of the Jewish people as a nation. Theodor Herzl was a Viennese reporter who wrote an emotional pamphlet titled *The Jewish State* (1896), in which he said that the only hope for the Jews was the establishment of a national homeland, preferably in Palestine itself. In 1897, the First World Zionist Congress met in Basel, Switzerland.

Although the leadership of the Zionist movement tended to be mainly nonreligious, Orthodox Jews supported it because it correlated with the Orthodox belief in the eventual restoration and rebuilding of Israel and the Holy City of Jerusalem. The Conservatives also were in favor of most points in the Zionist program. Reform Jews at first found little in it that was attractive, because it conflicted with their desire to be at home in whatever culture they found themselves and with their teaching that Judaism was a religion that could be at home anywhere.

After the Holocaust, virtually all American Jews supported Zionism wholeheartedly. When the state of Israel was founded in 1948, American Jews raised huge sums of money via United Jewish Appeal to help resettle refugees. This focus on Israel remains a powerful unifying force for American Judaism. The Six Day War of 1967, with Israel seeming to be threatened with annihilation from its Arab neighbors, further mobilized Zionist sentiment and action, virtually eliminating any remaining questions about the necessity and appropriateness of Zionism's program.[24]

Hillel International

The primary organization of Jewish students on United States college campuses is Hillel International. It is named after Rabbi Hillel, a noted Jewish rabbi who lived at about the same time as did Jesus. Founded at the University of Illinois in 1923, it has become the largest Jewish campus organization in the world. It reaches out to all Jewish students, those who are religious and those who are not.

> The Hillel network brings to the college world all the richness and diversity of Judaism and Jewishness. Its historical commitment to a pluralistic community encourages intellectual challenge and growth. Hillel maintains a presence on over 400 campuses, and is in the vanguard of those who are determined to build a fuller and stronger Jewish people in the 21st century.[25]

HOLOCAUST, MEMORY, AND PUBLIC RELIGIOUSNESS

American Jewish scholar Jacob Neusner notes that there are two different spheres of Jewish religiousness, both accorded equal legitimacy. There is, in the first place, the Judaism of home and family. This aspect of Jewish religious practice focuses on rites of passage and on the celebration of the Days of Awe (Rosh Hashanah and Yom Kippur), Passover, and Hanukkah.

Alongside the religion of home and family there is the second aspect of Jewish religiousness, the public and political sphere, which Neusner calls the "Judaism of Holocaust and Redemption":

> "The Holocaust" of the Judaism of Holocaust and Redemption refers to the murder of six million Jewish children, women, and men in Europe between 1933 and 1945 by the Germans. "The Redemption" is the creation of the state of Israel. . . .

---

[24]Gerald Sorin. *Tradition Transformed: The Jewish Experience in America* (Baltimore, MD: The Johns Hopkins University Press, 1997), pp. 213–214.
[25]Hillel International Web site (http://www.hillel.org).

The Holocaust then corresponds in the here and now to anti-Semitism, exclusion, alienation, which Jews experience solely by reason of being Jewish.

The creation of the state of Israel is also given transcendent meaning. It provides the answer to the existential question raised by the Holocaust:

> [N]early all American Jews identify with the state of Israel and regard its welfare not only as a secular good, but a metaphysical necessity. Nearly all American Jews are supporters of the state of Israel. But they also regard their own "being Jewish" as inextricably bound up with the meaning they impute to the Jewish state.[26]

It is this second, public manifestation of Jewishness that leads the majority of American Jews to contribute to the United Jewish Appeal and other Jewish charities. Many also contribute to the American–Israel Political Action Committee (AIPAC) and engage in other political action supportive of the state of Israel. Like participation in life-cycle rites and certain widely celebrated holidays, it helps to hold the community together and define it as a community, at the same time relating it to values perceived to be ultimate. It forms the core of a Jewish civil religion that exists distinct from the religion of religiously observant Jews, while not being antagonistic to it.

The Holocaust, as most of you know, refers to the German killing of over six million Jews during the Third Reich. Many other people whom the Nazis deemed "undesirable" were killed by mass extermination methods as well. Contemporary Jews often refer to this almost unspeakable event by its Hebrew name, *Sho'ah*. Both Holocaust and Sho'ah mean the same thing—burnt sacrifice. Gentiles sometimes criticize Jews for what they regard as an unnecessary preoccupation with what Gentiles regard as a past event. Why set apart a day every year to remember? Why establish courses and centers and museums? Why keep references to Sho'ah in the words of the liturgy?

There are religious, practical, and moral reasons to remember. Religiously, it is important that the dead be remembered. By remembering the victims, they are dignified. Practically, human beings tend to repress and conveniently "forget" that which is so horrible or to generalize it to make it easier to think about. Very specific remembrances counteract these tendencies. Morally, "Jews worry that to fail to remember Hitler is to risk the rise of anti-Semitism once again." Anti-Semitism still exists, and keeping its worst effects in mind may hasten the day when it will no longer do so.[27]

In many communities, Christians join with Jews in remembering in formal ceremonies and services on Holocaust Remembrance Day. While they would deny that Hitler's motives were in any way Christian, Christians nonetheless recognize the complicity of some Christian ways of thinking about Jews in the events that led to Sho'ah.

---

[26]Jacob Neusner, *Introduction to American Judaism: What the Books Say, What the People Do* (Minneapolis, MN: Fortress Press, 1994), pp. 115–117.

[27]Rabbi Morris N. Kertzer (revised by Rabbi Lawrence A. Hoffman), *What is a Jew?*, pp. 159–162.

ANTI-SEMITISM

Anti-Semitism—dislike or hatred of and aggressive acts toward Jews simply because they are Jews—still exists in the United States. Two things must be kept in balance: It is unlikely that anti-Semitism will ever disappear completely. However, the situation of Judaism as a religion and most Jews as individuals has been and is better in the United States than it was and is elsewhere. While there have never been pogroms nor respected anti-Semitic political parties, Jews are sometimes seen as outsiders in a predominantly Christian land.

One of the factors that led, and still leads, to anti-Semitism is the erroneous belief held by some Christians that Jews were responsible for Jesus' death. It is quite clear that Jesus was put to death by the Romans, not the Jews. Nonetheless, this idea persists. Many Christians also find it very difficult to understand why Jews do not accept Jesus as the savior of humankind. This leads to both anti-Semitism and efforts to convert Jews to Christianity.

A second historical facet of Jewish–Christian relations is that the Christian church in medieval times did not permit charging interest on money loaned. European Jews thus became associated with money and banking, and many people came to feel that the Jews were prospering at the expense of the Christians. This historical fact gave rise to a distrust of Jews in financial matters and to the stereotypes that "all Jews are rich" and "all Jews are stingy."

The Sephardic Jews who settled in what was to become New York found in Peter Stuyvesant a governor who referred to them as a "deceitful race" who would "infest and trouble" his colony. Civil liberties and the vote were denied to any except Christians in many of the colonies and in some states for a time after the Revolution. In 1861, when Congress established a chaplain corps for the Union army, it was restricted to ministers of any Christian denomination. President Lincoln succeeded in securing an amendment to that action that allowed for Jewish chaplains, but some damage had been done, nonetheless. The immigration bill adopted by Congress in 1924 was shamefully xenophobic, and that attitude was not eliminated until this measure was replaced by Lyndon Johnson's Immigration Measure. The Ku Klux Klan has been quite active throughout American history in anti-Semitic activities and diatribes. Henry Ford supported the publication of *The Protocols of Zion*. This classic piece of hate literature embodied an idea that also had currency elsewhere—that the Jews were engaged in a conspiracy to take over the world by overthrowing Christianity.

More general patterns of discrimination also occurred, such as quota systems that barred all but a few Jews from prestigious eastern colleges and restricted Jews to a handful of the professions. There are still private clubs that either restrict the number of Jewish members or do not admit them at all. Discrimination in housing has also been fairly commonplace. Synagogues have been defaced, frequently being spray-painted with Nazi swastikas, and crosses have been burned in the yards of synagogues and Jewish homes. Often, the attacks are verbal in nature, but there is also a pattern of physical attacks on Jewish property and Jewish people.

The Identity Movement (see Chapter 13) is staunchly anti-Semitic in its thinking, as well as advocating prejudice against Catholics, blacks, homosexuals, and various other people. People in the movement often describe the current situation as one in which a battle for the world is being fought under the direction of God, a battle between the whites whom God intends to inherit the earth and the Jews (and others) from whom they must wrest control of it. The close identification of some groups within this movement with the neo-Nazi movement is especially troublesome to Jews, as well as to other people.

Survey data demonstrate that a low level of general anti-Semitism continues. In the years 1990 through 1996, about 6 percent of people in the United States thought of Jews as "lazy," and 12 percent felt that Jews were "violent." Nine percent thought of them as "unintelligent" and 10 percent as "unpatriotic." Fourteen percent were opposed to living in a neighborhood in which half their neighbors were Jews, and 24 percent felt that Jews have too much influence in the United States.[28]

That there is less anti-Semitism now than at some other times in our history must not lull us into indifference. Remaining anti-Semitism, as well as other forms of discrimination, prejudice, and bigotry, whether religious or otherwise, must be blotted out.

Acceptance must not and cannot be contingent on differences being reduced to some sort of lowest common denominator or to minorities conforming to the majority opinion of how the minority ought to be. To do so dehumanizes the individuals in the minority and impoverishes the entire community, which is denied the richness of variety that healthy, culturally conscious minorities provide.

Community is in large part a dialogue, and for a lively dialogue to occur, there must be lively differences. To insist upon conformity as a condition of acceptance and as a criterion of membership in the community will ultimately destroy the dialogue upon which genuine community is based and which is its lifeblood. It will create strangers where there might have been neighbors, because they will have nothing to discuss.

JEWS IN AMERICA: PROMISE AND PERIL

The United States has offered Jews opportunities they have not found anywhere else. Constitutional separation of church and state meant that, at least in theory, all were equal before the law. And although that did not always translate into true equality on a day-in-day-out level, such equality was much more the case here than elsewhere. Political liberty and social acceptance, entry into the mainstream as defined by the majority culture—these have characterized the Jewish experience in America, particularly in the closing decades of the millennium. Therein is the promise.

[28]National Opinion Research Center General Social Surveys for 1990–1996.

At the same time, such liberty has meant that Judaism became a choice, and therein lies the peril. Two recent Jewish authors describe the situation poignantly:

> The curses, I believe, are in fact the "flip side" of the blessings: the price that Jews began to pay two centuries ago for the incalculable goods of emancipation from the ghetto, and pay still in our day for full participation in every aspect of American society and culture. Modernity, enlightenment, social acceptance, and political liberties—all of which we dearly treasure, and all of which have reached their greatest fulfillment in America—carry with them the consequence that Jews can choose *whether* as well as *how* to be Jewish. Inevitably many Jews will choose not to engage their ancestral tradition or participate in the Jewish community in any serious fashion, and some will even opt out altogether. There are many options for identity available, many paths to walk, and few people in any time and place ever opt to move against the currents of their society and culture.[29]

> The good news is that American Jews—as *individuals*—have never been more secure, more accepted, more affluent, and less victimized by discrimination or anti-Semitism. The bad news is that American Jews—as a *people*—have never been in greater danger of disappearing through assimilation, intermarriage, and low birthrates. . . .

> Jews have faced dangers in the past, but this time we may be unprepared to confront the newest threat to our survival *as a people*, because its principal cause is our own success *as individuals*.[30]

Two contending views have developed. One says that Judaism cannot survive the American experience, that it has survived centuries of persecution from without only to become the victim of its success. Others argue that what is happening to Judaism as a result of its success is not demise but change, reconfiguration, that has within it the possibility of transformation into new and even more vibrant forms.[31]

Nor has it been a one-way street. Not only has Judaism been influenced by America, but it has influenced America, as well. The prophetic ideal of caring for those less able to care for themselves meant that Jews have strongly supported liberal social legislation. Jews have been in the forefront of support for individual civil liberties. The non-Orthodox have frequently led the women's movement. Avant-garde tendencies in the arts have benefited from Jewish support. Popular

---

[29]Arnold M. Eisen, *Taking Hold of Torah: Jewish Commitment and Community in America* (Bloomington, IN: Indiana University Press, 1997), pp. x–xi. See also Robert M. Seltzer and Norman J. Cohen, eds., *The Americanization of the Jews* (New York: New York University Press, 1995); Gerald Sorin, *Tradition Transformed: The Jewish Experience in America* (Baltimore, MD: The Johns Hopkins University Press, 1997); and Alan M. Dershowitz, *The Vanishing American Jew: In Search of Jewish Identity for the Next Century* (Boston: Little, Brown and Company, 1997).

[30]Alan M. Dershowitz, *The Vanishing American Jew: In Search of Jewish Identity for the Next Century* (Boston: Little, Brown and Company, 1997), pp. 1–2.

[31]Gerald Sorin, *Tradition Transformed: The Jewish Experience in America*, pp. 4–5 and 235.

culture has been receptive to Jewish popular culture, with its distinctive foods and language ("that isn't kosher" applied to actions that aren't right or the advice to "be a mensch!").[32]

QUESTIONS AND ACTIVITIES FOR REVIEW, DISCUSSION, AND WRITING

1. In what different ways may someone be Jewish?
2. Be sure that you know the basic beliefs and practices shared by most religious Jews.
3. If possible, attend a service at a temple or synagogue. This might be done by the entire class together. Write an essay in which you describe what you observed.
4. If possible, arrange to interview an Orthodox Jew about her or his Sabbath and kosher practices. Do the same with a Reform or a Conservative Jew.
5. If there is a kosher restaurant nearby, arrange a visit there. Talk with the owner(s)/ employees about kosher dietary practices and what they mean to Jews in the United States.
6. In your own words, describe each of the expressions of Judaism. Of these, which seems the most attractive to you, and why?
7. Describe the attitude toward women in each of the major denominations of Judaism.
8. If possible, interview a Jewish woman about what being Jewish and female means to her.
9. Why is it important to Jews to remember the Holocaust?
10. What is the "promise and peril" of Judaism in the United States?
11. Visit the Web site of Jews for Jesus, a Messianic Jewish organization (http://www.jews-for-jesus.org). What is this group about? Visit the site of Jews for Judaism (http://www.jewsforjudaism.org). What is this group about? What is the issue between them?

FOR FURTHER READING

BRODY, LESLIE, ed., *Daughters of Kings: Growing Up as a Jewish Woman in America*. Boston: Faber and Faber, 1997. This is a collection of primarily first-person accounts from a variety of perspectives.

COHN-SHERBOK, DAN, and LAVINA COHN-SHERBOK, *The American Jew: Voices from an American Jewish Community*. Grand Rapids, MI: William B. Eerdmans Publishing Company, 1995. Like the previous book, this contains primarily first-person accounts. Both are highly recommended for this reason.

DINNERSTEIN, LEONARD, *Antisemitism in America*. New York: Oxford University Press, 1994. This book is a leading survey of the topic.

EISEN, ARNOLD M., *Taking Hold of Torah: Jewish Commitment and Community in America*. Bloomington, IN: Indiana University Press, 1997. Of the various general works on this topic cited in this chapter, this and the one following are the most accessible to the general reader.

SELTZER, ROBERT M., and NORMAN J. COHEN, eds., *The Americanization of the Jews*. New York: New York University Press, 1995.

ZWI WERBLOSKY, R.J., and GEOFFREY WIGODOR, eds., *The Oxford Dictionary of the Jewish Religion*. New York: Oxford University Press, 1997. Not a standard "dictionary," this reference volume contains substantial articles on nearly everything Jewish.

---

[32]Robert M. Seltzer and Norman J. Cohen, eds., *The Americanization of the Jews*, p. 9.

RELEVANT WORLD WIDE WEB SITES

Jewish Communications Network (http://www.jcn18.com).

Judaism and Jewish Resources (http://shamash.org/trb/judaism.html).

Judaism 101 (http://members.aol.com/jewfaq/index.htm).

Jewish Feminist Resources (http://world.std.com/~alevin/jewishfeminist.html).

United States Holocaust Memorial Museum (http://www.ushmm.org/).

Orthodox Union (http://www.ou.org/).

United Synagogue of Conservative Judaism (http://www.uscj.org/).

Union of American Hebrew Congregations (http://www.uahc.org/).

Zionist Organization of America (http://www.zoa.org/).

Women's Zionist Organization of America (http://www.hadassah.org/).

Hillel International (http://www.hillel.org/).

6

Humanism and the
Unitarian Universalists

The history of Western civilization shows us that most social and moral progress has been brought about by persons free from religion. In modern times the first to speak out for prison reform, for humane treatment of the mentally ill, for abolition of capital punishment, for women's right to vote, for death with dignity for the terminally ill, and for the right to choose contraception, sterilization and abortion have been free-thinkers, just as they were the first to call for an end to slavery.[1]

What associations, if any, does the word *humanism* bring to your mind? Does it have positive or negative connotations? What do you think about people who say that they are humanists? Do you think humanism necessarily excludes belief in God? Does your school have a college or department of humanities? Do you think these two words might be related? How?

There are many varieties of humanism. The group whose quotation appears above represents a thoroughly secular humanism, one that has no room for religion. Other forms of humanism are religious, as we will see.

WHAT IS HUMANISM?

Humanism can be defined briefly as a worldview or philosophy that derives its values from the experience of human life in this world, without reference to God as Jews and Christians understand God or to anything else supernatural. In order to fill in this brief definition, we will look at some recent statements of the meaning of humanism.

> Humanism is a celebration and a promise; it celebrates the integrity of human reason, responsibility and compassion, and it promises a satisfying lifestyle that can

---

[1]Freedom from Religion Foundation Web site (http://www.infidels.org/org/ffrf).

be counted on. No more deprecation of the human condition; rather, an opportunity to remain true to ourselves by having both feet in this world and responding to the challenges of existence with excitement and pragmatic service to others. Humanism is religion come of age; at long last we humans can live dignified lives, finite creatures though we may be. At long last, men, women and children can find ultimate fulfillment through bringing out the best in humanity for the sake of humanity.[2]

Humanists believe in what Robert Ingersoll called the trinity of science: reason, experience, and observation.[3]

Humanism is a rational philosophy informed by science, inspired by art, and motivated by compassion. Affirming the dignity of each human being, it supports the maximization of individual liberty and opportunity consonant with social and planetary responsibility. It advocates the extension of participatory democracy and the expansion of the open society, standing for human rights and social justice. Free of supernaturalism, it recognizes human beings as a part of nature and holds that values—be they religious, ethical, social, or political—have their source in human experience and culture. Humanism thus derives the goals of life from human need and interest rather than from theological or ideological abstractions, and asserts that humanity must take responsibility for its own destiny.[4]

Humanism is a democratic and ethical life stance which affirms that human beings have the right and responsibility to give meaning and shape to their own lives. It stands for the building of a more humane society through an ethics based on human and other natural values in a spirit of reason and free inquiry through human capabilities. It is not theistic, and it does not accept supernatural views of reality.[5]

Humanism is a philosophy, world view, or life stance based on naturalism—the conviction that the universe or nature is all that exists or is real. Humanism serves, for many humanists, some of the psychological and social functions of a religion, but without belief in deities, transcendental entities, miracles, life after death, and the supernatural. Humanists seek to understand the universe by using science and its methods of critical inquiry—logical reasoning, empirical evidence, and skeptical evaluation of conjectures and conclusions—to obtain reliable knowledge. Humanists affirm that humans have the freedom and obligation to give meaning, value, and purpose to their lives by their own independent thought, free inquiry, and responsible, creative activity. Humanists stand for the building of a more humane, just, compassionate, and democratic society using a realistic ethics based on human reason, experience, and reliable knowledge—an

---

[2]Beverley Earles, on the Friends of Religious Humanism Web site (http://humanist.net/frh/).
[3]African Americans for Humanism Web site (http://www.secularhumanism.org/aah/).
[4]The American Humanist Association, on their Web site (http://www.infidels.org/org/aha/).
[5]The International Humanist and Ethical Union, on the American Humanist Association Web site (http://www.infidels.org/org/aha/).

ethics that judges the consequences of human actions by the well-being of all life on Earth.[6]

There are a number of common themes that appear in these definitions; together they provide an outline of what humanism is:

- Humanism affirms human reason, compassion, responsibility, and the trustworthiness of human experience.
- Humanism affirms human life in this world, as a part of nature.
- It affirms the worth and dignity of each individual woman, man, and child, and the fundamental equality of all persons.
- It is possible for human beings to find meaning and fulfillment in life without recourse to the supernatural; people have the responsibility to engage in a search for meaning.
- Humanism supports the fullest development of democracy in all areas of life, human rights, social justice, and the expansion of individual rights to the fullest extent consonant with responsibility.
- Ethical and moral life is to be based on human experience, reason, and valuing.

Humanism, in other words, is based on the faith that people can live truly good lives in the here and now, that we have the capacity to cooperate to build a good society that balances out the needs of the individual and the larger group, and that we can find meaning and fulfillment without recourse to anything supernatural. Or, as one humanist puts it, humanism is "the use of reason in human affairs, applied in the service of compassion."[7]

Not all humanists are secularists, although many are. Jewish and Christian humanism also have a significant place in the story of American humanism. The humanist belief in the dignity and worth of every person, the emphasis on ethical conduct and human responsibility, and compassion in the context of human community are all shared by most religions. Liberal religion shares with humanism a belief in the basic goodness of human nature, its insistence that the context must be taken into account in making moral decisions, and its support for the use of reason and opposition to authoritarianism. Much of liberal religion agrees with humanism that supernaturalism in religion is outdated and that scientific inquiry can and should be used to evaluate claims to religious truth. Humanism and liberal religion also share the belief that the sacred and secular worlds cannot, in the final analysis, be separated. Social justice, opposition to prejudice in all forms, and an interest in peacemaking also characterize both.

"The adventure of religion," writes one advocate of religious humanism, "is not in the discovery of Eternal Truth or Absolute Meaning—arenas in which human beings do not and cannot deal—but in our individual and communal

---

[6]The Virtual Community of Humanists, on The American Humanist Association Web site (http://www. infidels.org/org/aha/).

[7]H. J. Eysenck, "Reason with Compassion," in *The Humanist Alternative*, ed. Paul Kurtz (Buffalo, NY: Prometheus Books, 1973), p. 91.

search for and creation of meanings and values that dignify and enhance life."[8] Another explains how humanism seeks to modify religion: "Humanism attempts to rid religious institutions, myths, creeds, prayers, and sacraments of superstitious beliefs, while enhancing their significance as expressions of human needs, hopes and values."[9]

HUMANISM IN THE UNITED STATES

The recent history of humanism in the United States is built on the foundation of centuries of earlier history, both in the United States and throughout the world. Rather than tracing this early history, however, we will look briefly at the more recent course of humanism in the United States. Humanism as a self-conscious movement began in the United States in 1933, when *Humanist Manifesto I* was written. There had been humanists and humanist philosophers in America as far back as the Declaration of Independence and even farther. Conscious attempts to articulate the principles of American humanism date from the first manifesto, however.

Three Humanist Statements

The first of these three statements is the *Humanist Manifesto I*, written in 1933 by a group of humanists in the United States who set out to draft what they understood to be the basic principles of the movement. It is an optimistic and upbeat document that expresses great confidence in humanism as the wave of the future. "In every field of human activity," they wrote, "the vital movement is now in the direction of a candid and explicit humanism." The humanism of this document is explicitly religious humanism. Its authors wanted to separate religion from doctrines and from methods that they believed were "outmoded" and not workable in the twentieth century. They intended it to be a "new statement of the means and purposes of religion." It is written in the form of a series of fifteen brief statements with an introduction and conclusion and deals with those themes that we have already seen in connection with humanism.[10]

The authors of the first major humanist statement *were* critical of the religious institutions of their day and regarded many religious beliefs and practices as unsuitable for life in the twentieth century. It is equally clear that they were not, on the whole, hostile to religion. Religion, while in need of dramatic transformation, would, once transformed, continue to serve many of the same functions it had served in the past. Their confidence in the capacity of human nature to accomplish what was needed was high. As a whole, the document carries its reader along on a tide of goodwill and optimism.

---

[8]Kenneth W. Pfifer, *The Faith of a Humanist* (Boston, MA: Unitarian Universalist Association, n.d.).
[9]Herbert W. Schneider, "Religious Humanism," in *The Humanist Alternative*, ed. Paul Kurtz, p. 65.
[10]Paul J. Kurtz, *Humanist Manifesto I* (Buffalo, NY: Prometheus Books, 1973).

By 1973, when *Humanist Manifesto II* was drafted, the events of the intervening forty years had made the first program seem far too optimistic. Still, its authors expressed great confidence in people's ability to solve the problems that existed. It calls for people to "fuse reason with compassion in order to build constructive moral values." A major change from the first document is that this manifesto states that religion cannot be reinterpreted sufficiently to be made viable; something radically new is needed. Promises of eternal salvation and threats of eternal hellfire are said to be especially harmful, because they distract people from their proper focus on life in this world. A closely related section deals with ethics. Ethics are derived from human experience in this world, and moral decision making must take the situation into account. Reason and intelligence are the best tools we have for making moral decisions, coupled with the cultivation of appropriate emotional attitudes of love and compassion.

The second manifesto was originally signed by 114 people and was later endorsed by many more. It is a statement sobered by a world war and by economic chaos in several places throughout the world. It has a much more clearly political tone than did its predecessor. Political and economic arrangements between nations receive more explicit attention. And, as previously noted, its attitude toward religion has changed. The changes between the two manifestos reflect the changes in the thinking of the humanist community in the United States and abroad. (The list of signers includes people from Great Britain, Canada, Germany, the former Soviet Union, India, France, and Sweden, as well as the United States.)

A Secular Humanist Declaration, written in 1980, is a very different sort of document. It outlines an explicitly secular humanism that clearly believes itself to be under attack and on the defensive. It attacks by name a variety of points of view and groups such as Christian fundamentalism, the Catholic papal hierarchy, Muslim clericalism, nationalistic Judaism, and many New Age beliefs and practices. It accuses these groups of promoting unthinking reliance on authority, restricting human freedom, and bypassing the use of reason and the scientific method to solve problems. It then moves on to a series of positive affirmations and calls for action that reflects the humanist values we have seen before.[11]

As these three documents reflect the evolution of humanist thought in the United States, we can see that the situation has become more and more polarized. As Christian fundamentalism has named secular humanism as the main focus of its attack, religious fundamentalism has become the focus of secular humanism's attack. There can be no doubt that the views of fundamentalists and humanists are sharply different at almost every point. Fundamentalists tend to oppose both secular and religious humanism, believing that both are examples of human rebellion against God's authority. The kind of society envisioned by the one would have no room for the other. Each provides a framework within which significant numbers of Americans live and attempt to construct a mean-

---

[11]Paul J. Kurtz, "A Secular Humanist Declaration," *Free Inquiry*, 1, no. 1 (Winter, 1980).

ingful life. If we really are to become neighbors and not strangers, there must be room in the neighborhood for both points of view. The tendency of each to view the other as an obnoxious enemy must give way to an appreciation of what each provides for those who live their lives by it.

HUMANIST ORGANIZATIONS IN THE UNITED STATES

Humanist organizations are not nearly as well known as more traditional religious organizations, but there are several such groups in the United States. They are more common in major urban areas than in smaller communities and along the coasts than in the heartland.

Felix Adler founded the **Ethical Culture Society** in 1876. He had been trained as a rabbi but left Judaism in favor of ethical humanism based on the dignity and worth of every individual. The member societies of the Ethical Culture Society hold Sunday meetings that are of an educational and morally uplifting nature. The group is also characterized by intense social activism in the areas of education, war and peace, and racism, among others.

The Statement of Purpose of the American Ethical Union describes the Ethical Culture movement:

> Ethical Culture is a humanistic religious and educational movement inspired by the ideal that the supreme aim of human life is working to create a more humane society.
>
> Our faith is in the capacity and responsibility of human beings to act in their personal relationships and in the larger community to help create a better world.
>
> Our commitment is to the worth and dignity of the individual, and to treating each human being so as to bring out the best in him or her.
>
> Members join together in ethical societies to assist each other in developing ethical ideas and ideals . . . to celebrate life's joys and support each other through life's crises . . . to work together to improve our world and the world of our children.[12]

The **American Humanist Association** was formed in 1941 as an effort to link the various humanist interests in the United States. Like the Ethical Culture Society, it supports an active program of social involvement that is based on the principles in the *Humanist Manifestos*. It publishes a periodical, *The Humanist*, and supports Prometheus Books, the largest American publisher of humanist literature.

The **Friends of Religious Humanism** publishes the journal, *Religious Humanism*. It was founded in 1962 as the Fellowship of Religious Humanists. It

---

[12]The American Ethical Union Web site (http://www.aeu.org).

is an affiliate of the Unitarian Universalist Association. One of its members articulates specifically religious humanism this way:

> Humanism can be religious; indeed, the most meaningful and liveable kind of humanism is itself a religious way of understanding and living life. It offers a view of [people] and [their] place in the universe that is a religious philosophy . . . overarching and undergirding it all, there can be a haunting sense of wonder which never leaves one for whom life itself is a mystery and miracle. Where did we come from, why are we here, where are we going with all the effort, frustration, the grief, the joy? To be caught up in this sense of wider relatedness, to sense our being connected in live ways with all the world and everyone in it, is the heart dimension of religion, whatever its name.[13]

The **Society for Humanistic Judaism** is the major Jewish humanist organization. It was founded by Rabbi Sherwin T. Wine in 1963 as a "nontheistic alternative in contemporary Jewish life." Several of the affirmations of the Society significantly reinterpret traditional Jewish teaching along humanistic lines. For example:

- "A Jew is someone who identifies with the history, culture and future of the Jewish people." There is no reference to *religious* Judaism.
- "Jewish history is a human saga, a testament to the significance of human power and human responsibility." Jewish history is more traditionally interpreted as the saga of God's power working in and with the House of Israel.
- "We possess the power and responsibility to shape our own lives independent of supernatural authority." Traditional Judaism is theocentric (God-centered) from beginning to end.[14]

The role of the black church has been central to the life of the African American community in the United States (see chapter 9). However, there is also an association of African Americans for Humanism. Although many of its goals are similar to those of the black Christian churches, its rationales and methods are those of humanism. The association

> . . . questions and challenges the religious beliefs which have been largely responsible for the many problems plaguing the African American community. Fights racism through humanistic education. Acknowledges the contributions of humanists of African descent to world history. Seeks to develop wisdom and good conduct through living in the African American community by using rational and scientific methods of inquiry. Believes that the "good life" can be achieved on Earth through positive thinking, the sharing of ideas and enlightened self interest. Acknowledges the various styles of thinking which exist among individuals and groups, and seeks to determine the best course of humane and rational action for the African American community through an open minded examination of all

---

[13]Peter Samson, on the Friends of Religious Humanism Web site (http://humanist.net/frh/).
[14]Quoted material is from the Society for Humanistic Judaism Web site (http://www.shj.org).

ideas. Does not seek to put forth the specific agenda of any religious, political, or economic organization.[15]

The Campus Freethought Alliance began in 1996 with "representatives of various student skeptical, secular humanist, atheist, agnostic, and freethought campus organizations." The students who joined to form the Alliance were in search of community for freethinkers among the college population:

> Given the fact that student religious organizations exist on virtually all college and university campuses (Campus Crusade, Newman Centers, Hillel, Muslim organizations and the like)—and that corresponding freethought, secular humanist, and unbeliever groups generally do not—we think it vitally important that freethought organizations be formed on every campus. Too many secular humanists, atheists, and skeptics face the demands of college life alone. A campus freethought organization can provide much-needed support, and when necessary, help to defend unbelievers' rights.[16]

These and other similar groups provide some organizational cohesiveness to the humanist movement in America and provide a means by which people in agreement with this point of view can find fellowship and engage in social action. They also provide a means by which humanists can voice their concerns. Humanist organizations work to get legislation passed that reflects their viewpoint, just as do other political interest groups, including religious interest groups.

There can be no doubt that humanism serves many of the same functions for its adherents that traditional religions do for theirs. It has many of the same emotional dynamics. Like the religions, humanism deserves a place among the myriad ways that Americans organize their lives in a meaningful fashion. It is a continuing element in the American landscape, one that will interact with religion for a long time to come.

ATHEISM AND AGNOSTICISM

Before you read further, stop and ask yourself what might lead someone to be an atheist or agnostic. Do those views seem to you to be reasonable ones for someone to hold, whether or not you, yourself, do?

Most people in the United States do believe in the existence of God as commonly understood. Most surveys indicate that 90 percent or more of adults hold such a belief in God, a Higher Power, or a Supreme Being, and the majority claim to hold such belief without doubt. It is to the nonbelievers that we now turn.

We'll begin with a brief definition of each word. **Atheism** is most often defined as not believing in any deity. In the United States, atheism usually means

---

[15]African Americans for Humanism Web site (http://www.secularhumanism.org/aah/).
[16]Campus Freethought Alliance Web site (http://www.secularhumanism.org/cfa/).

not believing in God as God is thought of in the Judeo-Christian-Islamic tradition. However, many atheists think that this definition is inadequate. While acknowledging that the word **atheist** is used to mean a person who *denies* the existence of God, they press for a distinction:

> Even an atheist would agree that *some* atheists (a small minority) would fit this definition. However, most atheists . . . would hold that an atheist is a person *without* belief in God. The distinction is small but important. Denying something means that you have knowledge of what it is that you are being asked to affirm, but that you have rejected that particular concept. To be *without* belief in God merely means the term "God" has no importance or possibly no meaning to you.[17]

Having said that, however, it is necessary to note that, usually, in the United States, most people use the words *atheism* and *atheist* with the meaning of not believing in God.

A typical definition, and one from a trustworthy source, is as follows:

> [A]theism is the doctrine that God does not exist, that belief in the existence of God is a false belief. The word *God* here refers to a divine being regarded as the independent creator of the world, a being superlatively powerful, wise, and good.[18]

Agnosticism has a number of meanings. Some agnostics hold that *they* simply do not know if God exists. Others believe that it is utterly *impossible to know* if God exists. Some would put it in terms of the *evidence* being *inconclusive*. Others believe that, even if we can say with some degree of certainty that some sort of higher being or power does exist, we can have absolutely no knowledge of the *nature* or *character* of that being.

Atheism, agnosticism, and various other types of "free thought" that are not in accord with the Judeo-Christian perspective have been a part of the religious and cultural perspective ever since Europeans came to the New World. Atheism and agnosticism were included in the plurality of religious views held by the early colonists and by the framers of the Constitution. Current survey data indicate that between 5 and 10 percent of the population does not believe in some higher power.

There are a number of different themes that appear repeatedly in people's reasons for disavowing belief in a supreme being or higher power. Some believe that people simply project their need for an eternal father figure onto the being whom believers call God. Following psychiatrist Sigmund Freud, for example, some atheists say that we as human beings want a father figure to protect us, to punish us when we deserve to be punished, and to reward us when we have been

---

[17]Gordon Stein, "Introduction," in *An Anthology of Atheism and Rationalism*, ed. Gordon Stein (Buffalo, NY: Prometheus Books, 1980), p. 3.

[18]George Alfred James, "Atheism," in *The Encyclopedia of Religion*, Vol. 1, ed. Mircea Eliade (New York: Macmillan Publishing Company, 1987), pp. 479–480.

good. We want, in other words, to remain in a childlike relationship with a powerful father. Because our earthly fathers inevitably die—and also fail to meet our expectations while they are alive—we create a God who is an omnipotent, all-knowing father. Alternatively, following Marx, people who are oppressed and mistreated project a God who will reward them in the future for present suffering and deprivation. This, then, invites abuse by the privileged and ruling classes, who can promise those they oppress future rewards in heaven for compliance and punishments in hell for disobedience. This dynamic was at work in some of the uses made of Christianity by slave holders.

Another alternative of this type is more sociological. Following sociologist Emile Durkheim, this view holds that a society (rather than individuals) projects a God as the source of its dearest values and social norms. The social norms and cultural values gain authority and sanction by being attributed to the deity. A very similar dynamic can be seen when proponents of various (and often opposing!) social positions claim that "God is on their side," as has been done by both sides in the abortion rights debate and the homosexual rights debate.

Some atheists believe faith in God is simply not consistent with a scientific view of reality and the methods that such a view entails. In other words, "God" cannot be proven by the methods of science, especially as refined and practiced by the natural sciences. Furthermore, the concept of God may be used to fill in where knowledge does not exist, as a substitute for knowledge, thus hindering the furtherance of knowledge. This is sometimes called a "God of the gaps" theology. "God" is brought in to explain that for which there is no other explanation. Thus, as human knowledge grows, God must necessarily shrink. Although most theologians do not support the "God of the gaps" view, it is fairly common among believers generally.

Some people think that the word *God* simply does not have a clear, unambiguous meaning. Statements about God cannot be verified or falsified in the usual ways and thus are an unacceptable use of language.

A particularly troublesome problem for many people is that they cannot reconcile the existence of an all-powerful and loving God with the presence of so much human suffering. Catastrophic disasters, pain and suffering endured by innocent populations, and horrifying illnesses that afflict apparently "good" people all have led to questions about God's existence. Even if they do not question God's existence, people may question God's simultaneous goodness and power (cornerstones of the Judeo-Christian-Islamic view). If God is both all-good and all-powerful, the argument runs, why does God allow things like this to happen? These questions run the gamut from individuals asking "Why?" after the death of a parent, child, or spouse, to those of Jewish faith who asked and continue to ask "Why?" after the Holocaust.

Other atheists argue that belief in God's existence is incompatible with the recognition of the autonomy and worth of humankind. The Christian insistence that people need a savior or the Jewish and Muslim avowal that people need the guidance of God to live truly good lives seems to some people to contradict human autonomy, freedom, and worth.

Some people feel that belief in God takes away from people's proper focus, which is to work actively for positive change in the social order. In some instances, this is a response to the perceived social conservatism of religion, religion's tendency to maintain the status quo rather than support change. As you have seen, some women feel very strongly that their churches and synagogues have been on the side of female oppression rather than on the side of women's rights. In other cases, this view stems from the shift in focus that sometimes goes along with belief in God and life after death. For some, although certainly not for most, believers, life in this present world is greatly devalued compared with eternal life with God. This devaluation then undercuts any attempt to better this life.

Finally, some people simply point to the fact that, the world around, many people, including many who espouse very high ideals, do not believe. If the whole experience of humankind is taken into account, there are just too many people for whom God is not a fact of their experience.

While several of these views are most likely to lead a person to atheism, at least three of them might also lead to agnosticism. Many agnostics simply feel that there is not enough evidence either for or against God's existence to warrant certainty. Some are disturbed by the ambiguity and lack of clarity that surrounds our use of the word *God*. And certainly some do wonder about how well people get along without such belief. Fewer agnostics than atheists tend to be militant about their position. For the most part, their "unknowing" makes them reluctant to try to make converts.

One of the sharpest statements of a militantly atheistic view comes from a pamphlet entitled "A Secular Humanist Declaration." In the Introduction, the authors state, "Regrettably, we are today faced with a variety of antisecularist trends." They then list a wide variety of manifestations of religion that they consider to be "dogmatic authoritarian . . . fundamentalist, literalist, and doctrinaire," choosing their examples from both the United States and around the world, and including aspects of virtually all religions. They continue:

> These religious activists not only are responsible for much of the terror and violence in the world today but stand in the way of solutions to the world's most serious problems. . . . [We] find that traditional views of the existence of God either are meaningless, have not yet been demonstrated to be true, or are tyrannically exploitive.[19]

This secularist attack on religion is every bit as immoderate as many secularists accuse religion of being in its attacks on secularism.

There are few **atheist organizations** in the United States, and, for most people, atheism is a matter of private belief and conviction. Probably the best-known American atheist was **Madalyn Murray O'Hair,** the twentieth-century

---

[19]Paul Kurtz, ed., "A Secular Humanist Declaration," *Free Inquiry,* 1, no. 1 (Winter 1980), pp. 9 and 18. Kurtz drafted the Declaration, which was signed initially by 58 people, the majority of whom were from the United States.

atheist whose name became for a time nearly synonymous with atheism itself. She founded **American Atheists, Incorporated**. The following list of principles comes from that organization. Although it begins with an emphatic denial of the existence of any deity, its basic tone is a positive consideration of human responsibility in light of that denial.

1. There is no heavenly father. Man must protect the orphans and foundlings, or they will not be protected.
2. There is no god to answer prayer. Man must hear and help man.
3. There is no hell. We have no vindictive god or devil to fear or imitate.
4. There is no atonement or salvation by faith. We must face the consequences of our acts.
5. There is no beneficent or malevolent intent in nature. Life is a struggle against preventable and unpreventable evils. The cooperation of man is the only hope of the world.
6. There is no chance after death to "do our bit." We must do it now or never.
7. There is no divine guardian of truth, goodness, beauty and liberty. These are attributes of man. Man must defend them or they will perish from the earth.[20]

Although most atheists do not try to persuade other people to join them in their denial of God, many do encourage this type of positive, humanistically based ethic alongside their denial of the God of the believers. Although they do not share the belief in God that most Americans have, they do share many of the same moral commitments.

These are some of the popular alternatives or supplements to participation in an organized community of faith. Woven into the tapestry of American religious life along with organized religion and the consensus alternatives, they help to make it a rich blend of colors and textures unrivaled anywhere else in the world.

UNITARIAN UNIVERSALISM

Unitarian Universalism is an organizational embodiment of the very liberal religious tradition in the United States. The present **Unitarian Universalist Association** is the result of a merger between the Universalists and the Unitarians. We will first consider the two separately and then look at the Unitarian Universalist Association today.

The Universalists

Simply put, **universalism** is the belief that all persons will eventually be saved by God; in other words, salvation is universal, not limited to an elect number. This belief is suggested by certain Biblical passages. For example, Acts 3:21 speaks of a

---

[20]J. Gordon Melton, ed., *The Encyclopedia of American Religions: Religious Creeds* (Detroit: Gale Research Company, 1988), p. 636. The gender-exclusive language is in the original.

time of restoration or restitution of all things. John 1:29 refers to Jesus as the Lamb of God who takes away the sins of the [whole] world, and Romans 5:18 speaks of the righteousness of Jesus being imparted to all people. In Revelation 21:5 God is said to say, "I make all things new." Clearly, traditional Christian teaching has not taken these and other similar passages in this light, but this interpretation was seized upon by those who could not reconcile the concept of a God of love with the idea that such a God would condemn anyone to everlasting punishment. Nonetheless, universalism usually has been regarded as a heresy (unacceptable belief) throughout Christian history.

By the time of the American colonies, universalism was already present on the American religious scene and would remain there. English-born John Murray (1741–1815) is sometimes considered the father of American Universalism. In 1770, he preached what may well have been the first Universalist sermon in America, in New England. The first covenant for a Universalist church was drawn up in Murray's church in Gloucester, Massachusetts, in 1779, and in 1780 he met with a group in Philadelphia to help draft a Universalist declaration of faith.

Elhanan Winchester (1751–1797) was another early leader, an intellectual and writer whose writing ability helped to spread the Universalist message and give it credibility. Both Murray and Winchester remained within the framework of trinitarian Christianity.

Hosea Ballou (1771–1852) was not a trinitarian, however, but a unitarian, who believed that God was one instead of three persons. Ballou's universalism was blended with his unitarianism in ways that prefigured the eventual merger of the two groups. Ballou's *Treatise on the Atonement* was the first American attempt to develop a coherent theology along Universalist lines. He became the pastor of the Second Universalist Church in Boston and held that post for over thirty years, becoming the chief spokesperson for Universalism in the new world. He also founded the *Universalist Magazine* and the *Universalist Expositor*, both of which helped to spread the universalist theology. During part of his pastorate in Boston, he worked closely with William Ellery Channing, who would become known as the father of American Unitarianism.

The denomination spread slowly in the nineteenth and twentieth centuries. It was especially successful in the rural and frontier areas, while the Unitarians were more concentrated in urban areas. By the mid-1900s, Universalism had become known as a liberalized and universalized form of Christianity, which it remained until its union with Unitarianism.

The Unitarians

While the universalists were teaching universal salvation as a clearer expression of the will of an all-loving God, the Unitarians reacted to other elements in traditional Christian teaching. First among these was the doctrine that God is a trinity, formalized at Nicaea in 325 C.E. This doctrine, you will recall from the discussion of basic Christian beliefs, holds that God is three distinct persons with but one substance. The **Unitarians** taught the oneness of God, against the trinitarians. Although their name derives from this one teaching, there were other Christian doctrines to which they objected. Among these were the infallibility of the Bible, human depravity and the inheritance of original sin, and the doctrine that some will be damned eternally. This last point aligned them with the Universalists. The Unitarians also encouraged the use of reason as a way of determining religious truth, a theme that we saw in our discussion of humanism and one that remains a hallmark of modern-day Unitarianism.

The first church in the United States that took an explicitly Unitarian view of God did so in the late 1700s. In 1785, the Episcopal King's Chapel in Boston appointed a young minister with Unitarian views, James Freeman. Freeman led his congregation in changing the Anglican Prayer Book to eliminate all references to the Trinity. The Episcopal Church refused to recognize the church as Episcopalian, and, in 1787, Freeman became the first American-ordained Unitarian minister. What had been the first Episcopal Church in Boston became the first Unitarian Church.

William Ellery Channing (1780–1842) is often said to be father of American Unitarianism. American religious historian Sydney Ahlstrom compares Channing's role in the Unitarian reformation in America to that of Martin Luther in the German reformation.[21] In 1819, Channing preached his famous sermon, "Unitarian Christianity," in which he defined the new movement. Channing's Unitarianism remained firmly Christian. In his interpretation, God the Father sent the Son and gives the Holy Spirit to those who seek it. These three are not to be considered three persons in one God, however. Six years later, Channing founded the American Unitarian Association. **Transcendentalism** played a large role in the early Unitarian movement. An American adaptation of English romanticism and German idealism, transcendentalism sought to refine Unitarianism and bring it into conformity with what it believed was the common substance of all the world's religions. Ralph Waldo Emerson (1803–1882) was the best-known leader of the Transcendentalist movement. Emerson preferred to be called a theist rather than a Christian, because the term was more general.

Harvard Divinity School and College (later, Harvard University) became the intellectual stronghold of Unitarianism. Most faculty and students were consciously Unitarian in their outlook, and, especially in the decade between 1811 and 1820, Harvard became the leading Unitarian training center in the United States. Unitarianism remained strongest in New England and in the more urban areas of the growing nation. In rural areas and along the frontier, where Universalism was stronger, Unitarianism was looked upon as an elitist religion. It was that aspect of Unitarianism that led someone to remark that Unitarians believed in "the fatherhood of God, the brotherhood of man and the neighborhood of Boston."

---

[21]Sydney E. Ahlstrom, *A Religious History of the American People* (New Haven, CT: Yale University Press, 1973), p. 398.

Unitarianism gradually transformed itself from the distinctly Christian Unitarianism of Channing's sermon into an ethically oriented, pragmatic, humanistic, and sometimes theistic, religion. Along the way, and indicative of the changes that were taking place, American Unitarians played a dominant role in organizing and supporting the Parliament of Religions in Chicago in 1893. It was this transformed Unitarianism that carried over into the present-day Unitarian Universalist Association.

The Unitarian Universalist Association

As we have seen, the Universalists and the Unitarians shared both a dissatisfaction with the prevailing religious orthodoxies of their times and a substantial body of common beliefs and religious sensibilities. Nonetheless, despite Hosea Ballou's repeated calls for unity, there was almost no interest in cooperation on the part of either group in the early years. They came from different social backgrounds, and, while many of their quarrels with traditional Christianity were similar, they arrived at their positions by different routes. The Universalists began with the conflict between the doctrine of God's love and the idea of eternal damnation. This gave their protest a different emotional quality than that of the more rational and intellectual Unitarian objection to what they saw as the illogic of the trinitarian viewpoint.

However, as both groups changed, in many ways moving even closer together, interest in cooperative efforts grew, spurred by the fact that neither group was large. Their small size meant that they needed each other. Finally, in 1947, a commission was set up to determine what kind of cooperation was actually possible. By 1951, this commission had drawn up a plan, which was accepted by both its constituencies, for cooperative work in several key areas such as religious education, public relations, and publications. They also recommended moving gradually toward a full merger. The merger was completed in the spring of 1961, bringing into being the Unitarian Universalist Association, the national organization for the church today.

Unitarian Universalism Today

Many of us, when we encounter a community of faith with which we are unfamiliar, want to know, "What, exactly, do you believe?" Unitarian Universalism has no specific creed. There is no official statement of beliefs to which members must give assent. There is no confession of faith that is repeated regularly in Sunday services. Rather than having a set of firm beliefs worked out and handed to people, the Unitarian Universalists support a set of very broad operating principles that serve as guidelines for individual and community decision making.

Individual freedom of religious belief is perhaps the most fundamental of all these guidelines. All people, following the guidance of their own best understanding and informed by the community of faith as a whole, are responsible for working out their own beliefs. There is no outside authority. Each person lives "by a thought-out covenant with himself [or herself] and with life as a whole," and people understand that their "beliefs may change as insights deepen and experiences broaden."[22] Unitarian Universalists believe that people are capable of doing this without divine revelation. This understanding of how religious beliefs come about leads Unitarian Universalists to a large measure of tolerance for differences within their ranks, as well as appreciation for religious views other than Unitarian Universalism. The emphasis, in other words, is not on having a correct set of beliefs handed down from church authorities or from a sacred book, but on responsibly working out one's own beliefs, subject to change as one's understanding grows.

Unitarian Universalists believe that religious beliefs should change as people change throughout the course of their lives, rather than saying that there are beliefs that should be clung to "through thick and thin." The process of arriving at religious beliefs is of central importance. For most, if not all, ethical action in the world, with and on behalf of other people, is of greater importance than belief.

The set of principles currently in use was approved by the member congregations in 1985. Many of these are humanist principles with which we are now familiar, such as the dignity and worth of every person, the importance of justice and compassion, freedom in the search for truth and meaning, the use of the democratic process in decision making at all levels, the goal of world community, and the affirmation of the interconnectedness of all life. Other principles highlight a variety of resources from which the church draws inspiration and guidance. A sense of wonder at the natural world and the people who inhabit it is the first such resource. The words and deeds of prophets, which, in a very wide sense of the term, includes all those people who have challenged injustice wherever they found it, are also important. The wisdom of all the world's religions is affirmed, with specific mention given to "Jewish and Christian teachings which call us to respond to God's love by loving our neighbors as ourselves." This item aroused considerable controversy among the congregations as they discussed the new statement. While some welcomed it, others believed strongly that setting Judaism and Christianity apart in this way implied an unacceptable ranking of them above the other world religions. Finally, the importance of humanist teachings is cited.

Unitarian Universalists summarize their beliefs on their Web site as follows:

> Unitarian Universalism is a liberal religion born of the Jewish and Christian traditions. We keep our minds open to the religious questions people have struggled with in all times and places.

> We believe that personal experience, conscience and reason should be the final authorities in religion. In the end religious authority lies not in a book or person

---

[22]Jack Mendelsohn, *Meet the Unitarian Universalists* (Boston: Unitarian Universalist Association, 1979), p. 6.

or institution, but in ourselves. We put religious insights to the test of our hearts and minds.

We uphold the free search for truth. We will not be bound by a statement of belief. We do not ask anyone to subscribe to a creed. We say ours is a noncreedal religion. Ours is a free faith.

We believe that religious wisdom is everchanging. Human understanding of life and death, the world and its mysteries, is never final. Revelation is continuous. We celebrate unfolding truths known to teachers, prophets and sages throughout the ages.

We affirm the worth of all women and men. We believe people should be encouraged to think for themselves. We know people differ in their opinions and lifestyles and believe these differences generally should be honored.

We seek to act as a moral force in the world, believing that ethical living is the supreme witness of religion. The here and now and the effects our actions will have on future generations deeply concern us. We know that our relationships with one another, with other peoples, races and nations, should be governed by justice, equity and compassion.[23]

These principles of belief lead most Unitarian Universalists to a lifestyle that includes engagement in social action. One notable characteristic of the members of this church is that they are, compared with their relatively small numbers in most areas, vastly overrepresented in those organizations that are identified with liberal social concerns. Organizations that work to make life better for all citizens can usually count on support from Unitarian Universalists. Groups that work on increasing civil liberties also attract Unitarian Universalists' interest. For most, political involvement, in the widest sense of that term, is a central way of working out their religious commitments in day-to-day life.

The freedom to work out one's own religious beliefs without pressure from any external authorities attracts the highly educated into Unitarian Universalism. They are the most highly educated, on the average, of any American church. This also means that this church includes many professional people among its members, both men and women. The freedom of religious belief that characterizes Unitarian Universalist churches also draws couples of mixed religious faith, because they can attend services at the same place without either of them compromising their own faith. People may also become part of a Unitarian Universalist congregation if they live too far from their own community of faith to participate in its activities.

Unitarian Universalists are also among the most culture-affirming people. They raise hard questions about the culture in which they live, especially when

[23]Unitarian Universalist Association Web site (http://www.uua.org/).

that culture seems less humane than it might be. Nonetheless, Unitarian Universalists believe in full participation in the life of the society of which they are a part. Restrictions on individual decision making about things like drinking alcohol, dress, and sexual arrangements between consenting adults are simply not a part of the Unitarian Universalist philosophy.

Unitarian Universalist congregations provide corporate ritual activity, but describing a "typical" service is difficult. The freedom that we have noted in belief translates into freedom in deciding what format religious meetings will take. Regular services usually occur on Sunday morning (Figure 6-1). It is not unheard of, however, for a church to hold services at some other time that suits the needs of the congregation better. In some churches, the service may be hard to distinguish from any other very liberal Protestant service. In others, greater experimentation and innovation are the rule. There is a *hymnal*, or hymn book, that includes traditional hymns that are modified to eliminate gender-exclusive language. Other hymns specifically reflect the church's own teachings. Readings in a typical service might be taken from many sources. The Jewish and Christian scriptures, the sacred writings of other world religions, contemporary poetry, and novels are only a few illustrations. It is not unusual to find a reading from the Christian New Testament and a reading from a John Updike novel side by side. The minister or a guest speaker gives a sermon, talk, meditation, or commentary (some churches do not use the more distinctly religious word *sermon*). It may concern a matter of ethical importance, social involvement, self-development, or human relationships, to name but a few examples. An offering is usually received. A person expecting prayers might be surprised; Unitarian Universalist church services sometimes do not include them.

Figure 6-1   Unitarian Universalist services attract people seeking freedom of religious thought. *(Joe Traver/Liaison Agency, Inc.)*

I have avoided using the word *worship* to describe the church services. Worship carries with it the idea that there is a god or supreme being that is being worshiped, an idea upon which not all Unitarian Universalists agree. There are no sacraments. Children are welcomed into the congregation and dedicated, at which time their parents and the congregation affirm their commitment to the child and celebrate the new life that has come into being. Other ceremonies such as marriages and funerals echo the liberal and humanistic perspective that is so much a part of the life of these communities of faith. Nearly all services include time for fellowship and refreshments before or after.

Fellowship is important for the members of Unitarian Universalist congregations. One Unitarian Universalist church in the Midwest, where midweek worship services are the order of the day for the Christian majority, sponsors a weekly Wednesday Revival Hour at which those who want to do so can get together for discussion and fellowship. The group meets at various local restaurants or cocktail lounges or may have a carry-in dinner at someone's home. Larger churches support a full range of activities from which members and friends can choose. Discussion, education, and debate characterize the life of these communities of faith. Education for adults, young people, and children is built into the Sunday morning activities, and other activities may occur during the week.

Organizationally, each local church is fully autonomous. The Unitarian Universalist Association, with headquarters in Boston, takes care of many operational details and serves as the central offices for the group. Its statements have only an advisory function where local congregations are concerned. There is a national conference annually. Beacon Press is the church's publishing house. The Association also supports a unique outreach program. Called the **Church of the Larger Fellowship**, this program was designed especially for religious liberals who live too far from a Unitarian Universalist church to attend. It makes available a news bulletin that contains sermons and inspirational writings, as well as reports on activities. A *Handbook of Services* for the major celebrations of life is provided for each member. A minister is available by mail or telephone. A religious education director provides parents with assistance in developing a religious education program for their children. There is also a lending library.

On some college campuses, there are organizations for Unitarian Universalist and other religiously liberal students, sponsored by a local Unitarian Universalist congregation.

Humanism and liberal religion provide meaningful alternatives to traditional religion for significant numbers of Americans. They have influenced more traditional religion in the direction of increased social concern. Humanism and humanitarianism have been and continue to be very closely linked in the United States, and the presence of humanism has encouraged the society to be more humanitarian. Atheists and agnostics, too, have contributed to the American cultural landscape. Like their sparring partners, the fundamentalists, humanists and freethinkers deserve a place in the community of neighbors, not strangers.

QUESTIONS AND ACTIVITIES FOR REVIEW, DISCUSSION, AND WRITING

1. Take a current ethical or moral problem of which you are aware. Think it through (1) beginning with the assumptions of Judaism or Christianity and (2) again from a humanistic viewpoint. What differences in the process and in the conclusions do you notice? You might want to organize this as a debate with a friend, each of you taking one point of view.
2. Humanism opposes all forms of authoritarianism. Do you agree, or do you feel that authoritarianism has a place in certain situations? Is it important to distinguish between authority and authoritarianism? For what reasons and in what circumstances might one person or group exercise authority over others?
3. In your opinion, is humanism a religion? Why or why not?
4. Which of the reasons given for atheism is most persuasive to you? Least convincing? Why?
5. Visit a Unitarian Universalist Church or Fellowship if there is one in your community or close by. In what ways is the Sunday service similar to others with which you may be familiar? How is it different? Many members of these churches became Unitarian Universalists after having been part of other religious groups. If possible, make arrangements to speak with the minister about how some of the people in the congregation came to their present religious outlook.
6. What might be the advantages and disadvantages of being a part of a community of faith that expects that religious beliefs will change throughout people's lives, rather than offering a set of beliefs that are expected to remain constant?
7. Visit the Web sites of two of the organizations listed under "Relevant World Wide Web Sites" below in order to learn something about each organization that goes beyond what is in this chapter.

FOR FURTHER READING

ALLEN, NORM R., JR., *African-American Humanism: An Anthology*. Buffalo, NY: Prometheus Books, 1991. Humanism has played a strong role in the development of the African American intellectual tradition. Allen's book has biographies of noted black humanists, essays, and interviews and is a thorough documentation of an aspect of humanism of which few are aware.

GAYLOR, ANNIE LAURIE, ed., *Women without Superstition: The Collected Writings of Women Free-thinkers of the Nineteenth and Twentieth Centuries*. Madison, WI: Freedom from Religion Foundation, 1997. Gaylor includes fifty mainly United States nonliterary figures whose writings are arranged chronologically by their year of birth.

HAUGHT, JAMES A, *2000 Years of Disbelief: Famous People with the Courage to Doubt*. Buffalo, NY: Prometheus Books, 1996. Major thinkers, scientists, scholars, reformers, politicians, and other world-changers who have also been freethinkers are discussed.

KNIGHT, MARGARET, ed., *Humanist Anthology: From Confucius to Attenborough*, rev. by James Herrick. Buffalo, NY: Prometheus Books, 1995. This book presents the full range of humanist thought, from the ancient world to the twentieth century.

MORAIN, LLOYD, and MARY MORAIN, *Humanism as the Next Step*. Amherst, NY: Humanist Press, 1998. This is a very basic introduction for the general reader.

WINE, SHERWIN T., *Judaism beyond God*. Hoboken, NJ: KTAV Publishing House, 1995. This is a good introduction to the development and philosophy of this movement.

WOLFE, GREGORY, ed., *The New Religious Humanists*. New York: The Free Press, 1997. This wide-ranging collection of essays provides an end-of-the-millennium portrait of this strand of humanist and religious thought.

RELEVANT WORLD WIDE WEB SITES

Unitarian Universalist Association (http://www.uua.org).

American Humanist Association (http://www.infidels.org/org/aha/).

Campus Freethought Alliance (http://www.secularhumanism.org/cfa/).

Friends of Religious Humanism (http://humanist.net/frh/).

American Ethical Union (http://www.aeu.org).

Society for Humanistic Judaism (http://www.shj.org/).

African Americans for Humanism (http://www.secularhumanism.org/aah/).

American Atheists (http://www.atheists.org).

The Secular Web (http://www.infidels.org).

Freedom from Religion Foundation (http://www.infidels.org/org/ffrf/).

7

Christianities That Began in the United States

Days later, I found out that Aaron died. . . . We were all part of a community of devout Christian Scientists, a faith that shuns doctors and medicine and relies on prayer alone to cure the sick. . . . I thought of other deaths and suffering I'd witnessed over the years in the name of Christian Science. Most painful of all, I thought of the time seven years before when I'd almost let my own daughter die.[1]

I would like to thank God for a healing that occurred just after my husband and I got engaged. . . . And immediately all of the pain vanished—my understanding of the unreality of the accident was so powerful that it wiped out all illusion of pain. . . . I witnessed a complete and permanent healing of the skin, and there was no trace of scarring. I was in rehearsals for a musical two weeks later, dancing and singing without any hindrance. This healing has been an inspiration to me ever since.[2]

The first of the accounts above is by an ex–Christian Scientist, the other by a college student who is a follower of that faith. They typify the controversy that has characterized people's opinions of Christian Science, one of the American-born forms of Christianity to be discussed in this chapter.

The religious groups that are the spiritual home of the majority of America's population came to the United States from Europe. By contrast, the four religious groups discussed in this chapter began in the United States, and the nature of each bears the marks of that beginning. The four communities of faith described below include somewhat less than 5 percent of Christians in the United States.

---

[1]Suzanne Shepard, as told to Marti Attoun, "Suffer the Little Children," *Redbook*, October, 1994, p. 66.
[2]Heidi Dittmar-Biever, in "Reports of Healing," *The Christian Science Journal*, August, 1994, pp. 54–55.

The communities of faith to which you were introduced in the first part of this book fit in with the culture of which they are a part, so much so that they have tended to disappear into that culture. More important, their way of seeing the world has come to be regarded as the normal view in the culture. It is necessary to distinguish **majority view** from **normal view**, even though the two are often believed to coincide. The *majority view* is simply the opinions held by the majority of those in a given population. It takes on a different status when it comes to be thought of as the *normal*, correct, proper, or appropriate view. Then, it is the only one given full respect in a society. When this happens, it becomes a handicap for those whose views do not happen to be those of the majority. The indigenous American Christianities have much in common with traditional Christianity. In this, they are aligned with the majority culture. However, they interpret the tradition differently than do most Christians. The ways in which indigenous Christianities depart from more traditional teachings and practices usually result from the views of the founder of each group. They are the result of Christianity being passed through the lens of the unique vision of one person or a small group of people. It is changed in the process, although it retains clear and obvious links with more traditional groups. In the community of neighbors, these are neighbors whose lives are centered in a faith that is different yet similar, clearly other and yet alike. The uniqueness of their insights and practices adds to the richness of religion in the United States. All of them, without exception, have been persecuted and looked down upon as a result of their nonconformity. Sometimes, they still are. They are living proof that the community of neighbors and not strangers has not been fully realized among us, because they are still looked upon as outsiders.

Have young Latter-day Saint (Mormon) missionaries ever come by your home asking to speak with you about their church? Have you perhaps seen them on your college campus? Have you seen a building in your community that is identified as a Kingdom Hall? It is the gathering place of Jehovah's Witnesses. Are you aware that Seventh-day Adventists worship on Saturday, or that followers of Christian Science do not rely on doctors and hospitals for medical care? All these people are representatives of the religions that you will learn about in this chapter. Ask yourself how you feel about people whose religion makes them stand out from the rest of the culture. Are you interested in why they behave the way they do?

These communities of faith contrast with consensus religion in several respects. Their members often have a sense of separation from the world. Although they may work very hard at making converts, their expectations for their members are high. The Mormons and the Jehovah's Witnesses are good examples of this. Members must be willing to accept more stringent rules and standards than those that apply outside the group. It is in this sense that they are somewhat exclusive. Their standards lead to a sense of separateness from the rest of the world, and members usually believe that they are following the one true way in religion while the rest of the world goes astray.

In addition to the Bible, other writings are often considered authoritative. They may be thought of as part of a group's scriptures or as interpretations of the Bible. These additional writings, usually those of the founder, may be regarded as new revelations or as interpretations inspired by God.

The material contained in the founder's writings gives rise to beliefs or practices—and usually both—that are distinctively different than those of more traditional Christianity. New revelations or new interpretations give rise to these new beliefs, rituals, and lifestyles and at the same time provide support for them.

A corollary of the sense of being set apart from the larger society is that these groups tend to be very close knit. Separation from those outside is complemented by closeness and community among those on the inside. They socialize together much more than they do with outsiders, and members of the group can count on strong support from other members in time of need. They often provide their members with a complete lifestyle and a full round of activities, not necessarily all of a religious nature. This reinforces the closeness of the community and limits contacts with outsiders.

Their lifestyles are frequently distinctive, making their separation from the culture somewhat obvious. There may be restrictions on dancing, gambling, and the use of alcohol and tobacco. There may be food regulations, and sometimes there are dress codes, especially for female members.

Authority in these religions is usually strictly enforced from the top down, with little room for innovation at the local or individual level. It would, however, be incorrect to conclude that members of these religious groups are blindly following their leader. For most, the acceptance of a strong religious authority and submission to that authority is in itself an important belief, one that has been consented to and taken as one's own.

LATTER-DAY SAINTS

When most of us think of the Mormons, we probably think of neatly dressed, clean-cut young men, most likely on bicycles or walking, going from house to house talking about their faith with all who will listen and hoping to make converts. Some may think of well-known U.S. citizens who are Mormon. Examples include the Osmonds; Ezra Taft Benson, former Secretary of Agriculture; and George Romney, former Governor of Michigan. Others might well think of the world-famous Mormon Tabernacle Choir or Brigham Young University. Mormons have grown from a group whose numbers could be counted on the fingers of one's two hands to one of the larger and better-known communities of faith in this country. Yet many people still feel that the Mormons are not a part of mainstream America. In some ways, they *are* different and choose to stand outside the mainstream. In other ways, such as their involvement in public life, they have moved into the center. In this section, some of the misconceptions that still surround this religious group will be dispelled. At the same time, some of the differences between their understanding of Christianity and that of their neighbors will be described. Some important ways in which their lives are different because of their faith will also be discussed.

The word **Mormon** itself is not the official name of the group. It is a nickname for members of the **Church of Jesus Christ of Latter-day Saints**. Mormon is believed by the church to have been a prophet in the area that would become the United States. In the concluding years of the fourth century C.E., Mormon compiled a book containing the records of the people of Lehi, a Hebrew who had led a colony of people from Jerusalem to America in about 600 B.C.E. Mormon's son Moroni added some information of his own, including a brief account of the people called Jaredites who had come to North America at the time that the Tower of Babel was built. This record is preserved as the ***Book of Mormon***.

The official name, Church of Jesus Christ of Latter-day Saints, tells us how this community of faith understands itself. They consider themselves to be Christians, members of the one true church that follows all the teachings of Jesus Christ. Although some more traditional Christian groups do not consider the Mormons to be fellow Christians, there is no doubt about their self-identification as Christians. They are neither Protestant nor Catholic nor Orthodox, however. The word **saints** is used in the Christian New Testament to mean "church members." "Latter-day" distinguishes this church from the church in the former days, which, according to Mormon teaching, fell away from the truth of Jesus Christ shortly after it was founded. About 2 percent of the population of the United States is Mormon.

The Latter-day Saints began in the first half of the nineteenth century in an area of New York State that scholars call the burned-over district. It has been given this colorful name because a large number of revivals swept the area with great fires of religious enthusiasm. **Joseph Smith** (1805–1844), who would become the group's founder, grew up in this climate of religious tumult. Confused, he earnestly tried to discover which of the many religious groups in the area was correct, so that he might join it. One day in his reading of the Bible, he read, "If any of you lacks wisdom, let him ask God, who gives to all men generously and without reproaching, and it will be given to him" (James 1:5, Revised Standard Version). Taking these instructions to heart, the young man went and knelt in an isolated grove of trees to seek God's guidance. God spoke to Joseph Smith, according to Mormon belief, telling him that none of the available religious groups was the true church, and that all had fallen away from the truth. Smith was to join none of them. Then, in 1823, the angelic messenger Moroni appeared to him and told him that he would be God's chosen servant to restore the church to the fullness of the Gospel. This restoration of the true church is an important Mormon belief.

Now, it is important for each one of us to know that the gospel of Jesus Christ has been restored to the earth through the Prophet Joseph Smith. Priesthood authority is once again upon the earth so that sacred ordinances may be performed for the eternal blessing of all those who will accept the blessings that the fulness of the gospel of Jesus Christ has to offer. Significant eternal truths have been restored, and they are the very foundation of our faith.[3]

Moroni appeared to Joseph Smith again in 1827 and revealed to him the location of golden plates upon which was written what would eventually become the *Book of Mormon*. Because they were written in an unknown script, Smith was also provided with something to assist in the translation (identified as the Urim and Thummim mentioned in Exodus 28:30). The *Book of Mormon* was subsequently published in 1830. According to Mormon history, the golden plates were taken up into heaven after Smith had completed the translation. The Latter-day Saints believe that their church is founded, not upon the human words and work of Joseph Smith, but on the direct revelation of God, as surely as the earlier Christian Church had been founded upon God's revelation in Jesus Christ.

The church was established in the spring of 1830, shortly after the publication of the *Book of Mormon*. It began with only five people. They were persecuted almost immediately. Persecution led to the long westward trek that would eventually take them to Salt Lake City. They first moved from New York to Kirtland, Ohio, and then to a place near Independence, Missouri. From there, their travels took them to Nauvoo, Illinois. Trouble again broke out, and several of their number were jailed at Carthage, Illinois. Among those imprisoned were Joseph Smith and his brother Hyrum, both of whom were murdered by a local mob while in jail. Some of Smith's followers, led by Brigham Young, then began the trek to what would become Salt Lake City, in the Utah Territory. Salt Lake City became the world headquarters for the Church of Jesus Christ of Latter-day Saints in 1847. Some, including Smith's widow and young son, disputed Young's leadership and stayed in Illinois, forming the nucleus of what would become the second-largest Mormon group, the **Reorganized Church of Jesus Christ of Latter Day Saints**.[4] The headquarters of this group is in Independence, Missouri.

One of the best-known and least-understood chapters of Latter-day Saints history is their practice of polygamy. Actually, it was polygyny, in which a man is permitted to have more than one wife. Some of the church's leaders believed that they had received a revelation from God in which God commanded this practice, which they began in 1843. It became public knowledge in 1852. It was met with public outrage, and the U.S. government moved quickly to undercut the power of the church in Utah and made the abandonment of multiple marriage a condition of statehood. In 1890, Mormon leaders announced that the practice was no longer approved. At any given time, probably less than 20 percent of the Church's leaders were actually involved in plural marriage. The only remaining

[3]Elder M. Russell Ballard, "Building Bridges of Understanding," (February 17, 1998), Latter-day Saints Web site (http://www.lds.org/).
[4]The Latter-day Saints use a hyphen and lower-case *d* in the spelling of their name. The Reorganized Church does not hyphenate and uses an upper-case *D*. When discussing characteristics that pertain to both groups, I will use the *Latter-day Saints* spelling.

polygynists are isolated in very small groups that are not recognized by the church. The era of plural marriage ended almost as quickly as it had begun.

Beliefs

Modern-day Mormons have beliefs that are similar to those of other Christians yet are in many ways distinctive. **The *Book of Mormon* is considered to be scripture, alongside the Bible**. In addition, new revelations were received at various times for specific purposes, and these were collected as the *Doctrine and Covenants*. The original edition was published in 1833, with subsequent editions containing additional material. Another book, *The Pearl of Great Price*, also contains revelations believed to have been received by Smith. Based on these writings, there are thirteen Articles of Faith that summarize the Church's beliefs. Some of these are discussed below, and others will be included in the discussion of lifestyle and organization.

Mormons **believe in God the Father, Jesus Christ the Son, and the Holy Spirit**, as do most other Christians. They are, however, **three separate individuals**, distinct from each other while being united in purpose. Further, the Father and the Son have physical bodies, "much like our own." The Holy Ghost is a spirit (Article 1). Thus, their understanding of God as Father, Son, and Spirit differs from the traditional Christian view that the trinity is but one God. Mormons do not hold people accountable for the sin of Adam and Eve, as do some Christians. Being held responsible for a sin in which one had no part is repugnant to Mormon sensibilities. The concept of "**free agency**" is a central aspect of Mormon belief. Human beings have free will and therefore will be punished for their own sins, not those of Adam. People have come to this earth from a pre-earth existence, and the "freedom to choose for ourselves between right and wrong is the most important thing we brought to the earth with us" (Article 2). Jesus' sacrificial death makes salvation available to all humankind. **Salvation comes by way of faith and works**. It may be lost from "lack of effort on our part to live the gospel" (Article 3). There are also **degrees of exaltation**. Heaven is divided into various realms or states of being. Mormons teach that the highest of these is available only to those who have followed all the laws and ordinances of the church. Those who attain this exalted status become gods, to whom all other things are subject, even the angels.[5]

A distinctive Latter-day Saints belief is that people exist in the heavenly realm before birth. Being given a human body is a unique opportunity to carry out the things necessary to return to God and higher degrees of exaltation:

> All human beings—male and female—are created in the image of God. Each is a beloved spirit son or daughter of heavenly parents, and, as such, each has a divine nature and destiny. Gender is an essential characteristic of individual premortal, mortal, and eternal identity and purpose.

[5] *The Doctrine and Covenants of the Church of Jesus Christ of Latter-day Saints* (Salt Lake City, UT: Church of Jesus Christ of Latter-day Saints, 1982), 132:20.

In the premortal realm, spirit sons and daughters knew and worshiped God as their Eternal Father and accepted His plan by which His children could obtain a physical body and gain earthly experience to progress toward perfection and ultimately realize his or her divine destiny as an heir of eternal life. The divine plan of happiness enables family relationships to be perpetuated beyond the grave. Sacred ordinances and covenants available in holy temples make it possible for individuals to return to the presence of God and for families to be united eternally.[6]

A cornerstone of Mormon belief is that God's will is revealed not only in the Bible, but to Joseph Smith, and, following Smith, to the leaders of the church throughout all the years of its existence. God will yet reveal many significant things (Article 9). The concept of **continuous revelation** allows the church's leadership to be flexible in responding to issues and questions that are not dealt with directly in the Bible or the other Mormon scriptures. At the same time, the authority of divine revelation is maintained.

Mormons also believe in the laying on of hands for the receiving of the Holy Spirit and in the other spiritual gifts such as speaking in tongues, prophecy, visions, healing, and the interpretation of tongues (Article 7).

This is a distinctively American church. The Book of Mormon gives America a scriptural past. Many religious groups in this country have believed fervently that America has a special role to play in God's plans for the world, but none has expressed that belief as concretely as do the Latter-day Saints. They look forward to a literal regathering of Israel, restoration of the Ten Lost Tribes, and the building of the New Jerusalem, to which they refer as Zion, on the North American continent (Article 10). Mormons believe in freedom of worship as a privilege for themselves and all other people (Article 11) and in obedience to the laws of the land and its leaders. People should protest against unjust laws but by using only "legal and proper" means (Article 12).

Lifestyle

If you are acquainted with many Latter-day Saints, you probably know them as people with an upbeat and healthful lifestyle. They participate wholeheartedly in the programs of their church. Honesty and truthfulness, chastity, benevolence, and doing good to all are affirmed (Article 13). The body is given by God and is sacred, and taking good care of it is a religious act. This is the reason behind the **Word of Wisdom**, a health code that Mormons teach was revealed to Smith in 1833. The code forbids smoking tobacco, drinking alcohol, drinking beverages with caffeine in them (such as coffee, tea, and many soft drinks), and taking drugs other than those prescribed by a physician for medical reasons. Meat is to be used sparingly, with the emphasis in the diet on grains, fruits, and vegetables. Physical exercise is encouraged, as is good grooming. They teach that following the Word of Wisdom will lead to great wisdom and knowledge, as well as to

[6]Latter-day Saints President Gordon B. Hinckley, "The Family: A Proclamation to the World," (September 23, 1995), Latter-day Saints Web site (http://www.lds.org/).

good health that includes moral, emotional, and spiritual dimensions along with the physical aspects of health.[7]

As many of you probably know, the **family is absolutely central in Latter-day Saints' thought and practice**. It is the basic unit of church and society and is held to be sacred. Local churches provide many family-oriented activities throughout the week, of both a religious and a nonreligious nature. In addition, families have "family home evening" once a week, using materials provided by their church. This is a time for families to be together for study and for worship and discussion of religious matters. They also simply enjoy being together and benefit from the interaction of parents and children. Church members called home teachers visit members' homes frequently to bring messages of hope and goodwill. They are the representatives of the church leaders in helping the family to solve problems.

Marriage is valued very highly by the Latter-day Saints. Everyone is enjoined to marry, and requiring anyone to remain celibate is specifically forbidden.[8] Adultery is grounds for dismissal from the Church, and premarital sex calls for severe repentance. Children are valued, and, however great a man's achievements, his highest goal and achievement is fathering children.[9] The husband and father presides over the family. As a male member of the church, he holds a position within the priesthood. The family unit functions as a small church in and of itself. Traditional roles for men, women, and children are encouraged. The husband is the provider and leader for his family. His wife is the primary caregiver in the home and is the emotional heart of the family. Parents expect children to contribute as much as they possibly can by helping with chores and participating in family home evening programs. Through a special sealing ceremony that takes place in temples, husbands and wives, along with their children, may be joined for eternity.

The Mormon emphasis on the family involves the **extended family through many generations**, as well as the nuclear family of those presently living. The Church sponsors one of the largest genealogical libraries in the world and assists millions of people with research into their family backgrounds. Faithful Mormons engage in Temple work on behalf of ancestors who died without being able to follow the ordinances for themselves. This is believed to be a great benefit to those who have died and confers a blessing on the living as well.

Latter-day Saints emphasize **education** for both men and women. Mormon children attend public and private schools but also participate in church educational programs that emphasize religious education. Home-study courses are available for those in isolated areas. A basic goal of the church is that every member will be able to read, write, do basic arithmetic, and study the scriptures

---

[7] *Doctrine and Covenants*, 89:19–20.

[8] *Doctrine and Covenants*, 49:15.

[9] James E. Talmadge, *A Study of the Articles of Faith* (Salt Lake City, UT: Church of Jesus Christ of Latter-day Saints, 1982), p. 443.

and other uplifting books.[10] The Church sponsors several institutions of higher education, the best known of which is **Brigham Young University** (BYU) in Provo, Utah. A publicity brochure for BYU describes the university this way:

> The uniqueness of Brigham Young University lies in its special role—education for eternity—which it must carry in addition to the usual tasks of a university. This means concern—curricular and behavioral—not only for the "whole man" but for the "eternal man." Where all universities seek to preserve the heritage of knowledge that history has washed to their feet, this faculty has a double heritage—the preserving of knowledge of men and the revealed truths sent from heaven.[11]

In addition to studying a full range of coursework, students are trained to become the type of people the Mormon tradition expects them to be. It may be of interest to many of you, because you are taking a religious studies class, to know that BYU students take at least one religious studies class every semester, ranging from world religions to Mormon theology.

Self-sufficiency is another trait encouraged by the Latter-day Saints. A detailed program of personal and family preparedness for self-sufficiency is spelled out, including education, career development, financial management, and home production and storage of necessities (sewing, gardening, food preservation, and the manufacture of some household items). These preparations will help individual families through hard times. The emphasis on self-sufficiency is balanced by readiness to help others who cannot help themselves. The church maintains storehouses, administered by local bishops, that are used to help those who have exhausted their own resources. The church also sponsors an employment clearinghouse, social services, and other assistance programs that weave together into a comprehensive program of assistance for both members and nonmembers. Mormons who receive assistance through these services are expected to work to help earn what they need and to help others who are in need. "There is," as the *Pressbook* states, "no dole. Instead, independence and freedom from idleness and its attendant evils are encouraged."[12]

As with all religions, Mormons vary widely in their adherence to Mormon beliefs and their practice of the lifestyle that their church advocates. Some take it very seriously, while others pay little if any attention to it. Most come somewhere in between the two extremes.

Ritual

When Mormons gather for worship on Sunday morning in local churches or chapels, they do many of the same things that are done in Protestant Christian services. Hymns are sung, prayers are spoken, a sermon is preached, and individuals

---

[10]*Pressbook* (Salt Lake City, UT: Church of Jesus Christ of Latter-day Saints, n.d.), p. 7.
[11]*B.Y.U.: The Mormon University*, (Provo, UT: Brigham Young University, University Relations, n.d.).
[12]*Pressbook*, p. 10.

may have the opportunity to tell how God has been especially active in their lives during the past week. Concerns of the church family are shared. Men and women, boys and girls participate in their own study classes. In the weekly sacrament meeting, communion is observed, using bread and water, because the Mormons do not use alcohol. Other religious services take place during the week, and other activities at the church abound.

The Latter-day Saints distinguish between these local churches and their activities and temples (Figure 7-1). The **temples** and the rituals that take place in them are the most distinctive feature of Mormon ritual life. The first of these special buildings was built in Kirtland, Ohio, and dedicated in 1836. It was built following a pattern that Mormons believe God revealed to Joseph Smith. It was a temporary structure only, without all the features found in modern-day temples. Temples are reserved for the performance of special ordinances of the church.

Figure 7-1   Salt Lake Temple of the Church of Jesus Christ of Latter-day Saints, Salt Lake City, Utah. Mormon Temples are used only for special Temple ordinances. Because they are regarded as sacred space, they are not open to the public. *Front left*: Tabernacle on Temple Square (egg-shaped building). *Center*: Salt Lake Temple (spired building). *Back center*: LDS Church Office Building (high-rise). (*Photograph copyright The Church of Jesus Christ of Latter-day Saints. Used by permission.*)

Many have been open to the public for tours for a time after they were completed, but after they are dedicated they are considered sacred space, and only worthy Mormons may enter.

Before Latter-day Saints can go to the temple, they must receive a **Temple Recommend** from the bishop. The bishop and the stake president, who is a local officer, conduct interviews to determine worthiness to enter the sacred place and to participate in its ordinances. Among other requirements, people must have "a testimony of the gospel," support the church and follow its programs and teachings, keep the Word of Wisdom, be morally pure, be members in good standing of the church, and be free of legal entanglements. Mormons who are judged worthy and go to the temple change from street clothing to clean, white clothing provided at the temple as a sign and symbol of purity. My descriptions of temple ceremonies are of necessity rather brief and very general. The details are not made available to non-Mormons, and those who participate in the ceremonies promise not to reveal the details of their experience. This reticence to discuss details stems in part from the long history of misunderstanding that has marked the career of the Latter-day Saints. It also reflects the sacredness that Mormons attribute to these special observances.

The first temple ceremony is the **endowment**. This is a prerequisite for any of the other ceremonies. The endowment is said to confer the knowledge necessary for a person to return to God after death. The history of the human race as the Latter-day Saints understand it is retraced, emphasizing the importance of the present time. Covenants or promises are made and obligations conferred, along with their accompanying blessings.

Another very important Temple ceremony is **eternal marriage**. People married according to the laws of the world, even if the wedding is performed in a Mormon church, are bound by the limitation of "until death do us part." Marriages that last a lifetime end with the death of one of the partners. Marriage and family ties can continue into eternity, according to Mormon belief. The relationship of husband and wife, and that of parents and children, can be made permanent by participation in temple ceremonies. Temple marriage is required for entrance into the highest degree of exaltation following death.[13]

Temple baptism is another temple ordinance. Temple baptismal fonts rest on the backs of twelve sculptured oxen that represent the twelve tribes of Israel. Mormons are baptized in fonts in their local churches or chapels in a service very similar to that of other Christian churches. Baptism is by immersion and is restricted to those who are old enough to understand its meaning for themselves. Temple baptism is performed by the living on behalf of the dead. Many people die without hearing the teachings that Mormons believe are necessary for exaltation. Mormons believe that the opportunity to do so can be made available to them in the spirit world by a living member of their family who undergoes temple baptism on their behalf. Only these baptisms on behalf of another are performed in the temple. Part of the significance of tracing one's genealogy as far

[13]*Doctrine and Covenants*, 132:15–19 and 131:2–4.

back as possible is to find those ancestors for whom temple work needs to be performed. Sealing ceremonies that join spouses, parents, and children for eternity can also be performed vicariously. In any case, the performance of a vicarious ceremony provides only the opportunity. The soul in the spirit world must give its voluntary consent. The concept of free agency applies even there.

Organization

There are several distinctive things about the institutional or organizational life of the Latter-day Saints. In many ways, the Church is a theocracy believed to be under the direct rule of God, because Mormons believe that the highest leaders of the Church continually receive revelations from God. No officer, however, serves without a sustaining vote from the people he serves, so that there are also democratic elements. There are no professional clergy, and lay members who serve as officers do so without pay. Now, however, both major branches of the church pay a living allowance to those people in the central administration. The Church has a president, considered to be a prophet of God. Former Secretary of Agriculture Ezra Taft Benson became the Mormon president in 1985. He is advised by two counselors who, along with the president, make up the First Presidency. There is a Quorum of Twelve Apostles that advises the First Presidency. The Church is highly organized along geographic lines, with no congregation being so large as to become impersonal.

Priesthood in the Mormon church simply means the authority to act in the name of God. The priesthood is open to all worthy males, twelve years of age or older. There are two divisions, the Melchizedek (the higher order) and the Aaronic (the lower order). Each is further divided into three subdivisions. Specific responsibilities and privileges come with each designation, and a man moves through the designations in order as he studies and carries out the duties of his present designation. Women are not priests. They have the blessings that Mormons believe are conferred by the priesthood through their husbands. The primary organization for women in the church is the Relief Society. Women are eligible to serve on the governing councils of the Church. Mormons believe that the pattern of organization that they have is the same as that found in the primitive church before it fell away from the true Church of Jesus Christ.

Restricting the priesthood to men is only one of the ways the Latter-day Saints emphasize the importance of traditional roles for women. Although their general support for education means that women are encouraged to continue their education beyond high school, careers are discouraged, and a woman is not expected to work outside the home once she is married. It should be noted, however, that many Mormon women do so, either out of choice or economic necessity. The role of women as wives and mothers is very highly respected. What distresses some Mormon women and angers the more militant among them is that this is the only approved role. Stepping outside it frequently leads to disapproval. Women who do so may be made to feel that they are endangering their eternal life with God. Speaking out publicly on feminist issues has occasionally resulted in dismissal from the church. Mormons have also joined Catholics and conservative Protestants in their support of antiabortion legislation.

Another unique feature of the Latter-day Saints is their **emphasis on missionary work**. The rapid growth of this community of faith can be attributed largely to this energetic program. Thousands of young men and women and retired couples accept missionary assignments for up to two years, normally serving at their own expense, often receiving financial assistance from family and friends. The main work of these missionaries is going from house to house seeking converts to their way of life.

Music is an important part of Latter-day Saints culture. The **Mormon Tabernacle Choir** is a 325-voice group that began in the mid-1800s. Its "Music and the Spoken Word" program has been carried by many radio stations since 1929. The choir's recording of "The Battle Hymn of the Republic" won a Grammy Award. There are also a Mormon youth symphony and a chorus, with 100 and 350 members, respectively. They, too, perform regularly.

The two major branches of the Mormon church grew out of a disagreement about who should be Joseph Smith's successor. The **Church of Jesus Christ of Latter-day Saints** (LDS) began with those who thought that Smith's successor should be a member of the Council of Twelve Apostles that advises the church president. This group chose Brigham Young as their leader. This branch is now based in Salt Lake City, Utah. The **Reorganized Church of Jesus Christ of Latter Day Saints** (RLDS) was founded by those who believed that Smith's successor should be his biological descendant. After Smith's death they chose his eldest son, Joseph Smith III, as their leader and established their headquarters in Independence, Missouri. The two groups are bound together by their shared commitment to the Christian Old and New Testaments, the *Book of Mormon,* and the *Doctrine and Covenants* as revealed scripture and the prophethood of Smith. They differ on several points. The RLDS church has a core of salaried local ministers. Both women and men have been ordained to both orders of the priesthood since 1984. Two women were recently appointed to the Council of 12 Apostles, a governing group second only to the three-member First Presidency in the church hierarchy. There is no baptism nor marriage of the dead by proxy, although Reorganized Mormons do believe that those who die without hearing the Mormon gospel will have the opportunity to do so after death. Unlike the LDS temples, to which access is restricted, the single RLDS temple in Independence, Missouri, "is a house of public worship, and entrance to the temple or participation in its ministries is open to all."[14] There are numerous smaller points of difference, as well.

These churches offer their members a stirring vision of how life can be. They provide firm guidelines for life and a set of ritual ordinances that members believe will lead to a greatly enhanced quality of life now and eternal life in the future, with the promise of becoming gods. They offer a strong community and a full program of activities with other like-minded persons. Their emphasis on

[14]Reorganized Church of Jesus Christ of Latter Day Saints Web site (http://www.rlds.org/).

the family and on traditional morality offer a clear-cut alternative to the problems many people see besetting modern society.

CHRISTIAN SCIENTISTS

Christian Scientists (members of the Church of Christ, Scientist) maintain a low public profile. They do not seek converts by missionary activity, but they do maintain Christian Science **Reading Rooms** where people can go and read the Bible as well as Christian Science literature. Christian Science is directly linked to the experiences of **Mary Baker Eddy**, its founder. In 1866, Mrs. Eddy reported a nearly instantaneous cure from a severe back injury after reading the account of one of Jesus' healings (Matthew 9:1–8). Along with the Bible, Eddy's *Science and Health with Key to the Scriptures* (first published in 1875) is the source of Christian Science teaching.

Christian Scientists believe that all that God creates is good, because a good God would not create that which was not good. Therefore, **the only reality that the evils of sin, sickness, and death have is that which we give them, because our erring human thought attributes to them a reality they do not have**. Christian Scientists rely on the power of God for healing rather than on medical treatment, although the church does not pressure those whose lesser faith leads them to see a physician. Such people are not dismissed from the church but are simply encouraged to strengthen their faith in God's healing mercy.

> Christian Scientists always have freedom of choice in caring for themselves and their families, just as anyone who normally resorts to medical care could choose to use spiritual means. When someone joins the Christian Science Church, he or she has already seen evidence of this means of healing and has determined to follow this way of life. If an individual departs from the use of Christian Science by choosing some other kind of treatment, he or she is neither condemned by the Church nor dropped from membership. In many countries, in order to meet legal requirements, Christian Scientists engage the services of a physician or a qualified midwife to attend the birth of a child in a hospital or at home.[15]

They *are* strongly discouraged from mixing the two types of care. Christian Science is based on the belief that the cause and the cure of illness are spiritual. Medicine looks at both cause and cure as primarily material. Trying to use both incompatible systems could compromise the healing process.[16]

Christian Science **practitioners** are specially trained by the church to assist those who seek Christian Science healing through prayer, and Christian Science in-patient facilities can provide supportive care to the seriously ill while treatment is given. Healing is by prayer but divinely natural, an integral part of the

---

[15]The First Church of Christ, Scientist Web site (http://www.tfccs.com/).
[16]The First Church of Christ, Scientist Web site (http://www.tfccs.com/).

harmonious order of the created world as God means it to be. Christian Science is not limited to physical healing but extends to psychological, emotional, and other problems.

Christian Scientists **think of God as divine Principle, Love, Mind, Spirit, Soul, Life, and Truth, which are the seven synonyms for God.**[17] God is understood to be wholly spiritual and not personalized. God includes qualities associated with both genders, and there is a tradition of gender equality on human terms that is echoed throughout the church's organization. There are no ordained ministers. **Readers elected from the congregation** serve for a period of three years, often without pay. It is preferred that one reader be female and the other male. Practitioners are more often female than male, and all church organizational offices are open to women.

The words *Christian* and *Science* in this church's name each tell us something important about it. It is a church *focused on Jesus, the Christ.* The tenets of the church include the following:

> We acknowledge Jesus' atonement as the evidence of divine, efficacious Love, unfolding man's unity with God through Christ Jesus the Way-shower; and we acknowledge that man is saved through Christ, through Truth, Life, and Love as demonstrated by the Galilean Prophet in healing the sick and overcoming sin and death.[18]

Christian Scientists distinguish between the human Jesus and his role as the Christ without separating the two:

> Christian Science draws a distinction between the Saviour's divine title of Christ and his human history as Jesus. But it by no means separates the two, for it fully accepts Jesus as the incarnation or embodiment of the Christ.[19]

Christian Scientists also believe that theirs is a **scientific religion**. *Science* is used to describe this religion because

> . . . it can be demonstrated. We see God as the universal, divine Principle underlying the life and healing work of Christ Jesus. God by His very nature must be unchanging Truth, invariable Love, operating through timeless spiritual laws rather than special miraculous acts. To understand these laws of absolute good is to find that Christianity can be scientifically applied to every human ill.[20]

The church meets for Sunday services that consist largely of readings from the Bible and *Science and Health*. Most of what takes place is determined by the

---

[17]Mary Baker Eddy, *Science and Health with Key to the Scriptures* (Boston: The First Church of Christ, Scientist, 1906), p. 465.

[18]Eddy, *Science and Health*, p. 497.

[19]*Christian Science: A Sourcebook of Contemporary Materials* (Boston: The Christian Science Publishing Society, 1990), pp. 102–103.

[20]*Questions and Answers on Christian Science.* (Boston: The Christian Science Publishing Society, 1974), p. 2.

Mother Church in Boston and is the same in all Christian Science churches. There is also music—organ music, hymns, and perhaps a vocal solo. The Wednesday midweek meetings also include readings from the Bible and from *Science and Health* but provide an opportunity for members and visitors to give and hear testimonies of healing. The First Reader chooses the subject and passages for the Wednesday evening meeting. One writer describes the two services this way:

> The Sunday service at a Christian Science church mingles something of the bare simplicity of the New England church services that Mrs. Eddy knew as a girl with a touch of the Quaker quietism and the Unitarian rationalism with which she came in friendly contact later. The midweek meeting . . . is chiefly known for the spontaneous "testimonies of healing" given by members of the congregation.[21]

There is a Board of Lectureship authorized to give public lectures explaining Christian Science and inviting further inquiry, but this is the extent of this group's missionary activity.

The Church of Christ, Scientist, has faced a number of challenges to its practices over the years. Currently, Christian Science healing is an accepted alternative to traditional medical treatment. Major insurance companies will usually reimburse those who receive Christian Science treatment. The Internal Revenue Service recognizes the cost of treatment as an income tax deduction, as it does medical fees. Christian Scientists do not claim that they have found the only way to God. They claim to have found a way that brings them peace and joy as well as physical healing, a way that they can recommend to others on that basis but that they do not ever attempt to force upon someone who is not interested.

Christian Science is also known to the public through its publication of the *Christian Science Monitor* newspaper, widely recognized as one of the best in the nation. There are also Monitor radio and television networks. A religious magazine, the *Herald of Christian Science*, is published in a dozen languages plus Braille. Religious periodicals and the *Monitor* are a part of the church's missionary activity.

SEVENTH-DAY ADVENTISTS

The Seventh-day Adventists are by far the largest single church within the group of churches that make up the adventist believers, a family that also includes the Latter-day Saints and the Jehovah's Witnesses. **Adventism** emphasizes the Christian teaching, found especially in the biblical books of Daniel and Revelation, that the return of Christ to the world will be a literal, physical event. Most adventists believe that this will happen in the near future. Those who rebel against God will be destroyed, while true believers will be saved.

---

[21] *Christian Science: A Sourcebook of Contemporary Materials*, p. 51.

The second coming of Christ is the blessed hope of the church, the grand climax of the gospel. The Saviour's coming will be literal, personal, visible, and world-wide. When He returns, the righteous dead will be resurrected, and together with the righteous living will be glorified and taken to heaven, but the unrighteous will die. The almost complete fulfillment of most lines of prophecy, together with the present condition of the world, indicates that Christ's coming is imminent. The time of that event has not been revealed, and we are therefore exhorted to be ready at all times.[22]

Adventism began early in the nineteenth century. Soon the United States was the location where its tenets and practices were best defined. Like many other movements that eventually became separate organizations, most adventists had no intention of breaking off from the churches of which they were a part. They set out to be an emphasis within a church, not a separate body. The emphasis created conflict, however, and many did break away. Adventism is sometimes linked with holiness (see Chapter 8), as believers seek to be prepared on a daily basis for the return of Christ.

Most of the divisions within adventism occurred when people set dates for the second coming. These dates passed, and nothing happened. In the sharp disappointment that followed such events, differences of opinion led to separations. A second major point of disagreement concerned whether the Lord's Day or Sabbath was properly celebrated on Saturday or Sunday. This difference contributed to the formation of the Seventh-day Adventist Church.

Some adventists predicted that Christ would return on October 22, 1844. When this prediction proved incorrect (sometimes known as the Great Disappointment), some of the people whose hopes had been dashed began meeting together. Among them were **Ellen G. White** and her husband. Mrs. White began entering into trance states in which she claimed to receive revelations, and she was soon accepted as a prophet by the group. Among the group's keystones was the **celebration of the Sabbath on Saturday rather than Sunday**. Mrs. White also confirmed the correctness of the 1844 date but redefined what happened on that date. Christ had not returned to the earth on that date, as was originally predicted, but had initiated the cleansing of the true, heavenly sanctuary described in Hebrews 8:1–2. This interpretation of the King James version of the text restored the adventist hope, and the effects of the Great Disappointment were overcome.

Seventh-day Adventists continue to celebrate the Sabbath on Saturday. "Seventh-day" in the group's name refers to this practice. Sometimes people who keep a Saturday Sabbath are called **Sabbatarians**. Adventists express the meaning of the Saturday Sabbath this way:

The beneficent Creator, after the six days of Creation, rested on the seventh day and instituted the Sabbath for all people as a memorial of Creation. The fourth

[22]Seventh-day Adventist Web site (http://www.adventist.org/).

commandment of God's unchangeable law requires the observance of this sev-enth-day Sabbath as the day of rest, worship, and ministry in harmony with the teaching and practice of Jesus, the Lord of the Sabbath. The Sabbath is a day of delightful communion with God and one another. It is a symbol of our redemp-tion in Christ, a sign of our sanctification, a token of our allegiance, and a fore-taste of our eternal future in God's kingdom. The Sabbath is God's perpetual sign of His eternal covenant between Him and His people. Joyful observance of this holy time from evening to evening, sunset to sunset, is a celebration of God's cre-ative and redemptive acts. [23]

Seventh-day Adventists believe that they are the "remnant church," a people called out in the last days to be the true church. Ellen G. White's gift of prophecy is recognized as a mark of such a remnant:

> The universal church is composed of all who truly believe in Christ, but in the last days, a time of widespread apostasy, a remnant has been called out to keep the commandments of God and the faith of Jesus. This remnant announces the arrival of the judgment hour, proclaims salvation through Christ, and heralds the approach of His second advent. This proclamation is symbolized by the three angels of Revelation 14; it coincides with the work of judgment in heaven and results in a work of repentance and reform on earth.

> One of the gifts of the Holy Spirit is prophecy. This gift is an identifying mark of the remnant church and was manifested in the ministry of Ellen G. White. As the Lord's messenger, her writings are a continuing and authoritative source of truth which provide for the church comfort, guidance, instruction, and correction. They also make clear that the Bible is the standard by which all teaching and expe-rience must be tested.[24]

Seventh-day Adventists are known for their **support of sound health practices**, because they believe that the body is the temple of the Holy Spirit. Good health practices are a religious obligation. They abstain from the use of alcohol and tobacco as well as illicit drugs, and they advocate healthy habits such as exercise and proper nutrition. They encourage a positive mental outlook. Many are vegetarians. For several years, they have sponsored a very successful stop-smoking program that is open to the public. Their emphasis on physical and mental health resembles that of the Latter-day Saints. Their awareness of the religious dimension of physical health has also led the Seventh-day Adventists to concentrate much of their missionary work, both in the United States and over-seas, on hospitals and other medical missions.

Men's and women's roles emphasize the traditional over the innovative. Both genders are encouraged to dress modestly and to manifest a "gentle and quiet spirit." Church and church-sponsored activities play a large role in most of

[23]Seventh-day Adventist Web site (http://www.adventist.org/).
[24]Seventh-day Adventist Web site (http://www.adventist.org/).

their lives. Especially in some areas of the country, Seventh-day Adventist children attend schools sponsored by their church.

JEHOVAH'S WITNESSES

Many Americans have become acquainted with the Jehovah's Witnesses through their aggressive program of **door-to-door evangelism**. The Witnesses believe that we are in a time of transition that precedes the reign of Christ on the Earth.

> When Jesus was on earth, his disciples came to him and asked: "What will be the sign of your presence and of the conclusion of the system of things?" He replied that there would be wars involving many nations, famines, pestilences, earthquakes, an increasing of lawlessness, false religious teachers misleading many, a hatred and persecution of his true followers, and a cooling off of the love of righteousness in many persons. When these things would start to happen, it would indicate Christ's invisible presence and that the heavenly Kingdom would be at hand. This would be news—good news! So Jesus added these words as a part of the sign: "This good news of the kingdom will be preached in all the inhabited earth for a witness to all the nations; and then the end will come."—Matthew 24:3–14.

> In themselves recent world happenings are bad, but what they signify, namely, Christ's presence, is good. Therefore, Jesus said: "As these things start to occur, raise yourselves erect and lift your heads up, because your deliverance is getting near." (Luke 21:28) These things started to occur in that widely heralded year 1914! It marked the end of the Gentile Times and the beginning of the transition period from human rule to the Thousand Year (Millennial) Reign of Christ.[25]

It is this understanding that we live in a "time between the times" that motivates the Witnesses to engage in such extensive door-to-door evangelism. They also seek other methods to spread the "good news," such as informal witnessing to people with whom they come into contact in daily life.

Although most of us know them best as Jehovah's Witnesses, their official name is the **Watchtower Bible and Tract Society**. The name Jehovah's Witnesses comes from Isaiah 43:12, which, in some translations, has God saying to the people that God is named Jehovah and they are God's witnesses. Jehovah's Witnesses do not consider themselves to be a church, but rather a group of Bible students and publishers of God's Word. *Publishing* here has two meanings. They translate and publish Bibles and religious tracts, and they publish (in the sense of making public) their understanding of God's message for modern-day people by every means at their disposal.

The group was originally organized by Pastor Charles Taze Russell (1852–1916), who is thought of as an organizer and not the founder, because God

[25]Watchtower Bible and Tract Society Web site (http://watchtower.org/).

alone is considered to be the founder. Unlike Joseph Smith and Ellen G. White, Russell disclaimed and condemned contemporary revelation, asserting that God's whole revelation was contained in the Bible. The Witnesses believe that theirs is the one true faith mentioned by Paul in Ephesians 4:5 (there is "one Lord, one faith, one baptism").

The group has never wavered from its focus on Bible study, and its teachings are supported by an elaborate system of references to scripture. When they meet, usually more than once per week, in Kingdom Halls (their meeting sites are not called churches), most of their time is spent in Bible study and discussion. They believe that the Bible was written by individuals who recorded God's message accurately. However, they hold that modern translations contain errors, and, in 1961, they published their own *New World Translation* of the Bible. Witnesses believe that their translation corrects the errors of earlier translations.

God is presently gathering the righteous together, in order to spare them from the disaster that will take place in the universal battle of Armageddon described in the book of Revelation in the Christian New Testament. This cataclysmic battle will inaugurate the reign of Jehovah God on the earth. The Witnesses understand themselves as the forerunners of this new kingdom.

Witnesses believe that only a limited number of people—the 144,000 mentioned in the Book of Revelation 7 and 10 —will live and reign with God in Heaven. The rest of the righteous will live in peace and harmony on an earth that has been restored to a paradisal state.

> The thought of persons living on earth as subjects of God's Kingdom may seem strange to many Bible believers who think of all those saved as being in heaven. The Bible shows that only a limited number go to heaven and that those who will live forever on earth will be a great crowd of unlimited number. God's Kingdom under Christ will fill the earth and reign over it.
>
> It is this Kingdom and the Scripturally supported hope of everlasting life on a cleansed and beautified earth that Jehovah's Witnesses wish to tell you about. Millions now living and many, many millions now in their graves will have opportunity to dwell therein forever. Then, under the Thousand Year Reign of Christ Jesus, Jehovah's original purpose for creating the earth and putting the first human pair on it will be realized. This earthly Paradise will never become boring. Just as Adam was assigned work in the garden of Eden, so humankind will have challenging projects in caring for the earth and the plant and animal life on it.[26]

Those who are gathered out are called to separate themselves from the world and form a **theocracy**, a community under the rule of God. To maintain this separation insofar as possible, the Witnesses avoid involvement in the political process by neither voting nor running for public office. They do not serve in the military. Technically, they are not pacifists; they claim that they would fight in God's war. They do not salute the flag nor sing the national anthem. They

[26]Watchtower Bible and Tract Society Web site (http://www.watchtower.org/).

believe that to do so is to worship the nation and make an idol of it. Oaths of any sort are forbidden. In an extension of the Christian Old Testament prohibition against drinking blood, they do not accept blood transfusions. Jehovah's Witness children do not participate in school celebrations of holidays such as Easter and Christmas, nor do their families mark these holidays, believing that there is no biblical reason for doing so.

> Jesus was not born on December 25. He was born about October 1, a time of year when shepherds kept their flocks out-of-doors at night. (Luke 2:8–12) Jesus never commanded Christians to celebrate his birth. Rather, he told his disciples to memorialize, or remember, his death. (Luke 22:19, 20) Christmas and its customs come from ancient false religions. The same is true of Easter customs, such as the use of eggs and rabbits. The early Christians did not celebrate Christmas or Easter, nor do true Christians today.

> The only two birthday celebrations spoken of in the Bible were held by persons who did not worship Jehovah. (Genesis 40:20–22; Mark 6:21, 22, 24–27) The early Christians did not celebrate birthdays. The custom of celebrating birthdays comes from ancient false religions. True Christians give gifts and have good times together at other times during the year.[27]

Jehovah's Witnesses are particularly critical of what they regard as the three strongest allies of Satan in his plan to destroy the world. These three Satanic allies are the government, big business, and churches that teach false doctrines (i.e., all those except the Witnesses). They must be destroyed in the coming battle before God can recreate the world. Although their aggressive missionary tactics anger and put off many people, Witnesses have earned a reputation for being honest, courteous, and industrious. Their conservative lifestyle stresses traditional roles for men and women. However, women participate fully in the door-to-door evangelism efforts of this group, and many times children are taken along. By the time they are ten years old or so, many children are accomplished Witnesses.

REFLECTION: COMMUNITY AND REASSURANCE

What is it that motivates the members of these communities of faith to live a life that distinguishes them sharply from the culture of which they are a part? To be sure, there are many reasons. Many followers of these ways of life live with a keen sense that the world is a wicked and evil place and that only by separating themselves from it can they have any hope of salvation. They take the idea of God's last judgment literally and seriously. Many believe firmly that the time is near when Christ will return to earth to judge all persons and make a final separation of the saved from the condemned. Therefore, it is necessary to be ready at all

[27]Watchtower Bible and Tract Society Web site (http://www.watchtower.org/).

times. They believe that they have increasing evidence of the work of the Holy Spirit in their lives and in the lives of their associates, and this helps to assure them that they will indeed be among the saved when that time comes.

Others have other reasons. For many, becoming a Mormon means joy and community in this life and the assurance that important family ties will remain intact on the other side of death. Christian Science offers not only an alternative to traditional medical care but an alternative way of understanding God and human nature. For many Scientists, their faith simply makes more sense out of their experience than do other alternatives.

These communities of faith offer their followers two very important things. They offer a strong sense of community that can be a refuge for those who are lonely and without other ties to the culture. It is a community of sharing among like-minded people whose goals and values are very similar. More important, many believe that they are called out of the world and into a small select community of faith. They believe that they are people who have heard and follow the message of the one true faith. The guidelines for life in this spiritual elite are clearly spelled out. The moral ambiguity that characterizes so much of contemporary society is absent.

Second, those who keep the faith and follow the guidelines are assured of salvation. Faith in justifying grace came as a great relief to Martin Luther, as it has to millions of other Protestants. It is nonetheless difficult to pin down. How does one know one is justified? How can one be absolutely certain of a place in heaven? These forms of Christianity emphasize true faith and an upright life. How to live an upright life is described in clear behavioral terms. This leads to a greater sense of security. Thus, these American-born religions offer their followers answers to some of the deepest and most pressing problems of human life, answers with fewer ambiguities and uncertainties than those proposed by the religions of their neighbors in the religious consensus.

QUESTIONS AND ACTIVITIES FOR REVIEW, DISCUSSION, AND WRITING

1. Think about how you would feel if you were a part of a religion that set very different standards for you than those followed by your classmates. Don't make this exercise too simple by concentrating solely on being different. Remember that such religions also offer security and the assurance that one is on the right path.
2. Most Latter-day Saints are very willing to discuss their faith with non-Mormons, and Mormon churches (chapels) welcome visitors eagerly. If possible, arrange to attend a service. You might also want to ask the missionaries to describe their experiences to you.
3. Visit a Christian Science Reading Room, and look over their literature. Report on what you find.
4. If you are not a member of one of the religions discussed in this chapter, write an essay about how your life would be different if you were a member. If you are a member, write about how your life would differ if you were not.
5. With a group, construct a chart that outlines the distinctive features of the communities of faith described in this chapter.

6. This chapter has touched on only the most central aspect of each of these groups. Visit the official Web site of each of these organizations to learn something that you did not learn from reading and discussing the chapter.

FOR FURTHER READING

EMBRY, JESSIE L., *Black Saints in a White Church: Contemporary African-American Mormons*. Salt Lake City, UT: Signature Books, 1994. Embry uses survey data and oral history to describe the positive and negative experiences of black Mormons in a church that did not always grant them full privileges.

KEPHART, WILLIAM M., and WILLIAM W. ZELLNER, *Extraordinary Groups: The Sociology of Unconventional Lifestyles*, 5th ed. New York: Saint Martin's Press, 1994. This book has chapters on several major alternative communities of faith. Kephart and Zellner's book is written from an objective, sociological point of view, yet it reads almost like a novel, fascinating and very accessible.

KNOTT, RONALD ALAN, *College Faith: 150 Adventist Leaders Share Faith Stories from Their College Days*. Nampa, Idaho: Pacific Press Pub. Assn., 1995. This book is valuable because it shows how nonconsensus faith plays out among college students.

MAUSS, ARMAND L., *The Angel and the Beehive: The Mormon Struggle with Assimilation*. Champaign, IL: University of Illinois Press, 1994. Mauss analyzes the last 40 years of Mormon history to focus on their transition from "outsider" status in the United States and their struggle with the resulting loss of distinctiveness. The result is a fascinating look at a dynamic that applies to many nonconsensus religions.

PENTON, JAMES M., *Apocalypse Delayed: The Story of Jehovah's Witnesses*. Toronto: University of Toronto Press, 1998. Penton grew up a Witness, became a professional historian, and was later disfellowshiped from the church. He offers a critical but not polemic view that nicely blends personal insight with professional distance.

WILLIAMS, JEAN KINNEY., *The Christian Scientists (The American Religious Experience)*. Danbury, CT: Franklin Watts, 1997. Williams includes history, beliefs, and practices, plus a review of Mary Baker Eddy's work, changes in belief and practice, and their location in American culture.

RELEVANT WORLD WIDE WEB SITES

Latter-day Saints (http://www.lds.org/).

Reorganized Latter Day Saints (http://www.rlds.org/).

Christian Science (http://www.tfccs.com/).

Electronic edition of the *Christian Science Monitor* (http://www.csmonitor.com/).

Seventh-day Adventists (http://www.adventist.org/).

Jehovah's Witnesses (http://www.watchtower.org/).

8

Alternative Themes in American Christianity

My dad was very "God and rule," and my mom sort of took it all with a grain of salt. But they were very strict about everything. They kept the sabbath on Sunday. You couldn't watch any TV or listen to the radio, or even just read a book that wasn't a religious book or listen to music that wasn't religious.[1]

After one year of disappointing results Demos [Demos Shakarian, founder of Full Gospel Businessmen's Fellowship International] decided to give up the Fellowship. While pouring out his heart in prayer the Friday night before the final meeting, he was lifted by the Spirit high into the air. In this vision, as the earth revolved each continent came into view.

"I could see people around the world—their race and color of skin," he said. "As a zoom camera can show minute details from a distance, I could see people close together but no real contact between them. Every face rigid, wretched, locked in his own private death."

Billions of lost souls from every nation. Demos cried out, "Lord, help them!" Suddenly God showed him these same men, faces radiant, their hands raised to heaven, praising the Lord. At that moment Demos' wife Rose gave the prophetic utterance, "My son, the very thing you see before you will soon come to pass."[2]

---

[1]Penny Edgell Becker and Nancy L. Eiesland, *Contemporary America Religion: An Ethnographic Reader* (Walnut Creek, CA: AltaMira Press, 1997), pp. 106–107.
[2]Full Gospel Businessmen's Fellowship International World Wide Web site (http://www.fgbfi.org/).

This chapter brings together a number of themes that are not confined to one denomination within Christianity. Neither are they specific groups, by and large, but movements and sensibilities that cut across groups.

FUNDAMENTALIST AND
VERY CONSERVATIVE CHRISTIANS

You have already been introduced to fundamentalism as a religious attitude. Some Protestant churches whose members have fundamentalist religious attitudes are part of the religious consensus. The increase in religious conservatism in the last several decades has brought many fundamentalists into the consensus. The type of fundamentalism with which this chapter deals is different. It is characterized by a strong desire to remain separate from other groups and individuals who do not believe as they do. Most of these churches are members of the **American Council of Christian Churches**, founded in 1941 by Dr. Carl McIntire. A periodical called the *Christian Beacon* reflects this organization's perspectives.

The self-understanding of this group and why its supporters believe it to be necessary are clearly described in one of its official statements. It describes the group's differences with the other two major ecumenical organizations.

The ACCC was formed to be a voice [for] Biblical Fundamentalism and to encourage and strengthen believers in their stand for the Truth. Churches, organizations and individuals wanted an organization that was completely separate from all trends and tenets of liberal theology. No church or individual can be a part of the ACCC and at the same time be connected in any way with the National Council of Churches (NCC) with its liberal theology, ecumenical apostasy, and leftist socio-political agenda. Neither can one be a part of the ACCC and be associated with the National Association of Evangelicals (NAE), which is noted for its compromise, confusion and inclusion of Charismatics. . . .

The apostle Jude mentions "the faith." This term refers to the Faith as a body of revealed truth from the Lord. Among the fundamental doctrines of the Faith are: the inspiration and inerrancy of Scripture; the deity of Jesus Christ, His virgin birth, substitutionary blood atonement, His literal bodily resurrection and His Second Coming "in power and great glory." We as Fundamentalists also affirm that the Bible teaches separation from unbelievers and erring brethren. To us, doctrinal purity is critical to the work of God. Therefore, when we see that which is in error, we must draw attention to it. That is what the ACCC has done and continues to do. As changes come in church groups, educational institutions, and mission agencies, we must expose compromise—even if it is not the popular thing to do.

It is easy for individuals and churches to conclude that they are standing alone in the battle for the Faith. We need to understand that there are churches and individuals all across our land that have not bowed the knee to Baal (I Kings 19:18). The ACCC is in existence to encourage Bible-believers in their practice of obedience to Christ. We need to stand together to expose Liberalism, New Evangelicalism, the Charismatic movement, and compromise in all areas of life and ministry.[3]

The word *fundamentalism* derives from a series of pamphlets called "The Fundamentals," written in the early 1900s as a reference point for conservative Protestants.[4] These pamphlets include the "fundamental doctrines of the Faith" held by the ACCC.

> The keystone was and is the inerrancy of Scripture, meaning not only that the Bible is the sole and infallible rule of faith and practice, but also that it is scientifically and historically accurate. Thus, evolution could not be true, miracles really did happen just as the Bible describes them, and on Judgment Day all who have ever lived will be assigned for eternity to heaven or hell, both of which really do exist. Any attempt to interpret these or other features of Scripture as myths or allegories strikes at the very root of Christian faith and must be resisted with every fiber of one's being.[5]

Separatist fundamentalists firmly believe that biblical Christianity is completely incompatible with Christian modernism or liberalism, as well as with anything secular. They try to keep the boundaries between themselves and the secular world drawn sharply. Nonfundamentalist Christians are regarded as part of the unsaved world, so fundamentalists remain separate from them, as well.

Fundamentalism is not just a style of religion, nor is it just a matter of religious belief. It is "a value-oriented, antimodern, dedifferentiating form of collective action—a sociocultural movement aimed at reorganizing all spheres of life in terms of a particular set of absolute values."[6] In the face of expanding pluralism and what fundamentalists and conservatives see as the takeover of society by rampant secularism, the movement seeks to make a single set of values (hence, "dedifferentiating") based on their reading of the Christian Bible dominant in the culture.

Fundamentalism reflects the reality that a substantial and significant part of the population of the United States feel themselves as cultural "outsiders" in contemporary American culture. Secularization, the privatization of religion, and the changes in moral standards that followed the turbulent decade of the 1960s helped to create a culture in which some people felt less than at home. "Fundamentalists would not be fundamentalists without deep-seated feelings of

---

[3]American Council of Christian Churches official Web site (http://www.amcouncilcc.org/).

[4]William H. Swatos, Jr., ed., *Encyclopedia of Religion and Society* (Walnut Creek, CA: AltaMira Press, 1998), p. 197.

[5]William Martin, *With God on Our Side: The Rise of the Religious Right in America*, (New York: Broadway Books, 1996), p. 11.

[6]Irving Louis Horowitz, "The Limits of Modernity," in *In Gods We Trust: New Patterns of Religious Pluralism in America*, 2nd. ed., ed. Thomas Robbins and Dick Anthony. (New Brunswick, NJ: Transaction Publishers, 1990), p. 79.

dispossession, resentment, and alienation, and it is important to understand . . . these emotions."[7]

Relatively more women than men are fundamentalists, by a ratio of about four to three. Fundamentalism as an outlook reflects the kind of passivity that our culture has traditionally associated with women. The fundamentalist emphasis on God rather than on human potential encourages that passivity and gives it divine support. Fundamentalism encourages women to be submissive to their husbands, remain at home, and accept a limited and traditional (although significant) role in the life of their church. While this seems restrictive to some women, for others it means the security of clearly defined roles that relieve the murkiness that cultural change has brought to women's lives in the last several decades.

Separatist fundamentalists have also been among the strongest supporters of the private **Christian school movement**, as well as of the home-schooling movement. Private Christian schools provide a way for parents to shield their children from the secular influence of the public school system. They also offer greater control over the curriculum. In most private Christian schools, children do not learn the Darwinian theory of evolution, nor do they study sex education and other subjects deemed inappropriate by fundamentalists. Their textbooks support traditional values and attitudes. More important, all subjects are taught from a Christian perspective. The school day begins with worship. The teachers are committed Christians, most of whom understand their work as a religious calling.

Perhaps most important in understanding why fundamentalist Christians view the Christian school movement as so important, Christian schools are a primary element in the advancement of fundamentalism's sociocultural goals. "By reuniting the three major socializing institutions of family, church, and school, [fundamentalists] hope to achieve a greater coherence in their own lives, bring their children up in the faith, and bring morality back to the United States."[8]

The private Christian school movement continues to grow but not as rapidly as the home-schooling movement. "**Home schooling**" means that parents teach their children at home, often using materials provided by Christian organizations. Individual parents have even more control with home schooling than with private schools. Both methods help to guarantee that children during their younger, most formative years will be socialized into the values that are central to fundamentalist Christians and into those values only.

Fundamentalist Christians also support a number of colleges in which higher education is carried out within the framework of their values and concerns. Among the best known of these schools is **Bob Jones University**. Students take required religion classes, and there is a dress code and careful control

---

[7]Joel A. Carpenter, *Revive Us Again: The Reawakening of American Fundamentalism* (New York: Oxford University Press, 1997), p. 242.

[8]Susan D. Rose, "Gender, Education, and the New Christian Right," *In Gods We Trust*, ed. Robbins and Anthony, p. 100.

of dating behavior among students. The University's charter statement expresses very well the spirit that animates these schools:

> The general nature and object of the corporation shall be to conduct an institution of learning for the general education of youth in the essentials of culture and in the arts and sciences, giving special emphasis to the Christian religion and the ethics revealed in the Holy Scriptures; combating all atheistic, agnostic, pagan, and so-called scientific adulterations of the Gospel; unqualifiedly affirming and teaching the inspiration of the Bible (both the Old and New Testaments); the creation of man by the direct act of God; the incarnation and virgin birth of our Lord and Savior, Jesus Christ; His identification as the Son of God; His vicarious atonement for the sins of mankind by the shedding of His blood on the cross; the resurrection of His body from the tomb; His power to save men from sin; the new birth through the regeneration by the Holy Spirit and the gift of eternal life by the grace of God.[9]

The Christian doctrines enumerated in the charter are a summary of the key elements of fundamentalist faith.

Many of the churches that fit this profile are independent, with no ties outside the local congregation. They believe that this most closely resembles the way in which the church was organized in New Testament times. It also affords each congregation the greatest opportunity to set its own standards of correct belief. Two groups of churches, however, do fit in here. In Chapter 3, you read about the Restoration Movement and the Christian Church/Disciples of Christ that is a part of it. Two other churches whose roots go back to the Restoration Movement embody the approach to Christianity described above.

The **Christian Churches/Churches of Christ** have no organization beyond the local congregation. There is less variation in belief among members of these independent churches than among the Disciples. Most are strongly conservative to fundamentalist. As in the other Restoration churches, the Lord's supper is served weekly. Like that of the Disciples, their worship includes instrumental music as well as the singing of hymns. The Christian Churches do not participate in ecumenical discussions or organizations, and the network of schools, colleges, and benevolent organizations they sponsor is supported entirely by local churches. They are located primarily in the lower Midwest and in Kentucky.

The **Churches of Christ** is the largest group within the Restoration churches. They are centered in the South and Southwest, although there are congregations throughout the United States. Like the Christian Churches, there is no organizational structure beyond the local church and no participation in ecumenical boards or groups. These churches seek "to speak where the Bible speaks and to be silent where the Bible is silent" in matters of faith and morality. They believe that this is the biblical pathway to Christian unity. As in the other Restoration congregations, the Lord's supper is a weekly celebration and believers are baptized by full immersion. Unlike the Disciples and the Christian Churches,

[9]*Bulletin*, Bob Jones University, 1995–96 (Undergraduate), n.p.

the Churches of Christ use no instrumental music in their worship. Instrumental music, these Christians believe, is not biblical but is instead one of the ways the church accommodated itself to the demands of more wealthy members.

EVANGELICAL CHRISTIANS

Evangelicalism is not new in the United States. Both evangelicalism and pente-costalism trace their heritage back to revivals that began in the eighteenth century. By the early 1700s, Puritan religion in the northeast had experienced a dramatic decline. In the mid-1700s, the northeastern and the mid-Atlantic colonies were the site of the first of a number of religious revivals that swept through America. Scholars have named this first outpouring of revival enthusiasm the **Great Awakening**.

The revivalists' messages were simple and straightforward. They concentrated on the outlines of the Christian message as Puritanism interpreted it: People are lost, trapped in sin, without any hope of saving themselves. God's free offer of salvation through grace and faith in Jesus must be accepted, because there is no other hope. Acceptance of God's gracious offer brings release from the terrible anxiety of the sin-stricken soul. The preaching style of Jonathan Edwards, George Whitefield, and other Great Awakening preachers assured that their hearers would be moved both intellectually and emotionally. Intense, abrupt experiences that people interpreted as conversion from their old lives to new lives in grace became the standard by which people's response was judged.

The **Second Awakening** occurred on the frontier in the 1800s. The basic theology and the simplicity of the message remained the same. The frontier population, however, was less educated and much less stable geographically; these factors brought about a change in revival preaching. The Second Awakening revivalists developed a style that was more emotional and less intellectual than that of their predecessors. A strong appeal to people's emotions, and equally emotional responses, were very common. Preachers pressed their hearers for immediate conversion, because many in the audience might well move on in a matter of hours. Conversion was often accompanied by emotional and physical manifestations, such as running and jumping about, unintelligible vocalizations, and fainting. Some preachers spoke out against these phenomena, believing that they were unseemly and excessive, but others encouraged them as signs of true conversion and the experience of God.

The simple message and the emotional style of the Awakenings continue in modern-day revivals. Testifying to one's faith and the centrality of the conversion experience are still important aspects of the evangelical way of being religious. Unusual physical manifestations attributed to the action of the Holy Spirit are a significant part of the contemporary pentecostal experience.

Consensus religion in the United States has usually been a relatively private matter. Who has not been reminded that it is "not polite" to discuss politics or religion? People's religion, like their political preferences, has been considered too personal to be discussed very much. Whatever may have been the fate of politics in recent years, religion has come front and center for many Americans. It has gone public. The upsurge of interest in evangelical religion, and its very public presence, has been one of the most noticeable features of American religion in the last decade and a half. Survey data indicate that, among Christians, over 80 percent have talked with someone about their faith with the aim of converting the other person to Christianity.

Recent surveys have helped to establish the criteria of the "minimal essence" of evangelicalism in the United States. They include the following characteristics:

> (a) salvation only through faith in Jesus Christ (the mechanism of the evangel); (b) an experience of personal conversion, commonly called being "born again" (the mechanics of the evangel); (c) the importance of missions and evangelism (sharing the message of the evangel); and (d) the truth or inerrancy of Scripture (the source of the evangel).[10]

It is very important to evangelicals to share their faith with other people. The word itself comes from the Greek and means "messenger of good news." Telling other people about the joy, peace, and happiness they have found in their relationship with Jesus is a top priority in the lives of most evangelicals. One campus evangelical organization, for example, is called Top Priority Outreach. In many ways, **witnessing**, or talking about their faith with other people with the intention of leading them to put their faith in Jesus also, defines evangelicalism. Evangelicals believe that the responsibility for missionary work rests on each and every Christian. They believe that Jesus' command to go into the whole world and preach (Mark 16:15) is directed to all Christians.

Most evangelical Christians also say they have been born again, and they emphasize the importance of this particular religious event. Being born again refers to a person's being able to point to a very specific event, a time and place in which they accepted Jesus Christ as their personal Lord and Savior. Being born again and asking Jesus to come into their lives establishes a warmly personal relationship with God that far exceeds anything they might have experienced prior to their conversion. Even those who had been active church members say that they became a Christian at that point in time. They distinguish sharply between being a member of a church and being a Christian. Usually, it is understood that virtually all Christians are church members, but not all church members are Christians. The emphasis on a datable, identifiable conversion experience goes back to Puritanism. The Puritans required testimony of such an experience as a condition of full church membership. Among all Christians, about half can identify such an experience in their religious lives.

Evangelicalism is very public in America in other ways as well. On college campuses, evangelical groups like Navigators, Campus Crusade for Christ, and

---

[10]William H. Swatos, Jr., ed., *Encyclopedia of Religion and Society* (Walnut Creek, CA: AltaMira Press, 1998), p. 176.

Intervarsity Christian Fellowship draw many students, many of whom have participated in Young Life in high school. Members of these groups often witness to other students in the library or student center. There are evangelical groups within professional fields, such as Christian Nurses and the Society of Christian Philosophers. Christian bookstores can be found in most cities. They offer a wide selection of books, music, videotapes, and jewelry that reflects the evangelical viewpoint. Christian music has become the music of choice for many listeners, and hymns such as "Amazing Grace" and "Morning Has Broken" have become easy-listening standards (Figure 8-1).

Christian music has its own awards program, the Dove Awards. Jewelry featuring crosses, fish symbols, and "One Way" and "Jesus First" slogans is a silent witness to all who see it being worn. Many cars have bumper stickers stating the driver's religious position. *Christianity Today*, a major weekly religious periodical, was founded to promote the evangelical viewpoint. Finally, public testimonies by leading figures in the sports, entertainment, and business communities have increased the public visibility of evangelicals.

Billy Graham (b. 1918) is the foremost contemporary exemplar of the evangelical and revivalist tradition in American religion and is the most public symbol of the style of evangelicalism that began in the 1950s and continues today. His radio program, "The Hour of Decision," began in 1950, and he was soon familiar to television viewers as well. The core of Graham's message is traditional: Repent and surrender to Jesus as Lord and Savior. However, his preaching also addresses social problems and national sins. He has spoken out strongly against racism and classism in the United States and supports nuclear disarmament. His style of presentation is restrained and theologically informed. He established a close working relationship with the White House in the 1950s during

Figure 8-1   Christian music is an important part of evangelical Christianity. *(Photo by the author.)*

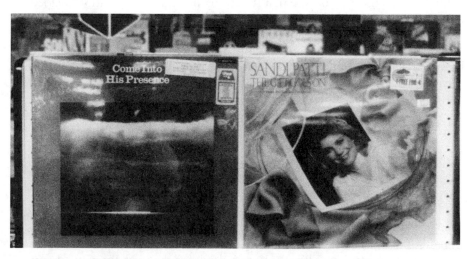

the Eisenhower administration, a relationship that has continued with Eisenhower's successors. Graham has since passed the responsibility for his ministry to his son, Franklin Graham.

Evangelicals usually distinguish themselves from fundamentalists, who are their closest ideological neighbors. Most evangelicals regard fundamentalists as too militant, too exclusive, and as having too low an opinion of modern scholarship. Evangelicals, although certainly conservative in both theology and ethics, do accept some compromise. The new style of evangelicalism is characterized by a cautious acceptance of some of the insights of biblical scholarship, while maintaining that the Bible is inspired by God. Evangelicals affirm the generally agreed-upon doctrines of Christianity in their traditional forms. Historically, evangelicals have emphasized personal morality, and this emphasis remains. There is a new spirit of sociopolitical involvement, too, that replaces the tendency of earlier evangelicals to remain outside the rough-and-tumble of political action.

Evangelicals preach a relatively simple message that emphasizes human sinfulness and the need for rebirth, the need for and joys of a personal relationship with Jesus, and the necessity of making a definite decision for Christ. Evangelicals certainly believe that conversion is a result of the action of God's grace upon a person. They also teach the important role of human free will in the process. Evangelicalism is more concerned with the quality of religious experience than with belief in particular doctrines. It is pietistic, emphasizing personal prayer, devotion, and Bible reading.

Most evangelicals believe in a supernatural God who constantly intervenes in the affairs of the world through miracles. For example, an evangelical who recovered from a serious illness would probably explain that recovery by referring to God's role in the healing process. A religious liberal or humanist would be likely to attribute healing to the skill of medical personnel and the effect of medication.

Most evangelical churches are not members of the National Council of Churches, because they believe that the strong desire for cooperation that led to the formation of the National Council also led to a compromise of biblical faith. Many, however, are members of the National Association of Evangelicals.

One contemporary manifestation of the evangelical spirit is "Promise Keepers," a men's organization founded in 1990 by Bill McCartney, former University of Colorado football coach. Unlike women, who have historically come together for spiritual support, men have lacked for such groups. Promise Keepers was founded in order to provide such fellowship and to provide specific structure for men seeking to live an evangelical Christian life:

> The Seven Promises are meant to be a guide to men who want to pursue godliness. The Seven Promises are not man-made rules but are each taken from biblical instruction on spiritual growth. The Seven Promises were formed as a response to the many men who were writing to us, asking how they could grow as Christians. These men had a clear desire to become like Jesus; however, it seemed that there was a vacuum of clear moral teaching in our society. After much prayer and deliberation, the leadership of Promise Keepers developed the Seven Promises as a way to

help men focus on specific areas of concern for Christian men. We believe that the Seven Promises are commitments to grow, rather than a set of rules to be followed.

Men in the movement make seven promises.

A Promise Keeper is committed to:
1. honoring Jesus Christ through worship, prayer and obedience to God's Word in the power of the Holy Spirit.
2. pursuing vital relationships with a few other men, understanding that he needs brothers to help him keep his promises.
3. practicing spiritual, moral, ethical, and sexual purity.
4. building strong marriages and families through love, protection and biblical values.
5. supporting the mission of his church by honoring and praying for his pastor, and by actively giving his time and resources.
6. reaching beyond any racial and denominational barriers to demonstrate the power of biblical unity.
7. influencing his world, being obedient to the Great Commandment (see Mark 12:30–31) and the Great Commission (see Matthew 28:19–20).[11]

The numbers of men drawn to this movement indicate that it meets a need that many feel keenly. Although Promise Keepers is a men's organization, women make up almost 40 percent of the national staff and 50 percent of the volunteers at a typical stadium conference and have been described as "indispensable" to the Promise Keepers ministry.

Evangelicalism is not limited to any one Christian church or denomination. Evangelical Christians are people who believe that their lives have been decisively changed for the better by a vibrant experience that they attribute to God's love, the saving grace of Jesus, and the working of the Holy Spirit. In their enthusiasm for their experience, they seek to share it with others (Figure 8-2).

SEEKER-SENSITIVE OR NEW PARADIGM CHURCHES

Seeker-sensitive churches specifically focus on drawing in people who otherwise do not attend church. They often begin by using survey data from a particular area to determine just what people are looking for in a church and then set about designing worship and other aspects of church life to respond to those desires.

One scholar refers to them as *"new paradigm"* churches and thinks that they are the harbinger of a "second reformation." While Martin Luther's Protestant Reformation challenged church doctrine, the second reformation focuses on the medium through which the doctrine is presented. They do not focus on reforming existing church structures but on developing new ones.[12]

---

[11]Promise Keepers Web site (http://www.promisekeepers.org/).
[12]Donald E. Miller, *Reinventing American Protestantism: Christianity in the New Millennium* (Berkeley, CA: University of California Press, 1997), p. 11.

Figure 8-2   Evangelicals seek many opportunities to share their faith with other people. On this business sign, PTL stands for "Praise the Lord." *(Photo by the author.)*

Although diverse in some ways, these churches do share a number of characteristics that help make them what they are and that situates them in the American religious landscape:

1. They were started after the mid-1960s.
2. The majority of congregation members were born after 1945.
3. Seminary training of clergy is optional.
4. Worship is contemporary.
5. Lay leadership is highly valued.
6. They have extensive small-group ministries.
7. Clergy and congregants usually dress informally.
8. Tolerance of different personal styles is prized.
9. Pastors tend to be understated, humble, and self-revealing.
10. Bodily, rather than mere cognitive, participation in worship is the norm.
11. The "gifts of the Holy Spirit" are affirmed.
12. Bible-centered teaching predominates over topical sermonizing.[13]

These are churches that have embraced three key features of contemporary culture: They are *therapeutic* in that they value openness and honesty and pro-

---

[13]Donald E. Miller, *Reinventing American Protestantism: Christianity in the New Millennium* (Berkeley, CA: University of California Press, 1997), p. 20.

vide a setting in which people can be vulnerable and admit their problems. They oppose many of the values of modern, particularly "pop," psychology and emphasize "biblical advice" over "counseling."

They emphasize *individualism* in that people are encouraged to interpret scripture for themselves, develop a personal relationship with Christ, and focus on religious experience more than shared beliefs. However, alongside this, they emphasize personal accountability and small group interaction in which people can be known face-to-face.

They are antiestablishment in that members and followers are frequently hostile to the bureaucratic aspects of the large denominational churches and to the more routine aspects of organized religious life. However, they strongly encourage community, and many members make the church and their friends there the center of their lives.[14]

This trend is too new to assess its impact on religion in the United States. It appears to be responding to a specific cultural situation. Hence, its continued success or its demise may hinge on how well it proves able to adapt as that cultural situation changes. In the meantime, it is a significant factor on the American religious scene.

THE RELIGIOUS-POLITICAL RIGHT

The involvement of evangelical Christians and fundamentalists in American politics is not a new occurrence. Evangelical religion was a strong force in American politics until the second decade of the 1900s. During the period between the end of World War I and the early 1970s, its influence on American government lessened dramatically. The early 1970s brought a renewal of evangelical and fundamentalist involvement in the political life of the nation, a trend that continued into the 1990s.

The **religious-political right** is a loose coalition of groups and individuals who are united by their conviction that the United States is in the midst of a severe spiritual and moral decline, a decline that could well snowball into a landslide that would lead to downfall of the United States and the defeat of democracy in the world. They believe that a return to the traditional values of American life, best safeguarded by fundamentalist Christianity, will prevent this landslide and again make America the strong and righteous nation that they believe existed in an earlier time. They are also united in their desire to use the legislative process to make their goals into the law of the land. One analysis of the movement has called it "a blend of old-time religion and far-right politics coordinated with Madison Avenue sophistication."[15]

Groups move in and out of the coalition depending upon which issue or issues are being dealt with at a given time. There are several groups whose

[14]Donald E. Miller, *Reinventing American Protestantism*, p. 20–22.
[15]Peter L. Benson and Dorothy L. Williams, *Religion on Capitol Hill: Myths and Realities* (New York: Oxford University Press, 1986), p. 173.

alignment with the goals and concerns of the religious-political right is fairly constant, however. The most reliable support, in terms of both programs and finances, comes from **those whose religious outlook is very conservative or fundamentalist**, some of whom are evangelicals and some of whom are not. Some are pentecostals, while some are not.

Protestants are clearly the backbone of this group. On certain issues, such as the movement to limit legal abortions, **support also comes from Catholics, Eastern Orthodox Christians, and even some Orthodox Jews**. On others, such as the campaign against ratification of the Equal Rights Amendment (ERA), the coalition has included support from the **Latter-day Saints**, who value traditional male and female social roles. **A second major segment of support comes from political conservatives**. They desire to see the balance of government power shifted from the federal to the state government and hope to return the responsibility for welfare programs to the private sector of American life. This leads them to support the religious right on these types of issues. A third group is related to the second. **Social and economic conservatives** share many of the same concerns that motivate the political conservatives' involvement with the religious-political right. Economic conservatives especially favor the modifications in the welfare program it encourages, as well as its support for private business interests. We can also cite a fourth group—those who, without any clearly defined religious motivation, subscribe to the **belief that America has a special role to play in the history of the world**. They describe this role using the biblical metaphors of a light to the nations and a city set on a hill. A final group is more difficult to define but just as important. We can call them the **social traditionalists**—those whose motivations are not clearly religious, political, or economic but who believe that a return to older values would be a beneficial course for America to follow. They comprise a loose back-to-the-basics interest.

The goals of the religious-political right are stated in various ways. However they are described, they revolve around the **intention to bring about major changes in American government and American life**. They seek to make the United States a moral and righteous nation, defining morality and righteousness in terms of the authority of the Christian Bible as the only legitimate guide.

The religious-political right also describes its goals as an all-out war on an enemy that they have identified as being at the root of America's moral problems: secular humanism (see Chapter 6 for a discussion of humanism). Secular humanism stands for nearly everything that the new right believes is wrong. Most supporters subscribe to an interpretation of recent history that holds that secular humanists in high government positions are conspiring to make secular humanism the official religion of the land. A significant part of this conspiracy centers on what is being taught and what is permissible in the public schools.

Not all the groups involved in this coalition fully agree about what its specific agenda should be. Nor do they agree on the relative importance of the various items. There are, however, certain planks that can be found in nearly all statements of their platform, and it is these that are described below:

1. A **call for a return to traditional values** means, first and foremost, support for traditional family structures. A number of other items, such as opposition to the ERA and to homosexual lifestyles, support their basic interest in traditional families.
2. A closely related category includes several issues relevant to the **public schools**, on one hand, and **support for a private Christian school system** on the other hand.
3. Third is their advocacy of **U.S. military superiority**.
4. **Direct political action**, such as lobbying, voter registration, and the election of candidates who are favorable to their views, is a fourth goal.

The religious-political right regards the family as the mainstay of American culture. They approve of only one form of family structure, which they identify as the **traditional form of family organization** in the United States. The traditional family is the family that consists of a man and a woman, married for life, with children. Women are encouraged to be full-time wives, mothers, and homemakers, and fathers should be the sole source of financial support for the family. The economic system should support this arrangement. Premarital chastity and marital monogamy are the only acceptable forms of sexuality. Both the Old and New Testaments of the Christian scriptures are cited in support of the position that homosexuality is a heinous sin and a prime contributor to America's spiritual degeneracy. Sex education should be taught only by Christians to ensure that proper values will be taught along with factual information.

Advocacy of the traditional family is reinforced by several other points. Perhaps foremost among these was the campaign of the religious-political right to block the ratification of the Equal Rights Amendment, a task in which they were ultimately successful. The ERA and the "feminist revolution" appear in every list of national errors that are said to threaten America. Opposition to abortion, especially government support for abortion in the form of Medicaid payments and federal funding for abortion clinics, is another important part of their family policy.

They also support a thorough cleanup of commercial television, not only to eliminate violence and the use of sexually suggestive advertising but also to eliminate the portrayal of alternative lifestyles. They oppose pornography in all its forms and want to have laws enacted that would mandate stiff penalties for those who create and distribute pornographic literature, films, videotapes, and so forth. Another priority is support for programs that will help to solve the problem of illegal drug use.

The concerns of the religious-political right obviously are shared by people who do not identify with it explicitly. Survey data indicate that approximately 90 percent of Americans believe that extramarital sex is always or nearly always wrong. About 80 percent feel that way about active homosexuality. Over half support at least some restrictions on the availability of legal abortion. Over half the population favors laws prohibiting the sale of pornography to people under the age of eighteen, and almost half oppose the sale of pornography to anyone, regardless of age. Many Americans are concerned about illegal drugs, as they are about sex and violence (and the frequent close association of the two) on commercial television.

The large role the federal government has assumed in administering welfare programs is another concern. The religious-political right does recognize that there will always be people who cannot care for themselves because of age or physical or mental infirmity. They want to shift the responsibility for the care of such people from the government to the private sector, including churches, businesses, and, above all, the families of the people themselves. For example, they support tax credits for those families who have a dependent elderly parent living with them. For all except those completely incapable of working, welfare "programs tend to destroy one's initiative, skill, work habits, and productivity."[16]

Government regulation of business and industry is yet another concern. Free enterprise, ambitious management, and competition unfettered by government regulation are held to be biblical values that are a part of God's plan for humanity. Restriction of the freedom of business and industry is often linked to the loss of other freedoms, such as freedom of speech, of the press, and of religion.

The religious-political right wants the nation to return to the values of an earlier, much less complicated period in history, when the population was much smaller. The members of this movement believe that the values that worked in that setting are what America needs now. Although not all Americans agree with them, their vision of a renewed America based on traditional values has captured the hearts and minds of a significant number of people. The religious-political right is one of the most significant religious and political movements of this century.

The **plan of action** that the religious-political right envisions **for educating children** is closely related to their hopes for a return to traditional values in American society. It is the schools, both public and private, that bear the responsibility, alongside the family and the churches, for rearing children who have a strong sense of and commitment to these values. Their approach to education has two main facets. The first is what they want to see happen within the public school system. The second is their goals concerning the establishment of a system of private Christian schools to supplement the public schools.

We will look at their goals for the *public schools* first. The public schools, according to this analysis, have been taken over by secular humanists and are being used as the main tool for indoctrinating youngsters with the values held dear by humanists. The U.S. Supreme Court decision that made mandated prayer and other school-sponsored devotional exercises in the public schools illegal is of particular concern. They want voluntary prayer and other devotional exercises returned to the public school classroom. They also want any

[16]Jerry Falwell, *Listen, America!* (Garden City, NY: Doubleday and Company, 1980), p. 78.

academic study of religion eliminated, because it maintains a position of neutrality concerning the truth of specific religions. This conflicts sharply with their belief that Christianity is the one true faith. To help accomplish these goals, they have increasingly focused on getting supporters elected to local school boards.

A related concern is that the public schools do not teach one absolute truth in any area. For example, in dealing with families in a high-school sociology class, a classroom discussion of many styles of relationships between adults and many approaches to parenting takes the place of the promotion of the traditional family as the only acceptable family. Rather than advocating that women remain at home as wives, mothers, and homemakers, the public schools attempt to prepare their students to assess the strengths and weaknesses of various arrangements. Rather than teaching the immorality of premarital sex, health teachers encourage their students to explore their own values and attitudes and introduce the cautions deemed necessary in the face of disease and the possibility of unwanted pregnancy. Government classes, instead of promoting democracy and condemning other forms of government, have students evaluate various forms of government.

Control over the textbook selection process is also an important agenda item for the new right. A few examples of their criticisms of schoolbooks used in the public schools will help make their position clear. Relativism has already been mentioned. Blurring of traditional sex roles, such as elementary schoolbook pictures of boys cooking and cleaning or girls building things and wearing hard hats, has been one of the things most criticized. Teaching about the European Renaissance is suspect because of its high estimate of humanity and human reason. The philosophy of the Enlightenment comes under the same criticism. Religion is not portrayed as a significant aspect of American history and culture; in fact, it is usually left out altogether. *The Wizard of Oz* portrays a witch as good, and *Cinderella* presents magical acts as if they were fact.

You might want to pause a moment here and think back over the textbooks from which you learned as a child. How was religion portrayed, if at all? What messages were being presented in the pictures of boys and girls, men and women? When you took the required (in most school systems, at any rate) government or civics course, were different types of government portrayed equally, or was democracy held up as an ideal?

The teaching of evolution is another focal point for the critique of public-school education. Some want the theory of evolution dropped from the curriculum completely in favor of teaching an account of the beginning of the world and humankind that is compatible with the creation stories in Genesis. Others want to see evolution and creationism or creation science taught alongside each other as theories. Again, think back to your high-school (perhaps junior-high or middle-school) biology, botany, or life-science classes. Were you taught about evolution? Were you taught the creation stories in Genesis? Was the entire subject ignored? Some textbook publishers and some schools have taken this last approach to avoid a confrontation over this very explosive issue.

A final point of contention with the public schools has to do with the teaching of sex education. In the first place, many supporters of the religious-political right want all sex education removed from the schools and left in the hands of parents and the churches. If sex education is to be taught in the public schools at all, the values of premarital chastity, marital fidelity, and lifelong monogamy should be the only things taught. Sex education cannot be separated from family life education, and the traditional family style must be upheld in the public schools.

An editorial reflection is in order here. The values of traditional Christianity have been a major influence in American life for many centuries. The Genesis accounts of how the world began have guided the thinking of uncounted millions of people and continue to do so. Sexual morality based on the teachings of the Christian Bible is the framework that has made family life meaningful and good for generations of Americans. These values deserve a place in public school education because they are a significant part of the story of humanity and of the history and present culture of the United States. In a pluralistic culture, they must be presented as one set of values alongside others from which people have chosen. They must not be taught as the only right values, to the exclusion of others. A similar point can be made concerning the omission of religion in descriptions of the history and present culture of the United States. Religion has been and continues to be an important factor in American life. To omit it is to present an inaccurate picture of both past and present. The distinction between teaching religion and teaching about religion must be scrupulously maintained, however, and the approach must always be descriptive rather than normative.

Every bit as important in the religious-political right's approach to public education is its support for a network of *private Christian schools*. You will recall that when we discussed Catholicism, we learned that the Catholic Church sponsors the largest private school system in the United States. It is usually called the parochial school system. Among Protestants, the Lutherans sponsor a number of schools. The network of Christian schools has grown steadily in the United States. Those who support Christian schools do so largely because they believe that home, church, and school should reinforce each other by presenting the same values and truths. Supporters of Christian schools want to see the development of a system that exists apart from the teacher training and licensing requirements enforced by the states. They do not want to be subject to the same curriculum requirements that guide the public schools.

There is more at stake, according to the supporters of private Christian schools, than simply being able to begin and end the school day with prayer and Bible reading or to say grace before lunch. Christian school advocates are asking for the right to control their children's education with minimal interference from the government. Government regulation is looked upon as harassment and as infringement on freedom of religion. For those whose values and home life are guided by the views and principles of fundamentalist Christianity, public-school attendance is a very real threat to their children's spiritual welfare. It threatens both their earthly happiness and their eternal life.

Catholics pressed for and won the right to their own schools because they believed that there was a clear Protestant bias in the public schools. Fundamentalist Christians believe there is a clear humanistic bias in the public schools. They seek the right to take decisive action to protect their youngsters. It is for this reason that education has become such a pressing issue.

The **military strength of the United States** and its position in relation to the other nations of the world are as great a concern to the religious-political right as are domestic issues. They believe that the United States must always be the first and foremost world military and economic power. They believe this is necessary mainly to protect the values of democracy and capitalism both in the United States itself and in the world. In this line of thought, the strongest possible national defense becomes not only a political necessity but a religious obligation. The United States has been chosen by God for a special destiny in the history of God's interaction with the world, and defending that destiny militarily is part of carrying out the divine plan. Any attempt at disarmament or compromise is seen as taking the United States one step farther along the road toward surrender or takeover by the forces of evil.

The religious-political right works through **direct political action** as well as through its efforts to educate people and persuade them to support their point of view. It seeks to elect public officials who are sympathetic to its programs and views. The role of government is described as the provision of "godly leadership."

Followers of this perspective believe that only by governing according to the Bible can a leader govern rightly. A direct practical implementation of this point of view came from the Christian Voice organization when it developed the Congressional Score Card to track the way that members of Congress voted on certain critical moral issues such as abortion support and the ERA. Voter registration drives have been another important focus, and voter registration has been done after Sunday-morning worship in some fundamentalist churches. After having done less well than they had hoped in national politics, their attention has turned more to local politics, where it remains, for the most part.

The Contract with the American Family

In 1994, the 104th Congress, the first Republican Congress in forty years, passed many of the planks that had made up the "Contract with the American Family." It was strongly supported by the Christian Coalition. Although not all of the items passed, and many of those that did passed in modified form, the document echoed many of the concerns of the religious-political right:

- There needs to be a constitutional amendment to guarantee religious liberty in public places, to prevent public institutions from being hostile to expressions of religion, and to prevent religion's being relegated to only the private sphere of life.
- Control of education should be returned to the local level by transferring funding from the federal level to families and local school boards.

- Legislation should be enacted that would empower parents to make school choices for their children, allowing parents to select the public school their children would attend and providing vouchers for those who chose to send their children to private schools.
- Parents' rights to control the upbringing of their children should be reinforced and the United Nations Convention on the Rights of the Child defeated because it interferes with parental control of their children.
- Greater tax relief should be provided for families with children by increasing the standard deduction for each child, equalizing the tax burden for married people and singles, and allowing homemakers to contribute to an IRA.
- A section on restoring respect for human life included a call for limits on late-term abortions, an end to "partial-birth" abortions, protection for those states that do not want to use tax funds to pay for abortion services, and an end to tax funding for organizations that promote and perform abortions.
- Individual support for private charities should be encouraged, for example by allowing people to designate that a limited amount of their taxes would go to private charities of their choice.
- Legislation should be enacted that will limit children's access to pornography on the Internet, via cable television, and by amending the federal child pornography laws to make any possession of child pornography illegal.
- Federal funding for organizations such as the National Endowment for the Arts, National Endowment for the Humanities, and Legal Services Corporation should end, requiring that they rely on private contributions.
- Work and study programs should be instituted for prisoners, with legislation enacted requiring restitution to crime victims and eliminating luxuries such as cable TV for prisons.

The Christian Coalition

The Christian Coalition is the largest and best-known among the many religious-political right groups. The Christian Coalition is "driven by the belief that people of faith have a right and a responsibility to be involved in the world around them. That involvement includes community, social and political action." Their organizational goals include:

- Strengthening the family.
- Protecting innocent human life.
- Returning education to local and parental control.
- Easing the tax burden on families.
- Punishing criminals and defending victims' rights.
- Protecting young people and our communities from the pollution of pornography.
- Defending the institution of marriage.
- Protecting religious freedom.

Its methods include many of those that have characterized religious right organizations, as well as other political interest groups, since their beginning:

- Nonpartisan voter guides and scorecard.
- *Religious Rights Watch* and other newsletters.
- Nationwide conferences and training seminars.
- A lobbying staff in Washington, D.C.
- Affiliates in every state—more than 2000 local chapters.
- Action Alert postcards, phone calls, and e-mail.
- Get-out-the-vote mailings and phone calls.[17]

A current major focus is the organization of grass-roots activists. Their "Families 2000 Strategy" seeks to recruit 100,000 volunteers to serve as liaisons between their local churches and Christian Coalition chapters. With this effort they hope to mobilize profamily activists by the November 2000 elections.

There are two pervasive and seemingly contradictory themes in the literature of the Christian Coalition.[18] There is a decidedly antipluralistic theme that calls for a restoration of Christian values as defined by the Coalition, a "reclamation" and "restoration" of the "Christian heritage" of the United States. A second theme apparently embraces pluralism when the Coalition calls for a "place at the table" for evangelical and fundamentalist Christianity and identifies its perspective as the victim of an increasingly secular and hostile culture. Many supporters of the Coalition and similar organizations seem to hold both values.

> There is an obvious and fundamental tension between the calls for the restoration of a Christian America and the demands for recognition of evangelical Christians as a persecuted group. The calls for restoration involve a rejection of the legitimacy of social and religious pluralism as an accepted norm of American society. The demands of recognition, in contrast, depend on the norms of pluralism for legitimation.[19]

Other Organizations

The Christian Coalition is the current flagship organization of the movement and politically its most influential group. There are others, however, that deserve mention in any discussion of the interaction between conservative religion and American culture. In addition to registering like-minded voters and electing agreeable government leaders, lobbying has been a central concern. The **National Conservative Political Action Committee** and the **National Christian Action Coalition** are primarily lobbying organizations. *Political action committees* (often referred to as PACs) are interest groups that engage in various activities. They often focus their attention on the election of sympathetic leaders. The Christian Voice Moral Government Fund and the Christian Voters' Victory Fund were

---

[17]The Christian Coalition Worldwide World Wide Web site (http://www.cc.org/).

[18]Justin Watson, *The Christian Coalition: Dreams of Restoration, Demands of Recognition* (New York: St. Martin's Press, 1997).

[19]Justin Watson, *The Christian Coalition*, p. 3.

formed expressly to help finance the political campaigns of people who would support fundamentalist and conservative values and programs.

The **Moral Majority**, founded by Jerry Falwell in 1979, was one of the earliest organizations in the religious-political right. As its interests expanded and it sought to draw in additional groups of people, it was renamed the **Liberty Foundation**. Late in 1987, Falwell turned over the leadership of the Liberty Foundation to Jerry Nims, an Atlanta, Georgia, businessperson and long-time Falwell associate.

The **Christian Voice** is the oldest national organization aligned with the religious-political right. It has concentrated largely on compiling information about candidates (Congressional Score Card) and providing voters with lists of approved and disapproved candidates. It provides financial support to those whom it approves.

At least two of the organizations were founded and are led by women. Best known is Phyllis Schlafly's **Eagle Forum**, which concentrated on the movement to defeat the ratification of the ERA. The lesser-known *Library Court* was organized in 1979, headed up by Connaught Marshner. It is named after the street in Washington, D.C., where it first met. Marshner worked very closely with Nevada Senator Paul Laxalt on the Family Protection Act, which he introduced into Congress in 1979. The Family Protection Act, which did not receive the necessary number of votes to pass, incorporated many of the family concerns of the religious-political right. Marshner has exercised a strong leadership role in the Library Court, as has Schlafly in the Eagle Forum. These organizations have also been leaders in the campaign to get an antiabortion amendment to the United States Constitution passed.

The Christian Reconstruction Movement

The Christian Reconstruction movement is a variation on the religious-political right theme. The Chalcedon Foundation is a nonprofit organization established in 1964 by R. J. Rushdoony. It seeks to educate people about the "Biblical standards for life, both individual and social." It supports the view that the only answers to individual and social problems can be found in the Christian Bible. Biblical standards as the Chalcedon Foundation interprets them apply to all people, not just to Bible believers, and the Bible gives God's blueprint for government as well as for individual and church life. The Rutherford Institute is the organization's legal defense arm.

Its presuppositions and its goals are further spelled out in its creed:

A Christian Reconstructionist is a *Calvinist*. . . . A Christian Reconstructionist believes the Faith should apply to all of life, not just the "spiritual" side. . . .

A Christian Reconstructionist is a *Theonomist*. Theonomy means "God's law." A Christian Reconstructionist believes God's law is found in the Bible. It has not been abolished as a standard of righteousness. . . . God's law is used for three main purposes: First, to drive the sinner to trust in Christ alone, the only perfect law-keeper. Second, to provide a standard of obedience for the Christian, by which he may judge his progress in sanctification. And third, to maintain order in society, restraining and arresting civil evil.

A Christian Reconstructionist is a *Presuppositionalist*. He does not try to "prove" that God exists or that the Bible is true. He holds to the Faith because the Bible says so, not because he can "prove" it. . . .

A Christian Reconstructionist is a *Postmillennialist*. He believes Christ will return to earth only after the Holy Spirit has empowered the church to advance Christ's kingdom in time and history. He has faith that God's purposes to bring all nations, though not every individual, in subjection to Christ cannot fail. . . .

A Christian Reconstructionist is a *Dominionist*. He takes seriously the Bible's commands to the godly to take dominion in the earth. This is the goal of the gospel and the Great Commission. The Christian Reconstructionist believes the earth and all its fullness is the Lord's: that every area dominated by sin must be "reconstructed" in terms of the Bible. This includes, first, the individual; second, the family; third, the church; and fourth, the wider society, including the state. The Christian Reconstructionist therefore believes fervently in Christian civilization. He firmly believes in the separation of church and state, but not the separation of the state or anything else from God. He is not a revolutionary; he does not believe in the militant, forced overthrow of human government. He has infinitely more powerful weapons than guns and bombs, he has the invincible Spirit of God, the infallible word of God, and the incomparable gospel of God, none of which can fail.[20]

Of these five items, the last is the most distinctive of the movement and has given rise to the term sometimes applied to it, "dominion theology." The dominionist viewpoint comes in the statement that not only individuals, families and churches must be "reconstructed" according to the Bible, but that all of society, including government, must be so transformed.

CHRISTIAN TELEVISION

Do you sometimes, or regularly, watch the television programs on any of the major Christian networks, such as PTL or FAM? If you do, why do you enjoy them? If you do not watch them, why not? What kinds of thoughts come to mind when someone uses the phrase, "television preacher" or "television evangelist"?

The religious message that is broadcast on Christian television is not new. Nor is religious broadcasting itself new. It began with radio and continued with commercial television. What *is* new is the medium. High-tech communications

[20]Chalcedon Foundation Web site (http://www.chalcedon.org/). The full text of the creed can be read on the site.

technologies, such as cable television and communications satellites, have revo-lutionized the religious broadcasting industry.

The early television evangelists such as Graham and Oral Roberts still use commercial programming. Some of the programs specifically identified with the religious-political right, such as Falwell's "Old Time Gospel Hour," are aired on commercial networks in some areas. So is Robert Schuller's "Hour of Power." However, Christian television is no longer primarily a matter of time purchased on commercial networks. The Christian networks, satellite connections, super high-tech studios, and computers have revolutionized Christian broadcasting. Three major Christian networks—the Family Network (FAM, formerly the Christian Broadcasting Network), Trinity Broadcasting Network (TBN), and the PTL (for "Praise the Lord" or "People That Love") Network—provide most of the programs that make up Christian television today.

The electronic church, as it is often called, has been hailed by those favor-able to it as the greatest tool the church has ever had for telling "the greatest story ever told." It has also been the most harshly criticized method of outreach the church has ever used. Whatever one's opinion of religious television, it now has a firm place in the overall landscape of the American love affair with both televi-sion and religion.

You have already been learning about Christian television, the electronic church, or "televangelism," because most of the programming on Christian tele-vision reflects the views of evangelical Christianity, fundamentalism, and the religious-political right. It is primarily an extension of the revivalist and evan-gelical tradition that has characterized American religion at least since the Awak-enings.

This particular form of religious broadcasting has often been referred to as **televangelism**. That word is somewhat inaccurate, because its main audience is composed of those who already share its point of view and religious beliefs. There is also a problem with the phrase **electronic church**, even though it is commonly used. There are some very important differences between *church* as most people think of it and what happens on the *electronic* church. I propose that we call it **Christian television**, using the phrase analogously to the phrase *Christian music*. Christian music is an outgrowth and an integral part of the con-servative/evangelical/fundamentalist point of view in American Christianity. It provides an alternative for those who are offended by contemporary secular music or who simply want music that reflects their own worldview. Similarly, Christian television provides alternative television for those who find it difficult to locate acceptable programs on the commercial channels. It reflects the same religious worldview that supports contemporary Christian music. Christian tele-vision, then, seems to be a logical choice.

This designation also helps us to understand the importance of the resur-gence in evangelical and fundamentalist Christianity in the United States for Christian television. There is now a group of consumers available who have clearly defined tastes in entertainment. It is this group of consumers that makes up the viewing audience for Christian television.

One of the best-known of the Christian television personalities is Jerry Falwell, founder of the Moral Majority. He is pastor of the 20,000-plus member Thomas Road Baptist Church in Lynchburg, Virginia, the site of the broadcasting empire he built. Thomas Road Church is an independent Baptist church, unaffiliated with any Baptist convention. Liberty Broadcasting Network, Liberty University, and the Lynchburg Christian Academy are all a part of the multifaceted program that Falwell supervises.

Pentecostal-turned-Methodist Oral Roberts has also put together a complex of operations, all of which revolve around his long-standing interest in religious healing. Known early as a television healer, he has downplayed this aspect in his later broadcasts. He built the City of Faith Medical Center in Tulsa, Oklahoma, to bring together medical research and treatment in a modern hospital facility and religious healing by prayer and the laying on of hands. Oral Roberts University, also in Tulsa, is one of the best-known of the conservative Christian colleges. Students attend required chapel and religion classes that are cast in the mold of the devotional study of religion rather than its academic study. They must agree to a strict code of personal conduct. Violations result in quick dismissal. Roberts' "Expect a Miracle" television program has been on the air for a quarter-century.

CBN (now FAM) was founded by Marion G. (Pat) Robertson, an early entrant in the field of Christian television who was among the first to offer a distinctively political orientation in his broadcasts. Following an unsuccessful bid for the 1988 Republican presidential nomination, he returned to his broadcasting career. Robertson built FAM into the largest Christian cable network, and his "700 Club" remains one of the most popular of the religious broadcasts.

Robert Schuller is an ordained minister in the Reformed Church in America. His twelve-story Crystal Cathedral in Garden Grove, California, is noteworthy for its architecture. It is a four-pointed star of reflective glass, 415 feet from point to point in one direction and over 200 feet in the other. One arm of the Crystal Cathedral slides open so that people can worship from their cars. He has focused his attention on the church and its congregation and has not expanded into educational or entertainment ventures. Schuller's sermons set him apart from the others. He freely acknowledges his debt to Norman Vincent Peale, famous for the "power of positive thinking." Schuller's "Hour of Power" makes much less of human sin than of human possibility. Peale's positive thinking has found new life in Schuller's "possibility thinking," which emphasizes that human possibilities are as vast as is our capacity to visualize them.

Who watches Christian television? Several studies have been done in the attempt to answer this question, and they all agree on the main points. Holding evangelical and fundamentalist or very conservative religious beliefs is the factor most strongly correlated with watching Christian television. Most viewers live in the South and the Midwest, with a disproportionate number in the South. The majority of viewers are female, and viewers are older than the general population. Between two-thirds and three-fourths are age fifty or over. Another important fact that emerges from these studies is that watching religion on television does not substitute for church attendance and participation. Most viewers are regular churchgoers and contribute to the financial support of their local congregation as well. The early predictions that Christian television would be the downfall of many a local congregation have not proven accurate. Christian television is used as a substitute for attendance by only one category of people—those who, for whatever reason, find it difficult to get out to attend church. Ratings indicate, finally, that there are fewer viewers by far than the massive audiences claimed by the broadcasters themselves. There are, especially, fewer regular viewers.

The fund-raising techniques used by Christian television have been widely criticized. Several methods are popular. Seeking donations is a common method. In return for a specified donation, donors may be memorialized in some fashion, such as by having their names inscribed in Oral Roberts' Prayer Tower or on chairs in Schuller's Crystal Cathedral. It should be noted here that donors' names have often been inscribed on pews or stained glass windows as local churches sought to raise money, too. Clubs such as the 700 Club or Faith Partners offer privileges and benefits in return for a specified sum per month. Besides a magazine or newsletter, participants gain a sense of being a part of something important, of being related in a personal way to the work being carried out by their favorite Christian television personality. Money is also raised by the sale of pens, bumper stickers, lapel pins, Bibles, records or audiotapes, and books. Frequently these items are not "sold" but offered in return for a donation. Most Christian television personalities are quite skilled at the personal-appeal style of fund-raising, in which they simply ask for donations. The "going off the air" appeal is a variant of this method, in which the personality makes a highly emotional appeal, in which it is said that only contributions over and above the usual will keep the program from having to go off the air. Again, contributors gain a feeling that they have helped to accomplish the work that the preacher set out to do.

For most of its founders, the initial goal of Christian television was evangelism. They wanted to bring their version of the gospel message to millions of viewers and win additional souls for Christ. Clearly, it does not work well as a tool for evangelism, because the great majority of its viewers already count themselves among those who agree with the viewpoint being presented. It does help to reinforce existing beliefs and behaviors. For the largely convinced viewing audience, what they see and hear models the behavior and beliefs they themselves are trying to live. It reinforces and supports, and many come away from its programs with renewed conviction and determination. As one of my students explained simply, "I watch it; I feel good."

There are important differences between Christian television and "church" as most people usually think of it. Christian television does not and cannot provide the personal dimension, the face-to-face contact that is a valuable part of a community of faith. In spite of "personalized" direct mail, clubs, and requests for contributions, Christian television is not a community. Its television-personality preachers are not pastors. They will not be there for their viewers when the viewers have marital problems or discover that a child is on drugs. They will not be there to baptize a new baby or to bury a grandparent or spouse. They are not accessible by telephone when someone wants to say, "Hey . . . I got the job! Thanks for your support." In a similar vein, an audience is not a congregation. Communities of faith provide their members with a group of people that is small enough to facilitate the development of intimacy. Many people find in their religious fellowships the kind of close interpersonal interaction that is necessary for emotional health. In communities of faith, attitudes and values are refined as people rub shoulders with like-minded others in an atmosphere that encourages trust and openness. Christian television cannot provide this vital dimension.

Why, then, Christian television? We can best think of it as viewer-supported alternative television. A significant number of people cannot find many programs on commercial television that do not run afoul of their values and tastes in entertainment. They want something more from television. One segment of the population turns to public television for what they want. A larger segment turns to Christian television. It is, in other words, a response to a very real need for viewing options other than commercial networks. As the percentage of conservative, fundamentalist, and evangelical Christians in the population has increased, so has the need for and the popularity of Christian television. The increasing conservatism and evangelicalism of American Christianity indicates that Christian television will continue to be an important element in the entertainment industry and in religion.

The 1980s was a decade of crisis for Christian television. Federal Communications Commission testimony demonstrated that funds collected by the several television ministries had been seriously misused. Allegations of sexual misconduct, actions that go to the very heart of the fundamentalist definition of sin, were hurled in several directions and later substantiated. The National Religious Broadcasters organization enacted new, tougher standards for its 1300-plus members.

Three things seems clear in the wake of that crisis. The problems of the 1980s and 1990s hurt Christian television. It appears unlikely that it will rebound to the level of financial support from viewers that it enjoyed prior to the 1980s. It is equally clear that the injuries were not fatal. The most likely scenario appears to be that Christian television will continue to be a significant aspect of our entertainment-oriented culture, providing programming for a segment of the population who cannot find acceptable television elsewhere.

The *Odyssey Channel* offers a different type of religious television. Its founders describe it as a "full-time national faith and values cable TV network." It is owned and operated by a coalition of over fifty national groups that represent a variety of Christian (Protestant, Catholic, Eastern Orthodox, and American-born) faiths, Judaism, and the National Council of Churches. There are three programming guidelines that distinguish Odyssey: no on-air solicitation of funds, no attempt to make converts, and no attacking of other faiths. Although it is not carried as widely as the better-known Christian networks, Odyssey does offer an alternative in some areas.

HOLINESS AND PENTECOSTAL CHRISTIANS

Holiness is a movement that involves several groups of Christian believers, rather than being a group in and of itself. It is rooted in Jesus' admonition that his followers be perfect, even as God is perfect (Matthew 5:48). To follow this directive means to work toward ever-increasing holiness and perfection of life in this world. Sin and the evidences of sin are to be progressively rooted out. The search for perfection usually has been accompanied by a sense of separation from those who are not engaged in a similar search. Holiness is a matter of both belief and lifestyle. Its adherents believe in the possibility and the necessity of sanctification, understood as a work of the Holy Spirit distinct from justification. By **justification**, a person is forgiven for past sin and placed in a new relationship with God. By **sanctification**, that new relationship becomes more and more evident in the person's life as the Holy Spirit continues to bring about growth in grace. Other people are likely to be made aware of someone's membership in a holiness church by their lifestyle, which reflects, in ways that vary somewhat from church to church, their understanding of how a sanctified life is to be lived.

When it began, the **holiness movement** in the United States took many of its cues from John Wesley's teaching about Christian perfection. Wesley, you remember, was the founder of Methodism in England. When Methodism came to the United States, it brought Wesley's emphasis on sanctification and perfection with it. Originally, Methodists had many of the characteristics that have come to be associated with the holiness movement. As Methodism grew in numbers and wealth and became more a religion of the middle class, outward holiness was downplayed. Groups that disagreed with this lessening of outward holiness broke away. They often referred to themselves as Wesleyans, in order to distinguish themselves from the Methodists and to express their loyalty to the original intention of John Wesley.

The rejection of that which is "of the world" in order to attain holiness brought with it disagreements over precisely what was to be rejected. Over time, these disagreements led to there being many divisions within the movement. There are now several holiness groups made up of many churches as well as many independent communities of believers without ties outside their own group.

What, then, are some of the things that holiness Christians reject as being too much of the world? The use of alcohol, tobacco, and illicit drugs are universally banned among such groups. They are very careful in their language, avoiding not only obvious swearing and blasphemy but much of the common slang used in our culture. Gambling, too, is universally forbidden. Attending movie theaters and sometimes watching television are not permitted. Dancing is avoided by most. Swimming, or swimming in mixed groups of males and females, is sometimes disallowed. Children often do not participate in physical education classes that violate their standards, such as those involving folk dancing or those that require girls to wear slacks or shorts. Some holiness students also ask to be excused from participating in regular classroom work that conflicts with their beliefs. Examples include the teaching of evolution in biology or botany classes, sex education in health classes, or when movies are shown in class.

It is especially important, according to holiness teaching, that women follow a virtuous lifestyle. Women's role in the home and in the rearing of children makes them the primary transmitters of holiness. Frequently, women are discouraged from cutting their hair or at least from wearing it shorter than shoulder length. The use of cosmetics and the wearing of much jewelry is frowned upon. A simple wristwatch and a wedding band are often the only permissible jewelry. High-cut necklines and at least elbow-length sleeves are the norm, and dresses or skirts are worn rather than slacks or shorts.

Those in search of holiness tend to socialize with like-minded people who reinforce their values and way of life and who support them in their difference from the world. Marriages usually take place within the group, and children are encouraged to find their playmates among church members' children. Families are often large, and divorce is strongly discouraged if not forbidden. This pattern of socialization has the twofold effect of reinforcing the sense of community within the group and maintaining the separation between those who are "of the world" and those who are not.

There are many independent churches within this movement. There are also some groupings of churches. Some of the better-known groups include several in the Church of God family, the Churches of Christ in Christian Union, and some conservative Mennonite groups. Two of the largest are the Church of the Nazarene and the Wesleyan Church, both of which are especially strong in the midwest. Several statements included in the Wesleyan statement of faith and practice, "This We Believe," illustrate the holiness perspective:

> . . . abstaining from all forms of gambling and by abstaining from using or trafficking (production, sale or purchase) in any substances destructive to their physical, mental and spiritual health, such as alcoholic beverages, tobacco and drugs (other than proper medical purposes of drugs).

> In the light of the scientific knowledge of our day concerning the actual and potential harm of these substances, total abstinence is more in keeping with these biblical principles than is moderation.

> . . . grow in the knowledge, love and grace of God by participating in public worship, the ministry of the Word of God, the Lord's Supper, family and personal devotions and fasting.

> The Wesleyan Church abhors the trend to ignore God's laws of chastity and purity, and vigorously opposes public acceptance of sexual promiscuity and all factors and practices which promote it.

> The Wesleyan Church protests the inclusion of such questionable items as social dancing in the public school curriculum and maintains the right of its members to seek exemption from participation by their children in all matters that are contrary to scriptural doctrines and principles as expressed in the Articles of Religion, Membership Commitments or Elementary Principles of The Wesleyan Church, without prejudice to academic standing.

The Wesleyan Church believes that its members should exercise responsible stewardship of their leisure time. This will include careful regulation of the use in the home of mass media, such as current literature, radio and television, guarding the home against the encroachment of evil. It will also involve. . . the refusal to participate in social dancing, the refusal to patronize the motion picture theater (cinema), together with other commercial ventures as they feature the cheap, the violent or the sensual and pornographic, and the refusal to engage in playing games which tend to be addictive or conducive to gambling.

The Wesleyan Church believes that our people should provide clear testimony to Christian purity and modesty by properly clothing the body and by dressing with Christian simplicity.[21]

Perhaps the best known of all the holiness organizations, because it maintains the highest public profile, is the Salvation Army. While most people probably associate the Salvation Army with thrift shops and Christmas bell ringers, it is also a fully functioning church. In addition to the social programs for which it is best known, Army Citadels hold Sunday and midweek services for a membership of about 500,000. Their wholehearted identification with the poorest of the poor and the outcasts of society make them able to reach out to people who are likely to be overlooked by other churches. The United Pentecostal Church is a major holiness denomination that is also pentecostal.

Some of you may feel that the restrictions that holiness imposes amount to a program for avoiding life in the real world. It certainly is true that there are fewer worldly temptations for people who conscientiously follow this path. Consider, however, the burden of difference that these people take upon themselves for the sake of the higher goals they seek. Students who are not a part of the ordinary round of school activities, and whose dress and behavior set them apart from other students, may be ridiculed, or at least misunderstood and socially isolated. Acceptance by others comes slowly or not at all under these circumstances. Those of all ages voluntarily limit social contacts and activities taken for granted by the majority culture. It is a life of difficult choices, the final validation of which must of necessity wait until an unspecified time in the future.

Part of the variety in American religion stems from variations in the way that different communities of faith balance out their appeal to the intellect, the will, and the emotions. Some services of worship are calm and dignified and offer stimulation primarily to the intellect. Those that emphasize ethical behavior and social service appeal to the will. Some offer more in terms of emotional satisfaction.

The experience of highly emotional worship and religious ecstasy is the foundation of pentecostalism. It has been a part of American religion for many years in the form of traditional pentecostalism and has gained in acceptance and visibility in the charismatic renewal movement. Pentecostalism is also one of the fastest-growing forms of Christianity, both in the United States and around the world. Two of the American denominations showing the most rapid recent

[21]The Wesleyan Church World Wide Web site (http://www.wesleyan.org/).

Figure 8-3 Pentecostal worship is emotional and enthusiastic. *(Guy Gillette/Photo Researchers, Inc.)*

growth—the mostly white Assemblies of God (1.8 million) and the mostly black Church of God in Christ (5 million)—are pentecostal.

The word **pentecostalism** refers to an event recorded in the Christian New Testament, in the Book of Acts. The disciples were gathered together following the devastating events of Jesus' crucifixion and death. They must have been a discouraged and disheveled band of men. As the biblical account goes, the Holy Spirit came to the disciples in a new and powerful way, described as "tongues like flames of fire, dispersed among them and resting on each one" (Acts 2:3, New English translation). They began to speak in languages other than those they usually used, and all present heard in their own languages. In the confusion that followed, Peter is said to have spoken, quoting the Hebrew prophet Joel (God is said to be speaking here): "This will happen in the last days: I will pour out upon everyone a portion of my spirit; and your sons and daughters shall prophesy; your young men shall see visions, and your old men shall dream dreams" (Joel 2:28, New English translation). Most Christian churches celebrate this event annually in the spring, on Pentecost Sunday, as the anniversary of the founding of the church. For some Christians, however, it has meant much more. Pentecostal Christians (whether traditional pentecostal or *charismatic Christians*[22]) believe that what God did at Pentecost continues to happen

[22]The *charismatic renewal movement* is discussed in the next section.

today. People can receive the Holy Spirit in the same way as did the disciples, according to the Book of Acts.

Pentecostals believe that certain phenomena accompany and give evidence of the work of the Holy Spirit. The principal evidence of this gift is usually said to be the ability to **speak in tongues**. This phenomenon is also called **glossolalia**. Speaking in tongues takes two forms. People may speak in a recognizable human language. On the other hand, some pentecostals say that their tongues are not recognizable human languages, but a private language given by God. Linguists who have studied this type of glossolalia have found that, although it is not a known human language, it has the characteristics that identify it as distinctly human speech. Pentecostal Christians are urged to expect and actively seek this gift: An Assemblies of God statement expresses it this way: "All believers are entitled to and should ardently expect and earnestly seek the promise of the Father, the baptism in the Holy Ghost and fire, according to the command of our Lord Jesus Christ. This was the normal experience of all in the early Christian Church. With it comes the enduement of power for life and service, the bestowment of the gifts and their uses in the work of the ministry."[23]

Pentecostals make another distinction as well. For some, tongues are a prayer language between the individual and God and do not call for interpretation. Others believe that tongues are a way that God uses to communicate with an entire congregation. In these instances, an interpreter is required to "translate" the message. Interpretation also is thought to be a gift of the Spirit. Usually, the speaker and the interpreter are two different people.

Speaking in tongues is regarded as the primary manifestation of the action of the Holy Spirit. The United Pentecostal Church International considers it "the initial sign of receiving the Holy Ghost," and "an immediate, external evidence" of the Holy Ghost's indwelling. Other gifts of the Spirit are mentioned in the New Testament. Examples of such lists can be found in 1 Corinthians 12:8–10, 28, and 29–30. The healing of physical and psychological illnesses is considered second only to tongues by most pentecostals. Prophecy and the interpretation of tongues receive considerable attention. Preaching and administration in the church are considered gifts. Exorcism, or the removal of unclean spirits, is practiced by some. Wisdom and knowledge are gifts, as is the ability to distinguish good from evil spirits. A very few pentecostals handle venomous snakes and drink poison in response to a statement attributed to Jesus in the Gospel of Mark, which says that believers can do these things without harm (Mark 16:17–18).

Some of the divisions that occurred within the holiness-pentecostal movement came about as churches began to differ about the role of glossolalia. The Wesleyan Church's statement on this topic illustrates the position that some churches take:

---

[23]Assemblies of God World Wide Web site (http://www.ag.org/).

We believe that the Gift of the Spirit is the Holy Spirit himself, and He is to be desired more than the Gifts of the Spirit which He in His wise counsel bestows. . . .

The Wesleyan Church believes in the miraculous use of languages and the interpretation of languages in its biblical and historical setting. But it is contrary to the Word of God to teach that speaking in an unknown tongue or the gift of tongues is the evidence of the baptism of the Holy Spirit or of that entire sanctification which the baptism accomplishes; therefore, only a language readily understood by the congregation is to be used in public worship. . . .[24]

Traditional pentecostalism began in America in the late nineteenth and early twentieth centuries. It was an outgrowth of the holiness movement. Like holiness, traditional pentecostalism usually emphasizes the necessity of outward holiness. More important, pentecostals focus on what they call the baptism of the Holy Spirit (often referred to in these churches as the Holy Ghost). This is said to be an encounter with God that may precede or follow water baptism. The specific religious experiences believed to be associated with the gift of the Holy Ghost became more important than the lifestyle associated with the holiness movement.

Two people are especially associated with the early history of pentecostalism in the United States. Charles Fox Parham was a traveling ex-Methodist preacher who settled in Topeka, Kansas, and founded a Bible school called the College of Bethel. In December 1900, some thirty or forty of Parham's students received the gift of tongues after studying Acts 2. The key person behind the development of pentecostalism as a movement, however, was William Joseph Seymour, a former slave who was at one time a student of Parham's. After receiving the gift of tongues himself in 1906, Seymour rented a run-down building on Azuza Street in Los Angeles, which became the site of the well-known Azuza Street Mission. Seymour held very enthusiastic religious revivals at Azuza Street, and many people received the various spiritual gifts under his leadership. The mission was eventually renamed the Apostolic Faith Gospel Mission, developed a missionary program both at home and overseas, and published a monthly newsletter plus several other publications. A movement had been born.

Several of the early pentecostal churches still exist in the United States, including the Assemblies of God (the largest), the Church of God (Cleveland, Tennessee), the Church of God in Christ, the Pentecostal Holiness Church, the Foursquare Gospel Church, and the United Pentecostal Church. Many still retain at least some emphasis on holiness, as well. There are also numerous independent churches in the pentecostal category, which are more likely to require a holiness lifestyle in addition to clear-cut evidence of the spiritual gifts. Their membership tends to come from the lower socioeconomic classes. Many congregations, although certainly not all, are predominantly black. Although they are

[24]Wesleyan Church World Wide Web site (http://www.wesleyan.org/).

not limited to any one geographical area, their greatest strength is in the Midwest, the lower Midwest, and the South.

Although linked by their pentecostal experiences, the various pentecostal denominations also have differences. As noted above, some, such as members of the United Pentecostal Church, affirm a holiness lifestyle, while others, such as members of the large Assemblies of God, do not. The United Pentecostal Church is also the largest of the "Oneness Pentecostal" churches, affirming the oneness of God rather than belief that God is a trinity of three persons in one God. People are baptized in the name of Jesus only, rather than with the more usual "in the name of the Father, the Son, and the Holy Spirit." Father, Son, and Holy Spirit are different manifestations of the one God rather than distinct persons united into a single God. By contrast, the Assemblies of God is trinitarian.

Although pentecostalism began as an interracial movement, segregated congregations and denominations became the norm. At present, new efforts toward racial unity are occurring. The predominantly white Pentecostal Fellowship of America, which includes several pentecostal churches, is reorganizing to include black churches, including the rapidly growing Church of God in Christ. Interest in unity has come about in part due to the necessity to work together in inner-city ministries.[25]

Pentecostal worship is emotional and enthusiastic, marked by frequent outbursts of pentecostal phenomena and shouts of "Amen!" and "Praise Jesus!" from the congregation. It addresses the human need for religious experience very directly. Traditional pentecostalism is, in its own right, a significant aspect of American religion. It also forms the background against which we can better understand the modern-day charismatic renewal movement. This movement shares important characteristics with traditional pentecostalism and at the same time has significant differences. An Assemblies of God college professor and former president of the Society for Pentecostal Studies summarizes his tradition this way: "This is the experiential religion par excellence. It fills a vacuum for meaning in life and does so at the deepest levels of one's experience. But it also incorporates one into a movement and community larger than oneself."[26]

THE CHARISMATIC RENEWAL MOVEMENT

The intense emotional involvement that characterizes pentecostal worship was not a part of consensus religion prior to the charismatic renewal movement. Since the revivals of America's early history, there have been sharp differences of opinion about the appropriateness of such "manifestations of the Spirit." Most of the consensus churches either ignored the pentecostals or criticized their worship as undignified and excessively emotional. The **charismatic renewal movement** refers to a group of Christians who have had pentecostal experiences but

---

[25]*Christianity Today*, April 25, 1994.
[26]Quoted in Don Lattin, "Touched by the Fire," *Common Boundary*, July/August 1995, p. 34.

who are not members of traditional pentecostal churches. The word **charismatic** is derived from a Greek word that means "gift" and refers to the gifts of the Holy Spirit enumerated in the Christian New Testament. The charismatic renewal movement began in the United States, as far as we know, in 1960. The reverend Dennis Bennett of Saint Mark's Episcopal Church in Van Nuys, California, his wife, and about seventy other members of his congregation received the gift of tongues during a prayer meeting. The phenomenon spread very rapidly and soon had appeared in every major Protestant denomination as well as in the Roman Catholic Church.

Richard Quebedeaux, in his study of the charismatic renewal movement titled *The New Charismatics, II*, explains its importance this way: The consensus Christian churches typically teach that God is present with the faithful, that new life in Christ is possible now, and that the Holy Spirit is present in the church, but they fail to make this message believable. There is no experiential evidence that would enable people to know beyond doubt that the message was true and that God was present to them personally. The charismatic renewal movement rejects both the "liberal, nonsupernatural god who really isn't there anyhow," and the "rational evangelical god of the intellect," whose specialty is propositional truth. It embraces a "God you can feel, respond to, and *love*." He continues, "It is the knowledge of this God, given through the experience of his Holy Spirit, that has bound charismatics together."[27] Modern-day charismatics are not content to be told about the presence of God in their churches and the presence of the Holy Spirit in their hearts. They seek knowledge and certainty, the certainty provided by the religious experience of the charismatic renewal movement.

There are several characteristics of the charismatic renewal movement that set it apart from traditional pentecostalism. For the most part, there has been no large-scale exodus of charismatics from noncharismatic churches. Usually they meet together in small prayer groups in addition to remaining involved in other church activities. In addition, however, the movement has given rise to charismatic groups that include charismatics from all sorts of church backgrounds. The movement emphasizes experience rather than doctrine and has become thoroughly ecumenical, with people of different backgrounds and theologies united in a common bond of experience.

The largest of the ecumenical organizations is the **Full Gospel Businessmen's Fellowship, International**, founded in 1951. Although founded before the rise of the new charismatic movement, it attracts people who count themselves among the new charismatics. The organization has grown rapidly and now has male and female members from all walks of life, a women's group (Women's Aglow Fellowship), and teen and youth groups. Members usually meet for a meal and to share experiences and testimony. Groups of charismatic students meet regularly on most college campuses in the United States. The charismatic renewal movement also holds nationwide conferences yearly, one of the largest of which is at the Catholic Notre Dame University in north-central Indiana.

---

[27]Richard Quebedeaux, *The New Charismatics, II* (New York: Harper & Row, 1983), pp. xiii–xv.

In contrast to the highly emotional outpourings of early pentecostalism, the charismatic renewal movement is quieter. This toning down clearly reflects the middle-class and upper-middle-class nature of the charismatic renewal movement, another feature in which it differs from traditional pentecostalism. Most charismatics say that they receive the Holy Spirit in quiet prayer with a small group of other Christians. Those who have already had such experiences gather around people who are seeking the experience, pray with them, and place their hands on the seekers' heads. There is an incident recorded in the Book of Acts in which Paul is said to have laid his hands on some of the disciples. When he did, "the Holy Spirit came on them, and they spoke in tongues and prophesied" (Acts 19:6, New International Version). The initial experience of tongues is usually followed by continuing to speak in tongues and receiving other spiritual gifts. Because it is ecumenical and experiential, it is theologically diverse as well, with very little commonly held theology. Charismatics (who are also called *neopentecostals* or *new pentecostals*) are bound together by their experience and by their belief in that experience.

The lifestyles of contemporary charismatic Christians differ little from the lifestyles of other people in their culture. The requirements of outward holiness that often mark traditional pentecostalism are absent. Charismatics share with evangelicals the desire to share the faith and joy they have found, and many actively witness to their experiences. For all their differences, though, modern-day charismatics are one with traditional pentecostals in their belief that God works experientially in the lives of believers now.

Both traditional pentecostalism and charismatic renewal offer people who participate in them the assurance that their God is present with them. Belief is superseded by evidence. Those outside the movement often wonder how those inside it can be sure that what they experience is in fact the work of the Holy Spirit. Nonparticipants often believe that phenomena such as speaking in tongues are the result of self-induced hysteria. There is a middle ground between the uncritical acceptance of the believer and the skepticism of the nonbeliever. When viewed from the empathic perspective of the academic study of religion, the heart of pentecostal religion, old or new, is seen to be both the experience itself and the **meaning** that it has for those who are a part of it. Whatever the explanation for the experience, it is clear that its meaning to those who are the recipients of it is religious and provides the certainty that they seek.

QUESTIONS AND ACTIVITIES FOR REVIEW, DISCUSSION, AND WRITING

1. What might be the advantages and disadvantages of the "separatist" position taken by the fundamentalists described in this chapter?
2. Has anyone ever "witnessed" to you? How did you feel, and why? If you yourself "witness" to other people, reflect on what doing so means to you.
3. What is your response to the views of the religious-political right? Be sure that you can state the reasons for your response.

4. Do you think that the Christian Reconstruction Movement is a good thing or a bad thing for the United States? Why?
5. If you are able to get cable television, or if you can get religious television on a commercial channel, watch two different programs and write an essay in which you reflect on what you observe.
6. If you are not a holiness Christian yourself, how would your life be different if you were? Try to see both positive and negative possibilities. If you are, reflect on what being a holiness Christian means to you.
7. If you are not a pentecostal or charismatic Christian yourself, discuss with friends or classmates who are what that experience means to them. If you are, reflect on what it means to you.
8. If possible, attend a pentecostal or charismatic worship service and write an essay in which you reflect on what you observed and experienced. Women: If you attend a traditional pentecostal service, remember that many of these churches do have a dress code for women. You may want to call first and inquire.
9. Several Web sites for denominations relevant to this chapter are listed below. Visit several of them to locate specific examples of the viewpoints and practices described in the chapter.

FOR FURTHER READING

JORSTAD, ERLING, *Popular Religion in America: The Evangelical Voice*. Westport, CT: Greenwood Press, 1993. Jorstad discusses the relationship of evangelical religion to several important issues such as family and economic values and the interaction of popular evangelicalism with the media. He sees a new diversity emerging in the evangelical movement as a range of individual churches find their places under what has become a rather large umbrella.

MARTIN, WILLIAM, *With God on Our Side: The Rise of the Religious Right in America*. New York: Broadway Books, 1996. This book describes the history, views, and methods of the religious right from 1960 onward.

MILLER, DONALD E., *Reinventing American Protestantism: Christianity in the New Millennium*. Berkeley, CA: University of California Press, 1997. Miller sees a "new reformation" going on in Protestantism in the United States and provides excellent descriptions of three major churches in the "new paradigm" church movement.

POEWE, CARLA, ed., *Charismatic Christianity as a Global Culture*. Columbia, SC: University of South Carolina Press, 1994. This edited collection of essays situates charismatic Christianity in the United States in its larger world context.

SCHULTZE, QUENTIN J., *Televangelism and American Culture: The Business of Popular Religion*. Grand Rapids, MI: Baker Book House, 1991. This book is a careful examination of televangelism as business, as religion, and as a significant form of American popular culture, and what this might mean for each.

SHERRILL, JOHN L., *They Speak with Other Tongues*. New York: Pyramid Books, 1964. Although this is an older book, it can be highly recommended. Sherrill is a reporter who was assigned to do a story on the charismatic renewal movement and became a part of it as a result. His account is fascinating and provides a unique look at his journey from skeptical outsider to convinced insider.

WATSON, JUSTIN., *The Christian Coalition: Dreams of Restoration, Demands for Recognition*. New York: St. Martin's Press, 1997. This carefully nuanced study of this central religious right group points out its contradictions without being polemic.

RELEVANT WORLD WIDE WEB SITES

Promise Keepers (http://www.promisekeepers.org/).
American Council of Christian Churches (http://www.amcouncilcc.org/).
Trinity Broadcasting Network (http://www.tbn.org/).
Christian Broadcasting Network (http://www.cbn.org/).
Full Gospel Businessmen's Fellowship International (http://www.fgbfi.org/).
Aglow International (http://www.aglow.org/).
United Pentecostal Church International (http://www.upci.org/).
Church of the Nazarene (http://www.nazarene.org/).
Wesleyan Church (http://www.wesleyan.org/).
Assemblies of God (http://www.ag.org/).
Church of God in Christ (http://www.cogic.org/).
Foursquare Gospel (http://www.foursquare.org/).
Christian Churches/Churches of Christ (http://www.cwv.net.christ'n/).
Christian Coalition (http://www.cc.org/).
Eagle Forum (http://www.eagleforum.org/).
Rutherford Institute (http://www.rutherford.org/).

9

Ethnic Christianity

Since the late 1970s, Chicago's black inner city has become a harsher place to live. In the same period, storefront churches have flourished. . . .

In the storefront church, low-income blacks create ways of thinking about the world and acting in the world that reverse degrading public assumptions about inner-city blacks. . .

Racist stereotypes about lazy, ineffective, immoral, and unresourceful blacks are contradicted by rigorous church protocols, steadfast commitment to work for the church, and creativity and skill on the part of the community of believers to maintain the storefront mission. . . . [Members] meaningfully address the problems they have securing work; the violence and crime they endure in their neighborhoods; the deprivation they see on the ghetto streets; and the hostility, indifference, and humiliation they suffer because they are poor and black.[1]

ETHNIC CHRISTIANITY

Ethnic Christian communities of faith are groups of people whose religion and ethnic, racial, or national identities are inextricably linked together. Eastern Orthodox Christians and black Christians in traditional black churches and black independent congregations are the two major representatives of ethnic Christianity in the United States.[2] Although both of these groups include converts whose ethnic heritage differs from that most closely identified with the group—Eastern Orthodox of non-Eastern European descent and whites who are members of black churches—the ethnic identity of the group as a whole remains clear and important in its self-understanding.

[1]Frances Kostarelos, *Feeling the Spirit: Faith and Hope in an Evangelical Black Storefront Church* (Columbia, SC: University of South Carolina Press, 1995), pp. 123–126.
[2]In the next chapter, we will take up more ethnic communities of faith.

These religious groups are important carriers of ethnic and cultural identity. For Eastern Orthodox Christians, the church often provides not only a place for worship, but a place in which native dress, language, food, and other cultural customs are preserved, understood, and appreciated. The church and its members become the primary social center for the group. Churches may also sponsor cultural festivals that help to bring the native culture of their members to the larger community. The church helps provide a link to "the old country," allowing its members to be both American and distinctively ethnic. By doing so, it plays an important role in easing the transition for new immigrants and in helping to keep the ethnic heritage from becoming lost in succeeding generations.

As you will learn, the black church played a central role in helping blacks become an integral part of American culture. At the same time, it helped to keep alive the traditions of distinctively black worship and religious life. It continues to do so today. The black churches provide a place in which black heritage and pride in blackness can be nurtured in an otherwise oppressively racist society. They also provide resources to help blacks advance in the predominantly white culture.

The ways in which religion and ethnicity are interrelated are too complex for full exploration here. Three important points can be noted, however, in addition to what has already been said. Religion is an important source of stability and comfort among immigrants and others who are not fully at home in American culture. Immigration—whether forced or undertaken by choice—means the loss of the familiar. Often it entails separation from not only friends but family as well. Although for many, coming to the United States has meant the hope of a new beginning, it has brought with it grief and a sense of loss. In the midst of such feelings, religion offers something of "home" that can come with the immigrant.

Another point at which religion and ethnicity intersect is in the role of religious leaders. The religious leaders are usually among the better-educated members of the ethnic community and have tended to be respected in this country simply because they are religious leaders. This puts them in an excellent position to serve as spokespersons for the ethnic, national, or racial group in question. This has been particularly evident in the role of articulate black ministers in the civil rights movement.

Research[3] indicates that links between religion and ethnicity in the United States will continue to decline in the next millennium, for several reasons. (1) Both religion and ethnicity are declining in social significance, although some individuals continue to assign great importance to one or both. What is important is that this is now a matter of choice, in most instances. (2) Both religion and ethnicity are also declining in "inheritability." What this means is that

---

[3]Phillip E. Hammond and Kee Warner, "Religion and Ethnicity in Late-Twentieth-Century America," in *Religion in the Nineties, The Annals of the American Academy of Political and Social Science*, vol. 527, ed. Wade Clark Roof (Newbury Park, CA: Sage Publications, 1993), pp. 55–66.

"genes may be inherited, but the social meaning of those genes" increasingly is not. (3) While intermarriage, increasingly common, need not weaken either set of ties, it often does. To sum up, "as religion becomes more and more a matter of individual choice, and as persons become increasingly selective in making that choice, ethnicity, along with other background characteristics, will have a declining effect in determining religious identity."[4] This trend could significantly increase the cultural diversity of America's congregations over time. If it does so, becoming genuinely multicultural communities of faith will almost certainly challenge those congregations in ways that cannot yet be fathomed.

EASTERN ORTHODOX CHRISTIANITY

Some of you reading this book are undoubtedly Eastern Orthodox Christians. The majority of you are not. For those of you who are, this chapter is an invitation to see your church in a new way, from the point of view of the academic study of religion. For those of you who are not, I invite you to imagine yourselves in the world of an Eastern Orthodox service of worship. Bearded priests dressed in ornate vestments (Figure 9-1) lead an impressive procession to the front of the church. The air is heavy with the smell of incense. Around the church are many icons—paintings of Jesus, Mary, and the saints done in glowing colors, embellished with gold. The priest and the people chant responsively in Greek, its measured cadences seeming to belong to the time that the Christian New Testament was written. An air of mystery makes you catch your breath.

Figure 9-1 The vestments of Orthodox Christian priests are ornately symbolic. *(Audrey Gottlieb/Monkmeyer Press.)*

[4]Hammond and Warner, "Religion and Ethnicity," p. 66.

The **Eastern Orthodox churches** are a group of churches whose members follow the teachings and practices of Christianity as it was practiced in the major cities of the Eastern Roman Empire in the first centuries of the Common Era. They include the Greek and Russian Orthodox Churches and churches with national ties to the former Yugoslavia, Ukraine, Serbia, Croatia, Armenia, Bulgaria, and Romania.

The word **orthodox** means "correct" or "right," and Orthodox believers understand the rightness of their religion in three ways. It is right belief, continuing an unbroken tradition that reaches back to the time of Jesus himself. It is also right worship, which is the key to the unity of these churches. Right worship is at the very heart of their lives. It also means right organization, maintaining the forms of church government that were common in the earliest centuries of Christianity, closest to the time of Jesus. We will explore each of these dimensions in turn. The **Eastern** in Eastern Orthodox Churches means fidelity to the faith and tradition of the early church that was centered in and around Jerusalem, Antioch, Alexandria, and Constantinople. It also refers to the locations of the seven ecumenical councils of Christianity. Two were at Nicea, three at Constantinople, and one apiece at Ephesus and Chalcedon. The Eastern Orthodox churches accept these seven councils as authoritative.

History

For the first ten centuries of its existence, the Christian church was essentially one and undivided, although there were certainly differences between various geographical locations. Within a few years of the beginning of Christianity, there were communities of believers in all the major cities of the Roman Empire, one body of Christians with a diversity of beliefs and practices. There was as yet no central leadership. Leadership was shared among the leaders in the different cities.

It is not necessary to trace the intricate political and religious differences that led up to the final division between Christianity in the West and in the East in order to understand American Orthodoxy. The political factors were at least as important in bringing about the final division as were the religious ones. In 1054 C.E., an emissary of the Bishop of Rome excommunicated the Bishop of Constantinople, who, in turn, excommunicated the Bishop of Rome, making formal and official a division that had been growing for centuries.

The first Orthodox church in the United States was a Greek Orthodox church in New Orleans in 1864, although there had been a colony of Greek Orthodox people at New Smyrna, Florida, a century earlier. Orthodox immigration into the United States came relatively late. The first significantly large numbers were not present until the nineteenth and twentieth centuries. The first archdiocese (a church governmental unit, usually a metropolitan center, headed by an archbishop) in the United States was the Orthodox Archdiocese of North and South America, incorporated in New York in 1921. Large numbers of Greek immigrants arrived in the United States at the turn of the century, bringing their

Orthodoxy with them. Large numbers of Russians arrived after 1917, when the Bolshevik Revolution began in Russia.

Two other events played significant roles in Orthodox history in the United States. First, missionaries from the Russian Orthodox Church established missions in Alaska as early as 1794, providing a base from which Orthodoxy could enter the United States. The large number of Orthodox Christians in Alaska meant that when Alaska became a state in 1959, the number of Russian Orthodox in this country rose dramatically. Second, thousands of Orthodox immigrants came from Greece, Asia Minor, Russia, and Eastern Europe between the Civil War and World War I.

In spite of the close national connections of the Orthodox churches, early archdioceses often included all the national churches, because the total numbers were small. Such archdioceses were incorporated in New Orleans in 1864, in San Francisco in 1867, and in New York City in 1870. As the numbers increased, national churches were organized. A Serbian Orthodox church was incorporated in 1926, a Romanian church in 1935, Antiochene and Ukrainian churches in 1937, and a Bulgarian church in 1938. These churches still have a strong national consciousness that plays a major role in keeping them apart organizationally.

EASTERN ORTHODOX CHRISTIANITY IN THE UNITED STATES

There are approximately 1 million Orthodox Christians in the United States. About 1 percent of Americans are members of Orthodox churches. Most are members of either the Greek or Russian churches. There are several monasteries, two schools of theology, a college, and several other institutions.

Belief

People of Orthodox Christian faith believe and practice in ways that are both like and unlike those of their Protestant and Catholic neighbors. Orthodox belief is based on the Bible and on the official teachings of the **seven ecumenical ("of the whole church") councils** of the Christian church, which took place during the first 1000 years of its history. Like Catholics but unlike Protestants, Orthodox Christians accept both the Bible and the church's tradition as genuine sources of revelation. Tradition is not found in a single document, but in many. The Nicene Creed is the principal creed. The creeds of the other councils are also believed to be true expressions of God's revelation. The Divine Liturgy (the principal act of worship) itself is an authoritative part of the tradition, as are the teachings of the early church Fathers. So is the Orthodox Churches' long history of **iconography**, the depiction of religious figures in special paintings. The veneration of icons will be discussed in the section on ritual.

The Christian belief in God as a trinity is important to Orthodox Christians. They also give **great honor to Mary as the Mother of God**. Although she is not God, Orthodoxy teaches that at one time she contained God in the person of Jesus. She is called **Theotokos**.[5] Jesus is believed to have been both fully human and fully divine during his earthly life. With other Christians, Orthodox believers hold that Jesus as the Christ plays the essential role in the drama of human sin and redemption.

God, according to Orthodox thought, remains **shrouded in holy mystery** and cannot be comprehended by human beings. Orthodox Christians believe that, because God is "absolutely incomprehensible and unknowable" (Saint John of Damascus, c. 675–749 C.E.), all that people can say about God is what God is not. Thus, God is *in*corporeal, *in*visible, and *in*tangible.

Like those of Catholic faith, Orthodox Christians believe that the grace of God is a divine, saving power available to persons through the sacraments of the church. **Divine grace requires human cooperation**. Salvation is not based on grace alone, as most Protestants affirm, but on both grace and human cooperation, another belief that the Orthodox share with their Catholic counterparts.

Orthodox Christians believe that the image of God in humanity is distorted and tarnished as a result of the disobedience of Adam and Eve that is recorded in Genesis. This ancestral sin continues to be transmitted to all people. **Although the image of God is in each person, sin distorts it and makes it unclear**. Orthodox Christians believe that by means of the cooperation between divine grace and human effort, the image of God can become clearer and clearer. By participating in the church as a worshiping community, human beings can become more and more like God. Although this process stops short of a full deification of humanity, the accent on the divine potential of human beings certainly tends in that direction in Orthodox thought and is an image of hope for all who follow it. **God did not become human to satisfy the demands of divine justice, according to Orthodoxy, but to enable other human beings to become like God. As people grow in God's grace, the image of God shines ever more brightly**.

Death means the separation of the soul or spirit from the body. Orthodox Christians believe that people immediately begin to experience something of heaven or hell—of being in communion with God or not. They also believe that there will be a final judgment. Based on the character of people's lives, their "resurrected existence will then live eternally in heaven in communion with God, or eternally in hell, out of communion with God."[6]

Ritual

Eastern Orthodox Christianity puts its greatest emphasis on worship and other **ritual**. Proper worship defines what it means to be Orthodox and links the various national churches together in close communion. The central act of worship

[5] *Theotokos* is Greek and means "Bearer of God."
[6] Stanley S. Harakas, *The Orthodox Church: 455 Questions and Answers* (Minneapolis, MN: Light and Life Publishing Company, 1988), p. 97.

Figure 9-2 This Greek Orthodox Church near Chicago incorporates the traditional domed roof over the sanctuary into distinctively modern architecture. (*Photo by the author.*)

is called the **Divine Liturgy**. It is a solemn yet joyful act that is stylized and highly liturgical. Originally, the language of the Divine Liturgy was Greek. In most churches now, the custom is to use the language of the people for most of the service or to use a combination of the two. In some churches, a choir chants most of the congregational responses. The Sunday morning liturgy is usually based on an order of worship developed by Saint John Chrysostom (347–407 C.E.), or on one developed by St. Basil the Great (c. 330–379 C.E.). All of its parts intend to express the holy mystery of God while maintaining it. God is present precisely as mystery. In worship, God is not so much to be understood as to be experienced and adored in mysterious holiness. The liturgy takes place in a church that is usually designed in the form of a cross, the arms of which project equally from the center, over which a dome is built (Figure 9-2). The Eastern arm of the cross is set apart by a richly decorated screen, the **iconostasis**, behind which the priest enacts the holy mysteries, shielded from the view of the congregation.

There are **three parts of the Orthodox liturgy**. The first, sometimes called the **morning service**, includes the preparation of the communion elements and recalls Jesus' birth and God's incarnation. The second, the **processions**, consists of responsive prayers, Bible readings, the sermon, and the Great Procession, in which the prepared communion elements are brought out. This symbolizes Jesus' coming to humankind to teach and to heal. The third part is the **communion** service itself. The priest goes behind the iconostasis, consecrates the elements, and places the bread into the chalice[7] of wine. The chalice is

---

[7]A *chalice* is a special cup or glass, often with a stem, used for the wine in the Eucharist.

carried among the people, and all those who are prepared to do so partake. This third part of the liturgy symbolizes Christ's sacrifice for humankind. As do Catholic Christians, the Eastern Orthodox believe that the bread and wine actually become the body and blood of Christ. The entire service may last up to three hours. Not everyone attends for the full service, and it is not uncommon for people to leave the church and return during the service. It is customary for families to worship together, with even the youngest children present for much of the service. Orthodox Christians believe that it is beneficial even for children who are too young to grasp its meaning to be present for the Divine Liturgy.

In addition to the majestic Divine Liturgy on Sunday morning, there are **various services throughout the day**, marking out the passage of time into a holy cycle. Most people, of course, do not participate in all these services, but in the monasteries, these rites pace the monks throughout the day and night.

The Orthodox Churches celebrate the seven traditional sacraments, which they call **Holy Mysteries**. The sacraments are believed to convey grace by the presence of the Holy Spirit within them. "God touches, purifies, illumines, sanctifies and deifies human life through the mysteries. . . . In them, we encounter Christ in order to be Christ."[8] People are **baptized by triple immersion**, symbolizing both the three persons of the Trinity and the three days Jesus is said to have lain in the tomb. Infant baptism is the usual practice, in which case baptism may involve only partial immersion. Confirmation, or **chrismation**, in which the person is anointed with oil that has been blessed for that purpose, follows immediately. Newly baptized people, infants or adults, then receive their first communion.

Leavened bread and wine are used as the **communion** elements. As noted above, Orthodox Christians believe that the elements become the body and blood of Christ. It is expected that all Orthodox Christians who are baptized and confirmed will partake regularly, and participants often fast from the evening meal prior to the service. Only Orthodox Christians who are in good standing with the Church may receive communion. The laity usually receive the bread and the wine together in a small spoon made for that purpose; priests receive the elements separately. In some churches, Orthodox Christians who did not receive the communion elements, and non-Orthodox people as well, are offered the "bread of fellowship" after the communion as a way of sharing in the service more fully.

The rite of **penance** as practiced in Orthodoxy reflects a number of themes that have already been mentioned. Baptism is only the beginning of a lifelong process of healing and restoring the damaged image of God within each person. This process is carried out in part through the sacrament of penance. The priest stands with the penitent, approaching God on the penitent's behalf and pronouncing God's forgiveness. Penance, writes one Greek Orthodox scholar, "is

---

[8]Alciviadis C. Calivas, "Orthodox Worship," in *A Companion to the Greek Orthodox Church*, ed. Fotios K. Litsas (New York: Department of Communication, Greek Orthodox Archdiocese of North and South America, 1984), pp. 31–32.

essentially a healing mystery, since sin is viewed primarily as a disease that needs to be healed, rather than a crime that needs to be punished."[9] The Orthodox are not altogether different from their Protestant and Catholic neighbors in this interpretation, although non-Orthodox Christians (and especially some Protestants) are more likely to emphasize a juridical interpretation of sin and forgiveness. The Orthodox focus on healing the separation between people and God and the restoration of the divine image in people.

The sacrament of **ordination** sets men apart for the priesthood. Married men may be ordained as priests, but priests are not permitted to marry after they are ordained. Bishops and other leaders in the hierarchy are always drawn from the ranks of the celibate monks. Priesthood is limited to men, because the ministry of Christ is carried out in the Church by the priests who are in Christ's image. Through the priest, Christ is present in and to the Church.

Marriage reflects the union of Christ with the faithful, of Christ and the Church. It is believed to be for life. However, because marriage involves human free will, there is always the possibility that a mistake will be made. When divorce happens, the Church usually holds that a true marriage did not occur. The marriage did not show its necessarily eternal character. The laity may have up to three attempts to establish a true and valid marriage. A fourth marriage is absolutely forbidden. The rites for marriages other than the first are subdued and have a penitential character. Clergy may marry only once, because they are expected to set as good an example as possible for the laity.

Customs surrounding Orthodox weddings vary from group to group, but two are widespread. At one point in the ceremony, crowns are placed on the heads of the bride and groom. The crowns are sometimes linked together with a ribbon. Although there are several meanings associated with the crowns, primarily they signify the new status of the couple as the King and Queen of a new Christian household. Orthodox Christians traditionally wear their wedding rings on their right, rather than their left, hands. The rings signify the couple's solemn pledge to each other, and the right hand is associated with strength and authority.[10]

The **sick are anointed** with blessed oil. Like the Catholic sacrament for the sick, this special service is intended to assist in recovery if that be God's will or to ease the passage from earthly to eternal life if that is to be the outcome.

Because the Orthodox churches follow the Julian rather than the Gregorian calendar, the **dates of the major festivals differ from those celebrated by other Christians**. For example, Holy Week (Palm Sunday through Easter) was a week later for Eastern than for Western Christians in 1999.

Orthodox ritual life, both in the church and in the home, is marked by the use of icons. **Icons** are special paintings that function as windows through which the sacred, without compromising its mystery, becomes visible. The painting of an icon is a devotional act carried out by a monk whose commitment to his work

[9]Calivas, "Orthodox Worship," p. 48.
[10]Harakas, *The Orthodox Church*, pp. 198–199.

is not only artistic, but spiritual. According to Orthodox belief, icons are not to be worshiped; to do so is idolatry. Orthodox Christians worship only God, as do other Christians. But Orthodox Christians affirm the **veneration** of icons. In becoming human in Jesus, God accepted everything pertaining to humanity, including "being depictable." Thus, "to refuse to venerate an icon is . . . to deny the reality of the Incarnation."[11] Icons are carried in procession and venerated by bowing in front of them, kissing them, and lighting candles before them.

Lifestyle

The lifestyles of Eastern Orthodox Christians are determined as much by their national heritage and the extent of their accommodation to American culture as by their faith. Except for the celibate priests, Eastern Orthodox Christians do not separate themselves from life in the secular world.

Marriage and family life are highly honored and respected. Deviations from this pattern, such as premarital or extramarital sex or active homosexuality, are regarded as inconsistent with a Christian life. Sexually abusive behavior is explicitly condemned.

Orthodox Christians may not marry non-Christians in the Church, but they may marry baptized non-Orthodox Christians. If married outside the Church, they may not participate in the Eucharist, nor may they serve as a god-parent for an Orthodox infant or as a sponsor at an Orthodox wedding.

Abortion is not permissible except in cases in which the pregnancy or birth of the baby would gravely endanger the life of the mother. Although children are valued and seen as an important part of marriage, conception and birth are not regarded as the only reason for physical intimacy. Therefore, birth control is left up to the conscience of the couple.

Eastern Orthodox Christians are encouraged by their church to uphold all just laws. They may in good conscience break an unjust law. Orthodox Christians, for example, participated in nonviolent civil disobedience during the civil rights marches of the 1960s. Involvement in public life is encouraged. Orthodox Christians support full human rights for all persons. Most churches officially supported the Equal Rights Amendment while simultaneously emphasizing the importance of the family. They remain, however, adamantly opposed to women being ordained to the priesthood, for the reasons noted in our discussion of ordination.

Organization

Organizationally, each of the nationally associated Orthodox churches is independent (the preferred word for this among the Orthodox is *autocephalous*, "self-headed"). Patriarchs lead the churches in each of the four ancient centers of

[11]Paul D. Garrett, "Eastern Christianity," in *Encyclopedia of the American Religious Experience*, ed. Lippy and Williams, vol. I, p. 328.

Orthodoxy: Constantinople, Antioch, Alexandria, and Jerusalem. Among these four, the Patriarch of Constantinople is said to have primacy of honor and spiritual leadership. He is called "first among equals" but has no more authority than the rest. He is often referred to by the honorific title of *His All Holiness Ecumenical Patriarch*. The current Ecumenical Patriarch is Bartholomew I.

In addition to these four patriarchates, each of which has divisions within it, there are other major autonomous bodies of believers, such as those of Russia, Greece, and Serbia. Although they are independent in their organizational structure, they are united on important liturgical and theological points.

The Pope has no authority for Orthodox Christians. They believe that the original Christian church was governed by bishops who presided over limited geographic areas. There was no one central authority. The Orthodox interpret the "rock" referred to in Matthew 16:18 ("upon this rock I will build my church") as Peter's faith rather than Peter himself, thus undercutting the primacy that the Catholic Church ascribes to the Bishop of Rome. This style of government has been maintained to the present time. Within each autonomous Church, government is hierarchical.

In practice, American Orthodox churches operate with considerable autonomy. National consciousness notwithstanding, there is a degree of unity among Orthodox Christians in the United States. Particularly in the United States, most Orthodox Christians long for greater unity:

> The more deeply the Orthodox strike roots in North America, the more they lament the ethnic foliage that conceals a united confession of faith. Immigration history, not theology, separates the Orthodox people. And in general they long for and anticipate their union in one organically Orthodox fellowship."[12]

The **Standing Conference of Orthodox Bishops in America** is one voice for American Orthodoxy. There are two views of how Orthodox unity in North America might come about. The **Orthodox Church in America** was formed in 1970 by the merger of several Russian churches. Its goal is to unite the Orthodox churches of the United States into a single body. It is headed by an archbishop who has the title, "Archbishop of Washington [D.C.], Metropolitan of All America and Canada." The fact that Russians were the first Orthodox Christians in the United States leads the Russian Orthodox Church to the belief that they have precedence in the United States. Greek Orthodox Christians, who far outnumber the Russians, however, have been reluctant to accept the Russian-founded group as representative. The **Greek Orthodox Archdiocese of North and South America** has become the center of the point of view that holds that all Orthodox Christians owe allegiance to the Patriarch of Constantinople (now Istanbul, in Turkey). In 1996, Archbishop Spryidon was elected as Archbishop of America. He is the fifth archbishop of America since the archdiocese was

[12]Anthony Ugolnik, "An Ecumenical Estrangement: Orthodoxy in America," *The Christian Century*, 109, no. 20 (June 17–24, 1992), p. 611.

organized in the 1920s. He is the first American-born Archbishop of America, having been born in Ohio in 1944.

Saint Vladimir's Seminary (Russian) in New York state has become a training center for Orthodox clergy of many national backgrounds. There is also a Greek Orthodox seminary in the United States, the Holy Cross Greek Orthodox School of Theology in Boston. There is also an Orthodox Theological Society of America, which includes members of all groups, and an Orthodox Inter-Seminary Movement. In worship, pan-Orthodox liturgies on the first Sunday of Lent have become an American tradition.

Eastern Orthodoxy is an embodiment of Christian faith centered in a rich liturgical life that vibrates with the resonances of a tradition as old as the Christian Church itself. For a significant number of American citizens, it is the faith that provides the sacred meanings that make life good. It relates the passage of time throughout the year and the passage of life through its various stages to God, providing a context of holy mystery that transfigures the mundane world.

AFRICAN AMERICAN CHRISTIANITY

If you worship or have worshiped in a predominantly black congregation, you have an idea about what black Christianity is.[13] If you have not experienced it directly, you may not know much about it. In that case, have you seen black Christianity depicted in the movies or on television? How is it portrayed? In either case, what comes to mind when you think of African American Christianity and worship?

The "Lost Third Theme" of the Religious History of the United States

A recent study of African American religion in the United States[14] advances the thesis that there have been two themes that have guided the interpretation of American religious history. One is pluralism—the existence of religious diversity and the extent to which it has been affirmed or at least tolerated. The other theme is Puritanism and the necessity that America have a collective purpose, a theme that appears to be fundamentally at odds with the first. These two, however can be seen as an evolving dialectic. As Puritanism and the sense of collective purpose and mission have lost ground, the affirmation of diversity has gained. When diversity has lessened, the sense of collective mission has gained.

There is, however, a third theme that cannot be subsumed under either of the other two: A major aspect of the religious history of the United States

---

[13]Both the term "black Christianity" and "African American Christianity" are current in literature written by African American Christians themselves. I will use the two interchangeably.

[14]David W. Wills, "The Central Themes of American Religious History: Pluralism, Puritanism, and the Encounter of Black and White," in *African American Religion: Interpretive Essays in History and Culture*, ed. Timothy E. Fulop and Albert J. Raboteau (New York: Routledge, 1997), pp. 9–10.

is the encounter between black and white. The Puritan theme has its primary locus in New England, and the pluralism and toleration theme begins in the middle colonies such as Pennsylvania, Delaware, and Rhode Island. The southern colonies and later southern states do not fit comfortably in with either of these.

> It is this problematic encounter of black and white—which tests the limits of all our views of pluralism and undermines every attempt to formulate a sense of collective purpose—that is the Southern theme in American religious history. . . . [And] it is not only a Southern theme.[15]

Further, while the religious history of the United States demonstrates a relatively steady increase in diversity and toleration and a relatively steady decline in the Puritan drive for collective expression of the sacred, the black–white encounter is "the story of a persistent and seemingly intractable gap." In spite of efforts to overcome it, some of which will be described below, the gap endures and remains "one of the foundational realities of our national religious life."[16]

The Ambiguity of Christianity for African Americans

Christianity has always been ambiguous for the descendants of the African slaves brought to this country in the holds of ships. They were first introduced to Christianity by those who enslaved them, and it was usually used to undergird obedience to the slave masters. One author describes the beginning of this ambivalence dramatically:

> This ambivalence is not new. It was ours from the beginning. For we first met the American Christ on slave ships. We heard his name sung in hymns of praise while we died in our thousands, chained in stinking holds beneath the decks, locked in with terror and disease and sad memories of our families and homes. When we leaped from the decks to be seized by sharks we saw his name carved on the ships' solid sides. When our women were raped in the cabins they must have noticed the great and holy books on the shelves.[17]

On the other hand, Christianity provided benefits for the slaves. Some of the slave holders allowed their slaves at least a measure of control over their religious expression, and patterns of worship developed that the slaves could claim as their own. Even being taken into town to the "white" church provided a social outing and some relief from the burdens of work. Later, especially as slaves and former slaves embraced the Exodus story of the Hebrews' escape from Egyptian slavery, Christianity provided a context for liberating action.

---

[15]Wills, "The Central Themes of American Religious History," p. 15.
[16]Wills, "The Central Themes of American Religious History, pp. 15 and 20.
[17]Vincent Harding, "Black Power and the American Christ," in *Black Theology: A Documentary History, 1966–1979*, ed. Gayraud S. Wilmore and James H. Cone (Maryknoll, NY: Orbis Books, 1979), p. 36.

The Three Sources
and Diversity of African American Christianity

We can identify at least three sources of African American Christianity. There are, in the first place, continuing influences from the tribal religions of Africa. We cannot understand African American Christianity without recognizing this background. Second, it has been influenced by patterns borrowed from white European American Christianity. Third, it has developed its unique character as African Americans responded, first to slavery and then to their ongoing history of living in an oppressive and racist society.[18]

There is a great deal of diversity within African American Christianity. There are also non-Christian manifestations of African American religion. (Islam, the primary one of these, will be discussed in a later chapter.) Within Christianity, four types may be distinguished.[19] *Mainstream churches* are the predominantly black denominational churches and predominantly black congregations within white denominations such as those discussed in Chapter 3, as well as black Catholic congregations. They often function to enable African Americans to become better integrated into the predominantly white society, whose culture they often accept as valid. Although their worship and other religious activities resemble those of their white counterparts, they are frequently more emotional, longer, and include more music and extemporaneous prayer and praise than one would usually find in a white church of a similar denomination. In the social and political arena, this perspective is exemplified by Dr. Martin Luther King, Jr.

Messianic-nationalist groups are distinguishable for their separatist and militant point of view. They are "generally founded by charismatic individuals who are regarded as Messiahs who will deliver black people from white oppression."[20] Their stance is one of critique of the position of African Americans in the white culture, and they often are quite critical of the more integrationist stance of the mainstream black churches. This point of view is found in the work of the black Christian militants described later in this chapter. Several of these groups are either Islamic or black Jewish, but there are a few Christian churches among them, such as the Black Christian Nationalist Church, founded by Albert Cleage in the 1960s.

Conversionist groups, as their name suggests, emphasize the experience of conversion. Most are holiness and/or pentecostal. They emphasize strict personal morality and are often not deeply involved with either social action or politics. As with members of other African American religious groups, members of conversionist or "sanctified" churches dedicate much of their Sunday to church activities:

---

[18]Hans A. Baer and Merrill Singer, *African-American Religion in the Twentieth Century: Varieties of Protest and Accommodation* (Knoxville, TN: The University of Tennessee Press, 1992), p. 1.

[19]Baer and Singer, *African-American Religion in the Twentieth Century*.

[20]William H. Swatos, Jr., ed., *Encyclopedia of Religion and Society* (Walnut Creek, CA: AltaMira Press, 1998), p. 9.

Sundays are extremely busy for Sanctified churches, beginning with Sunday school in the early morning and evolving into the Sunday worship service in the later morning and early afternoon. A special program . . . may occur in the afternoon. Finally, an evening service of two hours or longer often brings to a close the most sacred day of the week. This round of religious activities may be punctuated by more profane affairs, such as a midday dinner or a picnic. Many Sanctified churches also conduct services on Friday nights as a way of making the transition between the profanity of life in the larger society and the sacredness of the Lord's Day.[21]

Finally, *thaumaturgical* groups use religious ritual and esoteric knowledge to seek worldly prosperity, good health, and other benefits. Otherworldly dimensions take second place to their emphasis on improving life in their world. Thus, they promise benefits that their adherents have been denied or found difficult to obtain in the racist white culture. They offer a sharp contrast with the other types described above. They emphasize the individual over the group, embrace health and prosperity as an indicator of spiritual position, and do not seek to reform the larger culture.

The Christian Churches and the Civil War

Religion figured prominently in the events that led up to the Civil War, in the war itself, and in the various attempts at interpreting its meaning that followed it. Both North and South looked to their faith, their churches, and their religious leaders to justify their position on the matter of slavery and to sustain them in the terrible bloodshed that pitted American against American and kin against kin. Both were certain that God was on their side, that theirs was the righteous cause, and that God would help them to prevail over their opposition. Both attempted to demonstrate support from the Christian scriptures. And, in both South and North, religious people sought to minister to those caught up in the war. There were chaplains with both armies, and aid societies assisted them in their work by providing reading materials, visitation, and facilitating communication between soldiers and the families they had left behind. It fell to these volunteers to deal as best they could with the grief of those from whom the war had taken family members, friends, and neighbors. The accounts of their work, along with that of the chaplains and medical personnel, are a stirring record of humanity amidst the inhumanity of war.

Religious perspectives gave rise to some of the most memorable literary and artistic responses to slavery and to the Civil War. Harriet Beecher Stowe's staunch and thoughtful Congregationalism led to her writing of *Uncle Tom's Cabin*. James Russell Lowell's stirring "Once to Every Man and Nation," familiar to most Protestant churchgoers, reminds us of the prophets of the Hebrews when they called on their people to make a decisive, once-and-for-all choice

[21]Baer and Singer, *African-American Religion in the Twentieth Century*, p. 166.

between good and evil. And Julia Ward Howe's "Battle Hymn of the Republic," although it became an anthem of the North, spoke eloquently of God's judgment on any people who made the wrong choice in that decision.

After the guns of battle were silent, the religious categories of divine wrath and punishment and the religious overtones of sacrifice were brought into play by both sides to interpret the meaning of the war and of victory gained or defeat suffered. Others, keenly aware of the ambiguous nature of the entire situation, called for repentance on both sides and reconciliation of hearts as well as governments.

The Free Black Church

A major shift came with emancipation and the development of black religion in the context of official freedom coupled with social repression and oppression that continued long after the Emancipation Proclamation was signed. The Emancipation Proclamation was a statement issued by President Abraham Lincoln on New Year's Day, 1863, that ended slavery throughout most of the South.

The **Baptist** and **Methodist** churches carried out the most vigorous and successful work among the blacks after emancipation. The vast majority of freed blacks were a part of one of these two communities of faith. A smaller, yet significant, number, especially in Maryland and Louisiana, were Catholic. Following the war years, the black church grew rapidly. Rejection or segregation of black members by historically white denominations (such as the Baptists' and Methodists' insistence on separate seating) led to the growth of all-black congregations within these denominations as well as to the formation of a number of black denominations. It was in these black denominations and in the all-black congregations within predominantly white denominations that black religion continued to evolve its distinctive style and message.

The black churches played a unique role in the developing black community, in the North and South, in rural areas and cities, to which increasingly large numbers of blacks were moving in search of work. The black churches were much, much more than simply religious institutions, although their primary identification as religious institutions influenced everything else in which they were involved. As a landmark study of the black church in the United States describes it:

> The black church has no challenger as the cultural womb of the black community. Not only did it give birth to new institutions such as schools, banks, insurance companies, and low income housing, it also provided an academy and an arena for political activities, and it nurtured young talent for musical, dramatic, and artistic development . . . in addition to the traditional concerns of worship, moral nurture, education, and social control. Much of black culture is heavily indebted to the black religious tradition, including most forms of black music, drama, literature, storytelling, and even humor.[22]

[22]C. Eric Lincoln and Lawrence H. Mamiya, *The Black Church in the African American Experience* (Durham, NC: Duke University Press, 1991), p. 8.

As historian Sydney Ahlstrom points out, black churches also served as a "surrogate for nationality" that substituted religious identification for the tribal identity that had been left behind.[23]

The Christian ministry was the only profession open to blacks, and the black churches were the only institution controlled by blacks. As such, they served as schools for leadership training and development. Most of the black political leaders in the United States trace their roots back to the church and many to the ministry itself. Frequently in the history of the black church, the minister, who was the most highly educated member of the black community, served as the liaison between the black community and that of the dominant whites. This function remains important, even though blacks have joined the ranks of the educated and the professionals in increasing numbers.

The Reverend Jesse Jackson's 1984 and 1988 political campaigns for the Democratic presidential nomination illustrate both of these last two points. He was able to use the black churches to organize voter registration drives and political support, thereby transforming black religion into political power. His campaign speeches were reminiscent of some of the speeches of Martin Luther King, Jr., and they clearly reflected his training and experience as a black Christian minister. At the same time, particularly in the 1988 campaign, he became a spokesperson to the white voting community on behalf of not only blacks but of other poor and disadvantaged groups as well. His effectiveness in doing so is reflected in the support he had from white voters.

The Black Church and Civil Rights

Black religion was at the heart of the civil rights movement. It had helped the slaves maintain some sense of humanity and peoplehood. It had provided structure and organization in the years following emancipation. And it provided a framework in which hopes for civil rights could become political realities.

The **civil rights movement** became an integral part of black religion. Most of the significant events of the civil rights movement occurred in the period that is centered on the turbulent decade of the 1960s and extends for a few years on either side of it. The black churches, their people, and their leaders were intimately involved.

Dr. Martin Luther King, Jr., pastor of the Dexter Avenue Baptist Church in Montgomery, Alabama was the undisputed leader of the civil rights movement. He brought to the task his lifelong experience of the black church, the moving preaching style of the black minister, and a social conscience informed by the liberal Protestantism he had learned while obtaining his doctorate at Boston University. King advocated **nonviolent protest**. His reading of the lives and teachings of Jesus and of Mohandas Gandhi, the Indian Hindu politician, convinced him that nonviolence was the morally right way to deal with the

[23]Sydney E. Ahlstrom, *A Religious History of the American People* (New Haven, CT: Yale University Press, 1973), p. 710.

situation in which blacks found themselves. Nonviolence meant **civil disobedience** in the spirit of Christian love rather than hatred and revenge against whites. *Civil disobedience* meant deliberately breaking laws that were unjust but being willing to endure verbal and even physical abuse without fighting back and to go to jail if necessary for one's actions. It meant working for reconciliation, not encouraging separatism.

Within a few years, many blacks, especially students, had used King's nonviolent methods in sit-ins at segregated lunch counters throughout the South. Freedom rides began to protest segregation in interstate commerce facilities. Many blacks rode interstate buses and entered facilities such as eating areas and restrooms that were reserved for whites. Such segregation was by that time illegal, but the laws were not enforced.

In January 1957, the **Southern Christian Leadership Conference** (popularly, SCLC) was formed, with Martin Luther King, Jr., as its founder. It proved to be one of the most effective black organizations throughout the 1960s and early 1970s. Protests in Birmingham, Alabama, were among the largest organized by the SCLC. King's "**Letter from Birmingham Jail**," a classic of the movement, was written while he was jailed in Birmingham as a result of his participation in these efforts. In it, King distinguished between a just law and an unjust law. A just law is one that squares with the moral law or the law of God. An unjust law does not. Unjust laws also legalize inequality and difference and are inflicted upon a minority who, by reason of not being allowed to vote, had nothing to say about their passage. People should obey just laws. Unjust laws, on the other hand, should be broken, but in the spirit of nonviolence and love already indicated.[24]

In the late summer of 1963, a massive demonstration in Washington, D.C., focused on segregation in accommodations. The following summer, the **Civil Rights Act** was passed. This piece of legislation received strong support in Congress from leaders of Protestantism, Catholicism, Eastern Orthodoxy, and Judaism, and from blacks and whites alike.

March 1965 saw the well-known march from Selma to Montgomery, Alabama. With King's able leadership, clergy and laity from all the major branches of Christendom and Judaism, along with humanists and free thinkers, marched and sang together in protest. Many went to jail. In August of the same year, the **Voting Rights Act** was passed. When Martin Luther King, Jr., was assassinated in the spring of 1968, many of the goals of the early civil rights movement had been met. But there was yet more to do.

Black Christian Militancy and Black Power

Gradually, the mood of the civil rights movement changed. Leaders arose who felt that these methods worked too slowly. They believed King was too willing to compromise, too moderate, too willing to work with whites. Why the change in

[24]Martin Luther King, Jr., "Letter from Birmingham Jail," in *Why We Can't Wait* (New York: Harper & Row, Publishers, 1963).

mood? Black Presbyterian theologian Gayraud S. Wilmore puts it this way: By the mid-1960s, "many believed that following King meant to give more attention to loving the enemy than to doing something about the suffering of brothers and sisters." [25] In most respects, King was a moderate among Christian ministers. For many blacks, patience with moderation had worn thin. When it had been formed, the Student Nonviolent Coordinating Committee (SNCC) had been committed to King's nonviolent methods, but its early commitment to nonviolence had lessened. Its leaders and rank-and-file members alike were willing to accept and condone violence in the service of righting the wrongs of previous centuries. The passage of the Voting Rights Act in the summer of 1965 sparked an incident that drew national attention, and, in some quarters, outrage. There was a week of bloody and destructive race riots in several major American cities. The week of uprisings highlighted the great frustration of the black community and showed both whites and more moderate blacks how far the militants were willing to go to meet their goals.

In the summer of 1966, **James Meredith** was shot and wounded while leading a 220-mile voting rights walk from Memphis, Tennessee, to Jackson, Mississippi. **Stokely Carmichael** and others who took over leadership on that march led the marchers in chants of "black power!" with clenched fists raised in what would become a nationally recognized symbol. The chants of "black power" were often led by church people, and they were accompanied by talk of God's judgment upon America for the injustices done to blacks and of coming retribution for oppression.

In 1967, the National Committee of Negro Churchmen became the National Committee of Black Churchmen. In 1969, the committee sponsored a conference on black economic development. Most of the key leaders of the black religious community had long since come to recognize that economic freedom was one of the main keys to ending oppression, a key without which no amount of good intention was enough. At that conference, James Forman read the **"Black Manifesto."** It is a document that "burns with anger and despair," as Forman said his brothers and sisters did. It made demands, demands that white Christian churches and Jewish synagogues pay reparations that would begin to offset the damage done by economic oppression. It explicitly accused these communities of faith of conscious and willing participation in the processes of slavery and oppression and of not moving nearly rapidly enough to bring about change. Specifically, it demanded $500 million. The money was to be spent in a variety of ways. Loans for land and homes were a main goal. Publishing, printing, and television networks were to be established. Training and skills centers were to be built. A National Black Labor Strike and Defense Fund was to be established. A black university was to be established in the South.

On May 4, 1969, Forman read the Manifesto, uninvited, to the assembled congregation of New York's prestigious Riverside Church. The white churches

---

[25]Gayraud S. Wilmore and James H. Cone, eds., *Black Theology: A Documentary History, 1966–1979* (Maryknoll, NY: Orbis Books, 1979), p. 16.

and synagogues strongly resisted paying any money for reparations. Those that did discuss it seriously often found their congregations split. The Manifesto was an effective tool for drawing national attention to the economic problems that had not been solved. It also illustrated the distance that the civil rights movement had moved from King's style of leadership. No longer willing to work with white religious groups, the supporters of the Manifesto drew clear battle lines.

Not all black churches supported the black power movement, and the movement itself drew support from people and groups not associated with the churches. Nevertheless, the growing consciousness of Jesus as Liberator that would highlight black religious thought gave support and religious legitimation to a powerful new thrust in the ongoing struggle of the black community.

Since the Civil Rights Movement

Five important changes have taken place in the black church since the era of the civil rights movement. First, denominations are less important as a part of black Christian identity than they were. Second, the women's movement has increased tensions in black churches, as women have pressed for and gained greater leadership. This has alienated some black males. Third, blacks are less likely than before to accept a "white Jesus," preferring more culturally relevant symbols. Fourth, the emphasis on dealing constructively with inner-city problems has increased greatly. Finally, preaching focuses more on Bible stories than previously, and some preachers are taking on a more educational role in their preaching.[26]

Religion and Sociopolitical Views

The role of the black church in the public life of the African American community remains very important.[27] Further, there are substantial differences in how religious views and participation and social views are linked among white Americans and among African Americans. Religious group identifications have an impact on political party identification, voting behavior, and ideological identification (liberal/conservative) much less for black people than for whites. Race is the determinative factor. Religious identification has almost no impact on views on social issues such as gender equality, welfare, abortion, euthanasia, and views about pornography among black Americans, whereas there are links among whites. There are isolated exceptions to this general point, but no patterns.

The more literalist African Americans are in the way that they interpret the Bible, the more likely they are to be both Democrats and identify themselves as political conservatives. White literalists are more likely to identify themselves as conservatives but not nearly as likely to be Democrats. This translates to conser-

[26]*National Christian Reporter*, February 25, 1994.
[27]The material in this section is summarized from Michael Corbett and Julia M. Corbett, *Politics and Religion in the United States* (New York: Garland Publishing, 1999), chapter 9.

vatism on some social issues—abortion, school prayer, and euthanasia, for example—but not on others—sex education, gun control, and capital punishment. On the issues affected, biblical literalists are more likely to be conservative, as are their white counterparts.

Among white Americans, high religious commitment often is associated with conservatism in social views. Among black Americans, the same is often the case, but the pattern is more mixed. Religious commitment affects views on some social issues but not on others.

The Black Church at Worship

The black church's worship is distinctive, with links back to the African and slave experiences of its members' ancestors. It is worship in which the Holy Spirit is encountered by the worshipers as an experiential reality, in which they are transformed by the presence of their God. Theologian James Cone has noted the **six main elements in black worship** wherever it takes place. They are "preaching, singing, shouting, conversion, prayer, and testimony."[28]

Preaching is the most important, because the preacher speaks the word of God to the people. The black churches emphasize that preachers must be called by God to preach; it is not their decision but an answer to God's call. It is customary to give an account of this call to the congregation. The sermon is not a lecture; it is enacted, using the rhythms of body movement and voice to give life to the message in response to the Holy Spirit's leading. The people in the congregation participate by their shouts or more subdued responses of "Yes, Jesus," "Say it, Brother," "Amen!" and the like. This congregational responsiveness pulls preacher and listeners together in a common act of worship (Figure 9-3).

After preaching, **singing** is next in importance, because it prepares for, and then intensifies, the experience of the Spirit. It sets the mood, although it cannot force the Spirit to come. It is said that good singing can overcome poor preaching, and that, while there can be church without preaching, there must be singing. Some black churches, especially the larger ones, have regular choirs, but congregational involvement in singing is the rule. For white Christians accustomed to two or at most three hymns during a worship service, the sheer number of hymns and religious songs in a black church service, as well as the hand-clapping, hand-waving enthusiasm with which they are sung, may come as a surprise.

Shouting and **conversion** are closely related. Shouting, sometimes referred to as "getting happy," is understood in the black church as a response to the action of the Holy Spirit, a form of religious ecstasy. It is not the same as similar phenomena in white pentecostal churches, because it grows out of an altogether different sociopolitical background and set of life experiences. The white pentecostal is a member of the dominant race, whereas the black is oppressed. As

[28]James H. Cone, *Speaking the Truth* (Grand Rapids, MI: William B. Eerdmans Publishing Company, 1986), p. 22.

Figure 9-3 Easter Sunday service at Ebenezer Baptist Church, Poughkeepsie, NY. *(Kathy McLaughlin/The Image Works.)*

black theologian James Cone writes very pointedly, it is "absurd . . . to contend that the Ku Klux Klansman and the black person who escaped him are shouting for the same or similar reasons."[29] Blacks shout in joy over the authentic person-hood given by Jesus and participation in his life and liberation, experienced as a present, here-and-now alternative to oppression and depersonalization. "The Holy Ghost reaches into the heart and sets individuals on fire, purging evil from their hearts and restoring love, faith, and mercy."[30] Shouting usually accompanies and is evidence of conversion and recurs when that experience is renewed. The gaining of authentic identity *is* conversion, something so radical that the metaphor of dying and rising fits it. Conversion is, on the one hand, a one-time event; but on the other hand, it is an ongoing experience and process, and both events are signaled by shouting.

Finally, **prayer**, free and spontaneous rather than read from a book, is understood as communication with Jesus. Like so much else in black worship, it is rhythmic, echoing the rhythms of the African past.

During **testimony**, people speak in front of the congregation about their determination to stay with their lives in Christ and in the church in spite of dif-ficulties. They believe that they are called by God and testify to their intention to be worthy of that call. It is an encouragement both to the person testifying and to those who hear it. The congregational responses of "Yes, Sister" or "Tell it,

[29]Cone, *Speaking the Truth*, p. 27.
[30]Kostarelos, *Feeling the Spirit*, p. 89.

Brother" let the speakers know that the rest of the congregation is with them against the temptations that arise.

Black Religious Thought

Theologically, black Christianity is conservative and traditional, in both thought and practice. Black Christians affirm the traditional beliefs of the church, with minimal modification. For the average person in the pew, especially, "keeping the faith" is much more important than modernization.

Historically, the black church has been a place to which people could retreat from the dehumanization of white oppression. It has preached and sung that "You're somebody in God's eyes even if you're nobody here." Black churches still offer their people this sort of message. But even when its message has been otherworldly and has promised heavenly freedom more than encouraging the struggle for earthly freedom, it has been a place of healing, a place that helped people remain sane in the midst of the insanity of slavery and the problems of newly freed blacks. Being a somebody in God's eyes was a powerful incentive to work toward a society in which there are no longer any nobodies.

The distinctive contribution of the black churches to the American theological enterprise is **black theology**. Black theology is **not simply traditional Christian theology**, which has been overwhelmingly white, European, and male, **overlaid with the experience of blackness**. It is guided and informed by the experience of blackness right from the outset. The experience of blackness sets the agenda for this way of doing theology. This approach became self-conscious and came to public attention during the tumultuous 1960s, as a part of the civil rights movement. Noted black theologian James Cone writes:

> I still regard the Bible as an important source of my theological reflections, but not the starting point. The black experience and the Bible together in dialectical tension serve as my point of departure. . . . The order is significant. I am *black* first— and everything else comes after that. This means that I read the Bible through the lens of a black tradition of struggle and not as the objective word of God.[31]

It is also **thoroughly Christian**, taking as its starting point and focus the Christian New Testament, especially the gospels of Matthew, Mark, and Luke, that tell the story of Jesus' life, death, and resurrection. It is also part of the larger category of theologies called liberation theologies. Liberation theologies all deal with the message of the Gospels for an oppressed group, be it Third World, black, or female.

There are a number of themes upon which nearly all black theologians would agree. The theme of **freedom** is central. Black religious thought draws on both the Christian Old Testament and the Christian New Testament in this

[31]James H. Cone, *God of the Oppressed*, revised edition (Maryknoll, NY: Orbis Books, 1997), p. xi.

respect. As a recent study of the black church put it, "the Old Testament notion of God as an avenging, conquering, liberating paladin remains a formidable anchor of faith in most black churches." However, **Jesus as the liberator** of the poor and oppressed is unquestionably the controlling theme of black theology. The suffering of black people throughout their history finds "immediate resonance with the incarnational view of the suffering, humiliation, death, and eventual triumph of Jesus in the resurrection."[32]

Jesus as the liberator means liberation now, in this world, in terms of voting rights, jobs, equal access to good education, and adequate housing. The liberation that Jesus offers certainly includes freedom from the eternal punishment of unforgiven sin. It certainly includes a hoped-for future in which oppression and pain of every kind shall cease. But first and foremost, Jesus means liberation now, sociopolitical and economic liberation. He means full humanity for people who have never had full humanity.

God is a God of justice, especially concerned for the fate of the oppressed. God is believed to be on the side of the oppressed and against the oppressor. God does not support the ruling class and the status quo but instead supports the attempt to bring about a more just and equal society. This, too, reflects the importance of the prophetic books of the Christian Old Testament in black religious thought. In a similar vein, the Kingdom of God is seen in terms of justice and equality in this world. People, with God's help and guidance, are responsible for bringing it about. While it may not come in its fullness until God intervenes decisively in human history, it can be greatly advanced. Black theology is a theology of political action; concepts such as the Kingdom of God are politicized and translated into concrete changes in how people live.

Black religious thought is **thoroughly contextual**. Theology has usually been done by and for the privileged classes—in the United States, white men. It has usually been assumed that there was but one theology, and the problem was to get that one correct. Contextual theology recognizes that, although Christians believe that there is only one God, there are a vast number of ways that people may understand God, based on their own time and culture. Theology is a circular process in which the current situation and the Bible interpret and reinterpret each other. For black theology, the beginning point is the experience of slavery and oppression. Any theology that does not take that experience into account and does not ring true to people whose identity is marked by that experience cannot be valid.

In the United States, black theology was the first of the contextual, liberation-oriented theologies to come to national attention. It set the stage for other attempts to interpret the Christian message in terms of a particular people's history. The pioneering work of the black theologians helped all theologians in the United States to realize how much their social and cultural settings influenced their theologies. It made it much more difficult to justify doing theology as if time and place do not matter.

[32]Lincoln and Mamiya, *The Black Church*, pp. 3–4.

Descriptive Data

About 80 percent of blacks in the United States are Protestant. Not quite 10 percent are Catholic. Less than 1 percent are Jewish, and about 5 percent each claim no religious preference or claim some other religious preference. This 5 percent includes Black Muslims. Among the Protestants, two-thirds are Baptist and about 10 percent are Methodist. About 1 percent each are Lutheran, Presbyterian, and Episcopalian; about 15 percent indicate some other preference, and about 5 percent are nondenominational. Looked at from another perspective, about 30 percent of all Baptists are black, as are about 10 percent of all Methodists. All together, there are approximately 65,000 black Christian congregations, with about 24 million members.

Approximately 80 percent of religiously affiliated blacks in the United States are members of one of **eight major black denominations**:

- National Baptist Convention, U.S.A., Incorporated.
- National Baptist Convention of America, Unincorporated.
- Progressive National Baptist Convention.
- African Methodist Episcopal Church.
- African Methodist Episcopal Zion Church.
- Christian Methodist Episcopal Church.
- Second Cumberland Presbyterian Church in the United States.
- Church of God in Christ.

The list clearly reflects the success that Baptist and Methodist missionaries had among the slaves and later among the free blacks, both north and south. The first black church in the United States was Baptist, and the first black denomination was Methodist.[33] Both black worship and black theology have developed most fully in the historically black churches, although both are found elsewhere as well.

The **black pentecostal denominations, of which the Church of God in Christ (COGIC) is by far the largest**, have shown the greatest growth among black churches in the twentieth century. The founder of COGIC, Charles Harrison Mason, had been a part of the Azuza Street revival in the early 1900s. Pentecostalism is growing more rapidly among blacks than among others in the United States.

The **Congress of National Black Churches** was founded to promote unity, charity, and fellowship among member denominations. The Congress is a coalition of six major historic black denominations: African Methodist Episcopal; Church of God in Christ; National Baptist Convention of America, Inc.; National Missionary Baptist Convention of America; and the Progressive National Baptist Convention, Inc. It sponsors a number of programs including programs for theological education, economic development, a black family

---

[33]Lincoln and Mamiya, *The Black Church*, pp. 23 and 47.

program, and an anti-drug program, as well as facilitating unity among the nation's black churches.

There are also a number of black or nearly all-black congregations in Christian denominations that are predominantly white, such as the American and Southern Baptists, United Methodists, Presbyterians, Episcopalians, and Catholics. These black congregations worship in a style that is closer to that of comparable white congregations. As Cone points out, however, although the forms may be different, the white denomination's style of worship is not the central self-identification of the black congregations. They did not participate in the creation of those traditions of worship and cannot affirm them wholeheartedly. Their primary identification is with the experience of blackness, of suffering and oppression, and the word of liberation in the gospel of Jesus as Liberator.[34]

Black congregations reflect the same sort of social stratification as their white counterparts. For example, as affluence and education rise, they are more likely to have a formal service, with a robed choir, a highly educated minister, and a director of religious education. In other words, the black congregations become more like the white congregations. Many would say that they become less true to authentic black religious experience.

Data from surveys that include questions about frequency of attendance at worship, private prayer and Bible reading, strength of religious preference, and religious commitment typically show that blacks participate in both public worship and private religious acts more frequently than their white counterparts. Their religious preference and commitment are stronger. They are more likely to consider religion a very important part of life and are more likely to believe that it can solve most or all of today's problems. Blacks are much more likely to be fundamentalist in their religious outlook, by about three to two, and are half as likely to be liberal.

Women in the Black Church

Like their predominantly white counterparts, black Christian churches have historically had a majority of female members and an almost exclusively male pastorate. This pattern continues in black churches, for the most part, into the present. Women do have many other leadership roles in the black churches, such as evangelists, deaconesses, lay readers, Sunday School teachers, counselors, and the like.

There are at least two unique positions of honor for women in many black Christian churches. Women may be "mothers of the church," a position that derives from African-based kinship networks that carry over into the African American community. There is no parallel in white churches.[35]

---

[34]Cone, *Speaking the Truth*, p. 129.
[35]Lincoln and Mamiya, *The Black Church*, p. 275.

Frances Kostarelos describes the role of church mothers in her ethnographic account of an inner city storefront church in Chicago:

> The Mothers Board . . . is . . . separated into junior and senior groups; the former includes women between fifty-five and sixty-five; the latter is for women who are over sixty-five. These women are also called church mothers. As church women approach their mid-fifties, they are expected to take their place on the Mothers Board. . . . Members of the Mothers Board say that through the good and evil they have known and a lifetime of serving God and their families, they have developed the personal qualities and habit of mind required for service on the Mothers Board. Church mothers are expected to be sober-minded, temperate at all times, and emotionally balanced. They are to avoid calling attention to themselves through their clothing and manners. They are to dress and comport themselves in a reserved and discreet manner. On Sundays they wear white dresses or suits, hats, stockings, and dress shoes. Their outfits represent their spiritual elevation and humility before God. At all times they avoid wearing striking outfits such as those worn by younger women in the church.
>
> It is the duty of the church mothers to be moral and spiritual guides to others in the congregation, especially to young women seeking to live in the Spirit. . . . Church mothers have the responsibility of counseling younger women. They are women who have been wife to one husband, good mothers and housekeepers, and in the church working for the Lord. The hardships they have endured as wives, mothers, and servants of God are believed to have strengthened them and brought them closer to the Spirit. The church mothers are highly respected and enjoy a great deal of deference from younger women. Church mothers have a significant spiritual role in worship services.[36]

Women may also serve as nurses in the church. Usually, the nurses are women younger than those on the Mothers Board. Dressed in a recognizable white uniform for church services and funerals, they are responsible for helping anyone in the congregation who needs assistance. They particularly help members overcome with emotion during services, and women with children who need to be taken out because they are fussing. Kostarelos describes the way that the Nurses Board is an avenue for women gaining respect in the church: Women achieve respect by consistently demonstrating their excellence in traditionally "female" qualities such as compassion, helpfulness, and being good with children.[37]

It is clear that these women have positions of great power within their congregations. Equally clear is the fact that their respect and position come from their manifestation of traditionally feminine qualities. Some women, barred from ordination, founded their own churches, becoming powerful preachers and leaders in their own right.

---

[36]Kostarelos, *Feeling the Spirit*, p. 51.
[37]Kostarelos, *Feeling the Spirit*, p. 49.

Black feminist theologians have articulated a bleak picture of the position of black women in American culture and in African American churches. They are the victims of racial and gender-based oppression and make up a "disproportionately high percentage of the working poor and underclass."[38] One woman describes how black women suffer a triple oppression—race, gender, and inferior status in their churches.[39] The feminist movement, including feminist theology, has been largely white, middle to upper class, and educated. Black theology has been overwhelmingly male. Therefore, feminist theology has not usually addressed the concerns of *black* women (nor those of Latinas and other marginalized women), and black theology has usually failed to speak to the concerns of black *women*. Only recently has black feminist religious thought begun to find its own unique voice. Even more recently, a very few black feminist theologians have raised the issue of homophobia in the African American community. One such theologian, Kelly Brown Douglas, points out that if "womanist theologians continue to maintain silence concerning the oppression of our lesbian sisters, not only do we perpetuate their oppression, but we fall short of our own vision for wholeness."[40]

The black Methodist denominations were the first to ordain women as pastors. Congregational polity among the Baptist groups has limited the development of consistent policies on the ordination of women, but the tendency is for fewer women to be ordained there. While policy usually does not explicitly prohibit it, tradition does. Pentecostals remain firmly against it. Overall, the reluctance to grant full ordination to women has come under increasing criticism in the last two or three decades, and changes are coming about slowly.

QUESTIONS AND ACTIVITIES FOR REVIEW, DISCUSSION, AND WRITING

1. What seem to you to be the advantages and disadvantages of religion and ethnic, national, or racial consciousness being interrelated as they are in these communities of faith?
2. If there is an Eastern Orthodox church where you live or where you go to school, try to make an appointment to visit the church during the week. Notice particularly the architecture of the building, the icons, and the iconostasis. Most priests will be glad to have you visit and will be quite willing to answer your questions. You might also want to consider attending the divine liturgy on Sunday morning.
3. If you are accustomed to worshiping in a white congregation, attend a worship service at one of the historically black churches. If you worship in a mostly black congregation, attend a service in a mostly white congregation. Reflect on the differences you observe.
4. Get your class together in integrated groups of black and white students, and discuss your perceptions of each other's worship.

[38]Mark L. Chapman, *Christianity on Trial: African-American Religious Thought before and after Black Power* (Maryknoll, NY: Orbis Books, 1996), p. 149.
[39]Theressa Hoover, "Black Women and the Churches: Triple Jeopardy," in *Black Theology: A Documentary History*, 1966-1979, eds. Wilmore and Cone, pp. 377–378.
[40]Kelly Brown Douglas, *The Black Christ* (Maryknoll, NY: Orbis Books, 1994), p. 102.

5. In your opinion, what are the advantages and disadvantages of the nonviolent methods of Martin Luther King, Jr.?
6. Read and report on James Baldwin's autobiographical novel, *Go Tell It on the Mountain.*
7. If you can get a videotape of the movie, *The Long Road Home*, with Whoopi Goldberg, view it and write a brief essay on the roles that the black church played in the civil rights movement, as depicted in the film.
8. In what ways do the roles of church mother and church nurse allow women honor and position within the black church while remaining within traditional gender roles?

FOR FURTHER READING

CHAPMAN, MARK L., *Christianity on Trial: African-American Religious Thought before and after Black Power.* Maryknoll, NY: Orbis Books, 1996. This is a fifty-year review of thought on the question of whether Christianity has been a source of liberation, oppression, or both for the African American community.

CLENDENIN, DANIEL B., ed., *Eastern Orthodox Theology: A Contemporary Reader.* Grand Rapids, MI: Baker Book House, 1995. Thirteen essays are included on major themes of Orthodox theology by Orthodox scholar/practitioners.

CONE, JAMES H., *Martin and Malcolm and America: A Dream or a Nightmare.* Maryknoll, NY: Orbis Books, 1995. Cone explores the role and influence of Martin Luther King, Jr., and Malcolm X, undoubtedly the two most influential black religious leaders in the history of the United States.

HARAKAS, STANLEY S., *Living the Faith: The Praxis of Eastern Orthodox Ethics.* Minneapolis, MN: Light and Life Publishing Company, 1993. This book presents major themes in Orthodox ethical practice.

HARAKAS, STANLEY S., *The Orthodox Church: 455 Questions and Answers.* Brookline, MA: Holy Cross Orthodox Press, 1988. This older but concise and comprehensive handbook emphasizes Greek Orthodoxy but includes more general entries as well.

HAYES, DIANA, *And Still We Rise: An Introduction to Black Liberation Theology.* New York: Paulist Press, 1996. Hayes covers the traditional themes included in most discussions of the topic but also includes chapters on black Catholic theology and womanist theology.

KOSTARELOS, FRANCES, *Feeling the Spirit: Faith and Hope in an Evangelical Black Storefront Church.* Columbia, SC: University of South Carolina Press, 1996. This ethnographic study, offering a rich description of an inner-city storefront church, is well illustrated with photographs.

LEMOPOULIS, GEORGES, *Let Us Pray to the Lord: A Collection of Prayers from the Eastern and Oriental Orthodox Traditions.* Geneva, Switzerland: World Council of Churches, 1996. This is a rich sampling of the prayer tradition of the Eastern Christian churches.

LINCOLN, C. ERIC, and LAWRENCE H. MAMIYA, *The Black Church in the African American Experience.* Durham, NC: Duke University Press, 1991. Based on extensive survey and field interview data, this is the current definitive study and also has good historical material.

LITSAS, FOTIOS K., ed., *A Companion to the Greek Orthodox Church.* New York: Department of Communication, Greek Orthodox Archdiocese of North and South America, 1984. This is a good basic introduction to Eastern Orthodoxy in general.

MATSUOKA, FUMITAKA, *Out of Silence: Emerging Themes in Asian American Churches.* Cleveland, OH: United Church Press, 1995. Little has been written so far about Asian American Christianity, and this is a pioneering work based on a study of four Asian American Protestant congregations. Several themes that are important in black theology emerge here as well.

STEWART, MARIA W., et al., with an introduction by Sue E. Houchins, *Spiritual Narratives*. New York: Oxford University Press, 1991. This book includes autobiographical narratives by Stewart, Jarena Lee, Julia A. J. Foote, and Virginia W. Broughton, four black women who preached despite their having been denied formal ordination.

RELEVANT WORLD WIDE WEB SITES

Greek Orthodox Archdiocese of North America (http://www.goarch.org/).

Russian Orthodox Church in America (http://ra.nilenet.com/~russmonk/theocac.htm).

The Orthodox Church in America (http://www.oca.org/).

The Orthodox Christian Foundation (http://www.ocf.org/).

National Baptist Convention, USA, Incorporated (http://www.nbcusa.org/).

National Baptist Convention of America, Unincorporated (http://www.nbca.org/).

Progressive National Baptist Convention (http://www.pnbc.org/).

African Methodist Episcopal Church (http://www.amenet.org/).

African Methodist Episcopal Church Zion Women's Home and Overseas Missionary Society (http://www.nonprofit.net/whoms/index.htm).

Church of God in Christ (http://www.cogic.org/).

Congress of National Black Churches, Inc. (http://www.cnbc.org/).

10

Muslims in the United States

I didn't wear my religion on my sleeve, as many converts do. My approach to Islam took a subtler form. Any action I undertook began with a statement of intention, *Bismillah* ("In the name of Allah"); I fasted every Ramadan (the holy month of fasting); and I pray to Allah daily, feeling no compulsion to broadcast my conversion and thus become the subject of gossip. I'd weave my prayers into my frantic junior executive's schedule, disappearing every so often into a stockroom at JCPenney's corporate headquarters, where, barefoot on a flattened-out box and facing the direction I determined Mecca to be in, I whispered Arabic prayers as telephones rang and business buzzed as usual outside the tranquil little universe I'd created for myself.[1]

Adherents of all the major religions of the world live in the United States. Many of these religions fit our definition of ethnic religion. In the next two chapters, we will look at three of the larger and better-known world religions whose members live in this country. The first, Islam, began in the same general geographic area as did Judaism and Christianity and has much in common with them. The second and third, Hinduism and Buddhism, began in India and are in many ways very different from the Semitic religions. I have kept the use of unfamiliar words to a minimum, instead using more familiar equivalents that convey the sense of what is meant. I have used less familiar terms when doing so seemed warranted because (1) they are used often in discussing a particular religion, (2) you would be likely to encounter them in your other reading or experience, or (3) they are often used and/or greatly preferred by followers of the religions.

A new immigration bill passed in fall 1991 allows a greater diversity of religious workers from foreign countries to enter the United States. The bill liberalizes the qualifications for "religious workers" to include lay workers as well as religious professionals. The bill does require that the applicant be a member of a

---

[1]Steven Barboza, *America Jihad: Islam after Malcolm X* (New York: Bantam Doubleday Dell Publishing Group, 1994), p. 7.

recognized U.S. denomination. However, most religious groups now have at least small numbers in the United States, with some sort of organization. The bill also eases conflict between immigration officials and applicants from religious groups whose leadership does not necessarily fit the pattern established by American clergy.

Islam is the third of the major Semitic monotheistic religions, along with Judaism and Christianity. **Semitic** is a general term that refers to people and religions of Middle Eastern origin, and so includes Judaism, Christianity, and Islam, as well as others. **Ethical monotheism**, as you probably remember, means the belief in and worship of only one God, who is believed to be personal, righteous, and holy. People who are followers of Islam are properly called **Muslims**. The word **Islam** means the peace of one who submits wholly to God (or **Allah**, an Arabic name for God). A *Muslim* is one who submits to Allah. You may have heard Muslims referred to as "Muhammadans" or a similar term. This is incorrect and very offensive to Muslims, because they are followers of Allah, not of Muhammad.

Before you read further, think about what your own opinion of Muslims and of Islam is. Do you know any Muslims personally? What kinds of things have you heard about Muslims, or about Islam as a religion?

Muslims are still regarded by most people in the United States as outside the religious consensus. This may not be the case in the new millennium, according to one analysis:

> The 1990s may be the last decade in which Islam is viewed as a "non-mainstream" religious tradition in America. At its current rate of growth, by the year 2015 Islam will be the second largest religion in the United States, following Christianity. There are approximately four million Muslims in the United States and 650 mosques.[2]

Muslim college students have come to study in the United States from nearly every country in the world where Muslims live. The Muslim Student Organization was founded in 1963 to provide for the needs of Islamic students on American campuses and to help non-Muslim students come to know Islam and its followers better. It remains one of the largest and most active among Islamic organizations, appealing to both immigrant and American-born Muslims.

MUHAMMAD

The story of Islam begins with Muhammad, whom Muslims believe is the "Seal of the Prophets," the last and final prophet in a long line of prophets sent by Allah to bring God's truth to humankind. He was born about 570 C.E. Forty years later, in 610, while meditating alone, Muhammad had an experience in

[2]Gisela Webb, "Expressions of Islam in America," in *America's Alternative Religions*, ed. Timothy Miller (Albany, NY: State University of New York Press, 1995), p. 233.

which he believed that the angel Gabriel spoke to him, conveying the actual words of Allah himself. He was told that he had been chosen as a prophet and that he must repeat the words he would be given to all who would listen. The revelations continued until shortly before Muhammad's death in 632. Islam began as an oral tradition, passed from Muhammad to a few close associates and, finally, to the world.

Muhammad, the Prophet, was a human being, no more than that. The Christian identification of the person Jesus of Nazareth with God is blasphemous to Muslims because making a human being God's equal does not recognize the incomparable greatness and oneness of Allah. Muhammad is, however, regarded as the model for what an ideal person is, and the stories about his life are a source of inspiration for his followers. What Muhammad said and did, as recorded by his companions in the tradition (**Hadith**), provide a blueprint for the interpretation and application of the Qur'an to the various situations of life. Poetry in praise of the Prophet and his life exists in virtually every language spoken by Muslims, and love for him and for his family marks Muslim devotion. Standards for Muslim belief and action come not only from the Qur'an but from its application exemplified in the life and sayings of Muhammad.

THE QUR'AN

The sacred scripture of Islam is called the **Qur'an**, or the **Holy Qur'an**. It was originally written in Arabic, and most Muslims believe that it is fully authentic only in that language. Islam is a missionary religion like Christianity, however, and the Qur'an has been translated into many languages, including English.

The first chapter is recited at the beginning of prayers. It summarizes many of the principal themes of Islam:

> All praise is due to Allah, the Lord of the Worlds.
> The Beneficent, the Merciful.
> Master of the Day of Judgment.
> Thee do we serve and Thee do we beseech for help.
> Keep us on the right path.
> The path of those upon whom Thou hast bestowed favors. Not [the path] of those upon whom Thy wrath is brought down, nor of those who go astray.[3]

Allah commanded that Muhammad **recite** the Qur'an, and reciting still plays an important part in Muslim devotion. The words themselves, because they are believed to be the very words of Allah, have power:

> Recitation of the Qur'an is thought to have a healing, soothing effect, but can also bring protection, miraculous signs, knowledge, and destruction, according to Muslim tradition. It is critical that one recite the Qur'an only in a purified state,

[3]The Holy Qur'an, trans. M. H. Shakir (Tahrike Tarsile Qur'an, 1983) (http://www.hti.umich.edu/relig/koran/).

for the words are so powerful that the one who recites it takes on a great responsibility. Ideally, one learns the Qur'an as a child, when memorization is easiest and when the power of the words will help to shape one's life.[4]

Beliefs

The core beliefs of Islam, from which all others arise, are the oneness and unity of Allah and the prophethood of Muhammad. There are two primary subgroups within Islam, the **Sunni** Muslims (by far the larger subgroup) and the **Shia** Muslims. There is a nucleus of beliefs that is widely shared among Muslims in North America, and these form the basis for our discussion here.

Muslims, as stated above, believe in **the oneness of Allah**. "Oneness" here is not primarily a matter of arithmetic, of there being numerically only one God. Rather the emphasis is on the utter incomparability of Allah, there being nothing as great as Allah. It is also not simply an intellectual matter but requires trust in Allah, submission to the will of Allah, and reliance upon Allah for everything in life.

They also believe in the **angels of Allah**. Angels are spiritual beings whose entire role is to serve Allah. Each has a specific duty to perform. This belief arises from the prior belief that knowledge cannot be limited to what can be perceived with the senses, that there are in fact things that exist that we cannot know through the senses (Qur'an 16:49-50 and 21:19-20).

Muslims also believe in **all the books of Allah**, including the sacred writings of Judaism and Christianity, culminating in the Qur'an. There are specific references in the Qur'an to God's having given Tanakh to the House of Israel and the Bible to Christians. The Qur'an is the standard by which the others are judged. Insofar as they agree with it, they are true and are to be accepted. When they differ from the Qur'an, it has precedence.

As a result of this, Muslims also believe in **all the prophets of Allah**. There are approving references to many of the Hebrew prophets (Abraham, Moses, and David among them) as well as to John the Baptist and Jesus. Each age and each nation is believed to have had its messenger from Allah. **Muhammad**, as stated before, **is the last and final Prophet**. Allah entrusted him with the prophecy that completes and corrects those that have gone before.

Those of Islamic faith also affirm **life after death**. The Qur'an paints vivid pictures of both paradise and hell, as well as of a day of judgment in which all people will be called to account for their lives. Muslims believe that Allah keeps an accurate account of everything people do and think. Good deeds will be rewarded and evil ones punished.

Muslim **morality** is very similar to that of both Christianity and Judaism. Marriage and family are very important; marriage is considered a duty and is based on a legal contract to which both husband and wife agree. Sexual relations

---

[4]Mary Pat Fisher and Robert Luyster, *Living Religions* (Englewood Cliffs, NJ: Prentice Hall, 1991), p. 275.

outside marriage are strictly forbidden. Divorce is permitted but strongly dis-couraged. Anything injurious to oneself or to others—mentally, physically, or morally—is forbidden. Respect and care for the elderly is considered very im-portant, and people are expected to care for their parents in their later years. The equality of all persons and dealing with others with respect and total honesty is a fundamental moral value.

Thinking about Muslim morality brings up a much-misunderstood con-cept, **jihad**. *Jihad* is often translated as "holy war," and this has given rise to the popular misconception of Islam as a fanatical and war-hungry religion. The basic meaning of jihad is otherwise: It means the continual, inner spiritual struggle for submission to Allah, in which all people must engage daily. It is a mistake to think that all Muslims are religious fanatics bent on terrorism. All religions, including those better known in the United States, have given rise to fanaticism at times. But we don't identify Judaism and Christianity with their fanatic representatives. We should extend the same courtesy and moderation to our Muslim neighbors.

There is no doubt that factions within Islam itself have encouraged the perception of Islam as a fierce and warring religion. The following excerpt from a 1988 speech by the Ayatollah Khomeini exemplifies this characteristic:

> We must smash the hands and teeth of the superpowers, particularly the United States. And we must choose one of two alternatives—either martyrdom or victory. . . .

> Our war is one of ideology and does not recognize borders or geography. We must insure the vast mobilization of the soldiers of Islam around the world in our ideo-logical war.[5]

During the Gulf War in the 1990s, Saddam Hussein also used the language of "holy war" to describe the conflict between the United States and Iraq. The American media have tended to pick up on inflammatory rhetoric such as this, and their doing so makes it especially important that we listen to other Muslim voices that provide a more balanced account. One Muslim scholar, Sobhi Mah-massani, describes the Muslim view of warfare this way:

> Islamic law . . . is essentially a law of peace, built on human equality, religious tol-erance, and brotherhood.

> War, in theory, is just and permissible only as a defensive measure, on grounds of extreme necessity, namely to protect the freedom of religion, to repel aggression, to prevent injustice and to protect social order. . . . This defensive war, when per-missible, is moreover subjected by Islamic jurisprudence to strict regulations and rules. . . .

[5]Cited in Ann Elizabeth Meyer, "International Law and the Islamic Tradition of War and Peace," in *Just War and Jihad: Historical Perspectives on War and Peace in Western and Islamic Traditions*, ed. Fred M. Don-ner (New York: Greenwood Press, 1991), p. 207.

Thus, a declaration of war has to be preceded by notification sent to the enemy. Detailed provisions are laid down for the use of humane methods of warfare and fair treatment of enemy persons and property. Acts of cruelty and unnecessary destruction and suffering are expressly proscribed. Provision is also made for the termination of war and the settlement of its consequences.[6]

The late Sufi saint M. R. Bawa Muhaiyaddeen wrote poetically about the essence of Islam:

You must not oppress or harm any man, no matter what religion or race he may be. . . .

All the children of Adam . . . are brothers and sisters. They are not different. . . . You must not harass their places of worship, their bodies, or their hearts. You must protect them as you would protect your own life.

To comfort the hunger of your neighbor, no matter who he is or what religion he belongs to, is Islam. . . . To realize the pain and suffering of others and offer your hands in assistance, helping to alleviate their suffering, is Islam. . . .

Hurting another is not Islam. . . . The purity of Islam is to avoid hurting others; you must regard others as you regard yourself.[7]

The Five Pillars of Islam

Islam is second only to Christianity in its number of worldwide followers. Wherever they live, Muslims share five core practices, called the Five Pillars of Islam. The Five Pillars are **five specific acts required of all faithful Muslims**. Although they are classified as "required," their actual observance varies from one person to another, even in traditionally Muslim countries. There is tension between those who support strict observance as the only way to be a "good Muslim" and those who accept a wider range of observance. This tension is not unique to Islam but exists in all religions. The first pillar is **faith, shown in the repetition of the creed** (*Shahadah*): "There is no God but Allah, and Muhammad is the Prophet of Allah." Devout Muslims repeat this affirmation of faith daily. Doing so helps keep the major principles of their faith at the center of their lives. These are often the first words spoken to a newborn Muslim baby, and the last words spoken or heard by one who is dying. While saying the Shahadah is important, the faith which it expresses is the central concern.

The second pillar is **prayer five times daily**. Ritual cleansing precedes the prayers, and each prayer is accompanied by specific ritual actions such as sitting,

---

[6]Cited in Meyer, "International Law and the Islamic Tradition of War and Peace," p. 203.
[7]M. R. Bara Muhaiyaddeen, *The Golden Words of a Sufi Sheikh* (Philadelphia, PA: Fellowship Press, 1981), cited in *A SourceBook for Earth's Community of Religions*, rev. ed., ed. Joel D. Beversluis (Grand Rapids, MI: CoNexus Press—SourceBook Project and New York: Global Education Associates, 1995), p. 61.

standing, and prostrating oneself with the forehead touching the floor or ground. Muslims pray facing Mecca, the holy city of Islam, located in what is now Saudi Arabia. These are set, formal prayers. In addition, Muslims are encouraged to repeat these prayers more times than is required and to add their own personal prayers to the required ones. Prayers are said at dawn, at midday, midafternoon, dusk, and at night. There is some flexibility in the exact times; the idea is to have the prayers paced throughout the day. Doing so helps keep Muslims continually aware of Allah and of the need for submission to him. Those who can are encouraged to attend the **mosque (masjid)**, the Islamic place of worship (Figure 10-1) for the midday prayers on Fridays.

Islam does not have a weekly Sabbath, but the community of faith gathers to pray these prayers together and usually to hear the Qur'an read and explained in a talk by the **imam** or prayer leader. While the Jewish Sabbath is a day of rest, and Christians have traditionally interpreted Sunday (the Lord's day) similarly, Muslims are explicitly enjoined to attend to their work before and after Friday midday prayer.

Figure 10-1   The *Masjid*, or mosque, Islamic Center of Toledo, Ohio. The presence of Muslims, Hindus, Buddhists, and others of the less familiar religions in the United States expands the range of religious architecture, as well as of religious beliefs and practices. (*Photo courtesy of Richard J. Fears.*)

As you can imagine, the required prayers can be difficult for Muslims in the United States. Prayer times may conflict with work times, and there may not always be an appropriate place to pray in the workplace. Employers may not always want to make the slight accommodation necessary to allow time for prayers, and the curiosity of fellow workers can be embarrassing. On the other side, many Muslims appreciate the opportunity it gives for them to express their faith to non-Muslims.

The third pillar is the **giving of alms** to help those in need. This is not simply charity. It is more like a religious tax in that it is required. It amounts to about 2½ percent, based on a person's net worth. Muslims in the United States select a Muslim organization to which they will pay the alms; for many, it is the Muslim Student Association. They are encouraged to make other charitable contributions, as they are able. Muslims do not look down on wealth, as long as it is gotten honestly; the honest earning of money and wise management of it is a tribute to Allah. But Allah must also be worshiped through one's wealth, and this is the point of almsgiving.

Fourth is **fasting during the month of Ramadan**. The Islamic religious calendar differs from the civil calendar, so Ramadan occurs at different times in different years. Ramadan is the month in which tradition holds that the revelation to Muhammad began. Fasting, in this instance, means complete abstention from eating, drinking, smoking, and sexual activity from just before sunrise until just after sunset. A meal is eaten immediately before and immediately following the hours of fasting. This activity helps unite Muslims around the world, encourages empathy for those who are hungry or otherwise lacking, and reinforces submission to the will of Allah. Ramadan is also a time of increased spiritual awareness, when Muslims often spend extra time in reading and studying the Qur'an and in prayer. Fasting is not required of young children, women who are pregnant or menstruating, travelers, the elderly and those who are ill or frail, as well as others on whom it would impose an unreasonable burden.

The fast is followed by the Festival of Fast-Breaking. This is a joyous time in which families and friends gather together to rejoice in the end of this strenuous time and to celebrate the spiritual benefits gained from it. For many Muslim families in the United States, it is a time to invite non-Muslim friends to join in the celebration and share special foods from their religious and national cultures.

The last of the Pillars is the **hajj**, or **pilgrimage to Mecca**, a journey that Muslims are required to make at least once in their lives, as long as they are mentally, physically, and financially capable of doing so. Hajj brings Muslims from around the world together for a series of religious rituals in and around Mecca. Its center is the Grand Mosque and the Kabah, a large stone building that Muslims believe was built by Abraham and Ishmael for the worship of Allah. Most pilgrims also visit Medina, the city in which Muhammad found shelter after he was forced to flee Mecca because people there would not accept his teaching. After the Meccan tribes were defeated, Muhammad made a pilgrimage back to Mecca in 629. The rites that he performed then are the prototype for those carried out by Muslims today.

MUSLIMS IN THE UNITED STATES

Estimates of the number of Muslims in the United States vary considerably. It is not necessary to be a member of a mosque to be a Muslim. Too, some Muslims remain hesitant to identify themselves as Muslims because prejudice still exists. Another possible source of inaccuracy in the data is that there may be Christians from Arab countries who identify culturally but not religiously with the Muslim community. Most nonimmigrant Muslims in the United States are black, although this accounts for only about 2 percent of the black population in the United States. Contrary to what you might expect, most Arab Americans are Christians, perhaps because Christians tend to emigrate to the United States from Muslim countries in greater numbers than do non-Christians.[8]

Muslims have come to the United States from virtually all of the Middle Eastern countries in which Islam is common, as well as from India, Pakistan, China, the former Soviet Union, and elsewhere. There have been Muslims in the United States for many generations, as well as a steady influx of recent immigrants. There are also American converts to Islam. Thus, on the one hand, there is an Islamic *community* here: a group of people united by a common religion. On the other hand, there are several *communities* of Muslims here: American-born, descendants of immigrants, and recent immigrants, as well as Muslims of various national and ethnic backgrounds.

As the Muslim community becomes more thoroughly integrated into the larger culture of the United States, distinctions such as "immigrant" and "indigenous" are becoming less useful to describe Islam in America as sociological changes occur over time:

> "Immigrant" communities are becoming "establishment," children are growing and intermarrying, foreign-born Muslims are becoming American citizens, demarcation between the "older" immigrants and the new African and Asian immigrants taking on racist overtones.[9]

Recent analyses of the Muslim experience in the United States indicate that the two key problems facing both immigrant and native-born Muslims are deciding how they will live an Islamic life in America and dealing with prejudice.

> American societal patterns are often at odds with needs of Muslim life and practice: Work schedules do not easily allow for the five-times-daily *salat* prayers or Friday congregational prayers. Institutional eating facilities (schools, prisons, military) are not set up for Muslim dietary practices [for example, avoiding pork and a wide range of other foods considered unclean]. The pervasiveness of alcohol in America and the cultural acceptance of sexual permissiveness and immodesty (in clothing and comportment) are seen as negative influences on the faith community, particularly on its young people. The *shariah*, however, continues to be held

---

[8]*New York Times National,* April 10, 1991, p. 1.
[9]Webb, "Expressions of Islam in America," pp. 240–241, n. 2.

as the ideal pattern of life to be striven for, somehow, in the midst of contemporary American culture.[10]

There is a growing subculture of young Islamic Americans, children of immigrant Muslims in the 1960s and 1970s, who are determined to forge an integrated identity that is both Muslim and American. Their doing so calls into question the usual stereotype of Islam as a "foreign" faith. They are also finding new ways to formulate that faith, ways that might well be unimaginable in the Muslim nations from which their parents came.

> American Muslims are experiencing both exhilaration at the opportunity to increase their numbers and develop their institutions and frustration and dismay as they continue to experience prejudice, intimidation, discrimination, misunderstanding, and even hatred. . . . [Muslims in the United States] have unprecedented freedom to experiment with forms and structures for the separation of religion and state away from the watchful eyes of wary governments and the criticism of traditionalists. At the same time, this freedom is fraught with the danger of innovation and deviance; the great range of options available in the American context carries the threat of sectarian division and fragmentation.[11]

Like members of most other religious groups, Muslims in the United States range from liberals who seek accommodation with the surrounding culture to the very conservative who seek to preserve the inherited tradition and advocate separation from those who do not agree. There are also differences of opinion between Muslims who want to convert non-Muslims and those who do not.

The Muslim mosque (*masjid* is being used increasingly) has changed character in the United States. In most traditionally Muslim countries, the mosque is simply a place in which the community of the faithful gathers for the Friday midday prayers. The *imam*, or prayer leader, is a member of the community who is skilled in Qur'anic recitation and perhaps exposition. There is no professional clergy in Islam, and usually the imam holds another job. In the United States, the mosque has become much more like a church or synagogue, and the imam has become a professional clergyman, in most instances. Mosques offer a full range of activities, both religious and cultural, for the Muslim community. Besides the traditional prayer service, there will often be women's groups, classes for all ages and both genders, social activities, and day care. The imam is expected to function as the leader of the congregation, a counselor, an administrator, and the representative of the Muslim community to the surrounding culture.[12]

---

[10]Webb, "Expressions of Islam in America," in *America's Alternative Religions*, p. 237. See also Kambiz Ghanea-Bassiri, *Competing Visions of Islam in the United States: A Study of Los Angeles* (Westport, CT: Greenwood Press, 1997).

[11]Yvonne Yazbeck Haddad, "Introduction: The Muslims of America," in *The Muslims of America*, ed. Yvonne Yazbeck Haddad (New York: Oxford University Press, 1991), pp. 3 and 5.

[12]For an ethnographic study of the changes that have occurred in one immigrant Muslim congregation, see Rogaia Mustafa Abusharaf, "Structural Adaptations in an Immigrant Muslim Congregation in New York," in *Gatherings in Diaspora: Religious Communities and the New Immigration*, ed. R. Stephen Warner and Judith G. Wittner (Philadelphia: Temple University Press, 1998), pp. 235–261.

As traditionally interpreted, Islamic law covers every aspect of life for Muslims: religious and secular (a distinction that is itself alien to Islam), private and public, extraordinary and mundane. Muslims who live in a non-Muslim culture must decide the extent to which full adherence to Islamic law is possible or desirable. As you might expect, individual Muslims vary in how carefully they keep all the details of Islamic law. There are two sources of variation: (1) different aspects of observance receive different attention, and (2) different Muslim subpopulations vary in their observance.

In the first place, some regulations are kept much more fully than others. For example, Muslim law forbids the payment or receiving of interest on money. Using the American banking system makes this extremely difficult. Most Muslims in the United States do have bank accounts and do use credit when necessary. Muslim law also forbids the consumption of pork, pork products, and alcohol. The great majority of Muslims do not knowingly consume pork or pork products, and most Muslims make a conscientious effort to find out if prepared foods contain them. Fewer adhere absolutely to the alcohol prohibition, although a majority do. Whether or not Muslims themselves choose to use alcohol, they must decide whether to offer it to non-Muslim guests in their homes. Some do and some do not.

Muslims are discouraged or forbidden from dating as it is practiced in the United States. Youth meet prospective mates through their families and at activities at the mosque. Social interaction takes place only in a well-chaperoned group setting. Marriages are usually arranged. Women especially, but men also, are discouraged from marrying outside the faith. If they do, they may marry only a Jew or a Christian (other "peoples of the Book"). This makes finding a suitable partner within such a small population difficult. Muslim magazines often carry matrimonial ads in which families invite correspondence from potential partners for a daughter, sister, son, or brother.

There is no consensus among Muslims in the United States about the application of Muslim laws and values. There is no doubt that observance declines with a number of factors. Less strict observance is associated with being in the United States for a longer time, with interacting with non-Muslim Americans, and "apparently as a general result of living in American culture."[13] Age is also a factor. While 70 percent of adults aged 18 and older in a recent survey believe that Islamic values should be observed "strictly," among those under 18 only about half agreed.[14]

The Islamic community in North America has shown its adaptability to American culture in another way. In the spring of 1998, the Islamic Society of North America hosted the "Conference on Muslims and the Information Super-

---

[13]Yvonne Yazbeck Haddad and Adair T. Lummis, *Islamic Values in the United States: A Comparative Study* (New York: Oxford University Press, 1987), chaps. 3, 4, and 5.

[14]Kambiz GhaneaBassiri, *Competing Visions of Islam in the United States,* p. 49. This book provides considerable data on varying attitudes and degrees of observance among Muslims in the greater Los Angeles area.

highway: Tools for the 21st Century." A call for papers for this conference described the relationship between Islam and the "information superhighway":

> The information Superhighway is increasingly being used as a tool for Islamic da'wah [sharing the faith] and for sharing information among Muslims around the world.

> In recognition of the increasing importance of this sector, the Islamic Society of North America (ISNA) is organizing the first Muslims & the Information Super-highway Conference. . . . The Conference will bring together Muslim information technology practitioner [sic] to share experiences, make connections and share ideas on the potential of the information highway as a tool for promoting the understanding of Islam.

> ISNA believes that the potential interaction of these professionals will help create better channels of communications and contribute toward building a strong Islamic community in North America. This Conference will contribute toward opening opportunities for Muslim professionals and users to utilize the power of the Internet.[15]

An Islamic popular religion is also developing in the United States as more and more items become available as the market for them increases. The issue of *Islamic Horizons* cited above carried an advertisement for a video, "Muslim Scouts Adventures," the first in what would be a three-volume animated series intended for ages four and up and available in both English and Arabic. There are compact disc Qur'ans and Islamic art screen savers for personal computers. An "I [heart] Allah" mug has been spotted, as well as a "Praise Allah" bumper sticker. Several companies cater to the clothing needs of Islamic women who wish to maintain traditional dress in the United States.

Meanwhile prejudice and misconception continue to exist. Following the Oklahoma City bombing in 1995 (in which neither Middle Easterners nor Muslims were even involved), messages such as "you'll die" were left on answering machines in mosques around the country.[16] Media speculation immediately turned to "Arab terrorist" involvement. When the Saudi Islamic Academy wanted to build a school in Loudoun County, Virginia, in 1998, "an anonymous flyer circulated among Loudoun residents, warning that the school would attract 'Muslim and Arab terrorists' and bring 'thousands of Middle Eastern strangers roaming our streets.'"[17]

There are a number of Muslim organizations in the United States. I will mention only a few of them. Most of you who are reading this book are college students. Some of you are members of or active in campus religious organizations sponsored by your community of faith. The **Muslim Student Associa-**

---

[15]*Islamic Horizons*, Vol. 26, No. 6, p. 40.
[16]Carla Power, "The New Islam," *Newsweek*, March 16, 1998, p. 35.
[17]Christian Jacobson, "Islam in Virginia," *Religion in the News*, June 1998, p. 11.

tion, described above, is one of the constituent groups of **The Islamic Society of North America**, an umbrella organization of several groups. It is generally considered to be the primary national Muslim organization, especially by immigrant Muslims. It publishes a journal, *Islamic Horizons.* The **American Muslim Mission** is the largest organization of American-born Muslims. It publishes *The Muslim Journal.*

Recall that in the discussion of Muslim beliefs, we distinguished between Sunni and Shia Muslims. There is a third group of Muslims in the United States, the **Sufi Muslims**, or simply, **Sufis.** Sufism is the **mystical branch of Islam**, comparable in that respect to Hasidic Judaism and Christian mysticism. Sufism first came to the United States in 1910 with an Indian musician named Pir Hazrat Inayat Khan. There are now organizations throughout the United States. Their beliefs focus on the essential unity of all religions. They affirm that there is one God, one holy book ("the sacred manuscript of nature"), one religion, one law, one human brotherhood, one moral principle, one truth, and one path.[18] Meditation and ecstatic dancing facilitate communion with God. The Order accepts individual students as initiates, sponsors worship as the Universal Worship of the Church of All, and also has a Healing Order that works with group healing rituals.

Women in Islam and Muslim Women in America

It is clear that under Qur'anic law, women received more equal treatment than was otherwise common in Muhammad's lifetime. Religiously and legally, women and men were considered as equals. It is also the case that, while having equal standing before Allah and before the law, women and men were thought to be different from each other, with different primary spheres of responsibility. Even if she were active in the public realm, a woman's primary responsibility was in the home, while a man's primary area of influence was the public arena.

Most Muslims in the United States approve of a married woman's working outside the home if she chooses. Even more approve if financial circumstances require it. Traditional Muslim dress requires that women cover most of their bodies when outside the home. Most Muslim women feel free to adopt American clothing styles, while often avoiding the less modest ways of dressing that are common here. Many either are required or choose to wear more traditional dress in the prayer room of the mosque. Some wear traditional clothing as a way of identifying with the Muslim community and expressing their commitment to its values. It should be noted here that the Qur'an specifically enjoins modesty in clothing for *both* sexes (Qur'an, 24:30–31), a fact that is often overlooked in discussions of women's dress codes.

Traditionally, whatever else women's roles outside the home have been, women have had almost no opportunity to participate in the leadership of the mosque. In many Islamic countries, women rarely even attend the mosque. In

[18]"Sufi Thoughts," Sufi Order, Lebanon Springs, NY, n.d.

the United States, women may or may not attend Friday prayers; most likely, they do not. When they do, they are often required to remain in the back of the prayer room or in a balcony or basement. While some women accept this traditional separation of the sexes and feel that it enhances their own worship of Allah, others find it demeaning:

> Being excluded from the mosque, praying in the basement, even after the *Jum'a* [Friday midday prayer], it is not fair. I went to a masjid in Washington, D.C., after *Jum'a*. No one was even in there. Here is this extremely beautiful masjid that we weren't even able to pray in.

> In terms of praying separate, for me, it is a negative concept. It is like we can't act responsibly. Not only just women, but men and women cannot act responsibly together.[19]

Nonetheless, women do play an active role in most mosques, in fundraising, teaching, supporting its social life, and in both formal and informal influence on decision making. They serve on boards of directors in some mosques. Many believe that women should be eligible for any lay leadership position, including the presidency of the mosque. Women do not serve as imams.

Muslim thought about the appropriate roles of women, and the American understanding of the Muslim view both vary:

> Contemporary Islam is subject to several different currents, each strong and with articulate advocates. While some reaffirm the necessity of women remaining in the home to maintain [traditionally Islamic] values for the sake of Islamic society, others stress the importance of full female participation in the public life of the Islamic community. The latter perceive the traditional position of women vis-a-vis men as alien to Islam and argue for equal rights in the workplace as well as equal participation in the outward manifestations of Islam.

> These various strands of thought, along with the legacy of misunderstanding of Islam on the part of many Westerners, make it difficult for Americans to fully appreciate the position of women in Muslim society. Many . . . [Muslims feel] that Americans in general do not understand the role of women in Islam and their own conviction that the Muslim woman does, in fact, have a better situation than women in other religious traditions.[20]

Islam and Black Americans

Black Americans were attracted to Islam by its message of complete racial equality. Muslim tradition holds that a daughter of Muhammad married a black man. Islam also offered belief in one God and a strong ethical code, as did Christianity, but it was not identified with the white oppressors. The story of Islam as

---

[19]GhaneaBassiri, *Competing Visions of Islam in the United States*, p. 53.
[20]Haddad and Lummis, *Islamic Values in the United States*, pp. 125–126.

it relates to the struggle for black freedom and self-definition is complex, as is the history of black Muslims in the United States. It is clear that Islam offered American blacks an opportunity for a more positive self-identification:

> Although very few references explain how ideas about Islam became available in the black community, it is clear that this religion promised a new identity, a feeling of "somebodiness" denied by the dominant culture, a liberation from . . . relegation to insignificance. The new adherents shed Christianity, which they perceived as the root of their oppression in its glorification of suffering and promise of redemption in the hereafter.[21]

Islam was initially linked with the black power movement. Elijah Muhammad emerged in 1934 as the leader of what was then known as the Nation of Islam.

In the 1960s, a group arose within the Nation of Islam who did not fully agree with Muhammad. This group was led by Malcolm X (born Malcolm Little in 1925). Malcolm X had earlier accepted Muhammad as a "divine leader." However, especially later in his life, Malcolm X and his followers wanted to move the Nation closer to traditional Islam and away from complete separation from whites. They founded the Muslim Mosque, Incorporated, in 1964.

In 1975, Elijah Muhammad died and his son, W. D. Muhammad (b. 1933) assumed control of the Nation of Islam. Under his leadership, the Nation moved closer to the viewpoint of the Muslim Mosque. Followers of Warith Muhammad are now accepted by Muslims worldwide as followers of traditional, Sunni Islam.

It is Malcolm X who has retained, even after his death, a hold on the imagination of American blacks, Muslim and non-Muslim alike. A poll done at the time that Spike Lee's controversial movie, *Malcolm X*, came out indicated that although only about half of American blacks really understood what Malcolm X stood for, a majority consider him a hero. Most rank him second only to Martin Luther King, Jr., in importance to contemporary blacks.[22]

Although the themes of black power and separatism have been muted among most black Muslims, Islam remains a viable alternative for American blacks. It has important similarities with both Christianity and Judaism while not being identified with slavery and oppression.

People who were dissatisfied with the emphasis on racial equality in mainstream Islam came together around Louis Farrakhan in a movement to return to the separatist views and policies of the old Nation. Minister Farrakhan's followers have remained an outspoken minority among American Muslims. A list of their demands includes:

- Complete freedom, justice, and equality of opportunity, particularly equal opportunity in employment

---

[21] Beverly Thomas McCloud, "African-American Muslim Women," in *The Muslims of America*, ed. Haddad, p. 178.

[22] *Newsweek*, November 16, 1992, p. 68.

- The provision of land for the descendants of slaves to establish their own homeland
- The freeing of Islamic and other black prisoners, particularly those on death rows
- An end to police brutality
- Freedom from all taxation until equal justice is a reality
- Separate but equal education under all black teachers
- No intermarriage[23]

The Nation of Islam also links black separatism with traditional Muslim beliefs. For example, they affirm:

- A "mental resurrection" that will begin with "the so-called Negroes," who are identified as God's chosen people.
- The final judgment will take place in America.
- Master W. Fard Muhammad [an early leader of the black Muslim movement] was himself the incarnation of God, the "Messiah of the Christians and the "Mahdi" [a savior figure] of the Muslims." [24]

The Nation of Islam under Minister Farrakhan's leadership continues the themes of separatism and retribution that the Muslim Mosque, Incorporated, has muted or eliminated entirely. As such, the Nation of Islam gives expression to the anger, bitterness, and resentment of a group of people so damaged in body, mind, and spirit by centuries of oppression that all talk of cooperation and "friendship" with the oppressors must ring hollow and hypocritical.

QUESTIONS AND ACTIVITIES FOR REVIEW, DISCUSSION, AND WRITING

1. If you live or attend school close to an Islamic mosque (look in the Yellow Pages under "Religious Organizations," or perhaps "Churches"), make arrangements to attend the Friday midday prayer. Non-Muslims are welcome at mosques. There may be some dress restrictions for women; inquire before you attend.
2. Especially if visiting a mosque is not possible, try to arrange for a Muslim student who attends your college or university to come and speak to your class.
3. If you are not a Muslim, pick one of the Five Pillars of Islam and discuss what it might mean to you if you were. You may want to do some additional reading on the Pillar that you choose. If you are a Muslim, discuss what one of the Pillars means to you.
4. If your library subscribes to any periodicals published by United States Muslims, read through two or three issues, and write about what impression you form of Islam.

---

[23]The Nation of Islam World Wide Web site (http://www.noi.org/). The same material often appears in *The Final Call*, the Nation's newspaper.
[24]The Nation of Islam World Wide Web site (http://www.noi.org/). The same material often appears in *The Final Call*, the Nation's newspaper. The site has the full text of the demands and beliefs.

FOR FURTHER READING

BARBOZA, STEVEN, *American Jihad: Islam after Malcolm X*. New York: Bantam Doubleday Dell Publishing Group, 1995. This collection of essays, edited by an American convert to Islam, is a good treatment of both "ordinary" Muslims and "lives of the rich and famous" American Muslims.

McCLOUD, AMINAH BEVERLY, *African American Islam*. New York: Routledge, 1995. McCloud covers the history and contemporary functions of Islam in the African American community. Chapters 3 ("The Family Structure and Domestic Life") and 5 ("Women in Islam") especially have a wealth of ethnographic detail that makes African American Islam come alive for the reader.

YOUNG, WILLIAM A., *The World's Religions: Worldviews and Contemporary Issues*. Englewood Cliffs, NJ: Prentice Hall, 1995. This is an excellent introduction to the world's religions, written from a perspective that is compatible with that taken in this book. It covers all the basics and includes a section on each religion's response to contemporary ethical issues.

RELEVANT WORLD WIDE WEB SITES

Islamic Texts and Resources MetaPage (http://wings.buffalo.edu/student-life/sa/muslim/isl/isl.html).
CyberMuslim Information Collective (http://www.ou.edu/cybermuslim).
Muslim Public Affairs Council (http://mpac.org/).
Nation of Islam (http://www.noi.org/).

11

Hindus and Buddhists
in the United States

Identity is not just a name or appellation which other people can attach to you. Identity is based on who you are and how you relate to the world and other things around you. . . . Being Hindus gives us an outlook on the world which is holistic, universal, nondiscriminatory and more in tune with the thinking of the founding fathers of the American Republic. . . . Therefore, we, the Hindus living in the USA, should call ourselves Hindu Americans and live proudly by the Hindu ideals of *Ekam satya vipra bahudha vadanti* (Truth is one, sages call it by different names) and *Vasudhaivya kutumbhakam* (The whole world is a family).[1]

Women . . . are moving to create a distinctly Americanized, feminized, democratized form of Buddhist spiritual practice. In this effort lies the possibility for the creation of a religion fully inclusive of women's realities, in which women hold both institutional and spiritual leadership. This movement offers opportunities not found elsewhere.

But the more basic appeal of Buddhist practice to women resides in the fact that Buddhism posits no god, creates no I–Thou relationship with an all-powerful father figure. A central tenet is that one must trust one's own experience above all else. Nothing—no tradition, belief, or direction from a teacher—must be accepted unless it can pass the test of experience.[2]

Hinduism and Buddhism both began in India, a far different world than that which gave rise to Judaism, Christianity, and Islam. What we now call Hin-

[1]Yash Pal Lakra, "Let Us Call Ourselves 'Hindu Americans,'" *Hinduism Today* (October, 1997), p. 9.
[2]Sandy Boucher (ed.), *Turning the Wheel: American Women Creating the New Buddhism,* updated and expanded edition (Boston: Beacon Press, 1993), pp. 1–2.

duism began in India, sometime between 2000 and 1500 years before the life-time of Jesus. Buddhism began later, in the fifth century B.C.E. Hinduism and Buddhism each account for less than one percent of the U.S. population, but are religious minorities whose visibility is increasing.

HINDUISM

Unlike the religions you have studied so far, it has no single founder. The word **Hinduism** is an umbrella term for a vast collection of religious beliefs and practices that nonetheless have enough in common to warrant grouping them together. Indians themselves often use the term **Sanatana Dharma** for their religion. It means "original religion," because Indians believe that theirs is a form of religion that has existed since the dawn of humanity. Hinduism is, however, quite different from the religions that have been discussed thus far. One author, commenting on the challenges of teaching about Hinduism, calls it the "ism that isn't." He continues,

> Hindus . . . have little interest in specifying a single line of teaching authority that ought to be embraced by all. . . . Hinduism has no central authority, no unifying scripture, no verbal formula to which all its adherents give regular assent. . . . Yet . . . it still has a coherence that separates Hindus from other religious people.[3]

In what follows, you will learn the basic outlines of the Hindu worldview and then be introduced to some of the Hindu groups in the United States.

As noted above, there is no single sacred writing that absolutely all Hindus regard as equally central. The **Vedas**, however, are the oldest of the sacred writings and have influenced the entire development of Hinduism. Loyalty to the Vedas is regarded by many Hindus as the litmus test of authentic Hinduism. In addition, Hindus regard the **Agamas** as revealed scripture. While the Vedas help to define what Hinduism as a whole is, the various Agamas are important to specific groups within it. The **Bhagavad-Gita** is an important devotional classic and is the best known and best loved sacred writing among Hindus. It is a section of a much longer epic work, the **Mahabharata**.

The Hindu Worldview

Whereas the Semitic religions distinguish clearly between God as Creat*or* and everything else as creat*ion*, Hindus do not use this distinction. Rather, **every living thing is a manifestation of the sacred**. The divine can be seen and known in everything that is, and everything that is can be seen as a part of the divine. Everything else exists only insofar as it participates in the sacred; nothing has independent existence. This also means that, fundamentally, there can be no

---

[3]John Stratton Hawley, "Teaching the Hindu Tradition," in *Teaching the Introductory Course in Religious Studies: A Sourcebook*, ed. Mark Juergensmeyer (Atlanta, GA: Scholars Press, 1991), pp. 37–38.

sharp separation between things—between the divine and the human, or between people and all other beings. In the innermost core of our being, myself, my cat, and the fly annoying my cat are one.

Another distinctive feature of Hinduism is the related concepts of reincarnation and karma. **Reincarnation** means (1) that a person's present life was preceded by other lives and will likewise be followed by other lives. It also means (2) that these lifetimes do not happen randomly but are connected. The way that life is lived in one lifetime determines the quality of the next incarnation. **Karma** is the moral law of cause and effect that links lifetimes together. The principle of karma states that every action has a reaction. In our own culture, even if we ourselves are not a part of the Judeo-Christian-Islamic tradition, most of us are accustomed to thinking in terms of rewards and punishments: Good deeds will be rewarded and evil ones punished. Karma, by contrast, is a moral law that operates analogously to natural laws such as gravity. Certain results inevitably follow certain actions. As described in one of Hinduism's sacred writings,

> According as one acts, according as one conducts himself, so does he become. . . . As is his desire, such is his resolve; as is his resolve, such the action he performs; what action he performs, that he procures for himself.[4]

According to one recent analysis, the Hindu belief in karma provides answers to three major questions:[5]

- Why am I "me" rather than someone else?
- Why does what happens to me happen to me, rather than something else happening?
- And why does it happen to me, instead of happening to someone else?

This same analysis, which attempts to reinterpret central Hindu beliefs for the present time and for a context that transcends their Indian origins, offers a twofold reinterpretation of the doctrine of karma. The results of our actions affect not just ourselves, but the community of which we are a part. Karma has a *social* dimension as well as an individual one. The person who chooses to smoke turns other people into passive smokers. Second, karma can be reinterpreted to address the question of *why* people act as they do. Not only do the results of our actions affect us, but they become extended in the way that we treat other people, including people who had nothing to do with how we were treated. Both functional and dysfunctional family patterns, for example, tend to persist throughout generations.[6]

Dharma refers to the underlying order of the universe and also to the way that a person must live in order to fit into it. In India, the class and caste system plays a central role in determining a person's dharma. It is not nearly as much of

---

[4]*Brihadaranyaka Upanishad.*
[5]Arvind Sharma, *Hinduism for Our Times* (Bombay: Oxford University Press, 1996), p. 25.
[6]Sharma, *Hinduism for Our Times*, pp. 27–29.

a consideration among Hindus in the United States. Nonetheless, the basic idea that each person has a particular place in the overall scheme of things remains. Lessening karma's grip, then, is a matter of becoming aware of one's dharma and following it to the best of one's ability.

Belief in reincarnation brings up the question of what it means to be a person, according to Hindus. First, we must **distinguish between our empirical self and our real self.** Our **empirical self** is what we think we are, what ordinary experience tells us we are. Most of us think about it as including our physical body, our mind and personality, and our subconscious. All these aspects of us are individual and personal: They pertain to us as individuals and as personal beings. The **real self**, on the other hand, is that of the divine within each and every person. It is not personal, nor is it individual. The real self moves from lifetime to lifetime throughout successive incarnations:

> Just as a person, having cast off old garments, puts on other, new ones, even so does the embodied One [i.e., real self], having cast off old bodies, take on other, new ones. . . . For, to one who is born, death is certain, and certain is birth to one who has died. . . . As in this body, there are for the embodied One childhood, youth, and old age, even so is there the taking on of another body.[7]

> As a goldsmith, taking a piece of gold, reduces it to another, more beautiful form, just so the Real Self, striking down this body and dispelling its ignorance, makes for itself another and more beautiful form.[8]

A contemporary Hindu catechism, written specifically for Hindu young people in the United States, describes it this way:

> Our individual soul is the immortal and spiritual body of light that animates life and reincarnates again and again. . . . We are not the physical body, mind or emotions. We are the immortal soul, *atman*.[9]

The human problem, as it is expressed by Hindus, is not sin and disobedience (as in Judaism, Christianity, and Islam), but **ignorance and illusion**. We fail to understand the real nature of reality and of ourselves, and, in that misunderstanding, act in ways that reinforce the illusion of separateness. As long as we think and act as though we *are* our empirical selves, as long as we think and act as though we are separate from other beings and from the universe itself, we remain trapped in the cycle of death and rebirth.

The ultimate goal of human life is escape from the cycle of death and rebirth. Throughout however many lifetimes it requires, a person comes increasingly closer to grasping the unity of all things, including the real self, in the

---

[7] *Bhagavad-Gita.*
[8] *Brihadaranyaka Upanishad.*
[9] Satguru Sivaya Subramuniyaswami, *Dancing with Siva: Hinduism's Contemporary Catechism* (Kapaa, Hawaii: Himalayan Academy Press, 1997), p. 79.

divine. Eventually, when that unity is fully grasped, incarnation ceases and the real self is reunited with the divine, which, of course, it never really left. Most Hindus describe this as an uninterrupted communion between the real self and the divine, in which the distinction between the two is preserved while the separation is overcome. Others, however, prefer to picture it as a complete merger between the real self and the divine, in which both separation and distinction are overcome. For the majority of Hindus, this is a far-distant goal. Most look forward to living better lives throughout successive reincarnations.

A final feature of Hinduism that deserves mention here is its recognition of the **validity of all religious paths**. As there are any number of ways to climb a mountain, say most Hindus, so there are many paths to reunion with the divine. Differences of belief and practice are external only, in this view, and the inner essence of all humankind's religions is identical. Such a view does not rule out having personal preferences among these "externals," nor does it necessitate approval of them all. It does entail the belief that all sincere seekers, by whatever path or paths they choose, will in time arrive at their destination:

> The soul, in its intelligence, searches for its Self, slowly ascending the path that leads to enlightenment and liberation. It is an arduous, delightful journey through the cycles of birth, death and rebirth culminating in Self Realization, the direct and personal spiritual experience of God, of the Self, of Truth.[10]

Hindu Ways of Liberation

Within itself as well, Hinduism offers people more than one way to seek release and liberation. These ways are not exclusive; people usually follow more than one, accenting one over the others and perhaps changing emphases during a lifetime. People differ in their personalities, in their stage and station in life, and one method will not be best for all. Finding the *appropriate* path is more important than locating the right one.

One very popular way is **devotion to a god or goddess**. By increasingly identifying with their chosen god or goddess, people increase their intuitive grasp of the oneness of themselves and the divine. Many Hindus worship **Shiva**, and many others are devotees of **Krishna** or **Vishnu**, gods whose concern for human beings is paramount. Others are devotees of the **Great Goddess**, who takes many forms. Deities are worshiped by prayer and offerings to their images at home altars and in temples. Deity worship personalizes the divine, giving the devotee the opportunity for a warmly emotional relationship with the sacred. It satisfies the human longing for knowing and being known by the sacred in a way analogous to that shared with a lover, close friend, or family member.

Hindu religious art abounds with images of deities, both pictures and statues. Statues are especially important. It may be difficult for you to understand the role that images of gods and goddesses play in Hinduism. For Hindus, *seeing*

---

[10]Subramuniyaswami, *Dancing with Siva*, p. xxiv.

the divine is a basic way of experiencing communion with the sacred. The divine is present precisely *as* the image, giving itself for worship. These are not idols. The clay or the brass of the statue is not worshiped, but the deity whom it portrays and makes present to the devotee is worshiped.

A second popular way to seek liberation is through **duty**, **work**, or **action**. To follow this way means to do what is called for by one's position in life, without allowing oneself to become attached to the results of the action. Neither hope of reward or fear of punishment is the motivator here, but simply the presence of a duty to be done. Scripture says that people have a right to their actions but not to the fruits of those actions. Attachment to the results of what we do binds us in the cycle of reincarnation. To whatever extent we can give up attachment to the results of our actions, we can lessen the grip of karma, according to Hindu belief. This path to liberation makes the ongoing flow of daily life the way to liberation.

For countless generations of Indian Hindus, for whom survival in the face of extreme poverty and climatic conditions is problematic, this allows for religious fulfillment without having to do something additional. For contemporary Hindus caught up in the realities of professional and business life combined with family and community responsibilities, it offers the same hope. Beyond that, it affords the opportunity to transform the dailyness of life into something sacred and meaningful.

For students, this would mean, for example, studying, attending class, and doing homework simply because they are students, rather than in order to get a good grade on the test and out of the class. For professors, it would mean carrying out the tasks expected of us without having an eye on the next promotion or professional recognition.

Other, less widely practiced, ways of liberation include intense study and contemplation of sacred writings, the physical disciplines of yoga, and the intensive practice of meditation.

Women in Hinduism

Hinduism's attitude toward women has always been highly ambivalent. On the one hand, the Great Goddess is worshiped and adored in all her manifestations. The major gods have their female consorts. Female energy is important in the attainment of liberation in certain approaches to meditation. In Vedic times, women were educated, participated in religious rituals, and were recognized as scholars, poets, and teachers.

On the other hand, the particular way in which the female and male principles are related in the sacred makes it clear that the "male principle is necessary if the female principle is to be fertile and good. Alone, the female principle tends to be evil and dangerous." Further, docility and service to one's husband are honored above all else. Arranged marriages often took place when a girl was very young, even before puberty. In the classical period, the "most concise index of women's place . . . is the traditional common belief that no woman of any caste could gain salvation, except in a future life, when she had been reborn as a man."[11] The practice of a widow's burning herself on her husband's funeral pyre (now outlawed in India) highlights the dreadful situation of a woman without a man.

Hindu women in the United States are primarily cosmopolitan and educated. They move in social circles that include professionals, administrators, and managers. Their lives are less determined by the Hindu tradition regarding women than by their position in American society. Temple leadership is usually limited to male priests, with women having a role to play as teachers of children. Typically, women are the ones who maintain the tradition of worship at a home altar for the benefit of their families.

Hindu Life and Worship

In many ways, we have already been discussing Hindu life. Distinctions between religion and the rest of life are alien to Hinduism, so that the pathways to liberation described above are also descriptions of the lifestyles of Hindu people. Here, I want to concentrate on the ethical dimension of Hinduism and then on Hindu worship.

The **moral life** is one that coincides with the natural order of the universe, the dharma. What it means to live by the dharma differs, depending on a person's place in the society, stage in life, and gender. There are also ethical prescriptions and proscriptions that are constant.

The contemporary Hindu catechism describes good conduct with five virtues:[12]

- *Noninjury* and gentleness in thought, emotions, and actions are described as "the first and foremost ethical principle of every Hindu." This is why most Hindus refrain from eating meat or eat it very sparingly. Noninjury is practiced because there is the divine in everything and also because harm done to another returns to oneself by the law of karma.
- *Purity* means refraining from anger, keeping one's body clean, and maintaining chastity until marriage and faithfulness in marriage.
- *Devotion* means devotion to the divine, to one's guru or religious teacher, and loyalty to family and friends.
- *Humility* is also encouraged. It is "mildness, modesty, reverence and unpretentiousness." It means taking things as they come, not getting impatient with either circumstances or people.
- *Charity* means being generous without thought of reward, giving what one can to help others, even if one can give but a little.

The catechism offers this summary portrait of good conduct:

We should be uplifting to our fellow man, not critical or injurious. We should be loving and kind, not hateful or mean. We should express the soul's beautiful qual-

[11]Denise Lardner Carmody, *Women and World Religions* (Nashville, TN: Abingdon Press, 1979), chap. 4.
[12]Subramuniyaswami, *Dancing with Siva*, pp. 181–203.

ities of self-control, modesty and honesty. We should be a good example to others and a joy to be around, not a person to be avoided. Good conduct is the sum of spiritual living and comes through keeping good company. . . . The Hindu fosters humility and shuns arrogance, seeks to assist, never to hinder, finds good in others and forgets their faults.[13]

Hinduism recognizes four clusters of goals of human life, all consistent with the living of an ethical life. These goals pull together diverse elements of life into a unified whole. Each is appropriate in its place, as long as we recognize that only the last one can provide ultimate satisfaction.

The *joy* cluster (sensual, sexual, artistic, aesthetic joys, compatible with ethics), the *economic and social fulfillment* cluster, the *morality* cluster (duties, obligations, right action, law, righteousness, general virtues and supreme ethical virtues . . .), and the *spiritual goal of salvation/liberation* (union and oneness with God).[14]

Hindu worship life revolves around the **home altar** that is an important part of most Hindus' homes. The altar will probably have a statue or statues of the chosen deity or deities. After ceremonial cleansing, people make offerings of fruit, incense, or flowers to their deities. They see the deity in the image and in return are seen by the deity. The food offered to the deity may then be eaten by the worshiper as a part of the deity's blessing. Some people perform this ritual, or **puja**, twice daily, while some perform it only in the mornings. While approximately 75 percent of Hindu women perform daily devotions for the benefit of their families, only about half of Hindu men do so. Puja is also performed in **temples**, where it is more elaborate.

Each god and goddess has a festival day, and these are celebrated with worship at the temple. Other **religious holidays** are celebrated as well. Often, weekly worship is also held, usually fitted into the common Sunday morning time period. This is a distinctive feature of Hinduism in America, a key aspect of its accommodation to the non-Hindu culture. It resembles worship at the home altar, with the addition of readings from sacred texts, a sermon or lecture, and devotional songs. Many temples in the United States have become social centers for the Indian community, as well, and sponsor a number of social events, in addition to holding classes for children and adults.

The priest associated with the temple—who may hold another job as well—also performs **life-cycle rites** such as birth rituals, weddings, and funerals for Hindu families. Hindus who do not live close enough to attend a temple regularly can request that puja or other services be performed at a distant temple in return for a financial contribution. While most temples in India are dedicated to one primary deity, those in the United States are often dedicated to several.

---

[13]Subramuniyaswami, *Dancing with Siva*, p. 181.
[14]Dr. T.K. Venkateswaran, "A Portrait of Hinduism," in Joel Beversluis, ed. *A SourceBook for the Community of Religions* (Chicago: The Council for a Parliament of the World's Religions, 1993), pp. 62–66.

Hindus may accommodate to United States religious culture in other ways, as well. Some Hindus celebrate the five-day festival of Pancha Ganapati on December 21–25. *Ganesha* is a deity who is revered as a remover of obstacles. Families may build a shrine to Ganesha in their homes and decorate it with pine boughs, ornaments, tinsel, and lights. Christmas trees, Santa Claus, and other religious and secular symbols are not supposed to be used. Gifts are placed before the shrine daily and worship is offered to Ganesha. After the final puja on December 25th, the gifts are opened with great festivity and celebration. Gifts are also given to employees and employers, as well as friends.[15]

Hindus in the United States

There has been much less detailed research done on Hindus in the United States than there has been on Muslims. The number of Hindus remains quite small—less than 0.5 percent of the population. Nearly all Hindus are either immigrants or descendants of immigrants from Hindu countries; fewer Westerners have become Hindus than have embraced either Islam or Buddhism. As you saw with Arab Americans, most Asian Americans are Christians. With a few exceptions, Hindus have not sought converts. Most live in urban areas. The largest concentrations are in the Los Angeles, San Francisco, New York City, and Chicago metropolitan areas. Many Hindus now living in the United States are professionals, intellectuals, and upper-level management personnel.

There are a number of Hindu groups in the United States, many of which are quite small. The three discussed represent different emphases in Hinduism. These organizations, along with others, represent both ways for non-Indians to become involved with Hinduism and ways for Indian and other immigrants to maintain community. A member of the Organization of Hindu Malayalees (OHM) describes what the organization means to him:

> OHM is like an extended family. It helps to alleviate problems—it helps in crisis management, stress management. There are many problems here—job related, domestic. Before OHM I had around four or five people to turn to, but now I have around twenty families that I can trust. I have several close friends and we call each other one or two times a week for personal conversation, quite apart from official OHM business. Just talking to others helps so much.[16]

The **Vedanta Society** was founded in 1894 by Swami Vivekananda. It was the first Hindu organization in the United States and is arguably the most influential on an intellectual level, although it is neither the largest nor the best known. Each Vedanta Center in the United States is a branch of the Ramakrishna Order, the monastic organization that Vivekananda founded in India.

---

[15]*Hinduism Today*, 14, no. 12 (December 1992), p. 16.

[16]Prema Kurien, "Becoming American by Becoming Hindu: Indian Americans Take Their Place at the Multicultural Table," in *Gatherings in Diaspora: Religious Communities and the New Immigration*, ed. R. Stephen Warner and Judith G. Wittner (Philadelphia: Temple University Press, 1998), p. 49.

Vedanta seeks to incorporate the methods and ideals of all Hindu movements. It describes itself as "a federation of faiths and a commonwealth of spiritual concepts." It supports all the pathways to liberation that were described above. Vedanta teaches four basic principles:

1. Truth is one, although known by many names. Likewise, God is One, although worshiped in many forms.
2. People in their essential nature are divine.
3. The goal of human life is to realize this divinity.
4. There are innumerable ways to realize this divinity.

The Vedanta Society of New York summarizes Vedanta this way:

Vedanta is a way of living and realizing. It gives full freedom to each individual to evolve morally and spiritually according to his or her own faith and conviction. It includes various truths found in all religions of the world, including the teachings of the worlds great saints and sages. In Vedanta is found a reconciliation of religion with science, of faith with reason. A Vedantin is a seeker of truth who accepts and respects all religions as paths to the same goal.[17]

Vedanta Centers offer weekly worship that is similar to that already described for Hindu temples. They usually offer classes in various aspects of Hinduism as well. The leader, or *swami*, who is invited by a local Board of Trustees to come from the Ramakrishna Order in India, also gives private instruction to students. The organization also operates Vedanta Press, a source for Hindu religious literature and other relevant books.

The primary embodiment of Hindu devotionalism in the United States is the daily and weekly worship that Hindus perform in their homes and in temples. The **International Society for Krishna Consciousness** (also known as **ISKCON** or the **Hare Krishna Movement**) is an organizational embodiment of Hindu devotionalism. It was founded in the United States by His Divine Grace A. C. Bhaktivedanta Swami Prabhupada (1896–1977) in 1965. The Krishna Consciousness movement emphasizes union with the divine attained through ecstatic devotion to Krishna. The Movement describes its mission as

to promote the well being of society by teaching the science of Krishna consciousness according to the *Bhagavad-Gita* and other ancient Vedic scriptures of India.[18]

Members follow five rules of conduct: (1) No meat, fish, or eggs may be eaten. (2) No intoxicating drinks or plants may be used, including tobacco, alcohol, coffee, and tea. (3) There must be no gambling. (4) Illicit sexual activity (defined as any sexual activity between people who are not married to each other

[17]"What Is Vedanta?" Vedanta Society of New York, n.d.
[18]"International Society for Krishna Consciousness Fact Sheet," (Alachua, FL: ISKCON Foundation, 1990).

or marital sex except for procreation) is also prohibited. Finally, (5) the name of Krishna is to be chanted daily in a prescribed ritual.

Devotees who choose to devote full time to the movement and live in the temples follow a rigid schedule of devotion and work. There are also opportunities for those who cannot or do not wish to enter this fully into the community. Devotees, whether living in the temple or not, give very high priority to *sankirtan*, daily chanting of the **mantra**. Mantra chanting has been a part of Hindu religious practice since its earliest times. *Mantras*—spiritual phrases—help to focus the mind and are believed to have power in and of themselves to align the devotee's consciousness with the deity. Temples are always open to visitors, who are welcomed into a world that may make them feel as if they have been magically transported to India itself (Figure 11-1).

Krishna devotees affirm::

1. By sincere spiritual practice, we can be free of anxicty and experience the bliss of pure consciousness in this lifetime.
2. We are our eternal souls, not our perishable bodies, and because Krishna is our common father, all are brothers and sisters.
3. Krishna is the Godhead, the energy that sustains the whole of the universe. He is the eternal, all-knowing, omnipresent, all-powerful, and all-attractive Personality of the Godhead.

Figure 11-1 Congregational members of the International Society for Krishna Consciousness live and work in the general community, practicing Krishna consciousness in their own homes and attending the temple on a regular basis. *(Photo courtesy of the International Society for Krishna Consciousness* Back to Godhead Magazine.)

4. The absolute truth can be found in the scriptures of all the world's great religions. The *Bhagavad-Gita* ("Song of the Lord Krishna") is regarded as the oldest revealed scripture and as the actual words of God.
5. Vedic knowledge must be learned from a true, unselfish spiritual master.
6. Food is to be prepared for and offered to Krishna before we eat. The acts of preparing and consuming food thus become worship.
7. All actions are to be performed as offerings to the Lord Krishna, with nothing being done merely for sense gratification.
8. The recommended means for attaining consciousness of and union with the godhead in this age is the chanting of the holy names of the Lord. The Hare Krishna mantra, a song of praise to the Lord Krishna, is the best way for most people to do this. It goes like this:

Hare Krishna, Hare Krishna (Praise to Krishna, Praise to Krishna)
Krishna Krishna, Hare Hare (Krishna, Krishna, Praise, Praise)
Hare Rama, Hare Rama (Praise to Rama, Praise to Rama)
Rama Rama, Hare Hare! (Rama, Rama, Praise, Praise).

The *a* in Rama is soft, as *ah*, and *hare* is pronounced *ha-ray*. *Rama* is one of Vishnu's incarnations, the hero of the epic poem the *Ramayana*. The Krishna Consciousness Movement teaches that this one mantra is the mantra for everyone in this present age, rather than following the more traditional practice that requires that mantras be given individually by gurus[19] and kept secret.

According to the founder, chanting the name of Krishna using this mantra conveys all the benefits of the other Hindu practices and much more rapidly: "Simply by chanting the holy name of God, one can attain that perfect self-realization which was attained by the yoga system. . . . by performance of great sacrifices . . . and by large-scale temple worship."[20]

There are about fifty ISKCON temples in the United States, as well as six farm communities and six vegetarian restaurants. The organization claims about 3000 fully initiated members and an additional 500,000 lay members who participate in temple activities at least monthly. The number of Indian participants has increased, and the number of non-Indian devotees has dropped considerably.[21]

Besides the temples, farm communities, and restaurants, the Society operates the Bhaktivedanta Book Trust for the publication of literature on Indian philosophy and religion. It also publishes *Back to Godhead: The Magazine of the Hare Krishna Movement*. Its "Food for Life" program distributes meals at no cost to those who need food. This program is an outgrowth of the custom of sponsoring a free meal every Sunday at the temples, which began in the very early days of the movement.

---

[19]*Guru* is an Indian word that means a religious teacher and mentor.
[20]A.C. Bhaktivendanta Swami Prabhupada, *Krsna Consciousness* (New York: The Macmillan Publishing Company, 1970), p. 12.
[21]J. Gordon Melton, *The Encyclopedic Handbook of Cults in America:* revised and updated edition (New York: Garland Publishing, 1992), pp. 237–238.

The rigorous monastic life and the sometimes aggressive solicitation of Krishna's American devotees have marked them off as distinctive and unusual. Their way of life is a small slice of India in a very non-Indian culture. There can be little doubt, however, about the sincerity and devotion of these followers of an Indian deity whose main attribute is his desire to help struggling human beings attain release from spiritual suffering.

There are many different Hindu groups in the United States that are based on some form of yoga. **The Self-Realization Fellowship** is typical of these. It was founded by a Bengali Indian, Paramahansa Yogananda, in 1925. Yogananda (1893–1952) taught in this country for more than thirty years.

Yogananda taught the classical form of yogic meditation outlined in the *Yoga Sutras* of Patanjali. His teaching and the practices that he developed are based on the traditional Hindu belief that the divine is within each person and can be experienced directly through meditation. Having experienced it in meditation, people can come to manifest it increasingly in everyday life. According to the Self-Realization Fellowship:

> The science of Yoga offers a direct means of stilling the natural turbulence of thoughts and restlessness of body which prevent us from knowing what we really are. By practicing the step-by-step methods of Yoga . . . we come to know our oneness with the Infinite Intelligence, Power, and Joy which gives life to all and which is the essence of our own Self. . . . [The] inner fulfillment we seek *does* exist and *can* be attained. In actuality, all the knowledge, creativity, love, joy, and peace we are looking for are right within us, the very essence of our beings. All we have to do is realize this.[22]

The Self-Realization Fellowship emphasizes that the techniques they teach and practice do not have to be accepted on authority or faith but can be tested in the life of each person. It is a scientific method for self-discovery and realization. Awareness and consciousness, energy, are withdrawn from outward concerns and redirected inward toward the goal of self-realization. There are eight temples and about 150 smaller centers in the United States, as well as a program of correspondence study. The centers offer classes, workshops, and weekly devotional experiences. Besides laypeople who participate in the centers' activities, there are renunciants who have chosen to pursue liberation more arduously and remain celibate, spending quite a lot of time in meditation and study.

Why American Converts?

With the exception of the Krishna Consciousness movement, Hinduism has rarely actively sought converts, and most of the members of many of the Hindu organizations in the United States are Indians or of Indian descent. There are,

---

[22] *Undreamed-of Possibilities: An Introduction to Self-Realization: The Teachings of Paramahansa Yogananda* (Los Angeles: Self-Realization Fellowship, 1982), pp. 5 and 3.

however, a small number of Americans who become "Hindus by choice." What attracts them? The answer to this question helps to reveal the complexity of how new religions come to fit into the predominant Judeo-Christian culture of the United States. Hinduism attracts American converts due to its similarities to what Americans already know *and* due to the genuine alternatives it presents.

First the similarities: Many forms of Hinduism emphasize the necessity of self-effort, a common theme throughout American culture. Many are compatible with science, and some, such as the Self-Realization Fellowship, emphasize this compatibility. Most teach that theirs is a method to be tried and tested in each individual's experience, not accepted "on faith." This practical empiricism also runs throughout the culture. Some, such as the Vedanta Societies, offer a somewhat "Protestant" style of worship, often on Sundays. Those that focus on devotion to a deity are similar in their approach to Christian devotion to Jesus; the Vedanta Society even encourages the worship of Jesus along with other deities.

On the other hand, they attract by their differences. Hindu tolerance and universalism offer an alternative for people for whom exclusivist claims have become problematic in a religiously plural world. Hinduism's very positive view of human nature, "we *are* the divine," can be a relief to those accustomed to talk about sin and depravity. Reincarnation and karma appeal to some more than either the Judeo-Christian concept of life after death or the secular alternative. Most Hindu groups offer practical *techniques* for spiritual transformation, an approach that has characteristically been lacking in Judaism and Christianity. Often these techniques facilitate the attainment of calmness and inner peace despite life's busyness and frustrations. Finally, many Hindu approaches to personal spiritual life emphasize a close relationship with one's guru or religious teacher, who becomes a guide on the path of self-realization.

BUDDHISM

As a young man, the Hindu prince **Siddhartha Gautama** became very distressed over the inevitable suffering of human life—aging, sickness, and death, among other things. Although born to a noble life, he renounced privilege and set out in search of a resolution to the spiritual unrest that plagued him. According to Buddhist tradition, he found what he sought during meditation, discovering the way to release from the burden of suffering (Figure 11-2). He then went about teaching what he had learned to other people and founded an organization based on his teachings. His followers called him "**the Buddha**," which means "**the awakened** (or **enlightened**) **one**."

Like Hinduism, Buddhism has a number of different sacred writings. The **Pali Canon** records what Buddhists take to be the teachings of the Buddha himself after his Enlightenment. Its importance is agreed upon by the great majority of Buddhists. Beyond that, various Buddhist subgroups accept other scriptures as valid.

Figure 11-2   Statues of the Buddha show him in serene meditation.

Basic Buddhist Teachings

The Buddhist worldview is different than that of Hinduism in some important respects, although there are similarities as well. As do Hindus, Buddhists affirm that the principles of **rebirth** and **karma** operate in every human life. Where Buddhists and Hindus differ is that Buddhists do not believe that there is a real self that reincarnates. Rather than seeing the universe as myriad manifestations of an eternal, unchanging spiritual reality, Buddhists see it as a vast, interconnected process. Buddhists also teach that **there is an intrinsic, moral order of the universe**, akin to the Hindu concept of dharma.

Interbeing and impermanence are central attributes of everything that is. **Interbeing** means that nothing exists in and of itself, without connections to other things. **Impermanence** points to the Buddhist belief that everything changes. Everything in the universe, including ourselves, is part of this vast, interconnected process. What underlies the universe as we observe it is not the sacred absolute of Hinduism, but constant change, constant becoming.

This leads to a **reinterpretation of rebirth**, because there is no real self that goes through the rebirth process. Buddhists simply say that each lifetime is connected to the ones before it and will be connected to those that come after it in a **chain of causation**. The analogy of lighting the wick of one candle from the flame on another is often used. Nothing is transmitted from candle to candle, but the flame of the second is unarguably connected to the flame of the first.

A basic statement of Buddhist belief, attributed to the Buddha himself, is the **Four Noble Truths**. It is an application of the foregoing interpretation of the world to human life and the human problem. We'll take the Truths one at a time. I follow a brief explanation of each with a quotation from *The Heart of the Buddha's Teaching*,[23] a contemporary interpretation of basic Buddhist teachings by Thich Nhat Hanh, a Vietnamese Buddhist monk whose work is widely appreciated in the United States.

1. All of life is marked by suffering. The Buddha was not, and Buddhists are not, long-faced pessimists without joy and happiness. Quite the contrary! What Gautama had in mind here is that, no matter how good life is, there is always an element of dissatisfaction, suffering, or basic "out-of-whackness" about it. Birth and death, he said, cause suffering on either end of the life cycle. In between, there is illness, having to deal with things we do not like and being separated from things that we do like. There is wanting more than we have or wanting something different than what we have. However, suffering is not necessary:

> But suffering is not a basic element of existence. It is a feeling. . . . The Buddha taught that when suffering is present, we have to identify it and take the necessary steps to transform it. He did not teach that suffering is always present.[24]

2. We can know the causes of our suffering. The traditional interpretation holds that all suffering comes from inappropriately holding onto things that inevitably slip from our grasp. However, we can also see that there are other causes:

> If we use our intelligence, we can see that craving can be a cause of pain, but other afflictions such as anger, ignorance, suspicion, arrogance, and wrong views can also cause pain and suffering. . . . If we practice identifying the causes of our suffering, we will see that sometimes it is due to craving and sometimes it is due to other factors. . . . We need to say, "The basis for this suffering is such and such an affliction," and then call it by its true name. . . . How else will we find the cause of our suffering and the way to heal ourselves?[25]

3. We can end our suffering. By eliminating the cause, the effect is eliminated.

> If you think that Buddhism says, "Everything is suffering and we cannot do anything about it," that is the opposite of the Buddha's message. The Buddha taught us how to recognize and acknowledge the presence of suffering, but he also taught the cessation of suffering. . . . The Third Truth is that healing is possible.[26]

[23]Thich Nhat Hanh, *The Heart of the Buddha's Teaching: Transforming Suffering into Peace, Joy, and Liberation* (Berkeley, CA: Parallax Press, 1998).
[24]Nhat Hanh, *The Heart of the Buddha's Teaching*, pp. 131–132.
[25]Nhat Hanh, *The Heart of the Buddha's Teaching*, pp. 21–22.
[26]Nhat Hanh, *The Heart of the Buddha's Teaching*, p. 11.

4.   The Buddha proposed a method for accomplishing this goal. Buddhists call it the **Noble Eightfold Path**.

> The Fourth Noble Truth is the path . . . that leads to refraining from doing the things that cause us to suffer. . . . The Chinese translate it as the "Path of Eight Right Practices."[27]

Because the Buddha became enlightened by his own efforts, traditional Buddhists teach that people are responsible for bringing about their own liberation from suffering. The first two steps on the path refer to **wisdom**: right understanding and right motivation. Right understanding means increasing our ability to see things as they really are, changing and impermanent. Right motivation means sincere desire to work on bringing about change, steady effort, and determination. The next several steps have to do with **morality**. Right speech means to speak truthfully and compassionately, without exaggeration, harshness, or rudeness of speech. Right action means observing the basics of Buddhist morality. Beyond that, it means acting with a balance of wisdom and compassion, always seeking the good. Right occupation means that one's occupation (which takes up a significant part of one's time) should not involve violating the moral precepts and should be such that it encourages peace and harmony, again striving for the good of all beings. Right effort means steady attention to weeding out negative and unhelpful ways of thinking and acting and replacing them with positive and helpful ways. The emphasis here is on constancy; the Path is a map for minute-by-minute existence, not for occasional use. The last two steps have to do with **meditation**. Right mindfulness means being aware in every moment. Right meditation deals directly with meditation techniques. Buddhists do not practice meditation as a way of going inward to find a real self (which, remember, does not exist, according to Buddhism). Different schools of thought teach different techniques. What unites them is that meditation is used as a way of being fully aware in every moment, then letting that moment go, as a way of calming and focusing the mind and bringing home the fleeting nature of everything.

Buddhists believe that there can be an end to the cycle of death and rebirth. This is the ultimate goal of the Eightfold Path. The Buddhist word for that goal is **Nirvana**. The Buddha did not speak very much about Nirvana, believing that doing so was not useful in the search for liberation. It certainly means living without dissatisfaction and thus with complete peace. It means the elimination of anything that separates the individual from the interconnectedness of all that is, the end of the illusion of isolated existence. When someone who has reached this advanced state of spiritual awareness dies, he or she escapes from rebirth.

Another summary of what is of central importance in Buddhism is the **Three Treasures** (also, **Three Refuges**, or **Three Jewels**). Although there is no

---

[27]Nhat Hanh, *The Heart of the Buddha's Teaching*, p. 11.

affirmation of faith that is required to become a Buddhist nor any set formula that makes a person a Buddhist, the Refuges help to define what being a Buddhist means. Usually, when someone becomes a Buddhist by choice, they formally take the Three Refuges and the Five Precepts in the setting of a Buddhist community or *Sangha*.

For Buddhists, "faith" is not faith in an unseen deity nor in something that cannot be known. It is not assent to propositions that cannot be demonstrated. It is an expression of what practitioners can know and verify through the effects of the practice in their own lives.

"**I take refuge in the Buddha**." *To take refuge in the Buddha* means to place one's trust and confidence in the Buddha having become the Enlightened One. For traditional Buddhists, especially, the Buddha is a human being, nothing more. Thus, the fact that he, through his own effort and determination, was able to achieve liberation means that *any* person can do so, provided they are willing to make the effort. The Buddha's humanity also means that the Buddha nature is to be found in all persons, as well as other beings. A contemporary American Buddhist nun describes the optimistic view of human nature that this entails:

> Each of us has within us the seeds of perfection, the natural and evolving Buddha potentials, and these seeds can be neither stolen or destroyed. There is no reason for us ever to feel hopeless and helpless. Because our Buddha potential is inseparably within us, there is always a basis for self-confidence and positive aspiration. . . .

> This is the beauty of our human life: we have the indestructible Buddha potentials which have been with us since beginningless time, and we have the perfect opportunity to realize and develop them in this lifetime.[28]

"**I take refuge in the Dharma**." Buddhists use the word *Dharma* to refer primarily to the Buddha's teaching. *To take refuge in the Dharma*, then, means to have confidence in the Buddha's teachings as a true analysis of reality and as the way to accomplish what he accomplished. "**I take refuge in the Sangha**." *Sangha* has two levels of meaning. Narrowly, it is the community of Buddhist monks. For traditional Buddhists, liberation is possible only after one has become a monk. Monks work for liberation full time, and they symbolize the goal of Buddhists. On a broader level, the *sangha* means the entire community of people, living and dead, who have walked the path to enlightenment mapped out by Gautama. Buddhists live in the certainty that they are not alone in their quest for enlightenment. Others have been this way before them.

Thich Nhat Hanh describes the act of taking refuge this way:

> When we take refuge in the Buddha, we express trust in our capacity to walk in the direction of beauty, truth, and deep understanding, based on our experience of the efficacy of the practice. When we take refuge in the Dharma, we enter the path

---

[28]Thubten Chodron, *Open Heart, Clear Mind* (Ithaca, NY: Snow Lion Publications, 1990), pp. 119 and 123.

of transformation, the path to end suffering. When we take refuge in the Sangha, we focus our energies on building a community that dwells in mindfulness, harmony, and peace.[29]

Lama Surya Das, an American whose primary affiliation is with the Tibetan Dzogchen lineage, translates the Three Refuges in a way that links the traditional understanding with the practitioner's vow to practice:

> I go for refuge in the Buddha, the enlightened teacher;
> I commit myself to enlightenment;
> I go for refuge in the Dharma, the spiritual teachings;
> I commit myself to the truth as it is;
> I go for refuge in the Sangha, the spiritual community;
> I commit myself to living the enlightened life.[30]

Buddhist Morality and Worship

Buddhist morality has already been mentioned as one of the steps on the Eightfold Path. One standard statement of Buddhist morality is the **Five Precepts**.

1.   Do not kill. Buddhists expand this precept to include not harming any living being, insofar as it is possible to avoid such harm. Positively, it means doing all that one can for the good of all beings on the earth. Nonviolence and noninjury are central in any Buddhist system of ethics.

> For a lot of people in our school [that is, the KwanUm Zen school] and for a lot of Buddhists that means being a vegetarian. For some Buddhists, that doesn't mean being a vegetarian. Vegetarianism is not a strict rule that must be followed. . . . It is like visiting our parents on Thanksgiving and being served turkey—the wisdom and love that allows a vegetarian offspring to eat turkey often makes a parent very happy.[31]

2.   Do not steal. Again, Buddhists understand this as going beyond outright stealing. It also means not taking advantage, not appropriating anything in any way that does not belong to you. Avoiding paying legitimate taxes is another example, as is borrowing and not returning an item. The larger sense of the second precept is that we should not take anything that is not freely given.

3.   Refrain from wrongful sexual behavior. Complete abstinence outside of marriage is the traditional rule. Buddhist monks and nuns are celibate. Sexual activity is regarded as appropriate only for committed couples. Wrongful sexual behavior includes any behavior that degrades another person, as well as sexual behavior that might spread disease.

---

[29]Nhat Hanh: *The Heart of the Buddha's Teaching*, p. 151.
[30]Lama Surya Das, *Awakening the Buddha Within: Eight Steps to Enlightenment: Tibetan Wisdom for the Western World* (New York: Broadway Books, 1997), p. 56.
[31]From the KwanUm Zen World Wide Web site (http://www.kwanumzen.com/).

If you're a monk, certain things are very clear. If you're married, certain things are very clear. But for anybody, what it means is a vow that you are not going to manipulate others because of your sexual desire, and you are not going to use anybody else's sexual desire as a tool to manipulate them, and you are not going to allow anybody else to use your sexual desire as a tool to manipulate you.[32]

4. Do not lie. Expanded, this includes refraining from saying anything that is hurtful, such as slander and gossip, rude and harsh speech, impolite language, running down other people, as well as idle chatter when silence would be better.

5.   Finally, Buddhists **avoid the use of intoxicants** of all kinds, such as alcohol and intoxicating drugs. Using them clouds a person's mind and also increases the likelihood that other ethical principles will be violated. Not all Buddhists take this as an absolute prohibition on an occasional drink, interpreting the precept as a ban on *intoxication* rather than on intoxicants.

> A number of senior people in our school have no problem with a glass of wine with dinner. Some abstain completely from alcohol. . . . [For] some people, a moderate amount of alcohol may provide a simple pleasure . . . without indulging in it to the point of giving up the power of decision. But that line is very thin, and it is easy to delude ourselves into thinking that we are keeping things in balance when we are pushing toward the edge of "heedlessness." So, we must always pay attention.[33]

Buddhism presses home the importance of cultivating proper attitudes and a proper frame of mind, so that outward actions flow freely from internal dispositions. Four attitudes are especially valued. Buddhists strive to cultivate *loving-kindness and friendliness, compassion and empathy, joy and rejoicing,* and *equanimity and peace of mind.*[34]

Like Hindus, Buddhists often have a small **altar or shrine in their homes**. A Buddha statue represents the historical Buddha and helps devotees focus on the Buddha nature within themselves, as well. Flowers symbolize enlightenment and a candle or altar light symbolizes the light of wisdom. Incense is often offered in gratitude for the Three Refuges and other blessings. An offering of water represents cleansing and a food offering represents giving and the willingness to share what one has with other beings.

Meditation is central to Buddhist practice and is a main focus of practice for most Buddhists in the United States. There are three aspects to meditation. The first is developing one-pointed concentration, the ability to truly do one thing at a time. To do this, people often practice by concentrating on their breathing. The second is the development of insight into the true nature of reality. This allows them to experience reality as it is, without getting caught up in conceptu-

---

[32]From the KwanUm Zen World Wide Web site (http://www.kwanumzen.com/).
[33]From the KwanUm Zen World Wide Web site (http://www.kwanumzen.com/).
[34]This particular translation of the "four noblest qualities of mind" comes from Das, *Awakening the Buddha Within*, p. 292.

alizations of it. The third is the extension of these attitudes into daily living as mindfulness in everyday life. Put simply, although it is far from simple to attain, this means being fully present to whatever one is doing in the present moment.

> This is meditation: To resume our true nature and discover an enormous sense of rest and peace, a spaciousness in our heart and in the midst of life; to allow ourselves to become transparent to the light that is always shining. . . . This is not a matter of changing anything but of not grasping anything, and of opening our eyes and our heart.[35]

Buddhists who live where they can go to a temple participate in activities that center around the natural rhythms of the lunar calendar. The holy days occur at the new moon, the full moon, and eight days after each, making them about a week apart. Attendance at the temple is not required, and some Buddhists participate much more than others. There is a religious new year festival in the spring, and the Buddha's birthday is widely celebrated. Temples also offer classes, special rituals for the passages of life, and serve as social centers.

Like Hindus and other non-Christians in the United States, Buddhists may accommodate to the major Christian religious holidays that are part of the culture. For example, Shasta Abbey in California (Zen Buddhist) celebrates December 24 as the Festival of the Eve of the Buddha's Enlightenment and December 25 as the Festival of the Buddha's Enlightenment.

Women and Buddhism

Traditional ideas about women and women's capabilities persisted in Buddhism even as in Hinduism. At the same time, Buddhism allowed for the establishment of orders of nuns. The rules established for female sanghas, however, guaranteed submission of nuns to monks and ensured that the number of nuns would remain small. That they existed and continue to exist, however, is significant. Although men controlled the writing and codification of sacred texts (as in all the world's religions), the question of the legitimacy of women's quest for nirvana and full participation in religion arises again and again.

One of the ways that Buddhism has changed as it has come West has been that greater gender equality in the West has forced the issue within the Buddhist community. American women have been and continue to be interested in Buddhism, and there is evidence that their increased participation, especially in leadership positions, is contributing distinctive accents to the practice of American Buddhism, while helping to ameliorate things that have been difficult for female practitioners of the Dharma in the West.

> Seduced by a fascination with orientalism or a taste for the exotic, or programmed by their female training and family background, some American women practic-

[35]Jack Kornfield, *A Path with Heart: A Guide Through the Perils and Promises of Spiritual Life* (New York: Bantam Books, 1993), p. 164.

ing Buddhist meditation have accepted situations inimical to their own good and insulting to their common sense and human dignity. But the honeymoon is over, and the actual dynamics of the marriage are becoming increasingly more apparent. We are Americans, with a heritage of egalitarianism and resistance to authority, as well as a history of women's effort to define ourselves and realize ourselves fully in religious as well as secular life. None of this is inconsistent with the essential teachings and practice of Buddhism.[36]

Specific changes that can be traced to the influence of women include

(1) minimizing power differences and bringing warmth to all relationships, (2) working with emotions and the body, (3) group activity that promotes sharing experiences and open communication; "effort" and "striving" are being replaced by "healing" and "openness," and (4) an activist orientation based on a vision that the essential fact about the universe is interrelatedness.[37]

The influence of women in American Buddhism leads to changes in Buddhist thought, as well. Buddhist theologian Rita Gross enumerates four changes that she foresees in Buddhist thought as a result of the increasing presence of trained and respected female leaders and thinkers in the United States:

- Greater emphasis on Buddhism as a path to freedom within the world rather than escape from the world: Rather than freedom from rebirth (world-denying), Buddhism offers freedom from suffering within worldly life. Impermanent, conditioned existence itself is not the problem; the problem is our attitude toward it.
- Deeper appreciation of the centrality of the sangha: The sangha is traditionally seen as less important than the Buddha or the Dharma. Rethinking Buddhism along lines suggested by feminism makes the community the "indispensable matrix of spiritual existence," essential for spiritual life and growth.
- Seeing everyday life and work as practice: The ordinary *is* the sacred, not necessarily sacred but made so by mindful awareness. The life of the householder cannot be thought less spiritual than that of a nun or monk.
- Rethinking the role and necessity of meditation as spiritual discipline: Meditation is necessary, but it cannot be regarded as the only valuable human activity, nor as the only valuable religious activity. Taken to extremes, it becomes world-devaluing.[38]

Asian Buddhists in the United States

Less than 0.5 percent of the population of the United States is Buddhist. Like Hindus, Buddhists are found primarily in major metropolitan areas. Buddhists have come to the United States from every Buddhist country in the world

[36]Sandy Boucher, ed., *Turning the Wheel*, pp. 21–22.

[37]Joseph B. Tamney, *American Society in the Buddhist Mirror* (New York: Garland Publishing, 1992), p. 95.

[38]Rita Gross, "Buddhism after Patriarchy?" in *After Patriarchy: Feminist Transformations of the World Religions,* ed. Paula M. Cooey, William R. Eakin, and Jay B. McDaniel (Maryknoll, NY: Orbis Books, 1991), pp. 65–86.

and have tended to remain clustered in national groups. Buddhists came from China as early as the 1800s to work in the mines during the Gold Rush. Japanese Buddhists arrived later, but their impact has been greater. Even later, Buddhists came from Vietnam, Cambodia, Thailand, and Laos. Buddhists also came here from Tibet when the Chinese Maoist regime attempted to destroy Buddhism there. I will discuss representative Buddhist groups in each immigrant community to convey the scope of Asian Buddhism in the United States.

Buddhists came to the United States in the wake of the Khmer Rouge regime's attack on Cambodian Buddhists in the 1970s. Buddhists also came here from Laos, Sri Lanka, Thailand, and Vietnam, especially following the Vietnam War. There are a greater number of Vietnamese Buddhists in the United States than from other Southeast Asian countries. They are spread more widely across the country, as well, due to efforts to resettle the large numbers of Vietnamese refugees. The majority of Vietnamese in the United States are Buddhists, although a significant minority are Christians.

The **International Buddhist Meditation Center** in Los Angeles, California, is the largest of the Vietnamese Buddhist organizations. The center blends various Buddhist schools of thought and practice. Buddhist leaders and teachers from a variety of backgrounds teach there and many groups use the facilities. Ordination for monks borrows from a number of traditions as well. Worship services feature chanting of the scriptures in several languages, including English. In 1991, the International Buddhist Meditation Center had about 300 members in the one center, which is staffed by four priests.

The largest **Japanese** Buddhist organization in the United States is the **Buddhist Churches of America**, which has about 100,000 members in the United States. It is considered to be a mission outpost of the Japanese church, which is the largest Japanese Buddhist group. There are about 130 temples or branches. As with all the Mahayana schools of thought, life as a Buddhist layperson is emphasized:

> The principal aim in following [these teachings] is to achieve harmony between life as a religious follower of the Buddha Dharma and life as a secular layperson. . . . [The] very essence of its tradition addresses the difficulties of practicing the Dharma in a secular world of human relationships.[39]

This form of Buddhism teaches that faith in **Amida Buddha**, the Buddha of Infinite Wisdom and Compassion, will bring liberation and rebirth in the Pure Land, a state close to complete enlightenment. Rebirth in the Pure Land means becoming a Bodhisattva, dedicated to returning to earthly existence to assist the liberation of all beings.

In its "church" type of organization and focus on the importance of regular participation in the activities of the church, BCA has adapted Buddhism to its

---

[39]"Buddhist Churches of America: Jodo Shinshu Hongwanji-ha" (San Francisco, CA: Buddhist Churches of America, 1990).

American context. Its teaching about the importance of reliance on Amida Buddha to bring about liberation reflects its Mahayana roots. Because this is similar to Protestant Christians' reliance on the power of faith in Jesus as the Christ, it has not appeared completely alien to American religious sensibilities and has provided an important vehicle for the acculturation of Japanese Buddhists. It has also attracted some American converts and offers an outreach membership program for those who live far from any BCA church.

Zen, probably the form of Buddhism best known in the United States, also came here from Japan. One of the largest Zen centers is in Los Angeles, California. It has branched out into centers throughout the United States. Zen followers concentrate on meditation, practicing daily meditation and participating in periodic retreats in which many hours daily can be devoted to *zazen*, Zen "sitting meditation." The awareness developed during meditation is also practiced in everyday life. ZCLA offers daily zazen for practitioners, classes, regular talks and discussions, weekend retreats, and longer retreats. It also offers *sesshin*, the opportunity for practitioners to discuss their practice with leading monks.

Shasta Abbey is the headquarters of the **Order of Buddhist Contemplatives**, a Zen organization that consciously adapts traditional Zen practice to Western culture. It was founded in 1970 by a British-born Buddhist nun, the reverend Jiyu Kennett-Roshi. Its main focus is training women and men for the Zen Buddhist priesthood in the United States. The daily order of the monastery is a good example of life in a Zen monastery in the United States (Figure 11-3). The schedule is intended to provide variety while keeping the participants' attention focused on spiritual pursuits and ensuring a minimum of distractions. Meals are vegetarian. Participants are expected to conduct themselves mindfully, aware of the spiritual purpose of their being there and the need to respect that same purpose in others.

The largest organizational representation of Chinese Buddhism in the United States is the **Dharma Realm Buddhist Association**, founded in 1959. Although based on Zen Buddhism, it teaches all five major schools of Chinese Buddhism. As well as attracting Chinese Americans, it has a following among American Buddhists as well. Its emphasis on monastic Buddhism with strict discipline makes it unique among Buddhist organizations in the United States. Its Dharma Realm Buddhist University was the first Buddhist university established in the West. The moral principles that students are expected to follow reflect Buddhist values and make it dissimilar to most other United States colleges and universities:

> The ethical dimension of the curriculum is concerned with the student as a whole person: a member of a family; of a university community; of a religious community; of an extended local, national, and world community; and of a professional community for which the student is in preparation.

> To help students realize the responsibilities of each role, the University encourages them to preserve the purity of their bodies and minds by observing only the highest

Figure 11-3

TYPICAL DAILY SCHEDULE OF THE MOUNT SHASTA ABBEY

5:55	Rising
6:15	Meditation
6:55	Morning Service
7:25	Temple Cleanup
8:40	Breakfast
9:15	Work
10:45	Meditation (three periods)
12:30	Spiritual Reading Period
1:10	Lunch
1:40	Rest
2:45	Work
3:45	Midday Service/Meditation
4:30	Class
6:05	Dinner
6:35	Rest
7:30	Meditation/Walking Meditation
8:10	Meditation/Evening Office
10:00	Lights Out

standards of moral conduct. They are encouraged to be mindful of their opportunity to become inspiring examples for society and the world at large. The qualities of humaneness, integrity, filial respect, and responsible citizenship are emphasized both formally and informally. In addition, students learn to honor the Six Principles of cooperation, generosity, not seeking for personal gratification, unselfishness, service, and honesty. Within the University community, faculty and students all abstain from drugs and drinking alcoholic beverages, social dancing, smoking, gambling, and promiscuity. Unmarried men and women students live and study separately. All food on campus is vegetarian.[40]

Tibetan Buddhists fleeing the Maoist regime's purge of Buddhism in Tibet brought **Vajrayana** Buddhism to the United States. **Vajradhatu**, headquartered in Boulder, Colorado, is the largest of several such organizations in the United States, with about 4000 members. It sponsors a full range of ritual and educational activities and serves as a focus for the Tibetan Buddhist community in the United States. It also sponsors the **Naropa Institute**, one of the better-known Buddhist educational facilities in the United States. Its **Shambhala Press** is one of the major publishers of Buddhist literature in the United States.

[40]Dharma Realm Buddhist University World Wide Web site (http://www.drba.org/drbu.htm).

Americans and Buddhism: The Dharma in the West

Non-Asians in the United States become Buddhists in far greater numbers than they become Hindus, and there may well be more non-Asian Buddhists than Asian Buddhists here now. Non-Asians who have become Buddhists are almost uniformly white, middle-class, well-educated people between twenty-five and forty-five years old.[41]

European Americans have been interested in Buddhism at different times for different reasons. Sociologist of religion Joseph Tamney divides the American interest in Buddhism into four clearly definable phases:

> First, during the years 1800–1880, roughly, there emerged a serious interest among intellectuals in Eastern religions. The Transcendentalists incorporated Eastern ideas into their religious world view. Soon after, Theosophy was invented; this new religion was more Asian than European. The second period, 1880–1950, was the time when Buddhist institutions catering to European-Americans were established in the United States. For the first time, a significant number of Americans became Buddhists. The third period was 1950–1975, i.e., the years during which Buddhist institutions grew rapidly and Buddhism entered popular culture. "Beat Zen" was invented. The final phase, 1975 to the present, has been a time when Buddhist ideas and practices have been coopted by various professional groups as well as by those in the New Age movement.[42]

In the process, Buddhism has changed as it has interacted with American culture. We have seen this (to a lesser extent) in Islam and Hinduism as well. Such change is inevitable when a religion comes from one culture and enters into the life of a very different culture.

A recent analysis by Lama Surya Das, an American trained in the Tibetan Buddhist tradition, points out that Buddhism has always adapted itself to different cultures without losing its essence. In part, this has happened through the evolution of Buddhist leadership in the United States. American Buddhism is increasingly led by teachers who have trained in America with American-born Dharma teachers. This has led to a series of changes in how Buddhism is practiced here.

- Americans typically look to Buddhism as a meditation practice with the goal of improving our quality of life. We " want personal transformation, direct religious experience, and we want to integrate wisdom, goodness, and compassion into our daily lives."
- Ours is a practice oriented to lay or householder practitioners much more than it is to nuns and monks.
- Gender equality remains an unrealized goal, but one that appears to be attainable.

---

[41]Charles S. Prebish, "Buddhism," *Encyclopedia of the American Religious Experience: Studies of Traditions and Movements*, ed. Charles H. Lippy and Peter W. Williams (New York: Charles Scribner's Sons, 1988), p. 676.

[42]Tamney, *American Society in the Buddhist Mirror*, p. xviii.

- It is less institutional and hierarchical, and more democratic and personal, than its Asian predecessors.
- It tends to eliminate or minimize "complex, esoteric rites and arcane rituals designed for initiates only."
- It is ecumenical, with much less emphasis on specific schools of thought and practice and a willingness to combine old forms in new ways even as it invents new forms.
- American Buddhism is a "psychologically astute" Buddhism that focuses on individual spiritual growth and well-being.
- It encourages questioning and exploration. It is a Buddhist practice intent on "being . . . inquiring, skeptical, rational, and devoted to testing and finding out for ourselves." In this connection, Lama Surya Das quotes the Buddha as having said:

Do not believe in anything simply because you have heard it.
Do not believe in traditions because they have been handed down for many generations.
Do not believe in anything because it is spoken and rumored by many.
Do not believe in anything simply because it is found written in your religious books.
Do not believe in anything merely on the authority of your teachers and elders.
But after observation and analysis, when you find that anything agrees with reason, and is conducive to the good and benefit of one and all, then accept it and live up to it.

- The Sangha, in the largest sense of a "community of spiritual friends," is important. Participation in it is of the essence of the holy life.
- Contemporary American Buddhism is a "Lobby for Wisdom and Compassion," as it develops a strong social and ecological consciousness.[43]

QUESTIONS AND ACTIVITIES FOR REVIEW, DISCUSSION, AND WRITING

1. If you are fortunate enough to live or attend school close to a Hindu or Buddhist temple, arrange to visit, and write an essay on what you observe and your response to it.
2. Especially if attending a temple is not possible, try to arrange for a Hindu or Buddhist student who attends your college or university to come and speak to your class.
3. If your library subscribes to any periodicals published by United States Hindus or Buddhists, read through two or three issues, and write about what impression you form of the religion.
4. Yoga as a form of physical exercise and relaxation is taught in many physical education departments. If your school has such a class, invite the instructor to demonstrate some of the basic postures with class participation.
5. Discuss with a group of your classmates the ways in which the Four Noble Truths might apply in (1) your own lives and (2) American culture in general.

---

[43]Das, *Awakening the Buddha Within*, pp. 376–387.

6. What are some practical, concrete applications of the Hindu and Buddhist ideal of noninjury or nonviolence in our own culture? How could you as an individual put this ideal into practice?

7. How do you think you would respond to the daily routine of the Shasta Abbey?

8. How would your life as a college student be different than it now is if you attended Dharma Realm Buddhist University?

9. Visit the Web site of either the Association of American Buddhists or the American Buddhist Congress (or both). In what ways do they reflect a specifically American interpretation of Buddhism?

FOR FURTHER READING

CARMODY, DENISE LARDNER, *Religious Woman: Contemporary Reflections on Eastern Texts*. New York: Crossroad, 1991. Carmody's is a feminist analysis of Islamic, Hindu, and Buddhist sacred texts, as well as sacred writings from Japanese and Chinese sources dealing with women.

DAS, LAMA SURYA, *Awakening the Buddha Within: Eight Steps to Enlightenment: Tibetan Wisdom for the Western World*. New York: Broadway Books, 1997. This is an easily accessible work based on the Path of Eight Right Practices. Although Lama Das trained in the Tibetan tradition, his approach is not exclusively Tibetan. I recommend this book.

ELLWOOD, ROBERT S., and HARRY B. PARTIN, *Religious and Spiritual Groups in Modern America*, 2nd ed. Englewood Cliffs, NJ: Prentice Hall, 1988. There are good sections on Hinduism, Buddhism, and other Indian religions. Additionally, a vast multitude of other religious alternatives are described. This book is highly recommended.

HANH, THICH NHAT, *The Heart of the Buddha's Teaching: Transforming Suffering into Peace, Joy, and Liberation*. Berkeley, CA: Parallax Press, 1998. A presentation of very basic Buddhism, this book covers all the major Buddhist teachings and practices in a way that reflects Thich Nhat Hanh's gentleness of spirit.

JACKSON, CARL T., *Vedanta for the West: The Ramakrishna Movement in the United States*. Bloomington, IN: Indiana University Press, 1994. Valuable as a study of the Vedanta Movement itself, Jackson's book also focuses on the transformations undergone by Eastern religions when they come West.

SHINN, LARRY D., *The Dark Lord: Cult Images and the Hare Krishnas in America*. Philadelphia: Westminster Press, 1987. Shinn provides good descriptions of the lives and values of Krishna Consciousness members, contrasted with common perception of them.

TAMNEY, JOSEPH B., *American Society in the Buddhist Mirror*. New York: Garland Publishing, 1992. Tamney's thesis, which he ably supports, is that Americans have been interested in Buddhism at various times for various reasons, as Buddhism helped to compensate for characteristics of American culture. The author's method provides a good example of the benefits of studying religion in relationship to the larger culture.

YOUNG, WILLIAM A., *The World's Religions: Worldviews and Contemporary Issues*. Englewood Cliffs, NJ: Prentice Hall, 1995. This is an excellent introduction to the world's religions, written from a perspective that is compatible with that taken in this book. It covers all the basics and includes a section on each religion's response to contemporary ethical issues.

RELEVANT WORLD WIDE WEB SITES

Hinduism Today (journal) (http://www.hinduismtoday.kauai.hi.us).

Global Electronic Hindu Network (http://www.hindunet.org/).

Self-Realization Fellowship (http://www.yogananda-srf.org/).

International Society for Krishna Consciousness (http://www.harekrishna.com/).

Back to Godhead Online Magazine (http://www.krsna.com/).

Hindu Organizations (links) (http://www.hindu.org/).

Hindu Temple of Greater Chicago (http://www.ramatemple.org/).

Shasta Abbey/Order of Buddhist Contemplatives (http://www. obcon.org/).

Zen Mountain Monastery (http://www.zen-mtn.org/).

Zen Center of Los Angeles (http://www.zencenter.com/).

Dharma Realm Buddhist Association (Chinese) (http://www.drba.org/).

Dharma Realm Buddhist University (http://www.drba.org/drbu.htm).

Dzogchen Foundation (Tibetan) (http://www.dzogchen.org/).

Insight Meditation Society (Theravada) (http://world.std.com/~metta/index.html).

Naropa Institute (http://www.naropa.edu/).

The Association of American Buddhists (http://www.americanbuddhist.com/).

The American Buddhist Congress (http://www.wgn.net/abc.html).

Shambhala Sun (Journal) (http://www.shambhalasun.com/).

Tricycle: The Buddhist Review (http://www.tricycle.com/).

CyberSangha: The Buddhist Alternative Journal (http://www.hooked.net/~csangha/).

12

Other Religious
and Spiritual Movements

What is needed in today's world is to unleash the spirit's work of New Creation, of new possibilities for letting go and birthing, for being transformed and for transforming. In a culture that has lost its sense of Eros and celebration, the true prophets will come celebrating. Celebrating, sensuality and earthiness, passion and compassion, failures and imperfections, space, time, being, foolishness, our capacity to laugh, let go, and be young again. Play itself becomes a salvific act.[1]

For the first time in history there is a viable movement—the New Age Movement—that truly meets all the scriptural requirements for the Antichrist and the political movement that will bring him on the world scene. . . . The Antichrist's appearance could be a very real event in our immediate future.[2]

This chapter draws together several diverse movements that are significant in the United States at the beginning of the new millennium. They include the New Age Movement, the self-help movement and twelve-step programs, feminist spiritualities, the Fellowship of Metropolitan Community Churches, and cyber-religion. In one way or another, all link religion and other important features of United States culture at this time in history.

- All five share the American emphasis on individualism rather than large organization.
- All five also share the American passion for "what works" in identifiable, empirical terms.
- The New Age Movement and feminist spirituality pick up on the concern for the environment beginning to be felt through the culture.

[1]Matthew Fox, *Original Blessing: A Primer in Creation Spirituality* (Santa Fe, NM: Bear and Co., 1996), p. 300.
[2]Constance E. Cumby, *The Hidden Dangers of the Rainbow* (Shreveport, LA: Huntington House, 1983), p. 7.

- Feminist spirituality echoes women's work for full equality in the culture, and the Fellowship of Metropolitan Community Churches has grown out of homosexual persons' search for an authentic expression of Christianity in which they are regarded as equals.
- The abundance of twelve-step programs recognizes the extent to which many people in the culture are psychologically wounded in some way.
- Cyber-religion is located at the inevitable interface of religion with the growth in importance of the Internet, as well as being a dramatically individualistic form of religion.

THE NEW AGE MOVEMENT

The **New Age movement** is difficult to pin down, because it is not a specific group but a very loose network (a favorite New Age word) of groups, organizations, and individuals with a common set of concerns. At the same time, the new age movement is probably one of the two most popularly recognized movements; the other is the twelve-step movement. There are authors, psychologists, teachers, leaders, body workers, and the like who are well known to most New Agers. There is, however, no single authority. There are well-known and widely accepted books but no single authoritative text. There are several common beliefs and practices yet no absolutely definitive belief or practice. One author asks, "What is the New Age, anyway?"

> Is it a religious cult? No, although much of what the cults teach can be seen in new age doctrines. Is it a business? No, although thousands of entrepreneurs make money selling new age products. Is it a political movement? No, although it has an international political platform dedicated to world peace and ecological balance. Is it a social movement? No, although this comes closer to identifying it. It is too loose a conglomeration of separate groups to be considered a movement in any unified social sense. Perhaps it is best thought of as a phenomenon of cultural consciousness. It consists of a set of cosmological ideas and spiritual practices that nobody owns but that are widely shared by diverse groups and individuals.[3]

Joan Duncan Oliver, the editor of *New Age Journal,* recently described the New Age movement in the following words:

> The culture is changing. . . . Nearly one in four Americans—44 million of us—espouses a new set of values. Paramount among our concerns are health for ourselves and the environment, respect for the feminine perspective, serious spiritual searching, and a broad, multicultural—and ecumenical—view. . . . You want to take charge of your own healing and not leave it to your doctor or insurance company. You want to live amicably with others—and lightly on the earth. You want to slow down and savor life instead of running frantically to keep up. You want to

---

[3]Ted Peters, *The Cosmic Self: A Penetrating Look at Today's New Age Movements* (San Francisco: HarperSanFrancisco, 1991), p. 4.

rediscover the creative and spiritual urges you set aside while juggling jobs and family and pursuing the good life. You want to pass along the wisdom that you've gained.[4]

The near-total lack of organization and the flexibility of definition make it difficult to estimate the number of people involved in the New Age movement. There is also a problem about who, exactly, to count. Are only members of organizations identified with the New Age to be included? Or should we include anyone who likes to listen to New Age music? These two estimates would result in wildly different numbers. One recent survey indicates that adherents of the New Age movement add up to under 30,000.[5] It has been called the "most popular and widely publicized new religion in recent years."[6]

Its origin in the United States is often traced to the 1960s. Similar ideas, however, have been present throughout American history. The 1960s were a time of discontent with many of the values of the West, especially its spiritual values. At the same time, there was an increased interest in the religious and spiritual values of the East. Courses in world religions and Eastern religions became popular on college campuses. An influx of immigrants from the East brought many Americans into direct contact with ancient Eastern spiritual disciplines and teachings. At the same time, interest grew in the "alternative tradition" of metaphysical, occult knowledge, and practices that has been a part of the history of the West itself.

The key theme that unites New Age followers is one that links them with much of what has gone before in religion in the United States: "The New Age Movement," writes one observer, "can be defined by its primal experience of transformation. New Agers have either experienced or are diligently seeking a profound personal transformation from an old, unacceptable life to a new, exciting future."[7] Although in many ways very different, this same spirit animated the Puritans, those moved by the great revivals of the late 1700s and 1800s, and those who today experience being born again. It also informs the extensive secular self-help movement.

Beliefs

The teachings and practices of the New Age movement are diverse. There are, however, several major themes that stand out because they recur frequently in New Age literature. We can begin with the major beliefs and attitudes that characterize New Age thinking.

[4]"Body and Soul: New Age Journal's Annual Guide to Holistic Living—1998," *New Age Journal*, Vol. XVI, Issue 7 (Winter 1997), p. 4.

[5]*The New York Times National*, April 10, 1991, p. 1.

[6]Ruth A. Tucker, *Alternative Religions and the New Age Movement* (Grand Rapids, MI: Zondervan Publishing House, 1989), p. 319.

[7]J. Gordon Melton, Jerome Clark, and Aidan A. Kelly, *New Age Encyclopedia* (Detroit, MI: Gale Research, Inc., 1990), p. xiii.

One emphasis is the *need to overcome the dualism that has characterized much of Western thought*. Many of these dualistic ways of thinking have become part of how we view the world and ourselves: sacred or divine/profane or ordinary, religion/science, spirit/matter, mind/body, male/female, thinking/feeling. Virtually without exception, New Age thinkers believe that dualism must be replaced with a *holistic vision* of the world and ourselves that overcomes dualism while including legitimate differences.

An important corollary of this view is the belief in the *immanence of the divine within all things*. Western culture has traditionally taken its cues from a three-level view. At the highest level is a God who stands outside the created world and is very different from and vastly superior to it. In the middle are people, created by this God and thus most emphatically not God, yet at the same time thought to be higher than the rest of creation. The nonhuman world makes up the third level, different from and lower than both God and human beings.

In contrast to this understanding, New Agers believe that there is a single life force that is inherent in all living things. The New Age philosophy is *monistic*.[8] The same universal energy animates everything that is. This energy is usually thought of as psychic or mental in nature rather than physical.

Another important corollary of this view is that *all things are intimately interrelated*. The entire universe is a seamless web of life. Nothing happens in isolation, and anything that happens has an impact on the whole.

This leads directly to a great *concern for planet earth and an interest in ecology*. Because all things are interrelated, the fate of all hinges upon the fate of each. Everyone is responsible for the preservation of the earth's resources and species. "Think globally, act locally" is an often-repeated phrase.

The present time is a time of dramatic, far-reaching change. Some see this change coming in abrupt, cataclysmic fashion. Others see it more in terms of gradual yet sweeping change. Either way, the accent is on the present time as the beginning point for change at every level of being, from the individual through the entire universe.

The transformation of self will lead to a transformation of the culture and the planet. Almost without exception, New Agers believe that the changes that are coming about begin with individual transformation and radiate outward. Individuals have a responsibility to work to transform themselves in order to bring about planetary transformation. No one is exempt from this responsibility, and everyone can do something about the fate of the whole by working on themselves. Most of those who identify themselves as a part of the New Age share a nearly boundless optimism about the possibilities for both personal and communal transformation.

However, self-transformation is but one aspect of what the New Age calls upon individuals to do. *Compassionate service to individual people, to one's com-*

---

[8]*Monism* is a philosophical and religious view that holds that underneath the apparent diversity of life, there is but one reality. It is found in Hinduism as well as in New Age thinking.

munity, and on wider levels is a prominent theme, although one that receives relatively little attention from outside the movement. Through such service, people can have a dramatic impact on universal transformation.

The *underlying unity of all religions* is also a central belief. Although religion takes many forms in different cultures, beneath the differences is a universal religion that will eventually be recognized by all people. This universal religion is grounded in the cycle of the changing seasons and the cycle of human lifetime. It understands life as a continual process of transformation through which people grow into greater consciousness. Inner exploration, psychic development, and self-awareness are valued highly.

This is but one dimension of the belief that the *development of a planetary culture is both possible and desirable.* This worldwide (and some would say universe-wide) culture will not replace the distinctive cultures that now exist. It will complement them, both enhancing them and being enriched by them. Legitimate differences will remain. New Age believers look forward to a time when there will be one world government and a world language that is spoken and understood by all, facilitating communication and greater understanding among nations. Some favor the development of a worldwide monetary system to facilitate trade and a world court system as well.

This very large worldwide or planetary goal is echoed in the *development of the communal lifestyles* that have attracted some, bringing into being, in a small and local way, the type of organization that is foreseen on a much wider scale. Such communities are believed to provide the best context for personal transformation, for working toward greater transformation, and for demonstrating that these ideas can work.

Cooperation is more important than competition and much more to be desired. This relates back to the belief in the interconnectedness of everything. If everything is indeed interconnected, competition is simply the various parts working against the whole. Cooperation benefits the whole by eliminating conflicting actions of the parts.

Most followers of the New Age believe in some form of the Eastern teachings of *karma* and *reincarnation.* They often emphasize the karmic effects of actions in the present lifetime. Another way in which the New Age belief in reincarnation differs from most classical Indian teaching on the subject is that New Agers often believe that people can become aware of past lives through meditation, hypnosis, or past-life regression therapy. Doing so is held to be an important way of resolving present problems.

Rituals and Lifestyle

Several key practices are shared by many within the New Age movement. *Being on a spiritual path is important to most New Age believers.* For some, this means choosing a path and staying with it for a lifetime. For others, it means sampling a variety of spiritual disciplines. The path may be taken from Hindu or Buddhist practice. For some Americans, the importance of finding a compatible spiritual path has led to the study and practice of Native American (Indian) spirituality. Many in the New Age movement create their own spirituality by combining elements from several sources. Whatever path or paths are chosen, the goals are awareness of the life force and self-development. The goal of union with the mysterious reality that is both within and beyond can be attained more quickly if an intentional path is taken, rather than leaving it to chance.

The most important religious act is getting in touch with this life force through *ritual* and *meditation*. New Age believers seek communion with sacred reality. They believe that it is both within themselves and within the depths of all that is. Aligning oneself with the flow of the universe is both the goal and the means to the goal. Such alignment is said to produce physical and psychic healing, can bring about parapsychological experiences, and leads to strong feelings of well being and peace of mind.

People meditate for many reasons and by many specific means. Meditators seek to quiet and focus their minds. Doing so is said to bring a sense of peace and focus to all of life, a kind of heightened awareness and perspective that extends beyond the time spent in meditation, so that it infuses all activities and relationships. Many people believe that it also has significant health benefits. It is a primary way of being in touch with the sacred. It is a way to reenergize and replenish the energy spent in transformation.

There are nearly as many ways to meditate as there are people who meditate. Many people focus on their breathing, counting to a specific number and then starting over, being aware of how their breathing feels. This helps them stay focused on the present. Some may focus on other objects such as a statue of a deity, a candle flame, or a flower. Some use music for a focus. In mantra meditation, a word or phrase is used. By focusing on one thing with complete concentration, distractions are kept to a minimum.

Rituals of many kinds are also important elements of New Age practice. Meditation is itself a ritual. Rituals may be done to celebrate the changing seasons and the phases of the moon. The New Age movement offers the opportunity for people to construct their own rituals to mark events and occasions for which the larger culture does not have rituals or to develop creative, more personalized rituals to be used instead of more common ones. Many individuals develop private rituals for themselves. *Affirmations* seek to replace negative thoughts with positive ones. *Visualization* encourages people to "see" mentally and spiritually the goals they seek, believing that such seeing helps to bring them into being.

Holistic health and alternative healing are important dimensions of life for many people involved in the New Age movement. The underlying philosophical and religious assumptions of the movement lead people both to question standard medicine and to seek out alternatives to it. Chiropractic, herbal medicine, traditional systems of healing such as those of China and India, and nutritional approaches to healing are all part of the New Age healing repertoire. So are many kinds of body work and massage, done to benefit body, mind, and spirit. Aromatherapy makes use of the effects attributed to specific scents, and color therapy does the same with color. Healing through the use of crystals is popular with some. As with nearly everything in the New Age movement, there is a wide-ranging pragmatism in its approach to healing— "Try it, and see if it works." Different things work for different people and in different situations. Nontraditional health-care practitioners treat many New Age followers who are disillusioned by standard Western medicine and want therapies that attend to the entire person, not just the disease, and are usually less invasive.

Many advocates of the New Age try to follow what they describe as a *simple, natural* lifestyle. This means different things to different people but often includes a preference for clothing made from natural fibers such as cotton and wool over synthetics, natural cosmetics and household products, organic food and growing food at home, and limits on participation in America's consumer-based culture.

These themes are not new; most, if not all, of them can be found in various earlier groups and movements in the United States. But the New Age movement as it exists in the United States (as well as elsewhere) in the 1990s does have two characteristics that distinguish it from its predecessors and give it a distinctively "modern" flair: First, the basic ideas and themes of the New Age are being applied to distinctly contemporary issues, including world peace, nuclear war, ecological concerns, AIDS, hunger, and homelessness. Second, the very important concept of the immanence of the sacred has been cut loose from its moorings in Eastern religious thought so that it can be espoused by those whose basic religious orientation is in the Judeo-Christian-Islamic tradition.[9]

Organization

There is vast diversity within the New Age movement. Beliefs and, especially, practices range from the serious and thoughtful to the frivolous and mercenary. Prominent New Age author David Spangler helps us distinguish the serious from the less serious. Merchants have discovered that New Age sells and do not hesitate to take advantage of that fact. Most of the publicity surrounding the New Age movement has focused on many highly publicized teachers and adepts, a renewed interest in angels, channelers, popular self-help books and tapes, and occurrences such as the harmonic convergence of the late 1980s. The requirement for inclusion at this level seems to be that some glitzy aspect of the movement catches public interest.

Other followers of the New Age movement are genuinely committed to dramatic change in themselves and in their culture. Economics, politics, social institutions, education, and technology are all involved and are all changed to support planetary goals. People with this perspective speak about becoming able to see everything that is as holy, a reintegration of the human with the sacred and with the earth conceived as a living being. In Spangler's words, it is "a deepening

[9]Mary Ferrell Bednarowski, *New Religions and the Theological Imagination in America* (Bloomington, IN: Indiana University Press, 1989), pp. 17–18.

into the sacramental nature of everyday life, an awakening of the consciousness that can celebrate divinity within the ordinary and, in this celebration, bring to life a sacred civilization."[10]

A group of *journals and magazines* makes new information available and facilitates communication among New Age believers. Titles include *East/West Journal, Yoga Journal, Common Boundary,* and *New Age Journal.*

New Age followers are a diverse group of people for whom an authentic spiritual search has led generally eastward and inward. Their affiliation with the movement varies from being at its center to barely touching its edges. They are among those whose religious needs have not been met in the more usual religions. New Age believers do not meet in church buildings or have an organized hierarchy of leadership. It is a religion, however, in that it provides for its followers the four elements of belief, lifestyle, ritual, and organizations in a way that helps to make life meaningful and good.

How can we summarize such a diverse movement and perhaps locate it within the larger sweep of American culture? A review of several New Age books does so this way:

> It is not all that clear . . . what role the New Age movement plays in American culture. It functions in many ways. It can certainly be seen as another blossoming of the persistent metaphysical tradition in America. It is an arena in which people in a secular culture can ask and answer theological questions in nondoctrinal terms and outside the parameters of established religious institutions. It generates alternative perspectives on a variety of social issues, pollution and nuclear warfare among the most central. It provides insights into some of the effects of religious pluralism in American culture—in part, perhaps, the coming to fruition of popular knowledge about non-Western religious traditions. It offers a forum in which both experts and amateurs speculate about the relationships among religion, the physical sciences, and the social sciences. And it demonstrates the vitality of grassroots religion and what might even be called "grass-roots science" in American culture.[11]

When it is described in this way, we can see that the New Age movement is not something alien to its American context. It integrates themes and basic ways of approaching religion that have been a part of the culture almost from the beginning.

THE SELF-HELP MOVEMENT AND TWELVE-STEP PROGRAMS

Twelve-step programs such as Alcoholics Anonymous are only part of a larger movement that we can call the self-help movement. However, the founding of *Alcoholics Anonymous* marked the beginning of a new era in self-help movements

---

[10]David Spangler, *Emergence: The Rebirth of the Sacred* (New York: Dell Publishing Company, 1984).
[11]Mary Ferrell Bednarowski, "Literature of the New Age: A Review of Representative Sources," in *Religious Studies Review*, 17, no. 3 (July 1991), p. 216.

as well. Its twelve steps to recovery provide the blueprint for many such programs today.

A.A., as it is most commonly known, began in Akron, Ohio, in 1935. It was founded by a layman, William G. Wilson, and a doctor, Robert Smith (usually referred to as "Bill W." and "Dr. Bob," because anonymity is a cornerstone of group procedure). These two men, along with a third individual, began talking together about how to overcome their struggles with alcohol, and the organization was born out of their experience together.

Much of the basic philosophy of A.A. initially came from the Oxford Groups or Moral Re-Armament Movement, a fairly conservative Christian movement that had begun in England in the early 1920s. Stated briefly, the movement held that

> God could become real to anyone who was willing to believe. . . . Estrangement from God is . . . caused by moral compromise. People needed to examine their lives against the standards of absolute purity, unselfishness, and love. . . . [The movement] emphasized the need for sharing and guidance. Sharing consists of confession of one's sins and failures to another member of the group.[12]

At first, the members of "The Way Out" (as the group for recovering alcoholics was first named), remained part of Moral Re-Armament. However, the rather evangelical Christian bent of that group became a problem as interest in their approach to alcoholism spread to include people of other faiths and no faith at all. The group revised its approach so that a very clear spiritual element remained, without its being linked to any particular religion. In its essence, A.A. and its offshoots offer people

> . . . a nondenominational, nonpolitical approach to spirituality as the foundation for developing a positive self-image and arresting the illness that was manifesting itself in compulsive behaviors. These Twelve-Step Programs . . . [offer] the individual the opportunity to develop his or her own conception of a Higher Power, to build personal relationships, and to make a guided self-assessment so that major life changes could be made.[13]

The approach that A.A. takes to recovery from alcoholism is that alcoholism is a disease that has physical, mental, and spiritual dimensions. It can be best treated through its spiritual dimension. When alcoholics work on their spiritual lives, physical and mental recovery will follow as well. This is best done, say A.A. members, in the context of supportive groups of fellow sufferers. The strategy is summarized in the famous Twelve Steps.[14]

[12]J. Gordon Melton, *The Encyclopedia of American Religions*, 3rd ed. (Detroit: Gale Research, Inc., 1989), p. 964.

[13]Sandra Sizer Frankiel, "California and the Southwest," in *Encyclopedia of the American Religious Experience: Studies of Traditions and Movements*, ed. Charles H. Lippy and Peter W. Williams (New York: Charles Scribner's Sons, 1988), p. 1520.

[14]The Twelve Steps are listed in nearly every Alcoholics' Anonymous publication. The steps are in italic type. I have added comments to some of them.

1. *We admitted that we were powerless over alcohol, that our lives had become unmanageable.*
2. *We came to believe that a power greater than ourselves could restore us to sanity.*
3. *We made a decision to turn our will and lives over to the care of God as we understood him.*

A.A. regards the admission of one's inability to deal with the problem on one's own as the necessary starting point. It echoes the Christian belief in people's powerlessness apart from God. "As we understood him" is central to the spiritual view of A.A. People do not have to accept a particular belief in God or a Higher Power but are left free to conceptualize their Higher Power as they will. For some, however, this remains a stumbling block, and there have been a few groups formed that follow a similar approach to that of A.A. but without the overtly religious overtones. The largest of these self-consciously secular sobriety groups is S.O.S., or Secular Organizations for Sobriety (also, Save Our Selves).

Women and black people, especially, have questioned this emphasis on reliance on a Higher Power, feeling that it can reinforce their sense of oppression and powerlessness, which is often part of the problem. They have also asked if it simply substitutes one kind of dependency—albeit perhaps a less destructive one—for another.

4. *We made a searching and fearless moral inventory of ourselves.*
5. *We admitted to God, to ourselves, and to another human being the exact nature of our wrongs.* These two steps clearly reflect the movement's roots in Moral Re-Armament. They also reinforce the distinctive spiritual or religious nature of A.A.'s technique. Self-examination and confession to God and to another person are important dimensions in many religious groups.
6. *We became entirely willing to have God remove our defects of character.*
7. *We humbly asked him to remove our shortcomings.* Willingness to be helped is understood to be a necessary precondition of being helped. Again, this belief is a feature of many religions, as well.
8. *We made a list of all persons we had harmed, and became willing to make amends to them all.*
9. *We made direct amends to such persons whenever possible, except when to do so would injure them or others.* You may remember that the Jewish practice of repentance includes making amends to people who have been wronged. Buddhists, as well, believe that direct amends should be made whenever possible and whenever no further injury will result from doing so. The same is true of some other religions.
10. *We continued to take a daily inventory, and when we were wrong promptly admitted it.* Commitment to consistency and regular, mindful self-examination is also a feature of many religions. It was practiced, for example, by the Puritans who were in the New World from the earliest days of the colonies.
11. *We sought through prayer and meditation to improve our conscious contact with God, praying only for knowledge of his will for us and the power to carry that out.* The spiritual dimension of this step is obvious. It carries forward the theme of surrender of self-will to the will of a higher power.

12. *Having had a spiritual awakening as a result of these steps, we tried to carry this message to other alcoholics and to practice these principles in all our affairs.* Three of the major religions of the world—Christianity, Islam, and Buddhism—are missionary religions, carrying the message of spiritual awakening to other people. "Spreading the Gospel" has been an important feature of Christianity in the United States, as well as elsewhere.

This analysis of the twelve steps clearly delineates the spiritual character of the movement. Like organized religions, twelve-step and other self-help programs offer their followers something from each of the four dimensions of religion. Perhaps the most important *belief* is that human beings *can* transform their lives. Even when the situation appears hopeless—or most of all *when* it appears hopeless—people have the capacity to make a better life for themselves. Some programs, like A.A., advocate reliance on a power outside oneself. Other programs focus on self-effort. Certainly the reliance on "other power" is more in tune with the predominance of Christianity in this country. Reliance on self-effort, however, echoes a theme as old as the beginning of the United States: the self-reliant frontiersman or frontierswoman setting out to conquer the wilderness. Self-effort and individualism, although not always highlighted in American religion, are significant parts of the larger American cultural story. The importance of "working on oneself" and bettering oneself goes back as far as the Puritans, for whom growth in personal character was a highly prized goal. Taking responsibility for one's actions and their results is also a theme that is written large in both religion and secular culture in the United States.

There is yet another presupposition of the self-help movement that draws on an important feature of American religion. In self-help groups, people are aided in their own efforts by their peers. While a few groups have a professional leader or counselor, many do not. Even in those that do, the professional is there primarily as a facilitator, not as "the person whose responsibility it is to fix everything." Democracy in government in the United States has spilled over into many areas of life. We noted that even those communities of faith that are primarily hierarchical in their organization are usually less so in their American embodiments. There is a tendency to see the leaders as leading their congregations in ministry, rather than being the only ones involved in ministry. Many alternative popular spiritual groups are very democratic in their structure. Especially in recent years, trust in professionals has declined, and many people have sought to take a larger role in their religion, health care, education, or automobile repair. Many people no longer think that calling in a professional is the only or the best solution.

Alcoholics Anonymous teaches the importance of changing one's *lifestyle* if one is to stay sober. Lasting sobriety is not likely to be achieved if recovering alcoholics continue to go to bars, socialize with former drinking buddies, and engage in whatever other behaviors were associated with their drinking. Most self-help groups emphasize changes in lifestyle. The details of these changes depend upon the goal of the particular group, but lifestyle is a focus for nearly all. New habits must replace old, and new rewards must supplant old, negative ones. This reflects the importance that lifestyle and morality in general have for American religion. As a general rule, people's religious *beliefs* are not of great concern to most people, as long as those who hold the beliefs conform to the accepted canons of behavior.

The *ritual* dimension is there as well. Meeting together for mutual support and fellowship is central for the self-help movement. It is customarily believed that the best context for making important changes is a fairly small, supportive group of people who know what each other are going through because they're "all in the same boat." Some groups help people develop rituals to mark important changes of life, recognizing that rituals simply do not exist for many contemporary occasions that nonetheless need rituals. Alcoholics Anonymous groups celebrate the anniversaries of their members' sobriety, for example.

Certainly the *organizational* dimension is present. Alcoholics Anonymous itself spawned a number of other organizations such as Al-Anon (for families of alcoholics) and Alateen (specifically for teenagers), and, most recently, groups for adult children of alcoholics. Twelve-step groups have been formed to help people recover from other compulsive behaviors, including drug addiction, gambling, overeating, uncontrolled spending, and spouse and child abuse. These organizations have then developed groups for spouses and other family members of the recovering person.

A nearly limitless number of other kinds of support groups have formed, all based on the premise that the best support in a crisis comes from other people who have been through similar experiences.[15] Some direct all their energies toward helping the people involved. Weight Watchers is one example. There are also support groups for people with cancer (and for their families and friends), and those who are divorcing, chronically ill, or in chronic pain. Your campus may have a variety of support groups for students, such as a group for students who suffer test anxiety.

Other support groups have also developed a "political" dimension that complements their supportive function. Mothers Against Drunk Driving (MADD) began as a support group for parents whose child had been killed or injured in an alcohol-related accident. They soon began working actively to reduce the number of such accidents. Support groups for people who are HIV-positive or who have AIDS (and their families and friends) often undertake political activity on behalf of affected people.

As we have seen, the self-help movement, exemplified by Alcoholics Anonymous and other similar groups, is clearly a spiritual movement. For some people, it is an adjunct to participation in a community of faith. For others, it is a substitute for such participation. The specific format, and certainly the prolif-

---

[15]To get a sense of the range of recovery groups, visit http://www.jps.net/Sunflake/Support.htm. There is an extensive list of groups, including ones for people who think they may be spending too much time online, Internet Anonymous and Netaholics.

eration of these groups, is relatively new on the American scene. On the other hand, as we have seen, some of the themes and presuppositions are as old as the United States itself.

FEMINIST SPIRITUALITY

Most—although not all—of the religious groups and organizations in the United States share at least some of the patriarchal viewpoints and practices that continue to mark American culture in general. This has created concern for many women in these communities of faith. We can describe the responses that women make to this situation in terms of a continuum. At one end are those *many women for whom traditional structures, views, and rituals are meaningful and fulfilling.* Survey data strongly indicate that women are more traditionally religious than are men. Many women, perhaps the majority, are not disturbed by references to God as "He" and to humanity as "man." These women can and do remain within their traditional communities of faith and find meaning there, without seeking or desiring change. Some may feel threatened by people who *are* bothered by the questions and issues that do not bother them and who do seek change. The religious right has made upholding women's traditional roles a central theme.

As you learned in Chapter 3, most women choose to stay in their communities of faith, either accepting things as they are or working actively to change the things with which they disagree. But some women choose not to remain in their churches, temples, or synagogues and found or join *groups specifically based on women's spirituality.* This is the response that I will focus on in this section. More specifically, I want to look at *goddess worship and the Wiccan tradition* as it relates to feminist spirituality.

Women and men who consider themselves to be followers of the types of religion described below also do not agree completely on how the religion should be named. Some prefer *Wicca* (practitioners are *Wiccans*), a word meaning "Wise Ones." It has the same root as our word "wisdom." Some of its advocates believe that using this less familiar word helps overcome the negative connotations often associated with the word "witch." Others deliberately use *Witchcraft* and *Witch* in a bold move to reclaim the word from its detractors. Others prefer *the Craft*, with its emphasis on the ritual work that Wiccans do. For still others, *the old religion* signifies the ancient roots of this worldview. I will use these terms interchangeably.

Attempts to develop an agreed-upon statement of Wiccan belief have fallen far short of universal acceptance among actual Wiccans. Decentralization and the autonomy of individuals and groups is a primary organizing principle. However, it is possible to describe certain basic beliefs that are widely shared among Wiccans. In a similar fashion, I will describe common ritual practices.

Wicca is one form of a larger world view, that of *magick*. The basis of this view is that there are unseen, although completely natural, forces within the world that can control and manipulate people if people do not learn to control them. Sybil Leek, a contemporary American witch, defines magick as "the art of producing a desired effect or result through the use of various techniques such as incantations and presumably assuring human control of supernatural agencies or the forces of nature."[16] Ritual provides the primary tool for working with these forces. In a nation in love with technology (although perhaps less enamored of its promises than we once were), Witchcraft offers a "spiritual technology" with which to interact with unseen forces. At the same time, it runs against the primary grain of American thought about the divine. The Judeo-Christian tradition that has had the greatest influence on American religious ideas emphasizes that God cannot be manipulated nor controlled by human beings.

Most Wicca in the United States traces its roots back to British author and lecturer Gerald B. Gardner (1884–1964) and therefore it is called "Gardnerian Wicca." Although there are various accounts of exactly how Gardner developed his religious thought and practice, it blended together elements from Western occult and magickal traditions with various pieces of Eastern religions that he picked up while living in India and Southeast Asia. The Gardnerian tradition came to the United States with Raymond and Rosemary Buckland in the mid-1960s. The Bucklands formed a coven on Long Island, and Gardnerian thought and practice spread from there. Although there are many variations within the American Wiccan community, most of them retain at least the outlines of Gardner's world view and ritual. Among the most closely related schools is the Alexandrian, formed by Alexander Sanders (1926–1988).

One indication of the evolution of the Wiccan movement in the United States is that the well-known Wiccan practitioner and author, Starhawk (Miriam Samos) has written a new book, titled *Circle Round: Raising Children in Goddess Traditions*.[17] What this indicates is that Wicca in the United States is no longer just a movement of converts, of first-generation practitioners, but that a need has developed to address the issue of raising up the next generations.

Beliefs

The way in which the sacred or holy is thought about and spoken about, addressed in prayer and celebration, is one of the most central beliefs in any religion. Instead of the traditional habit of thinking and speaking of God in the Judeo-Christian-Islamic tradition as if God were male, some women have turned to belief in and worship of the goddess instead. Goddess worshipers believe in a female creator, often paired with a god as the male principle. Although it came to public attention in the 1970s, goddess worship had been explored much earlier by women in the Victorian period.[18] Followers of the god-

---

[16]Sybil Leek, *Diary of a Witch* (Englewood Cliffs, NJ: Prentice Hall, 1968), p. 4.

[17]Starhawk, Anne Hill, and Diane Baker. *Circle Round: Raising Children in Goddess Traditions* (New York: Bantam Doubleday Dell, 1998).

[18]Rosemary Radford Ruether and Rosemary Skinner Keller, *Women and Religion in America, Volume III: 1900–1968* (San Francisco: Harper & Row, Publishers, 1986), p. xiv.

dess look back to religions that predate Judaism and Christianity, in which the goddess was very important. Worshiping both a god and a goddess, with the emphasis placed on the goddess, restores a balanced view of ultimate reality or the holy for these people, in ways that simply altering traditional language cannot. Not all followers of the goddess are Wiccans, but virtually all Wiccans are worshipers of the goddess.

According to one feminist scholar, women need the goddess for four main reasons. (1) Her most basic meaning is the acknowledgment of female power as good and as independent of anything or anyone else. She provides a way that female power can be called forth in ritual and prayer. (2) She affirms the female body and the life cycles inherent in it that are also inherent in the earth. She appears in the roles of maiden, mother, and crone,[19] affirming virginity, motherhood, and old age. "Virginity" here does not refer to physical virginity, but to women as essentially independent of men. (3) The goddess encourages women to affirm that the will of the female can be effective in the world and to work to make it so. Through the goddess, women can believe in the female will as valid and not subordinate to the will of males. (4) The goddess is a revelation of female bonding, especially the mother–daughter bond, distinguished from the patriarchal heritage in which women's bonds are with men. The goddess helps women to affirm and celebrate "female power, the female body, the female will, and women's bonds and heritage."[20]

One practicing Wiccan woman puts it this way: Images of deity as goddess "inspire us to see ourselves as divine, our bodies as healthy, the changing phases of our lives as holy, our anger as purifying, and our power to nurture and create, but also to limit and destroy when necessary, as the very force that sustains all life."[21]

For many goddess worshipers, the goddess is a way to the recognition and celebration of the divinity within themselves. They experience the entire world as one divine whole and see themselves as a part of it. To address and celebrate the goddess is but a step on the way to "reclaiming [their] own divinity as part of the vastness of the natural world."[22]

Wiccans usually worship the Goddess in her threefold form, sometimes referred to as the *Triple Goddess*. She is *maiden, mother,* and *crone,* signifying the various ages of woman. She is frequently symbolized by the phases of the moon—the waxing or rising crescent, the full moon, and the waning or subsiding moon. Wiccans draw on the goddess traditions of many times and cultures, believing that all the names of the goddess are equally valid. She is invoked by many names in ritual:

---

[19] *Crone* is meant here as a term of respect that means "a wise old woman."

[20] Carol P. Christ, "Why Women Need the Goddess: Phenomenological, Psychological, and Political Reflections" in *Womanspirit Rising: A Feminist Reader in Religion*, ed. Carol P. Christ and Judith Plaskow (San Francisco: Harper & Row, Publishers, 1979), pp. 276–285.

[21] Starhawk (Miriam Samos), *The Spiral Dance: A Rebirth of the Ancient Religion of the Great Goddess* (San Francisco: Harper & Row, Publishers, 1979), p. 8.

[22] Hallie Inglehart, *Womanspirit: A Guide to Women's Wisdom* (San Francisco: Harper & Row, Publishers, 1983), p. 97.

Isis, Astarte, Diana, Hecate, Demeter, Kali, Inanna. . . .
Listen to the words of the Great Goddess, the Great Mother of the Universe—
Gaia, Yemaya, Spider Woman, Ishtar, Ashtoreth, Mary, Inanna, Demeter—
known by a thousand names across geography and time.[23]

Most also worship her consort, *Pan* or the *horned god* of the fields. He, likewise, has had many names in many times and places.

Wiccans also affirm the *divinity and holiness of all living beings and of the earth* itself (or, as many would put it, herself). There is disagreement about the relationship between Wicca and the Pagan religious traditions, but they have at least this in common.

> In the Wiccan worldview, there is no warring dichotomy between Spirit and Nature. Rather, they are part and parcel of one another; the sacred permeates all aspect of the cycle of life and death. Witchcraft takes its teachings primarily from Nature, in the cycle of the seasons, which we call the Wheel of the Year, we are inspired to see and experience the sacred dimension within the rhythms of life all around us. . . . Becoming aware of and in tune with the rhythms of Nature—the cycles of beginning, growth, and ending, learning how to work with these rhythms and not against them—these are the lessons of the Wheel of the Year.[24]

Witches believe that *people*, because we are conscious and have freedom of choice, *have a unique responsibility toward the environment*. It is up to people to live a lifestyle that reflects respect for the earth and to live in harmony with nature. Often, the earth is revered as a manifestation of the goddess.

Witches *do not worship Satan* or the Christian devil. The beginnings of Wicca predate Christianity, while Satanism relies on the development of the idea of Satan within the Christian tradition. Although they are often carelessly lumped together, there is no relationship between them aside from the underlying magickal worldview they share.

Nor do witches try to put evil spells and curses or hexes on people. Such behavior is always considered unethical. Self-determination, personal freedom, and autonomy are central values in Wiccan ethics and morality. Most witches feel that it is unethical even to work a spell for someone's benefit without their knowledge and agreement. There are two basic principles that guide behavior. One is the "Wiccan Rede," *An ye harm none, do what ye will. An* here is an ancient use of the word that means "as long as." The second is the principle that what people do returns to them. Many put this in terms of the *Threefold Law*: Whatever we do returns to us three times over, be it good or ill.

---

[23]The first listing of names is from a widely used chant, the origin of which is unknown at this time. The second is the beginning of the "Charge of the Goddess," cited in Nikki Bado, "Multiculturalism within the Women's Spirituality Movement: The Search for Female Deistic Images" (unpublished paper), p. 1.

[24]Nikki Bado, "Changing the Face of the Sacred: Women Who Walk the Path of the Goddess," in *Explorations: Journal for Adventurous Thought*, 8, no. 1 (Fall 1989), p. 7.

Practices

Witches often organize into *covens* or small groups of three to twenty people to perform rituals and enjoy fellowship. There are also *solitaries*, witches who, through personal choice or circumstances, practice alone. Some covens are all female (and a few are all male), and some are mixed. Although there are traditional rituals that have been handed down, most feel very free to improvise and create new rituals as occasions call for them.

"*Casting a circle*" is a fundamental ritual. The circle thus marked off becomes a sacred space. Wherever it is, indoors or out, city or farm, it becomes a place in which the sacred can be contacted and interacted with. Ritual purification of the circle removes negative energy from it, protects those within it, and helps to concentrate their own spiritual energies on the task at hand. This is most often done using the traditional elements of air, earth, fire, and water. Often, gods and goddesses are called upon to be present alongside the human participants.

The circle having been cast and purified, participants often *raise a cone of power*. This is done by chanting or dancing (or both) or running around the circle. The "cone of power" is really the combined wills of the group, intensified through ritual and meditative techniques, focused on an end collectively agreed upon.[25]

The focus can be any of a number of things. Healing, both physical and emotional, is a common focus. Healing can be directed toward individuals (within the circle or outside it), groups, or the earth itself. Sometimes the focus is simply to raise positive energy. Coven work often centers around directing positive energy toward the goals of the members and others—be it finding a job, a love relationship, overcoming a crisis, or simply living with grace and joy in everyday life. This type of work is done in *esbats*, coven meetings that are held traditionally at the time of the full and new moons, although they may be held at other times as well. Some covens, for example, meet weekly. The ritual work is most often followed by sharing a meal or at least refreshments and a time of fellowship.

There is also a series of *seasonal festivals or Sabbats* that reflect the natural cycle of the seasons and the positions of the sun and earth relative to each other. There are four *Great Sabbats*: (1) *Samhain* or the Celtic New Year on October 31; (2) *Candlemas* on February 2, a winter festival that focuses on purification and the beginning of spring; (3) *Beltane*, May 1, the great spring festival of fertility and renewal symbolized by the marriage of the god and goddess; and (4) *Lughnasadh* (in some accounts, *Lammas*), the August 1 festival of the first fruits of harvest that also looks toward the seasonal decline of winter. The four *Lesser Sabbats* celebrate the summer and winter solstices (June and December) and the spring and fall equinoxes (March and September).

---

[25]Margot Adler, *Drawing Down the Moon: Witches, Druids, Goddess-Worshipers and Other Pagans in America Today*, 2nd. ed. (Boston: Beacon Press, 1986), p. 109.

Initiation is an important ritual for individual witches. Although some witches believe that a person must be initiated by another witch, others support self-initiation, especially if the opportunity for initiation by a practicing witch is not available. However it is carried out, it is a rite of beginning, of accepting and celebrating one's status, and of becoming a part of the Wiccan community of faith and agreeing to live by its norms.

Organizations

When we try to estimate the number of people who are Wiccans, we encounter problems similar to those involved in counting New Agers. We also confront a different problem. Because of the negative associations that many people bring to witchcraft, many Wiccans are understandably reluctant to reveal their participation. Groups do not report membership figures. One survey puts the number of Wiccans in the United States at under 50,000.[26]

Most Wiccan covens are small, and there is no central organization. Those that I describe below are intended to be examples of some of the better-known ones. The *Church and School of Wicca* in New Bern, North Carolina, is one of the most accessible of the witchcraft groups. Its twelve-lesson home study course is widely advertised. Its members have campaigned energetically to promote what they believe is a correct understanding of the meaning of the craft and to help overcome centuries of prejudice and misunderstanding.

The *Church of Circle Wicca* is located in Mount Horeb, Wisconsin. Like the Church and School of Wicca, it has maintained a much higher public profile than have most Wiccan groups. It is believed to be the largest network for such groups, and its Circle Sanctuary is the site of many intergroup conferences and celebrations.

The *Covenant of the Goddess* in Berkeley, California, is a national organization that encourages cooperation between various covens and traditions within American Wicca. Its members also work for the legal recognition of Wicca as a religion. Such recognition would make the same benefits available to Wiccan groups that are enjoyed by other communities of faith, such as tax exemption.

Dianic Wicca, exemplified by the Susan B. Anthony Coven Number One, is a collective term for covens that have developed a strongly feminist emphasis. They consider themselves completely separate from the Gardnerian lineage. Dianic Witches worship the ancient goddess *Diana* (identified with the Greek goddess Artemis). Diana was a deity of woods and forests and the special patron of women and childbirth. She is a virgin, and her virginity symbolizes female independence from males. Since its organization beginning in the early 1970s, Dianic Wicca has been recognized as an important dimension of American Wicca. Its followers unite in Dianic covens or participate in non-Dianic covens.

Our Lady of Enchantment, Church of the Old Religion also sponsors correspondence courses. Its center near Nashua, New Hampshire, includes a book-

---

[26]*New York Times National,* April 10, 1991, p. 1.

store, library, museum and a seminary for training priestesses and priests in the Wiccan tradition. Some members live at the center itself. Members and non-members, residents and sympathetic nonresidents, may participate in the ritual and educational life of the community and share in its fellowship.

What are we to make of Wicca? What does it offer its adherents? It seems to me that there are several things. (1) As a part of the magickal tradition, it offers people techniques for dealing with the mystery of the divine in constructive ways that people believe allow them to benefit from sacred forces. (2) It offers an alternative to the patriarchalism of the prevailing Western and most Eastern religions. (3) It teaches the immanence of the divine in all things and thus seems to many to be more "earth-friendly" than the monotheistic religions. Its seasonally based ritual calendar gives people ways to celebrate their closeness to the natural world. (4) Similarly, its emphasis on the sacred within every person suggests new ways of understanding what it is to be a human being. (5) For many women, Wicca provides a way to affirm and celebrate being a woman in a culture that has not always valued women as highly as men.

THE UNIVERSAL FELLOWSHIP OF METROPOLITAN COMMUNITY CHURCHES

The Universal Fellowship of Metropolitan Community Churches, which celebrated its thirtieth anniversary in October, 1998, is a Christian community of faith for "lesbian, gay, bisexual, and transgendered" persons:

> The Universal Fellowship of Metropolitan Community Churches (UFMCC) plays a vital role in addressing the spiritual needs of the lesbian, gay, bisexual, and transgendered community around the world. For those of us who were raised in a religious atmosphere, homosexuality was usually associated with shame and guilt. As a result, many of us were cut off from the spiritual dimension of our lives. Metropolitan Community Churches provide an opportunity to explore a spiritual experience that affirms who we are.

> Today, as self-aware and self-affirming gay men and lesbians, we reclaim the fullness of our humanity, including our spirituality. We find great truths in the religious tradition, and we find that our encounter with God is transformational and healing. . . .

> Throughout the . . . history of the Universal Fellowship of Metropolitan Community Churches, thousands of gay, lesbian, bisexual, transgendered, and heterosexual people have found hope, and have lived the joy, reverence, and excitement of our fellowship and faith in God. We have seen how people have been changed by this experience. Quite simply, we make a difference in people's lives.

Within the context of the mainstream Christian tradition as far as belief and worship are concerned, the Fellowship acknowledges that traditional Christianity has routinely excluded other than heterosexual persons from full fellowship. In contrast, it teaches that God's promises of salvation and fellowship are offered to all persons, without regard for sexual preference or orientation. Homosexuality is regarded as neither a sin nor an illness, but as one part of oneself that one neither can nor should try to change. As God creates some people heterosexual, others are created homosexual. The Bible does not condemn "loving, responsible homosexual relationships," and therefore these relationships should be encouraged, affirmed, and celebrated.

RELIGION IN CYBERSPACE

We have already seen that the consensus religions, and many of the nonconsensus communities of faith as well, have pages or sites on the World Wide Web. Religious organizations have found the Web a useful place on which to present their views to others and to keep their own constituencies informed. Individuals motivated by religious concerns maintain sites and pages to present their views.

When I use the term *religion in cyberspace* I have something else in mind. There are manifestations of religion that have developed specifically on and for the Internet or World Wide Web. This section provides a description of some of them, with URLs. To explore this dimension of religion further on your own, a good place to begin is Yahoo's category, "Cyberculture Religion."[27]

In February, 1998, three Tibetan Buddhist monks at the Namgyal Monastery in New York state prayed for a half-hour, conducting a formal Buddhist blessing of cyberspace.

> In the monks' view, cyberspace resembles space in general, which Tibetan Buddhists characterize more as the absence of obstructions than as a distance between two points. Also, cyberspace, like ordinary space, can be defined as something that cannot in and of itself be seen or measured, yet which can be conceptualized and used. That is, it has no inherent existence for its own part, yet it exists as a field for mental activity.
>
> Where there is an absence of obstructions, there is the potential for something to arise, the nature of which depends on the motivation of those who use it. In blessing cyberspace, the monks reasoned, they could offer prayers that the motivation of Internet users become more positive and that the benefits of using the Internet become more positive.

They chanted a traditional Buddhist prayer for the welfare of all, in the hope that the positive potentials of cyberspace would develop in such a way that they would outweigh the negative ones.

---

[27]http://dir.yahoo.com/Society_and_Culture/Cultures_and_Groups/Cyberculture/Religion (remember that URLs are often case-sensitive).

May all beings have happiness and its causes.
May all beings be separated from suffering and its causes.
May all beings never be separated from happiness.
May all beings have equanimity toward the eight worldly dharmas.

May people be happy and their years be blessed.
May the crops grow well and may religion prosper.
I pray that all happiness arises for everyone.
And that whatever they desire shall come to pass.[28]

There are a number of "virtual congregations" on the Web, existing only in cyberspace. *Havienu L'Shalom* is a Jewish virtual congregation. It offers many of the things that one would find in a "real world" congregation, such as a library, a social hall, calendar, and opportunities for forums and study with the rabbi.

> Havienu L'Shalom has won international recognition for its unique merger of advanced technology and traditional chaplaincy, increasing access to Jewish services, education and guidance worldwide. The "virtual" congregation has developed a worldwide community devoted to helping its members achieve their highest human potential within a framework of Chassidus-based Torah learning and Jewish meditative prayer. It provides an opportunity for peoples of all faiths to experience a foretaste of, and work toward, that peace which is the hallmark of the Era of Redemption. The name itself, Havienu L'Shalom—bring us in to peace, signifies the Congregation's promotion of spiritual purpose and fulfillment within a context of material security.[29]

The First Church of Cyberspace, founded by a Presbyterian minister, is Protestant Christian.[30] It offers a sanctuary (sermons, music, prayers), movie reviews, bulletin boards, galleries, and discussions of contemporary issues, among other things. You can listen to Bach's "Jesu, Joy of Man's Desiring," a classical Christian composition, by clicking on an audio icon. Shin Buddhism has a cyberspace temple, the White Path Temple.[31] Its offerings include an online Buddhist dictionary, information on Buddhism, a virtual meditation hall, altar, and art gallery, sacred diagrams called mandalas, texts and sutras, and other resources. There is even a "meditation channel" (#meditation) on the Internet Relay Chat that is "scarcely ever empty, but it is always silent. No one types messages on this site. Its de facto purpose is to function as an electronic meditation hall."[32]

---

[28]An account of the ceremony and its rationale, along with sound clips of the chant and an image of the Kalachakra mandala, can be found at http://www.namgyal.org/blessing.html, from which both the citations are taken. The eight worldly dharmas are four pairs of things that we experience: gain and loss, pleasure and pain, praise and insult, and fame and infamy. Buddhists believe that human beings tend to be attached to the "pleasant" pole, while trying to avoid the "unpleasant" one.

[29]http://www.havienu.org/

[30]http://www.execpc.com/~chender

[31]http://www.mew.com/shin/

[32]Jeff Zaleski, *The Soul of Cyberspace: How New Technology Is Changing Our Spiritual Lives.* San Francisco: HarperSanFrancisco, 1997, p. 219.

There are other virtual communities of faith that are not as immediately recognizable. One is the Church of All, a cyberchurch with a strong planetary and ecological emphasis, with a sense of the urgency of taking the needs of the planet seriously. It teaches that "religion and science were once one, and so shall they be again."

> The church of All is a modern religion for modern times. It is a church for all people. We breathe the same air, we drink the same water, this is our world. We all suffer when our fellows starve, are sick, are under-educated, are drug addicted, are the victims of crime.
>
> This religion preaches, that we must do god's work, save the people, save the land, save the ocean, save the atmosphere, save the planet. The power is there. Believe in it, tap in to it, act like the god you are.
>
> We do the thinking here. We are the doers here. Become part of the universal power to do positive work. You are a part of the infinite life form, god, you are a part of All.
>
> Join us. Join the truly universal religion. Accept responsibility for yourself. Don't wait for an abstract god to save our planet. Link to the power, use it, become strong from it. Do god's work now, before it's too late.[33]

The Church of All offers a sermon of the week, previous sermons, a questions-and-answers page, personal guidance, and the "Verse of All." It also offers a number of "internet chapels" that focus on brief devotionals that encourage appreciation of the natural world.

A serious attempt at creating an internet religion, although with an unlikely name, is the Church of Virus. It is an atheistic religion with a scientific emphasis:

> Virus was originally created to compete with the traditional (irrational) religions in the human ideosphere with the idea that it would introduce and propagate memes which would ensure the survival and evolution of our species. The main advantage conferred upon adherents is Virus provides a conceptual framework for leading a truly meaningful life and attaining immortality without resorting to mystical delusions. . . .
>
> Virus is a collection of mutually-supporting ideas (a meme-complex) encompassing philosophy, science, technology, politics, and religion. The core ideas are based on evolution and memetics because one of the primary design goals was survivability through adaptation (religions die, not because they grow old, but because they become obsolete). If a new religion is designed around the premise of continuously integrating better (more accurate, more useful) concepts while ensuring the survival of its believers, it could conceivably achieve true immortality.[34]

[33]http://netzone.com/church.html
[34]http://www.lucifer.com/virus/lb_index.html

Its founders chose the name "Church of Virus" because the word "virus" has such a negative connotation, particularly among computer users acquainted with the havoc that computer viruses can cause. It was chosen to "deliberately antagonize" people and to warn people that it might "infect" them with the truth.

Another distinctly Internet-related manifestation of religion is the inclusion of methods to ask questions on some religious organization sites. Lama Surya Das, an American dharma teacher in the Dzogchen lineage, includes "Ask the Lama" on his site. The Zen Mountain Monastery features Cyber-Monk, a similar means whereby visitors to the site can e-mail questions to the monastery.[35]

There is also a "Prayer of Internet Connecting," modeled on the Christian Lord's Prayer, that many people who use a modem a lot can appreciate.[36]

What are we to make of religion in cyberspace? It would seem to be very difficult to replicate some of the features of "real world" religion in virtual religion. There is communication, to be sure, some of it very personal, in cyberspace. However, it is not face-to-face. It is far too easy, as recent incidents have shown, for people to deceive others about their identity when the only connection is through words on a computer monitor. Accountability is seriously lacking, or wholly absent. Despite the development of screen symbols to indicate emotions (*emoticons*), {{{ }}} falls far short of a real world hug, and :=), while cute, lacks the warmth of a human smile.

One of the things that is most often used as a marker for something being religious is the presence of ritual. In spite of some few attempts, ritual has shown itself to be hard to do in cyberspace. So much of ritual is about embodiment—about bread and wine as the body and blood of Jesus in the Christian Eucharist, for example, or about offerings of flowers or fruit or rice. And virtual reality is very much *dis*embodied reality.

That having been said, if virtual religion seems to be a questionable matter at this time, the role of the Internet—the Web, bulletin boards, chat rooms, newsgroups—in providing a forum for people to share their religious views, to advocate for their particular community of faith, to learn about religions other than their own, to find support among those with similar views has become an important part of religion in the United States.

---

[35]http://www.zen-mtn.org and http://www.dzogchen.org
[36]http://www.spiritone.com/~stephenk/prayer.html

QUESTIONS AND ACTIVITIES FOR REVIEW, DISCUSSION, AND WRITING

1. If there is a New Age bookstore in your community, visit it and note the types of literature, music, and other items that are available. If you can, speak with the owner, manager or someone who works there about their clientele and the purpose that they believe the store serves.
2. What might be some advantages of overcoming the dualistic ways in which we usually think about ourselves and the world? What might be the disadvantages?
3. If you have been a part of a twelve-step or self-help group, reflect on the extent to which it was based on spiritual presuppositions or had a spiritual impact on you.
4. If you can locate one in your community, attend a Wiccan ritual or meeting. Write an essay on what you observe and how you respond to it. If this is not possible, try to find a Wiccan who is willing to come and speak to your class.
5. What effect do you think that ritual observance of the changing seasons and phases of the moon would have on you?

FOR FURTHER READING

ANDERSON, SHERRY RUTH, and PATRICIA HOPKINS, *The Feminine Face of God: The Unfolding of the Sacred in Women.* New York: Bantam Books, 1991. Based heavily on interviews with "spiritually mature women in our time and culture" who describe "the unfolding of the sacred in their lives in their own words, in the language of their own hearts," this book includes minimal commentary with a focus on the process rather than the result. It's a good read.

ELLER, CYNTHIA, *Living in the Lap of the Goddess: New Feminist Spiritual Movements.* New York: Crossroad, 1992. This major effort at reporting on and analyzing the religions of goddess-worshiping feminists combines sociological analysis and reporting with material from interviews and description of rituals. It comes highly recommended.

FERGUSON, DUNCAN S., ed., *New Age Spirituality: An Assessment.* Louisville, KY: Westminster/John Knox Press, 1995. This is a collection of essays assessing the meaning and impact of New Age spirituality, written both from within and outside the movement.

HARDMAN, CHARLOTTE, and GRAHAM HARVEY, eds., *Paganism Today: Wiccans, Druids, and the Goddess: Ancient Earth Traditions for the 21st Century.* San Francisco: HarperSanFrancisco, 1996. Hardman and Harvey describe the history of the pagan movement, including Wicca and explore its many facets.

LEWIS, JAMES R., and J. GORDON MELTON, eds. *Perspectives on the New Age.* Albany, NY: State University of New York Press, 1992. This book begins with a thorough historical overview that relates the present movement to its historical predecessors and covers various aspects of the movement. It includes essays on the New Age in several foreign countries.

MELTON, J. GORDON, with JEROME CLARK and AIDAN A. KELLY, *New Age Encyclopedia: A Guide to the Beliefs, Concepts, Terms, People, and Organizations That Make up the New Global Movement toward Spiritual Development, Health and Healing, Higher Consciousness, and Related Subjects.* Detroit, MI: Gale Research, 1990. What can a reviewer add to the subtitle?! As with Melton's other encyclopedic works on religion in the United States, this is thorough, accurate, and very well indexed.

ZALESKI, JEFF, *The Soul of Cyberspace: How New Technology Is Changing Our Spiritual Lives* (San Francisco: HarperSanFrancisco, 1997). This is a diverse look at religion in cyberspace and its implications. Some of the chapters deal with sites related to specific religions, while others assess the implications.

RELEVANT WORLD WIDE WEB SITES

New Age Journal (http://www.newage.com/).

Voice of Wellness (http://www.vow.com/).

SpiritWeb (http://www.spiritweb.org/).

Real (http://www.real.org/).

Alcoholics Anonymous (http://www.alcoholics-anonymous.org).

Covenant of the Goddess (http://www.cog.org/).

Cleome's Wiccan Resources (http://www.geocities.com/Athens/Agora/7515/wicca.htm).

The Witches' Voice (http://www.witchvox.com/).

Grant Me the Serenity: Addiction and Recovery (http://www.jps.net/Sunflake/RecoveryPage/html).

Pentacle: Pagans 12 Step CyberMeeting (http://members.aol.com/JehanaS/recovery.html).

Universal Fellowship of Metropolitan Community Churches (http://www.ufmcc.com/).

13

Religion as an Individual and Cultural Problem

Traditionally, in Asia, vows and moral precepts have protected teachers and students from sexual and other forms of misconduct. In Japan, Tibet, India, and Thailand, the [Buddhist] precepts against harm by stealing, lying, sexual misconduct, or abuse of intoxicants are understood and followed by all members of the religious community. Even where certain precepts have been relaxed or modified (such as allowable drinking in China or Japan), everyone understands certain strict cultural norms for the behavior of teachers. Whole communities support this, for example, by dressing modestly to protect the teacher and student from sexual interest, by jointly knowing the appropriate limits concerning the use of intoxicants or power.

In modern America these rules are often dispensed with, and neither TV preachers nor Eastern spiritual teachers have clear rules of behavior regarding money, power, and sex. . . . Spiritual practice without any common commitment to traditional precepts and vows can lead both teachers and students astray.[1]

What kind of a man would tape a plastic bag over a terrified 8-year-old girl's head, secure it with duct tape, and then dump the child's suffocated body in a swamp? What kind of person bombs newspaper offices, robs banks, and then warns his jury that God is coming and they'd best repent? Who shoots the fingers off a victim one by one before killing him, orders the sexual abuse of a child and then has the boy murdered?

The answer in each case, officials say, is a Christian Identity man.[2]

---

[1] Jack Kornfield, *A Path with Heart: A Guide through the Perils and Promises of Spiritual Life* (New York: Bantam Books, 1993), pp. 259–260.
[2] "Identity Crisis: Expanding Race-Hate Faith Underlies Movement," *Intelligence Report* (Winter, 1998), Southern Poverty Law Center.

Religion can become a problem for individuals, or for society as a whole, when it leads to violence, terrorism, addiction, or other dysfunctional behaviors. There are religious groups in the United States that frighten a lot of people. They have beliefs and practices that are unusual in our culture. Many people call them *cults*. It is important to note two things at the outset: (1) Religions are not the only organizations that may become a problem in these ways. Virtually any organization has this potential. (2) The great majority of the time, religions *do not* lead their followers to violence or other criminal activity, nor into addictive behavior.

The word *cult* has strongly negative associations. Despite our cultural affirmation of religious pluralism and the legal right of a variety of religious groups to exist within the law, there is a definite bias that also exists. Even when we support the idea of religious freedom and pluralism, we are often uneasy when confronted with communities of faith that depart too far from the usual or average ways of being religious.

The mass murder-suicide episode that occurred at Jonestown, Guyana, in November 1978 in the People's Temple group creates near-panic reactions whenever nonconventional religions are mentioned. To a greater or lesser extent, those feelings continue today. Jonestown again captured public attention on the occasion of its tenth anniversary in 1988. The People's Temple tragedy certainly served to remind all of us that things labeled "religion" could at times be dangerous.

Similar questions and fears were raised yet again in the spring of 1993 when a violent confrontation between federal Alcohol, Tobacco, and Firearms agents and members of the Branch Davidian religious group led to a fifty-one-day standoff that ended as the group's compound outside Waco, Texas, burned, a conflagration in which about eighty people, including a number of children, died. A year after the devastation at Waco, five Davidians had been convicted of voluntary manslaughter, two more on weapons charges, and four had been acquitted of any responsibility in the deaths of the four Alcohol, Tobacco, and Firearms agents who died when they stormed the compound. The appropriateness of the government's actions is still being debated.

These topics forcefully came to public attention yet again in 1997 when the media reported the mass suicide of members of the Heaven's Gate religious group.

There seem to be four things that cause the most difficulty for religious groups and teachers. The first is the "misuse of power." In some religious groups, the teacher has a great deal of power, and there is very little accountability. In some instances, this leads to an isolationist, us-against-them attitude that is in itself detrimental. Money is the second problem area. People are understandably grateful for religious teachings and teachers that have a profound effect on their lives, and for some, this leads to a desire to give very generously of their money or other material possessions. In some religious groups, people are expected to divest themselves of many of their worldly goods. This influx of wealth into a group can lead to mismanagement. Sexuality is the third problematic area. Religious communities and teachers are not immune from the misuse of sexuality that occurs throughout the culture. Finally, in some instances, there are problems with alcohol or drugs, either on the part of a teacher or leader or in the group. Clearly, these four problem areas are not mutually exclusive, and oftentimes abuses in one area are accompanied by abuses in others.[3]

Events such as those described above raise difficult questions in a pluralistic culture that prides itself on its religious freedom. This is especially so in light of the distinction between freedom of religious belief and freedom of action motivated by religion. The Supreme Court's decision in the *Reynolds* case (discussed in Chapter 2) meant that matters of religious belief are beyond the concern of the government. What people believe may not be restricted. However, when that belief is translated into specific actions, the government may intervene to stop actions that are held to be very damaging to society or repulsive to commonly agreed-upon moral standards.

The consternation in the public mind over these religions and their activities has led to polarization in the community of religious studies scholars as well.

> The majority of the scholars involved in the debate have concluded that the fears and impressions prevalent among the general public and worried parents of "cult" members are overblown; their research has tended to debunk the widely held perception that many alternative religions engage in brainwashing and mind control, leading them to conclude that, although abuses do occur in some specific situations, by and large the alternative movements are, if unorthodox, worthy of the general protection of the First Amendment enjoyed by larger, more accepted faiths. Other scholars, however, have come to very different conclusions and argue that something like mind control *does* exist at least occasionally and that significant numbers of the nonconforming contemporary movements in question do present a real threat to the public.[4]

A VERY BRIEF HISTORY

In the half century since the end of the Second World War, we can discern five distinct phases in the history of nonconventional religions in the United States.[5] The first period, 1946–1964, was one in which nonconventional religions had only minimal impact in the United States. The groups whose names are common household words now—the Unification Church or the "Moonies," Scientology, the Branch Davidians and Heaven's Gate, for example—were either nonexistent, unknown, or very little known.

Between 1965 and 1969 a wave of Asian spiritual teachers came into the country after immigration restrictions were relaxed. They easily became part of the counterculture of the 1960s. Small and not-so-small groups of nearly every

---

[3]Jack Kornfield, *A Path with Heart*, pp. 256–258.

[4]Timothy Miller, "*Nova Religio* Symposium: Academic Integrity and the Study of New Religious Movements: Introduction," *Nova Religio* 2, no. 1 (October, 1998), p. 8.

[5]Based on Benjamin Zablocki, "The Blacklisting of a Concept: The Strange History of the Brainwashing Conjecture in the Sociology of Religion," *Nova Religio* 1, no. 1 (October, 1997), pp. 109–14.

imaginable ideological approach proliferated in the climate of experimentation and questioning of the "establishment," including its religion.

Between 1970 and 1977, the situation became more polarized. The well-publicized trial of Charles Manson and his group caught the public's attention. "Anticult" groups began to form, and forcible deprogramming came into being and widespread use.

The anticult movement gained attention and credibility between 1978 and 1986. The People's Temple mass suicide and murders convinced many people that alternative religions were dangerous. Several leaders were successfully prosecuted. Simply being a nonconventional, new, or alternative religious movement was enough to bring a group under public suspicion and scrutiny.

The decade between 1987 and 1997 brought substantially increased study of these religions. Scholars who researched this area felt "that the very foundations of religious liberty and freedom of religious choice were in grave peril." The mood shifted from one of suspicion to one of the defense of the right of nonconventional religions to exist.

Perhaps, in the final years of this millennium, we are moving closer to a more balanced perspective that avoids the excesses of either side. The treatment of nonconventional religions and the perceived/real threat of violence below is an example of a new willingness to leave the questions open and not rush to arrive at premature answers. At least some scholars in the field are prepared to follow the advice that German poet Rainer Maria Rilke gave to a young friend when he advised him to live and love the questions, because the answers could not yet be given him.[6]

NONCONVENTIONAL RELIGIONS AND THE ACADEMIC STUDY OF RELIGION

One of the characteristics of religious studies as an academic discipline (see Chapter 1) is that it is an interdisciplinary, cross-disciplinary or multidisciplinary approach defined more by its subject matter than by its methodology. In order to understand nonconventional religions, it is especially helpful to keep this in mind.[7]

Looking at nonconventional communities of faith from a psychological perspective, several questions become obvious: Who is likely to join and why? Is joining such a group always a sign of there being something wrong, or can it grow out of a psychologically healthy personality? How *do* people join, free choice or "brainwashing"? Does life within the group tend toward emotional health or its opposite? While there are conflicting answers to these questions, as

---

[6]Rainer Maria Rilke, *Letters to a Young Poet*, trans. M. D. Herter Norton (New York: W. W. Norton & Company, 1954), p. 35.

[7]John Saliba, *Understanding New Religious Movements* (Grand Rapids, MI: William B. Eerdmens Publishing Company, 1997)

we will see, psychological investigation of nonconventional religions helps to frame the questions themselves.

Nonconventional communities of faith are often of particular interest to sociologists. They allow researchers to observe how a new religion comes into being and develops and how it interacts with the larger cultural environment. These groups are often more volatile than the established religions, particularly in their early years, and sociologists can observe in a relatively short time changes and developments that in more established groups might take decades or have already taken place. Sociologists can watch as a new group begins to make the transition from being a complete cultural outsider to a position of some accommodation with the larger culture.

Conventional and established religions usually interact with the legal system only in rare instances. Newer, less-understood and less-accepted communities of faith have often found themselves involved in litigation. Such litigation has increased dramatically. This makes it necessary to approach the study of nonconventional religions from the perspective of law, as well. Questions about the autonomy of a religious group and its members versus the degree that they may be subject to governmental control often arise. Suits may be brought by disgruntled ex-followers or by their families. Child custody cases come about when a custodial parent joins a religious group of which the noncustodial parent does not approve.

This multidisciplinary perspective has been followed throughout this book, and it will be very apparent in this chapter.

THE WORD *CULT*: PROBLEMS OF DEFINITION

In looking at the word itself from the standpoint of definition, we should first note that **cult is always an outsider's word.** People use it to describe a religious group with which they disagree, of which they are suspicious or frightened, or toward which they feel hostile. No one describes their own religion as a cult!

Beyond this, however, there is simply no agreed-upon definition of the word, and different individuals and groups use it to mean very different things. There are **three major types of definitions**.

1. **Social scientists** typically divide religious organizations into "churches," "sects," and "cults." Each of these classifications has a very specific meaning within sociological literature. The sociological meaning of the word *cult* focuses on religious innovation within a culture; cults are the locus of innovation and religious change within the culture. When sociologists use the word in a sociological context, they intend it to be neutral, neither favoring nor maligning the religions. It simply identifies what type of religious group it is.

2. The second type of definition is theological, usually from a **Christian** perspective. A *cult* is defined as a deviation from Christianity, based on the assumption that Christianity is the only true religion. On these terms, a cult is heretical, follows false beliefs, and is a distortion or perversion of biblical Christianity. This applies to both alternative interpretations of Christianity (Latter-day Saints and Seventh-day Adventists, for example) and to religions that have no connection with Christianity (Islam, Hinduism, and Buddhism, for example).

3. The third approach to definition came about with the **secular anti-cult movement** in the 1970s. It grew out of the disappointment, fear, and anger of parents whose daughters and sons had abandoned family traditions and parental hopes in favor of a new and often radically different religion and the lifestyle that went with it. This definition emphasizes a variety of characteristics that are judged to be destructive, such as secrecy, authoritarian leadership, thought control, deception, and financial misdealing.

A type of definition that differs from the three above is that used by William Whalen in *Strange Gods: Contemporary Religious Cults in America.*[8] Whalen defines a cult simply as a group whose beliefs and/or practices differ greatly from those that are common in the rest of the culture. This definition has the advantage of pointing to what most people think of when they hear the word. It does, however, have at least two problems. On the face of it, at least, it is not pejorative. However, there is often a lurking idea, whether implicit or explicit, that what is *usual* is also *normal* or *right*. In that case, definitions based on a group's similarity to or difference from the prevailing culture have the same sorts of problems associated with the second and third definitions mentioned above. The second problem with such definitions is that they permit the inclusion of a wide variety of groups, beliefs, and practices that are very different from each other. Whalen, for example, includes groups as diverse as the Unification Church, Children of God, Jehovah's Witnesses, the Way, and the Unitarian Universalists.

In my opinion, the word *cult* no longer has any place in the description and discussion of religious groups and people in the United States (or elsewhere). Its definitions are too varied and the emotional responses that it evokes are too strong and unreflective. As an essay in a volume on the Waco debate summarizes well,

> In current popular usage . . . the term [cult] is applied to a disparate array of groups and has no clear and consensual denotation. It does, however, have the sensational *connotation* of an authoritarian, mind-controlling movement in which convert-victims are mentally enslaved and can be made to perpetrate violence and crime as ordained by a charismatic prophet or guru. A label possessing an unclear denotation but a sharp negative connotation becomes primarily an emotive vehicle for conferring a stigma.[9]

---

[8]William J. Whalen, *Strange Gods: Contemporary Religious Cults in America* (Huntington, IN: Our Sunday Visitor, 1981).

[9]Thomas Robbins and Dick Anthony, "'Cults,' 'Mind Control,' and the State," in *From the Ashes: Making Sense of Waco*, ed. Lewis, pp. 125–135.

As the authors go on to note, however, there is quite possibly "no fully adequate alternative" yet, a judgment with which I would agree. In what follows, *nonconventional religion* will be used to denote these groups.

VIEWS ON NONCONVENTIONAL RELIGIONS

Whatever they may be called, nonconventional religions are the subject of ongoing controversy. There is no clear agreement on just how much of a threat nonconventional religions pose, nor on what to do about them. The following are representative of some of the positions taken.

Researchers do not agree on something as basic as the number of such groups active in the United States. The Cult Awareness Network (CAN, a leading secular anticult[10] organization) claims there are about 2500, and the number is growing. On the other hand, the Institute for the Study of American Religion, headed by J. Gordon Melton, cites approximately 700.[11] Clearly, the threat, if such exists, increases as the number increases. At the same time, it is easy enough to understand the variation in these estimates. Many of these groups are small, and, because of the threat of retribution, tend to maintain a very low profile. Some groups form and disintegrate rather quickly or are reborn with a new name. Anticult organizations have a vested interest in claiming a large number of groups and adherents, whereas those who want to downplay the problem have a similarly vested interest in claiming the opposite. Lack of agreement on what groups to include adds to the problem.

Anticult organizations portray nonconventional religions as a new and radically different aspect of American religion, usually beginning in the 1960s. Others point out that "new religious groups, far from being new to the American social landscape, have been one of its most perennial features. . . . Religious diversity and the flowering of new religious groups are actually hallmarks of American history."[12]

There is a tendency to lump all new and unusual religious groups together and portray them as exercising near-total control over every aspect of their members' lives and thoughts. In reality there is, as you would expect on further reflection, a wide range in the degree of control exercised.

Scholars also do not agree fully on the extent and exact nature of "mind control," undoubtedly the characteristic most associated with the term *cult* in the minds of many people. One model holds that people completely lose their capacity for independent action, becoming puppets or robots with no free will whatsoever. Usually included in this model is the idea that the brainwashing tactics of an experienced recruiter are virtually irresistible and the convert a hapless victim. This explanation has not held up to scientific investigation, which has

---

[10]The word *anticult* is used extensively by these organizations themselves and will be used here.
[11]"Cults in America," *CQ Researcher*, 3, no. 17 (May 7, 1993), p. 387.
[12]David G. Bromley, "The Mythology of Cults," in *From the Ashes*, ed. Lewis, pp. 121–136.

shown that there are no techniques capable of completely overwhelming free will under the conditions that pertain in the United States.

The association of the brainwashing theory with recruitment is itself debated. One researcher points out that in its proper usage, the term has a great deal more to do with "socio-emotional exit costs."

> The brainwashing conjecture is concerned with whether something happens to a member while he or she is in the group to make it emotionally not impossible, but very difficult to get out again. Does something occur to create, in the mind of the person, a social-psychological prison without guards or walls?[13]

This theory is still *accepted*, however, and has important legal ramifications. If the members of these groups have had their freedom of choice totally disabled, then tactics such as "kidnaping" them and deprograming them to free them from the influence of the group are likely to be regarded as appropriate and even necessary techniques. Court-ordered conservatorships and guardianships for legal adults can easily be justified in these circumstances. It has also been noted that this "explanation" of someone's involvement with a group deemed unacceptable by the member's family explains it in terms that put no stigma on either the family or the group member, thus freeing them from any hint of self-blame.[14] This view also supports the corollary that members have in effect had their money stolen from them by the group when they made contributions or turned over assets to the group.

The second model does not assert that free will has been lost in any legally or ethically defensible sense that would support and even require dramatic intervention. The responsibility for behavior remains with the member of the group, who continues to be seen as a functional adult.[15] This view is substantiated by the fact that the majority of people who become part of such a group do eventually leave it; the defection rate would be much lower if the thought control were as effective as the first model claims. And, although many and perhaps most people in the United States would feel that turning over all of one's assets to such a group is an unwise choice, it remains a choice, freely made, on this model.

The issue of thought control is related to the question of how people join religious groups. It is helpful to have a historical perspective on how the process of religious conversion has been described. The standard way of interpreting what happens in conversion has been based on the model provided by the biblical accounts of Paul's conversion on the road to Damascus. It was sudden, highly dramatic and emotional, and it was said to result from God's action. Paul had little control over the process (Acts 9:1–18). When this model of conversion is used to interpret conversion to an unusual religious group, God's intervention in

---

[13]Benjamin Zablocki, "The Blacklisting of a Concept," pp. 100–101.
[14]David G. Bromley and Anson D. Shupe, Jr., "The Future of the Anticult Movement," in *The Future of New Religious Movements*, ed. David G. Bromley and Phillip E. Hammond (Macon, GA: Mercer University Press, 1987), p. 224.
[15]Robbins and Anthony, "'Cults,' 'Mind Control,' and the State," pp. 125–137.

Paul's life is replaced by devious tactics of brainwashing, hypnotism, and coercive persuasion applied against helpless and passive people without their control or consent.

There is a newer model of conversion that is much more accurate. In a highly pluralistic culture such as ours, conversion is frequently not a one-time event. Most people join and leave several groups, religious and nonreligious, over the course of their lifetimes. Only a small number of people who have some initial contact actually join, and few of those who do remain for very long. Those who do join often have serious reservations about the group and their membership in it. Their participation is an experiment. People often behave as group members for a time, trying out a new role and way of life, while changing their beliefs and values very little. Participating in a group and accepting its teachings are not the same thing. On this model, affiliation with a religious group is seen along the same lines as affiliation with other groups, as a part of the human search for fellowship and identity. In other words, it is a normal, even necessary, process, one that cannot be taken as evidence of mental incapacity. Potential members and converts are active participants in the process, not passive victims of some deceptive and mysterious mental blackmail.[16]

Like other groups that actively recruit members, nonconventional religions have developed ways of attracting people to their causes. When the Bill of Rights was added to the Constitution and religion became a matter for voluntary association rather than birth, religious groups had to seek converts. They had to make their particular way of being religious attractive to people. In line with the accepted style of consensus religion, most of this competing for members in the United States is rather low key. Some communities of faith have sought members more aggressively and more visibly and have been criticized for using a hard-sell approach. The Latter-day Saints and Jehovah's Witnesses have concentrated on door-to-door solicitation of members. Other groups have chosen instead to focus on recruitment through existing friendship patterns, in which people who are already members invite their friends. They also seek new members in public places such as airports and bus terminals. Some seek members on college campuses.

Some groups *have* used deceptive techniques, not revealing the true identity of the group when approaching a prospective member. People have become involved in weekend retreats and longer conferences without full disclosure of what they would be doing once they arrived. There have been instances in which isolation and dependence upon the group leaders for transportation made leaving in the middle of such events difficult. Seeking to build group spirit quickly and firmly, leaders have at times overlooked or denied participants' legitimate needs for privacy and time to reflect on what was happening. Many people

---

[16]David G. Bromley and James T. Richardson, *The Brainwashing-Deprogramming Controversy: Psychological, Legal, and Historical Perspectives* (New York: Edwin Mellen Press, 1983), pp. 3–4. Other relevant studies include those reported in David G. Bromley and Anson D. Shupe, Jr., *Strange Gods: The Great American Cult Scare* (Boston: Beacon Press, 1981), and Larry D. Shinn, *The Dark Lord: Cult Images and the Hare Krishnas in America* (Philadelphia: Westminster Press, 1987).

regard these sorts of practices as unacceptable and inappropriate. However, the evidence does not support the accusations of brainwashing that have routinely been leveled against these groups.

One of the most common allegations about socially unacceptable religious groups is that there is a great deal of sexual abuse, including abuse of children, that takes place within the walls of the usually communal living arrangements. Leaders are charged with taking advantage of members and with encouraging sexual abuse among members themselves. However, other scholars point out that there are actually *fewer* serious accusations of sexual misconduct than against "mainline" priests and ministers.[17]

Those who fear the impact of nonconventional religions advocate constant vigilance and sometimes government intervention to "control the menace." One prominent spokesperson for the anticult movement states that these groups pose "very real threats to public health, mental health, political power, and democratic freedoms—as well as growing concerns over consumer issues—that become apparent as we learn how these manipulative and often unethical groups have spread into . . . the major sectors and institutions of our society."[18] Another observer of new religions worries that the coming millennium will encourage the rise of groups such as the Branch Davidians.[19]

Others fear the abridgement of constitutionally guaranteed freedoms at least as much as they fear the religions that provoke them. A representative of the Christian Legal Society writes that "the government is forbidden from interfering or abridging individual or organizational religious liberties. The anticonversion legislation proposed by various states does in fact intrude upon the very core of individual liberties and religious freedom."[20] According to a national survey carried out by People for the American Way, more than 50 percent of the attempts to censor school and public library books and public school textbooks now involve books that contain material that the would-be censors believe to be Satanic or occult.[21]

WHO JOINS AND WHY

Most research on nonconventional religions shows a common set of demographic traits among members. The vast majority are between the ages of eighteen and twenty-five. They are middle-class, reasonably intelligent people with some college education, although not usually college graduates. They are male

[17]J. Gordon Melton, *Encyclopedic Handbook of Cults in America*, Revised and Updated Edition. (New York: Garland Publishing, Inc., 1992), p. 189.

[18]Margaret Thaler Singer, with Janja Lalich, *Cults in Our Midst* (San Francisco: Jossey-Bass Publishers, 1995), p. 5.

[19]Hal Mansfield, quoted in "Doomsday Cults: Only the Beginning," *Newsweek*, April 3, 1995, p. 40.

[20]Thomas S. Brandon, Jr., *New Religions, Conversions, and Deprogramming: New Frontiers of Religious Liberty* (Oak Park, IL: The Center for Law & Religious Freedom, 1982), p. 1.

[21]Jeffrey S. Victor, *Satanic Panic: The Creation of a Contemporary Legend* (Chicago, IL: Open Court, 1993), p. 156.

and female in approximately equal numbers. Most are white. Most come from intact homes. All segments of the religious population of the United States are represented. Although most come from homes in which religion was a part of life, few were themselves active as teenagers. Many more people with these same demographic characteristics *do not* become members of nonconventional religions. Why some people and not others?

The age range of eighteen to twenty-five helps to point us to some—not all—of the answers to the question about why people may join nonconventional religions. This a time of passage, a time of transition in most Americans' lives. It may be a time of uncertainty. It is most definitely a time when forging our own identities as people different from our parents is of great psychological importance. It is a time of vulnerability for many. Having left the security of home or the college environment, people search for new sources of stability and security. Having left old friendships and groups that answered the need for human fellowship and intimacy that we all share, people seek new connections. It is a time when they may see their old lives and views as very outmoded and no longer useful and a time when new patterns of living and values need to be acquired.

Other factors may influence a person's decision to join a religious group very different from the one in which they were raised or to join a religious group for the first time. When we are confronted with a host of new choices, choices that, once made, will influence the rest of our lives, choice fatigue may set in. We are confronted daily with more choices than our grandparents could even imagine. In this situation, the promise of "six simple steps to love and acceptance now and salvation in the future" is alluring. In the present climate of uncertainty and doubt, many people are sincerely looking for an authority. They want a person or a philosophy of life that says with conviction, "This is it!" Some religions provide a comprehensive environment that reaches into every corner of life and offers an answer to every question. Once the major choice to join is made, other choices are sharply reduced. This comes as a welcome relief to the person suffering from choice fatigue.

Religions that are outside the cultural consensus offer an alternative, often something that seems much simpler. Many of those to whom such groups are attractive are sincerely seeking something better. Some people join such a group in search of answers to the dissatisfactions with everyday life that we all experience from time to time.

Others of those who join are engaged in a genuine spiritual quest and a search for an understanding of life's meaning that they can call their own. Many have found the more ordinary religions, the ones they and their friends grew up with, to be lacking in religious experience. Consensus religion has tended to devalue religious experience. Many of the nonconventional religions, especially those that developed in the East, emphasize techniques of spiritual experience, such as meditation, visualization, and chanting.

Specific psychological or emotional predispositions may lead people to join. Those with an unusually low tolerance for ambiguity may be drawn in by the promise of certainty. Those who have stronger-than-average needs for dependency may see the highly authoritarian structure of some religious groups as a good way of meeting this need. Those with an unusually strong need for approval from others will be susceptible to the instant friendship and acceptance sometimes offered. For some, the assurance of being in a group that believes itself to be the only true religion provides a bulwark against insecurity.

In other words, people choose membership in a nonconventional community of faith as a way of meeting needs that most people in the culture find met in consensus religions. These are important needs that all people have, simply because we're human beings. The emotional need for love and acceptance, the intellectual need for understanding and a framework of beliefs and values within which we can make sense of our world and our lives, and the moral need for a sense of purpose and direction all give rise to questions for which all of us search for answers. In many ways, the members of these communities of faith are no different from those of you who are reading this book. They may be somewhat more vulnerable because of their life circumstances or emotional makeup, or they may be experiencing an uncomfortable transition in their lives. They may have found ordinary answers unsatisfactory. They are people very like ourselves, with similar needs, hopes, and fears. They are persons who have chosen a different way of answering life's questions. Factors similar to these influence people to change their political party identification, switch from one consensus religion to another, make drastic changes in lifestyle, or even have cosmetic surgery. In other words, the influence of these factors is not restricted to people's decisions to join unusual religious groups.

NOT JUST NEGATIVES

It is common to see lists of the "negative" features of nonconventional religions. A person reading these lists—with their emphasis on thought control, tyrannical leaders only looking out for their own aggrandizement, and demands for long hours spent performing ritual activities or soliciting funds—might wonder why anyone would join such a group in the first place.

The answer is that these groups do offer their followers things that are not always found in more conventional communities of faith. They encourage (or demand) great enthusiasm, commitment, and dedication. New converts can see this as a challenge and as an alternative to more nominal membership. They also tend to emphasize religious or spiritual experience, ways for followers to experience religious feelings or at least feelings that are experienced and understood as such. They also offer new and sometimes exotic spiritual disciplines that again present the follower with a clear-cut alternative to what conventional religion offers.

Even the "negatives" are not necessarily completely negative. Someone with strong needs for an authority figure may respond very positively to a religious leader or teacher who claims near-absolute power and authority. Someone whose life feels out of control may find genuine comfort in the rigid schedules of many nonconventional communities of faith.[22]

NONCONVENTIONAL RELIGIONS
AND COLLEGE STUDENTS: TWO VIEWS

As we noted above, many college students are at a stage in psychosocial and faith development that is quite challenging and often threatening. According to some researchers, this makes college students especially vulnerable to recruiters for nonconventional religions and campuses particularly fertile sites for such recruiting. One college official describes them as "a major threat to the welfare, human rights, and indeed the very futures" of college students.[23] Nonconventional religions, he alleges, "lay siege to" college campuses and "prey upon students." While the more commonly accepted religious groups on campuses "support the spiritual life of students and assist them in their college endeavors, cult groups seek students to assist only the cult organization."[24]

Those who see nonconventional religions as a special threat to college students also point out that their effects go against what colleges try to do. "Cults, through the conversion process, close off and break down the logical faculties of the mind by narrowing the attention span of their members, robbing them of freedom of thought, intellectual growth, and personal development. . . . There is no question that destructive religious cults rob students of the very things we have joined together in universities to teach."[25]

In contrast to this approach, others point out that nonconventional religions, like other groups, have the legal right to be where they are. Students have a constitutionally guaranteed right to practice their faith, whatever that faith may be. They have as much right to organize for religious purposes as for any other purpose. Student religious groups have the same rights and responsibilities as other student groups. Ministers and other religious advisors have the right to work with college students. "The only restrictions which the college places on these advisors are those dictated by fair play for each other and by consideration for the orderly processes of the college."[26]

According to this view, the way to deal with whatever problems exist from the presence of nonconventional religions on college campuses is not suppres-

[22]John Saliba, *Understanding New Religious Movements*, pp. 11–20.

[23]Carl J. Rheins, "Why This Book?" in *Cults on Campus: Continuing Challenge*, ed. Marcia R. Rudin (New York: American Family Foundation, 1991), p. 1.

[24]Gregory S. Blimling, "The Involvement of College Students in Totalistic Groups: Causes, Concerns, Legal Issues, and Policy Considerations," in *Cults on Campus*, ed. Rudin, pp. 33–59. When the word *cult* occurs in a direct quote, I have retained it.

[25]Gregory S. Blimling, "Cults, College Students, and Campus Policies," in *Cultism on Campus: Commentaries and Guidelines for College and University Administrators*, ed. Robert E. Schecter and Wendy L. Noyes (New York: American Family Foundation and The National Association of Student Personnel Administration, 1987), pp. 5–20.

[26]George W. Jones, "Students and the Practice of Religion on Campus," in *Cultism on Campus*, ed. Schechter and Noyes, pp. 71–80.

sion or repression. Universities and colleges should be centers of openness to variant perspectives—all perspectives. They should be centers for the free expression of ideas—all ideas. Limiting access or forcing it into rigidly structured, narrow boundaries often causes more problems than it solves and runs the risk of violating students' constitutional rights. Forcing any group into covert activity increases the likelihood that it will come to be a threat. When freedom of speech prevails, "cult leaders can be heard and their beliefs and practices openly challenged and debated by the educational community."[27] This approach helps to diffuse anxiety about the little known, may keep groups from going underground, and facilitates exposure to new and controversial ideas, thus enhancing the educational process.

RELIGIOUS ADDICTION
AND NONCONVENTIONAL RELIGIONS

The literature on religious addiction gives us one way to understand how it is that religion sometimes becomes a problem in an individual's life or in the life of a society. *All* religions, without exception, are subject to being used in an addictive way. However, some, by their structure and the types of beliefs and lifestyle they advocate, may be more prone than others to being used in this way.

Like drugs, food, or personal relationships, religion can be addictive. Here, *addiction* means using

> ... something outside to escape from and control something we're afraid of inside.... [We] can use religion or religious things in exactly the same way as drugs or alcohol, to escape from what is real within. Religious addiction attempts to control painful inner reality through a rigid religious belief system.... What better drug of choice than a perfect, all-powerful, all-knowing God out there who controls everything and everybody?[28]

Other religious "drugs of choice" can include a powerful, charismatic religious leader, ritual practices, and religious beliefs.

The painful feeling from which addicts (religious or not) seek escape is most often *shame*. Shame is not the same thing as guilt. Shame, as it is being used here, is "a toxic, debilitating core sense of being unlovable and inferior as a person.... Guilt says I *made* a mistake; shame says I *am* a mistake."[29] Hurts that people receive as children and adults may lead to feelings of inadequacy and shame and to an unwillingness to risk more hurt and shame. When people are told often enough that their own reality is wrong, they learn to mistrust their

---

[27]Blimling, "The Involvement of College Students in Totalistic Groups," p. 55.

[28]Matthew Linn, S. J., Sheila Fabricant Linn, and Dennis Linn, *Healing Spiritual Abuse and Religious Addiction* (New York and Mahwah, NJ: Paulist Press, 1994), pp. 2–13. The Linns' book deals only with Christianity, but the basic dynamics of religious addiction that they describe apply to any religion.

[29]Linn, et al., *Healing Spiritual Abuse*, p. 43 (emphasis added).

sense of reality itself. This, then, makes people unwilling and indeed unable to question what they are told in the name of religion.[30] This may make religious groups and leaders that discourage questioning more attractive than they otherwise would be. It can also lead to the use of religious practices such as prayer and chanting as a way to escape and shut off the hurtful feelings.

There is no sure way to identify when religion is being used addictively. What is healthy for one person, at one stage of his or her life's development, may signal addiction for someone else. We also need to keep in mind that passionate commitment to one's religion is *not* the same as addiction, even when that commitment exceeds what other people might consider "reasonable."

An important corollary of this view is that when religious addicts become religious leaders, they become spiritual abusers. Spiritual abusers perpetuate the heritage of shame. When a religious leader, doctrine, ritual, or writing makes us

> feel ashamed of our feelings, our desires, our call in life, or any other aspect of our real self, then we are [encountering] it with blinders of spiritual abuse. We need to stop and question . . . how [religion] is being interpreted to us.[31]

Religion challenges us, calls us to examine our lives in the light of the best in the religious tradition and the experience of the community of faith, but it should not shame us.

One implication of the research on religious addiction is that "nonconventional religions" and "consensus religions" are not two entirely separable things. The leaders and the followers of nonconventional religions are not all that different from those who follow more conventional religions. Everyone has the potential to turn to religion in an addictive way, and every religion has the potential for abuse. This said, it is also the case that religions that require unquestioning loyalty to the leader, the teaching, and the community and those that require followers to spend great amounts of time in ritual practices seem to invite the addictive use and abuse of religion by those so inclined. This becomes even more likely if shame and other negative means of social control are used.

The results of research on religious addiction mean that in evaluating the harmful potential of a religious group, or of *any* group, we need to look not only at the characteristics of the group, but at how *we* relate to the group, what our purposes and motives are for being involved in it. Harmfulness is at least as much a function of the relationship of a follower to the group as a characteristic of the group.

Lama Surya Das, a Tibetan Buddhist teacher in the United States, offers a list of ten questions to consider about one's own motives.[32]

---

[30]Linn, et al., *Healing Spiritual Abuse*, p. 118.
[31]Linn, et al., *Healing Spiritual Abuse*, pp. 129–130.
[32]Lama Surya Das, *Awakening the Buddha Within: Eight Steps to Enlightenment: Tibetan Wisdom for the Western World* (New York: Broadway Books, 1997), pp. 391–392, adapted.

- Are we sincerely trying to follow a spiritual path that balances wisdom and compassion?
- Are we fascinated by exotic, extraordinary religious experiences, at risk of becoming "an experience junkie or bliss addict"?
- Are we seeking instant enlightenment without being willing to commit to the necessary effort and discipline?
- What are our real motivations and goals for selecting the teacher or leader whom we select?
- Are we using religion or spirituality to withdraw from the world or to hide from ourselves?
- Are we turning our back on life and genuine personal growth in our search for some extraordinary spiritual state?
- Are we motivated by egotistical ambition to search for leadership roles?
- Do we idealize the foreignness or exoticness of the cultural trappings of a religious group, the "Shangri-La Syndrome"?
- Are we over-utilizing either head or heart, hiding from feelings by thinking too much or from the responsibility for serious thought by an overemphasis on feeling?
- Are we operating out of spiritual pride or arrogance?

Again, a caution: As human beings, we are beings of mixed and variable motivations. Each of us can probably recognize some of our less admirable qualities in the above list, at least sometimes. As with the characteristics of groups and leaders, below, extent and intensity both matter here.

RECOGNIZING THE POTENTIAL FOR HARM

The radical pluralism that characterizes religion in the United States today means that we live in an "open market" in which many groups, religious and secular, mostly benign but some potentially destructive, compete for our attention, time, and money. Part of becoming an "educated consumer" of group membership is making intentional choices rather than drifting unreflectively into participation. It does not come within the purview of the academic study of religion to evaluate religions, nonconventional or otherwise. Many groups—both religious and secular—offer lists of the characteristics of potentially damaging groups, each from its own point of view.

The list below reflects many sources, and includes those characteristics most frequently mentioned as warning signals. I would emphasize again that these features are not restricted to religious groups, and that such considerations should be kept in mind when dealing with secular groups as well. It should also be emphasized that specific groups will probably not display all these characteristics, nor will all groups display them to a high degree. Many can be found to some extent in conventional religious and secular groups.

1. Exclusivity and isolationism: Groups that claim or imply they have the only right answers, that encourage sharply either/or thinking, that encourage an

us-against-them attitude, that encourage or require extreme isolation from the "outside world," particularly from members' former friends and family, that define outsiders as the enemy.

2. Groups that exert a high degree of control over members' lives, require them to follow a very rigid schedule, control the information to which they have access, expect unquestioning allegiance to and obedience of the leader or a small group of leaders, require complete conformity in behavior and/or belief.

3. Groups in which any sexual manipulation or sexual abuse of adults or children occurs.

4. Groups in which violence inside the group or against outsiders is encouraged or supported.

5. Groups in which problems that arise are not discussed openly but are ignored or "resolved" arbitrarily by the leaders or a small inner circle.

6. Groups that make followers feel bad about themselves, ashamed of who they are, unworthy, in which leaders treat followers with contempt or inhumanity.

7. Groups that appear to be primarily interested in acquiring wealth and/or power for the group itself.

8. Leaders who claim infallibility, make decisions based on "divine knowledge" that followers in principle cannot know or attain, claim special spiritual powers or attainments, or who are simply self-appointed without any outside confirmation.

9. Leaders who fail to "practice what they preach," who claim that moral standards expected of the followers do not apply to leaders because the leaders are "beyond" such expectations.

10. Leaders who lie to followers and/or encourage followers to lie to each other.

Some version of what Jews and Christians know as the "Golden Rule" ("Do unto others as you would have them do unto you") is endorsed by most, if not all, of humankind's major communities of faith and by nonreligious persons as well. In considering involvement in any group, it's always well to ask yourself, "Does the group treat me the way I wish to be treated? The way I would wish my mother/father/sister/brother/spouse or partner/child to be treated? Does it expect me to treat other persons in the way that I wish to be treated, humanely and with respect for their personhood?

SEXUAL MISCONDUCT BY THE CLERGY

Since the mid-1980s, media reports of sexual abuse by clergy have become increasingly common. There is considerable agreement that this problem is extensive.

> . . .most professionals agree that the problem is far-reaching not only in Catholic, Protestant, and Jewish congregations but in Buddhist sanghas and Hindu ashrams [monasteries] as well. Abuse by spiritual leaders is nondenominational, and the dynamics between clergy and parishioners, between gurus and devotees, between spiritual teachers and students, bear striking resemblances to one another. . . .

clergy sexual malfeasance is an ecumenical reality, one that has probably been with us as long as civilization and one that is not about to go away.[33]

Since that time, news reports of priests, ministers, rabbis, roshis, or swamis being disciplined or resigning amid charges of sexual misconduct have been a near-monthly event. Most of the attention to the problem in the United States comes from Christian churches, simply because they are such a majority. However, there have been sufficient reports from non-Christian communities of faith to support the view that this is truly an interfaith problem. There is ample evidence from "mainstream" communities of faith to make it clear that this is a problem not limited to those groups that people label "cults."

There are a number of reasons for the problem, according to a recent article in *Common Boundary*, a journal that integrates spiritual and psychological concerns.[34] Religious groups have historically been patriarchal in orientation, and many continue to maintain this stance. This pattern may even be understood as divinely sanctioned, with males dominant over females. This pattern, "combined with a cultural assumption of male sexual access to women and children" sets up a situation in which abuse can happen.

Spiritual leaders also are seen by their followers as authority figures, and in some communities of faith, spiritual knowledge and experience are believed to come through the relationship between teacher and student, guru and follower. On the one hand, this can encourage the leader to seek an inappropriate sexual relationship with a follower. On the other hand, it may also make followers vulnerable to exploitation; a "special" relationship with a revered guru can be a temptation in itself. It is, of course, the responsibility of the leader to keep the proper boundaries intact, but not all choose to do so, and not all are strong enough to resist the adoration and flirtation of a devotee. As indicated in the section above, leaders may come to believe that the rules which apply to others do not apply to them and to claim special privileges for themselves, privileges that are sometimes sexual.

Writing specifically about clergy sexual abuse, one author points out the religious impact of such abuse:

> No matter how self-confident we may be, our systems of meaning are always fragile because they are made up of the many tiny fragments of our lived experience, the many loves, small and great, of our lives. Sexual abuse is a bulldozer gouging a road through this fragile ecosystem of sexuality, love and meaning that [a] person has been painfully constructing. This, I believe, is the major spiritual harm caused by sexual abuse, the destruction of a delicate and elaborate system of meaning. What ought to be positive becomes negative, what ought to be love becomes a using of a person, what ought to be trustworthy can no longer be trusted. . . . In

---

[33]Anne A. Simpkinson, "Soul Betrayal," *Common Boundary* (November/December, 1996), from the Common Boundary World Wide Web site (http://www.commonboundary.org/ARTICLES/961101.html).
[34]Simpkinson, "Soul Betrayal," (http://www.commonboundary.org/ARTICLES/961101.html).

sexual abuse there is always spiritual harm because, no matter what other particular things may be destroyed, the abuse always destroys the person's sense of wholeness and connectedness, and hence the person's sense of meaning.[35]

Religious organizations and communities of faith are beginning to take
action, to establish policies and procedures to lessen the chance that violations
will occur and to deal with violations when they do occur. Codes of ethics name
sexual contact between leaders and followers as a violation of professional boundaries, and place the responsibility on the leaders to prevent it from happening.
Ways to handle allegations are also being developed. Increasingly, the subject is
being addressed in the seminary training of clergy and in clergy workshops. Help
is being provided for both survivors and perpetrators. Mutual accountability
among leaders is seen as a way to lessen the likelihood of violations.[36]

One of the larger organizational attempts to address this problem is the
Interfaith Sexual Trauma Institute, a project of Saint John's Abbey and Saint
John's University in Minnesota. They publish a newsletter and journal, maintain
a resource center, and sponsor conferences and other educational programs, as
well as other activities. Unlike secular agencies, the Institute specifically
addresses the religious and spiritual ramifications of sexual abuse by clergy. Its
mission statement gives an overview of the Institute's approach.

> The Interfaith Sexual Trauma Institute affirms the goodness of human sexuality
> and advocates respectful relationships through the appropriate use of power
> within communities of all religious traditions. ISTI promotes the prevention of
> sexual abuse, exploitation, and harassment through research, education, and pub-
> lication. In the area of sexuality, ISTI offers leadership, gives voice, and facilitates
> healing of survivors, communities of faith, and offenders, as well as those who care
> for them.

The Institute's goals address many of the concerns noted above:

1. to collect and disseminate accurate information about issues of sexual misconduct
2. to develop models of intervention, psychological and spiritual healing, restitution and recovery of community trust in collaboration with such persons as
   survivors, offenders, religious leaders, and those in the helping professions
3. to advance research on sexual abuse, exploitation, harassment, and their pre-
   vention
4. to publish materials regarding survivors and healing, offenders and rehabilita-
   tion, and spiritual communities and transformation
5. to encourage understanding of sexual misconduct through interdisciplinary
   seminars, conferences, and seminary instruction

---

[35]Most Reverend Geoffrey James Robinson, "Sexual Abuse: Spiritual Harm and Spiritual Healing," The Interfaith Sexual Trauma Institute, Collegeville, MN, at the Institute's World Wide Web site (http://
www.osb.org/isti/robinson2.html).

[36]Simpkinson, "Soul Betrayal," (http://www.commonboundary.org/ARTICLES/961101.html).

6. to support the systematic study of and theological reflection on healthy human sexuality and appropriate use of power
7. to network with other professional organizations and agencies that deal with issues of sexual misconduct.[37]

FEAR OF NONCONVENTIONAL RELIGIONS
AND THE QUESTION OF VIOLENCE

Why do we fear and mistrust alternative religious movements? Part of it is simply fear of the unknown, the unfamiliar. Part of it is the real potential for violence and abuse that exists, although there is less of this than media attention would lead us to believe. Part of it is the horrifying image of the Branch Davidian compound engulfed in flames. Two other perspectives deserve our attention, as well, for they are thought-provoking and help us to set the discussion in the context of the larger role of religion in American culture.

The first is provided by Jeffrey Victor, a New York sociologist whose own son was wrongly labeled a "Satanist" because of his preferred taste in clothing. This personal encounter with the public reaction to Satanism led Victor to employ his sociologist's training in the attempt to understand what was going on with what he came to call the "Satanic panic" in the United States.

Briefly, the claim of a "Satanic conspiracy" in the United States asserts

> . . . that there exists a secret organization, or network, of criminals who worship Satan and who are engaged in the pornography business, forced prostitution, and drug dealing. These criminals also engage in the sexual abuse and torture of children . . . kill and sacrifice infants, and sometimes adults, and commit cannibalism with the body parts . . . kidnap children for ritual sacrifice and commit random murders of indigents. . . . Satanists have infiltrated all the institutions of society in order to subvert society, create chaos, and thus promote their beliefs in Satan worship.[38]

While there certainly have been crimes committed by people who claimed to have committed them in the name of Satan, and while people draw and wear symbols associated with Satan and sometimes leave these symbols at the site of ritualistic activities, there is "no reliable evidence" of the avowed conspiracy.

FBI Supervisory Special Agent Kenneth V. Lanning, Behavioral Sciences Unit, National Center for the Analysis of Violent Crime, explains the problem from the perspective of one who has investigated these allegations for twenty years:

> It is simply too difficult for that many people to commit so many horrendous crimes as part of an organized conspiracy. Two or three people murder a couple of

---

[37]Interfaith Sexual Trauma Institute World Wide Web site (http://www.osb.org/isti/).
[38]Victor, *Satanic Panic*, pp. 3–4.

children in a few communities as part of a ritual, and nobody finds out? Possible. Thousands of people do the same thing to tens of thousands of victims over many years? Not likely. Hundreds of communities all over America are run by mayors, police departments, and community leaders who are practicing satanists (sic) and who regularly murder and eat people? Not likely. In addition, these community leaders and high-ranking officials also supposedly commit these complex crimes leaving no evidence, and at the same time function as leaders and managers while heavily involved in using illegal drugs.[39]

In that case, what's going on here? Victor explains it this way. The Satanic conspiracy scare is symptomatic of something deeper, the collective perception of a moral crisis in American society. The precipitating factors include economic decline, uncertainty and the stress that accompanies it, and family disintegration, which has been endemic in the United States in recent history. There is little agreement about whether such a moral decline actually exists or how severe it is if it does exist. What is crucial here is the *perception* that it exists, because it is the shared perception that has behavioral consequences.

Many of the factors underlying the Satanic scare are believed to have a particularly strong impact on children. Parents fear for the welfare of their children, not only from economic uncertainty and family problems, but from "child molesters and drug dealers, violent teenage gangs and teen suicide." Even more, parents' "deepest fear is that their children may 'go wrong' due to 'outside influences' over which parents have little control: influences from their children's peer group, teachers, and the mass media."[40]

Victor's thesis is that Satanists involved in a huge Satanic conspiracy have been culturally invented as "scapegoat deviants for the social stresses and internal social conflicts which currently beset American society." Satan proves to be an ideal metaphor with which to express the collective perception of serious moral decay. The conspiracy theory arises "from people's socially constructed predisposition to find Satanism in many unrelated incidents and activities." In the face of cultural conflict of the magnitude people experience today, it is socially necessary to find a scapegoat upon which to focus the conflict in order to prevent the conflict from tearing the culture asunder. In a time of widespread disagreement over what constitutes moral conduct, *Satanists* have been culturally defined as

> . . . traitors to, or deviant from, the over-arching moral values of the United States. When moral values are in dispute in a society, a witch hunt for moral subversives serves the purpose of clarifying and redefining the limits of moral conduct.[41]

Victor points out (it seems to me, correctly) that scapegoating as a general pattern has increased in the United States in recent years. Targets have included

[39]Kenneth V. Lanning, "Investigator's Guide to Allegations of 'Ritual' Child Abuse," January, 1992 (http://web.mit.edu/harris/www/lanning.html).

[40]Victor, *Satanic Panic*, pp. 155–156.

[41]Victor, *Satanic Panic*, p. 194–198.

homosexuals, blacks, Jews, immigrants from a variety of places but most notably Hispanics and Haitians, feminists, and environmentalists. Not only alleged Satanists but followers of nonconventional religions in general get caught up in this trend.

The above addresses the specific issue of there being a Satanic *conspiracy* of substantial magnitude. To question the existence of such a widespread conspiracy is *not* to claim that there are *no* cases in which children or adults are abused by persons acting on the basis of religious beliefs or practices. To say that there is no *conspiracy* does not mean discounting the claims of survivors, and to do so is dangerous:

> To realize the danger in not taking patients' accounts of satanic [sic] abuse seriously, one only has to consider instances in which reports of atrocities were initially denied and later found to be true. Two vivid examples from this century are the tragedy at Jonestown, Guyana, and the Holocaust. In both instances, accounts of the events unfolding were available long before they were believed.[42]

To completely discount the reports is to allow the problem to continue, and perhaps to grow.

> Sadistic ritual abuse exists. We don't yet know how prevalent it is. We don't know that every report is accurate. But we do know that survivors are suffering from its effects. It is painful—devastating—to face this reality. But unless we face it, we allow it to continue. The [Jewish] Talmud asks, "To look away from evil: Is this not the sin of all good people?"[43]

In my opinion, it is not possible at this time to give a definitive statement about this troubling problem. From the standpoint of the study of religion and its place in the culture of the United States, we need to see both sides of the issue, to remain open to both sides of the disagreement, realizing that the truth probably lies somewhere in between the views of the conspiracy theorists and of those who would deny that any problem exists.

A very different sort of explanation of our cultural reaction to nonconventional religions comes from Dean M. Kelley, Counselor on Religious Liberty to the National Council of Churches. Kelley's reflections on the topic emerged in response to the Waco tragedy. Kelley's point is that as a culture, we tend to distrust and misunderstand religions that elicit great personal investment from their followers, and we question the sanity of those followers. Kelley writes,

> Few people invest themselves fully in anything. . . . But new religious movements can often attract and enlist higher levels of energy for longer periods of time in

---

[42]Susan C. Van Benschoten, "Multiple Personality Disorder and Satanic Ritual Abuse: The Issue of Credibility," *Dissociation* 3, No. 1 (March, 1990), p. 25.

[43]Ellen Bass and Laura Davis, *The Courage to Heal: A Guide for Women Survivors of Child Sexual Abuse*, 3d ed., revised and updated. New York: HarperCollins Publishers, 1994, p. 522.

commitment to their spiritual vision than any other form of human endeavor. They seek to harness every waking thought and action of their adherents for the advancement and enhancement of their cause. This can be very threatening to their neighbors. . . . But this highly structured high-energy phenomenon can be very attracting to people with intense needs for ultimate meaning. . . . These high-energy movements are the forms of religious behavior at the same time most in need of legal protection and least likely to receive it.[44]

Stephen Carter makes a similar point in his very popular book, *The Culture of Disbelief*. Religion, Carter asserts, has come to be trivialized and regarded as a "hobby" in American culture. Through "all of this trivializing rhetoric runs the subtle but unmistakable message: pray if you like, worship if you must, but whatever you do, do not on any account take your religion seriously."[45]

Both points of view—religion as a very intense, all-consuming experience that sets its members apart from the rest of society and religion seen as one part of life without comprehensive claims on its members—have been present in the United States since the beginning. The passionately religious were a small minority then, and they remain so today. They often incurred the mistrust and persecution of the more moderate then, as they do now. It is worth noting as well that we tend to mistrust and devalue passion and radical commitment in general, not just in the religious sphere. Put-down terms such as *tree-huggers* and *feminazis* come to mind. Passionate commitment to causes, people, and ideals is "messy." It doesn't fit in well with our image of a smoothly flowing society. And it *may* lead people to rash actions. It challenges our spoken affirmations of a pluralistic culture in which all points of view can find a home in a community of dialogue.

At the same time, as Carter also points out, the passionately religiously committed may not want to engage in dialogue on the terms usually set by modern culture. When individuals seek to engage in dialogue or to influence public policy in the public square, goes this line of thought, their views must be justified and justifiable in secular terms, no matter how they arrive at those views. It is precisely these terms that the passionately committed are often unlikely to accept as the fundamental rules of the game.[46]

How is it that the canons of public discourse have come to be defined in secular terms in a nation in which over 90 percent of people claim belief in God or a higher power? Survey research on religious commitment sheds light on this apparent contradiction. When religious commitment is measured on the basis of standards drawn from within religion itself, the vast majority of Americans are found to be "effectively secular." These standards include such things as attendance, membership, personal devotional activity, religious salience, and the

---

[44]Dean M. Kelley, "Was Religious Liberty Violated at Waco?" *ACRM Info*, American Conference on Religious Movements (April 1994), pp. 8–9.

[45]Stephen L. Carter, *The Culture of Disbelief: How American Law and Politics Trivialize Religious Devotion* (New York: HarperCollins Publishers, 1993), p. 15.

[46]Carter, *The Culture of Disbelief*, pp. 53–56.

importance of religion to the respondent. The "committed" report at least some activity on all five of the above indicators. This category includes about one-fifth of the adult population. People with limited religious commitment have attitudes and views that are much closer to those with no religious commitment than they do to their committed peers. They are in effect, "functional secularists."[47] A further factor is that those involved with entertainment and media—the opinion setters and gate keepers—demonstrate a higher degree of secularism than does the general population. Secularism is more prevalent among the highly educated, as well, who are more likely to be in leadership positions in the culture.

Both Kelley and Carter provide additional perspectives on the matter of religion and violence. Having noted that many people feel that religious groups cannot be put above the law, Kelley notes that, while all citizens are bound by law, not all laws are enforced or enforced equally; police officers in fact use considerable discretion in what laws will be enforced and against whom. (To make this point salient, try observing the speed at which the majority of people drive and compare it with the speed limit!) In this situation of differential and partial enforcement, enforcement decisions become a matter of priorities. Which violations will be selected? And which perpetrators?

In this situation, Kelley argues that religious groups should, by-and-large, be let alone. Carter points out that everything the Davidians did has also been done by secular people (and more often). Their crimes, if proven, must not be confused with their religiosity. "In other words, we must not assume that it is *the fact of believing deeply* that made the Davidians dangerous, even if it is true that *what they believed deeply* made them dangerous."[48] We must, as a predominantly secular society with a secular legal system, be careful to distinguish the content of belief from its source in belief. Violence or other criminal activity committed with religious motivation is no different than when it is done out of secular motives.

CURRENT CONCERNS

There is an almost countless number of religious groups that have been, or are, called cults by their detractors. The list has varied throughout history. Currently, the two groups, or better, groups of groups, that seem to be of greatest concern are Satanism and the Christian Identity movement. Those who characterize themselves as religious conservatives tend to be more concerned about Satanism. Those who consider themselves religious, political, and social liberals are more likely to voice concerns about Identity Christians. Because these two groups are

[47]Lyman A. Kellstedt, John C. Green, James L. Guth, and Corwin E. Smidt, "Religious Traditions and Religious Commitments in the U.S.A." Paper presented to the XXIIth International Conference of the International Society for the Sociology of Religion, Budapest, Hungary, July 1993.
[48]Carter, *The Culture of Disbelief*, p. 277.

prominent now, they are discussed extensively here. For a much more exhaustive discussion of nonconventional religions, see J. Gordon Melton's *Encyclopedic Handbook of Cults in America*.[49]

Satanism

Satanism has received a lot of negative publicity in recent years, especially in some areas of the country. We can distinguish between two types of Satanism. Anton LaVey (1930–1997) founded the **Church of Satan** in 1966. He collected standard occult and magical teachings around the motif of the worship of Satan. The thrust of **magick** (spelled with a "k" to distinguish it from stage magic) in general is the use of ritual to tap into the power of the universe and use that power to control what happens in one's life. In addition, these forces are believed to manipulate and control people; unless they are the control*lers*, people are the control*led*. There are no other options, according to this worldview. Secrecy is part and parcel of this perspective. It is a defense against hostility and misunderstanding, as well as against curious people who might become involved for shallow reasons (e.g., the chance to participate in an orgy). More important, believers in magick feel that most people simply are not ready for the knowledge that they themselves possess.

The Church of Satan teaches that those things that Christianity has usually condemned as sins (such as pleasure seeking, vengeance, and pride) are actually virtues. Logically, the Church of Satan is dependent on Christianity; it is a reaction to it. LaVey's teachings are contained in three books: *The Satanic Bible* (1969), *The Compleat Witch* (1970), and *The Satanic Rituals* (1972). A list of Nine Satanic Statements at the beginning of *The Satanic Bible* summarizes LaVey's teachings:

1. Satan means indulgence, not abstinence.
2. Satan means living fully now, not vague spiritual aspirations for a future life.
3. Satan means self-knowledge, not hypocrisy and self-deceit.
4. Satan stands for kindness to those who deserve it, not love for the unworthy.
5. Satan stands for vengeance, not forgiveness.
6. Satan means responsibility for those who are responsible, not misplaced concern for "psychic vampires."
7. Satanism teaches that humans are simply animals, animals whose intellectual and spiritual development can make them more vicious than the other animals.
8. Satan encourages gratification of physical and mental desires.
9. "Satan has been the best friend the church has ever had, as he has kept it in business all these years!"

The Church of Satan, in other words, encourages individuals to seek the greatest gratification of their desires and feel free to practice "selfish virtues." The followers of Satan developed a religious framework for a pleasure-seeking life, without violating laws. For the most part, they maintain a very low profile in

---

[49]Revised and updated edition (New York: Garland Publishing, 1992).

society. The shock value of something that calls itself Satanism has made its members the target of persecution. At the same time, it has been an ideal vehicle for those who wish to rebel against the predominant culture. (Remember that one of the characteristics attributed to Satan is that he is the arch-rebel.) Although membership figures are not made public and members are often understandably reluctant to reveal their affiliation, membership in the Church of Satan is not widespread.

The individual's birthday is the most important holiday celebrated. Walpurgisnacht (April 30) marks the rebirth of nature in the spring, and Halloween is celebrated as well. Various other magickal and celebratory rituals round out the ritual calendar. In line with its orientation to magick, ritual is the central focus of Satanism in any of its forms.

The second form of Satanism consists of **ritual magick groups**. These small and loosely organized groups believe that people can use the power attributed to Satan to enhance their own power. These groups are responsible for much of the animal sacrifice, sexual rituals, desecration of graves, and human sacrifice that are attributed to Satanism. They are not connected with the Church of Satan. Members of the Church of Satan have sometimes assisted law enforcement officers in investigating such incidents.

Participating in these groups is often a way that their members act out psychological and emotional disturbances. It is important to distinguish cause and effect here. One model depicts Satanism itself as leading to violent, criminal, and antisocial behavior. Another, more accurate model, posits a prior cause—anger and rage, alienation, social maladaptation—that leads both to membership in a Satanic group and to the violent, criminal, and antisocial behavior.

The Christian Identity Movement

"Soldiers of the far right are engaged in a struggle for the hearts, minds and souls of men and women across the Pacific Northwest."[50] The **Christian Identity movement** is a coalition of groups with two primary interests: (1) They have developed their own interpretation of the Bible to justify and encourage racism and violence against all people other than whites of European descent. Blacks and Jews are especially targeted. (2) They emphasize the importance of paramilitary training, so that members are prepared to defend themselves in the collapse of order that the organization believes will soon occur. Christian Identity includes several different groups, many of which have ties to the Ku Klux Klan. Among them are the following:

- The **Christian Conservative Churches of America**, which teach the coming collapse of the United States government and encourage members to band together for their survival and the survival of the white race. Associated organizations include **The Christian-Patriots Defense League**, "dedicated to preserving Anglo-Saxon culture against any form of miscegenation" [mixing of the races, especially

[50]Don Duncan, "Thunder on the Far Right," *Grapevine*, July 1987 (New York: Joint Strategy and Action Committee of the National Council of Churches), p. 1.

through interracial marriage] and **The Citizen's Emergency Defense System**, a private military force ready to be activated should the situation demand it.

- **Church of Jesus Christ Christian, Aryan Nation**, a "white racial theo-political movement whose aim is the establishment of white Aryan sovereignty over the lands of Aryan settlement and occupation."
- **The Covenant, the Sword, and the Arm of the Lord**, perhaps the most militant of the groups that comprise the movement. "It fully expects a major internal war in which white Christians will be set against Jews, blacks, homosexuals, witches, and Satanists, as well as foreign enemies."[51]

There are similar organizations in Great Britain and Canada.

This movement believes that it is the birthright of white Europeans (whom they call Israelites) to be the wealthiest, most powerful nations on earth and to dominate other countries in all ways, using whatever force is necessary to accomplish that goal. The basis is not the covenant that is so important in Judaism, in which the people of God are pledged to obedience and brought into being as a nation by God's choice. The basis is race.

The biblical interpretation that serves as a theological backing for their views is complex and idiosyncratic. According to Christian Identity, when the Lost Tribes of Israel were carried off into captivity, they did not remain in Assyria. They escaped in several waves and moved westward, across Asia Minor, into Europe, the Scandinavian countries, and the British Isles. Identification of the Lost Tribes with modern-day British/German/Celtic countries, including the United States, is the key to their understanding of their role. Jews are believed to be the offspring of Satan. Blacks and other people of color are referred to as pre-Adamic, that is, a lower form of life than whites. Pluralism of any sort is seen as a great evil.

Christian Identity uses its view of the end of history to justify its paramilitary activity. Many Christians believe that Christ will return to earth, accompanied by both a period of upheaval and conflict and a period of peace and blessedness, "when the lion will lie down with the lamb." Christian Identity teaches that the time of trial and upheaval will precede the return of Christ. There will be no "rapture," in which the faithful are rescued from the earth before it is wrapped in conflict. Rather, the faithful are expected to remain and help fight the battle as God's agents and soldiers. Identity followers claim that humankind has already entered the period of tribulation. They teach that it is of great importance to be ready to take up arms in God's cause. Being ready to fight for the coming Kingdom means being racist and anti-Semitic in the Identity interpretation of Christianity. In Idaho, for example, pop-up targets bearing the Star of David symbol have been seized.[52]

Many Americans feel threatened by the problems that confront us all: inadequate health care funding, AIDS, the threats inherent in nuclear proliferation, problems in the farm economy, unemployment and underemployment,

[51]Melton, *Encyclopedic Handbook of Cults in America*, pp. 71–76.
[52]Duncan, "Thunder on the Far Right," p. 3.

homelessness, and discipline problems among youth, to name but a few. In this situation, it is easy to look for a scapegoat. Christian Identity focuses this scapegoating and gives it a violent edge, at the same time assuring its followers that they are the only ones who are truly doing God's will.

The movement has been criticized on several grounds. Biblical scholars point out that its theology cannot be supported from any evidence. More pointed criticism has been directed against the racial views and policies of its constituent groups. Because the movement's theology inherently contains the potential for violence, its activities are closely monitored in areas where groups exist. Some members have been indicted on charges ranging from murder to burglary and conspiracy, with some convictions resulting from the charges.

THE WAY, FAITH ASSEMBLY, AND THE UNIFICATION CHURCH

The following three nonconventional religions are less extreme in their views than is either Satanism or the Christian Identity movement. They are important examples of less controversial nonconventional religions.

The Way, International, was founded in 1942 by a former Evangelical and Reformed Church (now a part of the United Church of Christ) minister, Victor Paul Wierwille (1916–1985). He gave the organization its present name in 1974. Headquarters are near New Knoxville, Ohio, and colleges are maintained near Rome City, Indiana (Figure 13-1), Emporia, Kansas, and at other sites. They are quite active on some college campuses. The group's beliefs are stated in

Figure 13-1   The Way, International, has an extensive training program for its members. (*Photo by the author.*)

the language of traditional Christianity. While these beliefs agree with those of more traditional Christians on many points, some are distinctively different.

1. The Old and New Testaments are held to be inspired by God and perfect as originally given. The various books are said to pertain to different periods in God's relationship with humankind. The Way uses its own translation of the Bible and emphasizes the books of Ephesians, Colossians, Philippians, and Galatians.
2. Belief in God, Jesus, and the Holy Spirit is affirmed, but Jesus is not believed to be God and is not considered divine. The Spirit is the power of God and is impersonal, rather than personal.
3. The Way is pentecostal, believing in the gifts of the Holy Spirit such as speaking in tongues, healing, and prophecy.
4. They believe in one baptism, that of the Holy Spirit, and reject water baptism.
5. The organization of The Way reflects the way in which they believe that the earliest Christian church was organized.

The Way offers a thirty-three hour tape and film course called **Power for Abundant Living**. With further instruction people may become members of The Way Corps, which is a leadership program, or the worldwide missions program, **Word Over the World**. The **American Christian Press** publishes its written materials, including *The Way Magazine*.

The Way has often been the target of deprogrammers when parents have charged that their daughters and sons were being held by the group against the children's will. It has also been criticized for its financial policies, and in 1985 its tax-exempt status was revoked by the Internal Revenue Service. The revocation was overturned by the Supreme Court in 1990.

Faith Assembly was founded near Warsaw, Indiana, by Hobart Freeman. Its headquarters are now in Wilmot, Indiana. There are now Faith Assembly branches in all forty-eight connecting states and at least six foreign countries. Freeman, a former professor at Grace Theological Seminary, had begun collecting a group of devoted followers around him even before he lost his teaching position because his views were no longer acceptable to his colleagues and his church. He then devoted all his time to developing the point of view that he had begun to believe while at Grace and to gathering an even larger band of followers.

The new church existed for some time without attracting much public attention. Then a public health nurse noticed that the infant mortality rate and the death rate for women in childbirth were much higher for Faith Assembly members than for the population at large. The investigation that followed thrust the Faith Assembly into the public eye. Controversy followed as newspapers, especially the Fort Wayne *News-Sentinel*, published reports of more deaths, along with rigid control over members by Freeman and a "Gestapo-like" mentality within the leadership ranks. The unsolved murders of an editor of the *News-Sentinel* and his family added to the controversy.

Freeman taught the complete avoidance of all conventional medical care and reliance upon prayer to Jesus for all healing. He told those who listened to him that if they died, or if their children died, it was because their faith was deficient. Adequate faith, coupled with the positive confession of that faith, guaranteed results. One of Freeman's own daughters and her husband left the group after their baby died. Freeman himself died in 1986, and leadership passed to the remaining son-in-law. Under his leadership, the group's views moderated somewhat. While they continued to teach and practice reliance on religious healing, they became less opposed to medical care, especially for children. In part, this came about because the deaths of children led to several court cases and a number of convictions on charges ranging from child neglect or abuse to manslaughter.

The charges and convictions arising from Faith Assembly cases raise the thorny question of the relationship between religious belief and practice in a nation that declares itself to be on the side of religious freedom. The courts have held that if an adult wishes to abstain from traditional medical care for religious reasons, that is not the concern of the government. It has become clear in the Faith Assembly cases that it *is* the government's concern when minor children are deprived of medical care that could have saved their lives. In these instances, the state has charged, and the courts have agreed, that the state does have a compelling interest in protecting the lives of helpless children, an interest that overrides the parents' freedom of religion.

The **Unification Church** is a Korean import that has worked very hard at attaining greater acceptance in American culture. The Unification Church (also known as the Holy Spirit Association for the Unification of World Christianity) was organized in 1954 by the Korean Sun Myung Moon ("Shining Sun and Moon"). Its members are frequently called Moonies, usually a derogatory term. According to Unification Church teaching, Adam and Eve were created by God, sinless, and could therefore have been the parents of a perfect human race. However, as the story in Genesis portrays it, Eve was led astray by the devil (in the form of the snake) and then led Adam astray also. Thus, sin and death came into the world.

Seeking to restore humanity to fellowship with God, God sent Jesus as the Messiah, the savior. Jesus was not able to complete his mission and bring about salvation that was both physical and spiritual, however. According to the Christian Bible, Jesus did not marry and thus could not provide the foundation for the beginning of a new and perfected humanity. Another messiah was needed. This messiah must be male, to reflect God's masculine nature, and must marry a wife who reflects God's feminine nature; together they will produce the children that will be the beginning of the perfected race. The key role of perfected, sinless families in bringing about a restored world order is the reason for the mass weddings for which Moon became famous.

The key text for Unification theology is *Divine Principle*. It is an interpretation of the Christian Bible that is said to clarify the divine principle that Unification followers believe the Bible contains. All of the group's teachings are drawn from this book and others that enlarge upon its principles.

The church carries out a complex program of activities in the United States. Many of its organizations take different names. Some of these are the

International Cultural Foundation, the Conference on the Unity of the Sciences, Professors World Peace Academy, Washington Institute for Values in Public Policy, National Council for the Church and Social Action (CAUSA, an anti-communist group), Paragon Press, Rose of Sharon Press, and CARP (Collegiate Association for the Research of Principle, its college evangelism branch). National headquarters are now in New York City. There are about 5000 members in the United States, with more in Japan and Korea.

Moon spent thirteen months in prison for tax evasion in 1984–1985. While this event hindered the group's quest for acceptance, it should be noted that many organizations and individuals within the framework of consensus religion came to Moon's defense, on the basis that the government's interference in the internal affairs of any religious group was a threat to all religious groups.

It is too early to determine if the Unification Church's bid for acceptance will be successful. Its American followers have a clean-cut "all-American" quality about them that will certainly help their search for a place in the mainstream. The church's outspoken support for causes such as the antiabortion movement, anticommunism, and government noninterference in church-operated schools has lessened antagonism from conservative Christians, to whom these issues are very important. Many of their leaders have been trained in theology at some of our leading graduate schools of religion. Their conferences are instrumental in bringing together scholars from many areas. The church's beliefs differ considerably from the average, as do some of their practices. Yet they have had at least limited initial success in forging links with other religious groups. They may move into a position in society parallel to that occupied by the Latter-day Saints. They will be accepted or tolerated by the consensus without actually being admitted as a part of it.

Nonconventional religions have been a part of the religious scene in the United States almost since its beginning. They will continue to be present, probably in increasing diversity. In this situation, it seems important to maintain a balance between naive, uncritical acceptance of everything that wears the label *religion*, and unreflective negative reaction to everything that appears to be *nonconventional* religion.

QUESTIONS AND ACTIVITIES FOR REVIEW, DISCUSSION, AND WRITING

1. Think about how you would feel if you had joined a community of faith that meant a lot to you and then you were forcibly removed from it and deprogrammed.
2. Think about how you would feel if someone you loved joined a particular religious group and refused to see you anymore. If, on the other hand, they were willing to help you, would you be eager to try to understand their new community of faith and what it meant to them?
3. Find out if any nonconventional religions are represented in your community. If so, try to arrange to visit them, and, if possible, talk with some of the members about what their participation means to them. Instead of visiting, you might invite one of their members to speak with your class.

4. For both Satanism and Christian Identity, write a paragraph in which you discuss what you think are the main reasons for their appeal to people today.

5. Write brief essays in which you respond to the views of (1) Jeffrey Victor concerning Satanism and scapegoating and (2) Dean M. Kelley and Stephen L. Carter concerning passionate religious commitment and our cultural response to it.

6. Write a paragraph in which you reflect on your responses to the section on clergy sexual abuse.

7. Visit one or two of the Web sites for nonconventional religions listed below, or find others. Do they seem to emphasize their differences from or their similarities to more conventional faiths?

8. Visit the Ontario Consultants for Religious Tolerance page that deals with "cults." Write a paragraph in which you summarize their position.

9. Visit the Web site of the Interfaith Sexual Trauma Institute and read the article "Sexual Abuse: Spiritual Harm and Spiritual Healing" (http://www.osb.org/isti/robinson2.htm). In what way does the author understand the spiritual harm and healing of sexual abuse?

FOR FURTHER READING

RICHARD ABANES, *American Militias: Rebellion, Racism, and Religion* (Downers Grove, IL: Inter-Varsity Press, 1996). This thorough study of the American militia movement and the religious dimensions of it usually provides a balanced and accurate portrayal of the movement.

DEIKMAN, ARTHUR J., M.D., *The Wrong Way Home: Uncovering the Patterns of Cult Behavior in American Society*. Boston: Beacon Press, 1990. The author's thesis is that "cult behavior" is something in which all people may engage, not just those in specific religious groups. He builds a convincing case and offers suggestions for lessening such behavior in the culture.

LEWIS, JAMES R., ed., *From the Ashes: Making Sense of Waco*. Lanham, MD: Rowman & Littlefield Publishers, 1994. These essays from a variety of perspectives in response to the Branch Davidian tragedy are usually critical of how the situation was handled.

MELTON, J. GORDON, *The Encyclopedic Handbook of Cults in America*, revised and updated edition. New York: Garland Publishing, 1992. This is undoubtedly the single best reference on this topic. In spite of the author's continued use of the outdated word *cult*, Melton maintains a thoroughly even-handed approach throughout. There are good references in each chapter.

Nova Religio: The Journal of Alternative and Emergent Religions. This relatively new journal published by Seven Bridges Press, LLC, began publication in the fall of 1997. It is devoted solely to the examination of new religious movements from a variety of academic perspectives. Its cross-cultural and interdisciplinary approach makes it highly recommended.

PALMER, SUSAN J., *Moon Sisters, Krishna Mothers, Rajneesh Lovers: Women's Roles in New Religions*. Syracuse, NY: Syracuse University Press, 1994. This first entry in a series on women and gender in religion in North America is an engaging exploration of the bonds between women's sexual and religious identities. The author makes good use of first-person accounts.

SALIBA, JOHN, *Understanding New Religious Movements*. Grand Rapids, MI: William B. Eerdmans Publishing Company, 1996. In this thoughtful examination of nonconventional religions from a variety of perspectives, including history, psychology, sociology, theology, and the law, the author "aims to raise the general level of the argument which has, to the detriment of all concerned, so often degenerated into an unrelenting diatribe" (Preface). This book is recommended.

SINGER, MARGARET THALER, with JANJA LALICH, *Cults in Our Midst*. San Francisco: Jossey-Bass Publishers, 1995. This book deals with what nonconventional religions are, how they work, and helping "survivors recover." Singer is one of the leading spokespersons for the contemporary anticult movement and writes from that perspective.

RELEVANT WORLD WIDE WEB SITES

Ontario Consultants for Religious Tolerance Page on "Cults" (http://www.religioustolerance.org/cultmenu.htm).

American Family Foundation (http://www.csj.org/).

Light of Truth Ministries (http://www.ltm.org/).

Heaven's Gate (http://www.heavensgatetoo.com/).

Interfaith Sexual Trauma Institute (http://www.osb.org/isti/).

The Anton Szandor LaVey Page (http://hem.passagen.se/baphomet/lavey.html).

Hr. Vad's Homepage on Satanism (http://www.image.dk/~vad/).

Scriptures for America (http://www.identity.org/home.htm).

Kingdom Identity Ministries (http://www.kingidentity.com/).

Right of Israel Christian Identity Resource Page (http://home.arkansasusa.com/dlackey).

The Way, International (http://www.watchman.org/).

Unification Church Official Page (http://unification.org/).

Epilogue

Neighbors, Not Strangers

I hope that this book has left you with a continuing interest in religion in the United States. Knowing our neighbors, religiously speaking, does not guarantee our appreciation of them. However, living in ignorance may well guarantee, or at least substantially contribute to, intolerance and lack of acceptance. Ignorance allows prejudice, preconceptions, and misunderstanding free rein. Strangers may easily become enemies.

For the kind of world in which we all will live in the new millennium, we need to grow into being a *community of neighbors, not strangers*. Neighbors are people who are part of the same community. It is no accident that the words *community* and *communicate* stem from the same root. *Neighbors* are those who can and do communicate with each other. Communication in the community of neighbors must be based on several things. There must be the *willingness* to communicate—to share ideas, beliefs, and feelings openly. There must be openness to receive what is shared. This requires an open space, as it were, free of prejudice and preconceptions. There must be accurate information, in order for communication to be meaningful. And, there must be difference. The community of neighbors, not strangers, is not based on sameness, on uniformity. It is based on respect for differences. It cannot be based on an attitude of weighing differences to see who is right and who is wrong. People in the community of neighbors, although committed to their own communities of faith and the values they uphold, are also committed to the larger endeavor of understanding and appreciation, not to judgment.

The idea of treating others as we ourselves wish to be treated (which is affirmed in all of the major religions of the world), *if actually lived out*, would go a long way toward bringing about a climate in which strangers can become neighbors.

Index